Communications
in Computer and Information Science 1581

More information about this series at https://link.springer.com/bookseries/7899

Constantine Stephanidis · Margherita Antona ·
Stavroula Ntoa (Eds.)

HCI International 2022 Posters

24th International Conference
on Human-Computer Interaction, HCII 2022
Virtual Event, June 26 – July 1, 2022
Proceedings, Part II

 Springer

Editors
Constantine Stephanidis
University of Crete and Foundation for
Research and Technology – Hellas (FORTH)
Heraklion, Crete, Greece

Margherita Antona
Foundation for Research and Technology –
Hellas (FORTH)
Heraklion, Crete, Greece

Stavroula Ntoa
Foundation for Research and Technology –
Hellas (FORTH)
Heraklion, Crete, Greece

ISSN 1865-0929   ISSN 1865-0937 (electronic)
Communications in Computer and Information Science
ISBN 978-3-031-06387-9   ISBN 978-3-031-06388-6 (eBook)
https://doi.org/10.1007/978-3-031-06388-6

This Springer imprint is published by the registered company Springer Nature Switzerland AG
The registered company address is: Gewerbestrasse 11, 6330 Cham, Switzerland

Foreword

Human-computer interaction (HCI) is acquiring an ever-increasing scientific and industrial importance, as well as having more impact on people's everyday life, as an ever-growing number of human activities are progressively moving from the physical to the digital world. This process, which has been ongoing for some time now, has been dramatically accelerated by the COVID-19 pandemic. The HCI International (HCII) conference series, held yearly, aims to respond to the compelling need to advance the exchange of knowledge and research and development efforts on the human aspects of design and use of computing systems.

The 24th International Conference on Human-Computer Interaction, HCI International 2022 (HCII 2022), was planned to be held at the Gothia Towers Hotel and Swedish Exhibition & Congress Centre, Göteborg, Sweden, during June 26 to July 1, 2022. Due to the COVID-19 pandemic and with everyone's health and safety in mind, HCII 2022 was organized and run as a virtual conference. It incorporated the 21 thematic areas and affiliated conferences listed on the following page.

A total of 5583 individuals from academia, research institutes, industry, and governmental agencies from 88 countries submitted contributions, and 1276 papers and 275 posters were included in the proceedings to appear just before the start of the conference. The contributions thoroughly cover the entire field of human-computer interaction, addressing major advances in knowledge and effective use of computers in a variety of application areas. These papers provide academics, researchers, engineers, scientists, practitioners, and students with state-of-the-art information on the most recent advances in HCI. The volumes constituting the set of proceedings to appear before the start of the conference are listed in the following pages.

The HCI International (HCII) conference also offers the option of 'Late Breaking Work' which applies both for papers and posters, and the corresponding volume(s) of the proceedings will appear after the conference. Full papers will be included in the 'HCII 2022 - Late Breaking Papers' volumes of the proceedings to be published in the Springer LNCS series, while 'Poster Extended Abstracts' will be included as short research papers in the 'HCII 2022 - Late Breaking Posters' volumes to be published in the Springer CCIS series.

I would like to thank the Program Board Chairs and the members of the Program Boards of all thematic areas and affiliated conferences for their contribution and support towards the highest scientific quality and overall success of the HCI International 2022 conference; they have helped in so many ways, including session organization, paper reviewing (single-blind review process, with a minimum of two reviews per submission) and, more generally, acting as goodwill ambassadors for the HCII conference.

This conference would not have been possible without the continuous and unwavering support and advice of Gavriel Salvendy, founder, General Chair Emeritus, and Scientific Advisor. For his outstanding efforts, I would like to express my appreciation to Abbas Moallem, Communications Chair and Editor of HCI International News.

June 2022   Constantine Stephanidis

HCI International 2022 Thematic Areas and Affiliated Conferences

Thematic Areas

- HCI: Human-Computer Interaction
- HIMI: Human Interface and the Management of Information

Affiliated Conferences

- EPCE: 19th International Conference on Engineering Psychology and Cognitive Ergonomics
- AC: 16th International Conference on Augmented Cognition
- UAHCI: 16th International Conference on Universal Access in Human-Computer Interaction
- CCD: 14th International Conference on Cross-Cultural Design
- SCSM: 14th International Conference on Social Computing and Social Media
- VAMR: 14th International Conference on Virtual, Augmented and Mixed Reality
- DHM: 13th International Conference on Digital Human Modeling and Applications in Health, Safety, Ergonomics and Risk Management
- DUXU: 11th International Conference on Design, User Experience and Usability
- C&C: 10th International Conference on Culture and Computing
- DAPI: 10th International Conference on Distributed, Ambient and Pervasive Interactions
- HCIBGO: 9th International Conference on HCI in Business, Government and Organizations
- LCT: 9th International Conference on Learning and Collaboration Technologies
- ITAP: 8th International Conference on Human Aspects of IT for the Aged Population
- AIS: 4th International Conference on Adaptive Instructional Systems
- HCI-CPT: 4th International Conference on HCI for Cybersecurity, Privacy and Trust
- HCI-Games: 4th International Conference on HCI in Games
- MobiTAS: 4th International Conference on HCI in Mobility, Transport and Automotive Systems
- AI-HCI: 3rd International Conference on Artificial Intelligence in HCI
- MOBILE: 3rd International Conference on Design, Operation and Evaluation of Mobile Communications

List of Conference Proceedings Volumes Appearing Before the Conference

1. LNCS 13302, Human-Computer Interaction: Theoretical Approaches and Design Methods (Part I), edited by Masaaki Kurosu
2. LNCS 13303, Human-Computer Interaction: Technological Innovation (Part II), edited by Masaaki Kurosu
3. LNCS 13304, Human-Computer Interaction: User Experience and Behavior (Part III), edited by Masaaki Kurosu
4. LNCS 13305, Human Interface and the Management of Information: Visual and Information Design (Part I), edited by Sakae Yamamoto and Hirohiko Mori
5. LNCS 13306, Human Interface and the Management of Information: Applications in Complex Technological Environments (Part II), edited by Sakae Yamamoto and Hirohiko Mori
6. LNAI 13307, Engineering Psychology and Cognitive Ergonomics, edited by Don Harris and Wen-Chin Li
7. LNCS 13308, Universal Access in Human-Computer Interaction: Novel Design Approaches and Technologies (Part I), edited by Margherita Antona and Constantine Stephanidis
8. LNCS 13309, Universal Access in Human-Computer Interaction: User and Context Diversity (Part II), edited by Margherita Antona and Constantine Stephanidis
9. LNAI 13310, Augmented Cognition, edited by Dylan D. Schmorrow and Cali M. Fidopiastis
10. LNCS 13311, Cross-Cultural Design: Interaction Design Across Cultures (Part I), edited by Pei-Luen Patrick Rau
11. LNCS 13312, Cross-Cultural Design: Applications in Learning, Arts, Cultural Heritage, Creative Industries, and Virtual Reality (Part II), edited by Pei-Luen Patrick Rau
12. LNCS 13313, Cross-Cultural Design: Applications in Business, Communication, Health, Well-being, and Inclusiveness (Part III), edited by Pei-Luen Patrick Rau
13. LNCS 13314, Cross-Cultural Design: Product and Service Design, Mobility and Automotive Design, Cities, Urban Areas, and Intelligent Environments Design (Part IV), edited by Pei-Luen Patrick Rau
14. LNCS 13315, Social Computing and Social Media: Design, User Experience and Impact (Part I), edited by Gabriele Meiselwitz
15. LNCS 13316, Social Computing and Social Media: Applications in Education and Commerce (Part II), edited by Gabriele Meiselwitz
16. LNCS 13317, Virtual, Augmented and Mixed Reality: Design and Development (Part I), edited by Jessie Y. C. Chen and Gino Fragomeni
17. LNCS 13318, Virtual, Augmented and Mixed Reality: Applications in Education, Aviation and Industry (Part II), edited by Jessie Y. C. Chen and Gino Fragomeni

18. LNCS 13319, Digital Human Modeling and Applications in Health, Safety, Ergonomics and Risk Management: Anthropometry, Human Behavior, and Communication (Part I), edited by Vincent G. Duffy
19. LNCS 13320, Digital Human Modeling and Applications in Health, Safety, Ergonomics and Risk Management: Health, Operations Management, and Design (Part II), edited by Vincent G. Duffy
20. LNCS 13321, Design, User Experience, and Usability: UX Research, Design, and Assessment (Part I), edited by Marcelo M. Soares, Elizabeth Rosenzweig and Aaron Marcus
21. LNCS 13322, Design, User Experience, and Usability: Design for Emotion, Well-being and Health, Learning, and Culture (Part II), edited by Marcelo M. Soares, Elizabeth Rosenzweig and Aaron Marcus
22. LNCS 13323, Design, User Experience, and Usability: Design Thinking and Practice in Contemporary and Emerging Technologies (Part III), edited by Marcelo M. Soares, Elizabeth Rosenzweig and Aaron Marcus
23. LNCS 13324, Culture and Computing, edited by Matthias Rauterberg
24. LNCS 13325, Distributed, Ambient and Pervasive Interactions: Smart Environments, Ecosystems, and Cities (Part I), edited by Norbert A. Streitz and Shin'ichi Konomi
25. LNCS 13326, Distributed, Ambient and Pervasive Interactions: Smart Living, Learning, Well-being and Health, Art and Creativity (Part II), edited by Norbert A. Streitz and Shin'ichi Konomi
26. LNCS 13327, HCI in Business, Government and Organizations, edited by Fiona Fui-Hoon Nah and Keng Siau
27. LNCS 13328, Learning and Collaboration Technologies: Designing the Learner and Teacher Experience (Part I), edited by Panayiotis Zaphiris and Andri Ioannou
28. LNCS 13329, Learning and Collaboration Technologies: Novel Technological Environments (Part II), edited by Panayiotis Zaphiris and Andri Ioannou
29. LNCS 13330, Human Aspects of IT for the Aged Population: Design, Interaction and Technology Acceptance (Part I), edited by Qin Gao and Jia Zhou
30. LNCS 13331, Human Aspects of IT for the Aged Population: Technology in Everyday Living (Part II), edited by Qin Gao and Jia Zhou
31. LNCS 13332, Adaptive Instructional Systems, edited by Robert A. Sottilare and Jessica Schwarz
32. LNCS 13333, HCI for Cybersecurity, Privacy and Trust, edited by Abbas Moallem
33. LNCS 13334, HCI in Games, edited by Xiaowen Fang
34. LNCS 13335, HCI in Mobility, Transport and Automotive Systems, edited by Heidi Krömker
35. LNAI 13336, Artificial Intelligence in HCI, edited by Helmut Degen and Stavroula Ntoa
36. LNCS 13337, Design, Operation and Evaluation of Mobile Communications, edited by Gavriel Salvendy and June Wei
37. CCIS 1580, HCI International 2022 Posters - Part I, edited by Constantine Stephanidis, Margherita Antona and Stavroula Ntoa
38. CCIS 1581, HCI International 2022 Posters - Part II, edited by Constantine Stephanidis, Margherita Antona and Stavroula Ntoa

39. CCIS 1582, HCI International 2022 Posters - Part III, edited by Constantine Stephanidis, Margherita Antona and Stavroula Ntoa

40. CCIS 1583, HCI International 2022 Posters - Part IV, edited by Constantine Stephanidis, Margherita Antona and Stavroula Ntoa

http://2022.hci.international/proceedings

Preface

Preliminary scientific results, professional news, or work in progress, described in the form of short research papers (4–8 pages long), constitute a popular submission type among the International Conference on Human-Computer Interaction (HCII) participants. Extended abstracts are particularly suited for reporting ongoing work, which can benefit from a visual presentation, and are presented during the conference in the form of posters. The latter allow a focus on novel ideas and are appropriate for presenting project results in a simple, concise, and visually appealing manner. At the same time, they are also suitable for attracting feedback from an international community of HCI academics, researchers, and practitioners. Poster submissions span the wide range of topics of all HCII thematic areas and affiliated conferences.

Four volumes of the HCII 2022 proceedings are dedicated to this year's poster extended abstracts, in the form of short research papers, focusing on the following topics:

- Volume I: User Experience Design and Evaluation; Visual Design and Visualization; Data, Information, and Knowledge; Interacting with AI; Universal Access, Accessibility, and Design for Aging.
- Volume II: Multimodal and Natural Interaction; Perception, Cognition, Emotion, and Psychophysiological Monitoring; Human Motion Modelling and Monitoring; IoT and Intelligent Living Environments.
- Volume III: Learning Technologies; HCI, Cultural Heritage and Art; eGovernment and eBusiness; Digital Commerce and the Customer Experience; Social Media and the Metaverse.
- Volume IV: Virtual and Augmented Reality; Autonomous Vehicles and Urban Mobility; Product and Robot Design; HCI and Wellbeing; HCI and Cybersecurity.

Poster extended abstracts are included for publication in these volumes following a minimum of two single-blind reviews from the members of the HCII 2022 international Program Boards. We would like to thank all of them for their invaluable contribution, support, and efforts.

June 2022

Constantine Stephanidis
Margherita Antona
Stavroula Ntoa

24th International Conference on Human-Computer Interaction (HCII 2022)

The full list with the Program Board Chairs and the members of the Program Boards of all thematic areas and affiliated conferences is available online at

http://www.hci.international/board-members-2022.php

HCI International 2023

The 25th International Conference on Human-Computer Interaction, HCI International 2023, will be held jointly with the affiliated conferences at the AC Bella Sky Hotel and Bella Center, Copenhagen, Denmark, 23–28 July 2023. It will cover a broad spectrum of themes related to human-computer interaction, including theoretical issues, methods, tools, processes, and case studies in HCI design, as well as novel interaction techniques, interfaces, and applications. The proceedings will be published by Springer. More information will be available on the conference website: http://2023.hci.international/.

General Chair
Constantine Stephanidis
University of Crete and ICS-FORTH
Heraklion, Crete, Greece
Email: general_chair@hcii2023.org

http://2023.hci.international/

Contents – Part II

Perception, Cognition, Emotion and Psychophysiological Monitoring

Human Motion Modelling and Monitoring

IoT and Intelligent Living Environments

Multimodal and Natural Interaction

Simulation Object Edge Haptic Feedback in Virtual Reality Based on Dielectric Elastomer

Jiyao Chen[1]([✉]), Jun-Li Lu[1,2], and Yoichi Ochiai[1,2]

[1] Research and Development Center for Digital Nature, University of Tsukuba, Tsukuba, Japan
jiyaoc@digitaonature.slis.tsukuba.ac.jp,
{jllu,wizard}@slis.tsukuba.ac.jp
[2] Faculty of Library, Information and Media Science, University of Tsukuba, Tsukuba, Japan

Abstract. With reduced prices of VR device, consumers are increasingly purchasing VR devices. As a result of this, increase in the popularity, device makers are seeking new methods for VR interaction. Current haptic feedback gloves such as CyberGrasp, Haptx glove, and Demo focus on the positioning of the hand in the virtual environment, as well as the feedback of the force haptics of the hand on virtual objects. Users can use haptic gloves to determine the shape and size of virtual objects. However, while touching some tiny objects in the virtual environment, haptic gloves achieve cannot provide a good user experience. In this paper, I propose a new method to enhance haptic resolution from centimeters to millimeters, which can improve user experience with haptic device.

The goal of this study is to create a device that can be worn on the fingertip, which can reflect the subtle haptic sensations received by the user's fingertip in the virtual space built on UE4. This device enhances the user's haptic experience in a virtual space.

Keywords: Virtual reality · Human interface · Dielectric elastomer · Unreal engine

1 Introduction

Virtual reality has attracted increased attention in recent years. Oculus, Sony, HTC, and other hardware manufacturers have already launched their head-mounted displays and game controllers. At the same time, researchers have developed more feedback devices, such as haptic gloves, to provide an immersive experience. However, to date, most commercial VR devices developed by manufacturers focus only on visual enhancements, overlooking the need for adding information beyond the visual field.

As a very important bridge between people and the external environment, using haptic information as a complement to the visual can provide a more complete and immersive virtual experience. Currently, haptic feedback focuses on the positioning of the hand in a virtual environment and force feedback. Users can use haptic feedback gloves to experience the shape and size of virtual objects. However, while touching some tiny objects in the virtual environment, such as edges, unable to provide good feedback.

C. Stephanidis et al. (Eds.): HCII 2022, CCIS 1581, pp. 3–9, 2022.
https://doi.org/10.1007/978-3-031-06388-6_1

Dielectric elastomers are polymers, that deform in response to electric fields and widely used in aerospace, soft robotics, braille readers and sensors. These polymers have good bio-affinity, are soft, lightweight, inexpensive, can fit on the skin surface, and are easy to carry. Therefore, I propose that dielectric elastomers can be used in human-computer interaction devices. This research aims to find a suitable DE material and use an array of haptic response units based on the materialized to enhance haptic resolution. This tactile pad consists of DE units that can simulate the surface of small objects and provide a more realistic tactile sensation to users (Fig. 1).

Fig. 1. Haptx glove

2   Related Work

2.1   Dielectric Elastomer (DE)

Currently, dielectric elastomers studied in laboratories are either silicone rubber (SR) or polydimethylsiloxane (PDMS, etc.), or composites based on them. These two dielectric elastomer materials exhibit major differences in performance in terms of parameter such as dielectric constant, viscoelasticity, response time, and degree of deformations. For example, silicone rubber has the advantages of fast response, low viscoelasticity, and high resilience; however it has the disadvantages of a low deformation and a base dielectric coefficient. PDMS and other materials also have the advantages of a high deformation, high dielectric coefficient, slow response, and high viscoelasticity.

2.2   DE Synthesis

Huang et al. [1] combined HO-PDMS and CB materials to produce a film with a higher dielectric coefficient and displacement than a normal PDMS film. On the one hand, dielectric elastomers have a certain viscoelasticity. Reducing the negative impact of viscoelasticity in human-computer interaction devices will be a research focus in the future. Dielectric elastomers also exhibit different deformations when subjected to electric fields, even with the same chemical structure. Therefore, another focus of this study is to limit the deformation of dielectric elastomers such as that the variation between different dielectric elastomer units is consistent. Most current academic research on dielectric elastomers has focus on dielectric elastomer films. Given their relative ease of availability in the market, dielectric elastomer films are favored by university researchers. Deformation of dielectric elastomer films has been used to create grippers, Braille readers, and soft robots.

2.3 DE Fabrication

Sasaki et al. [2] fabricated multilayer elastomer films that achieved a response speed of up to 10 ms while reflecting a 50% increase in the peak value. Therefore, this property can be exploited to produce larger elastomers; that are easier to handle. In addition, the shape of the dielectric elastomer can be using mechanical structures such that its deformation is oriented toward the target.

3 Tools

3.1 Flexible Electrode

Since DEAs (dielectric elastomer actuator) undergo deformation over time, the electrodes used to drive DEAs should be made of deformable electrode material. At the same time, for DEAs with a thickness of several millimeters, the thickness of the attached flexible electrode is negligible. Conductive rubber [4] is preferred as the flexible electrode. Conductive rubber mixed with carbon black has high toughness and tear resistance, and is therefore suitable as a flexible electrode material for DEA in this study.

3.2 Wire

Conductive tape has the advantage of being lightweight and easy to operate. It is also negligible in thickness compared to DEA. Therefore, conductive tape was chosen as the conductor for the DEA. The conductive tape was processed to match the width of the DEA, thereby facilitating the post-processing of the DEA (Fig. 2).

3.3 DEA Structure

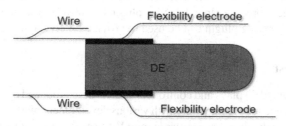

Fig. 2. DEA structure sample

3.4 DE Array

Using DEA to form a reaction array, we can respond to the surface shape of the virtual object and perform deformation at the corresponding parts for the simulation (Fig. 3).

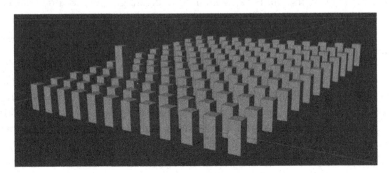

Fig. 3. DE array sample

4 Platform

4.1 Blender

In 3D modeling software, Blender, triangles were used to construct the mesh bodies. The surface structure of an object was stitched from triangles, which have a wide range of applications in computer graphics.

4.2 Unreal Engine

In addition to being a popular game engine, Unreal Engine (UE) has a large user base because it free. Many game developers use UE for virtual space construction. Because of the nature of its game production engine, it can perform calculations at a high frequency. Rosskamp [3] and others have developed the UnrealHaptics plugin, which is based on the UE4 engine Andrew is able to detect collisions between objects in the virtual space at a high frequency of up to 1000 Hz. At the same time, communication between the haptic feedback device worn by the user and computers occur at a high frequency of up to 1000 Hz. Furthermore, the UnrealHaptics plugin can also be used to calculate force and torque. Therefore, the plugin can be used to provide timely haptic feedback.

4.3 Oculus Quest

A set of head-mounted displays and controllers, which were produced by the Meta Quest Company, were found to be compatible with various development platforms. In addition, these head-mounted displays are popular among VR users because of their affordability (Fig. 4).

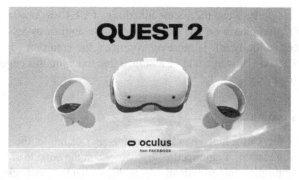

Fig. 4. Oculus Quest II

5 Method

First, Blender wash used up to model irregular objects for experimental material as the experiment. Second, in the UE4 engine, a VR space template was created, and the irregular object models created in the previous step were imported. An external camera (Oculus Quest2) was used for hand positioning. When the position of the hands overlaps with the surface of the virtual object in the virtual space, the distance between the surfaces of the overlapping part and the relative position of the hand is obtained. Using acquired angle data, the DE unit corresponding to a negative distance was determined. The voltage that should be applied was calculated, and was applied to this DE unit to complete a haptic simulation.

5.1 DE Pre-treatment

Because dielectric elastomers can deform, it is necessary to stretch the DE material before processing. A stretching device [5] was used to hold the DE material in place and stretch it in the direction of the desired deformation. This procedure provided prior knowledge of the degree of deformation of the DE material and helped evaluate the DEA performance.

5.2 DE Material

Commercially available liquid silicone rubber and conductive carbon black powder were purchasers. Conductive carbon black powder, which can be easily purchased, is typically used as a pigment. Liquid silicone rubber can also be purchased from chemical material manufacturers. The liquid silicone rubber was poured into a beaker, and a certain percentage of carbon black powder was added as needed, stirred until fully mixed, measured to the proper thickness, and placed in a drying apparatus until solid. After cutting and polishing the solid DE material, it was used an experimental DE material [6].

5.3 Angle Recognition

The position information of the three Rs vertices of each plane in the mesh body was used to calculate the normal data of each plane by interpolating each vertex after rasterization of the GPU. The angle between the vector functions of UE4 was used to calculate the angle between the two planes on the mesh body. If the angle was less than a certain number of degrees (initially 90° is more appropriate), the common edge between the two planes was marked. Thus, it could be assumed that touching this edge was required to provide edge haptics.

5.4 Hand Localization

There are various ways to achieve hand positioning. For example, the Oculus Quest2, now available in the market, is equipped with a camera on the outside of its body, which can be used to capture the finger optically. In addition, haptic feedback gloves can be used for hand position capture. Therefore, this study directly combines the existing methods for hand localization and focuses on matching and calibrating the position of the dielectric elastomer on the hand device.

This study used Meta Quest's Oculus Quest II as the experimental platform; therefore, the camera on the Meta Quest was used for gesture tracking (Fig. 5).

5.5 Workflow

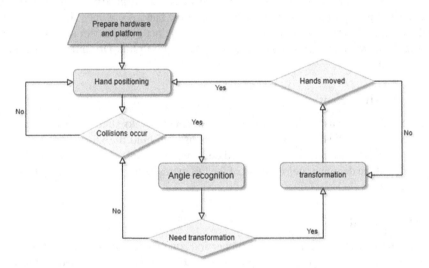

Fig. 5. System workflow

First, hardware was prepared using the experimental platform described in the previous sections. Then, spatial localization of the user's hands was performed in the experimentally prepared virtual space. After the position was determined, the imminent collision of the hands was predicted using UnrealHaptics plugin. If a collision occurred, the surface angle of the object that touches the finger was identified. Haptic feedback was provided if the angle was less than a certain number of degrees. If the hands moved, collision prediction and haptic feedback were performed again.

References

1. Li, M., et al.: Polymer actuator based on silanized graphene/silicone hybrid elastomer. Polym. Mater. Sci. Eng. **37**(7), 172–180 (2021). https://doi.org/10.16865/j.cnki.1000-7555.2021.0159
2. Mulembo, T., et al.: Linear-quadratic regulator for control of multi-wall carbon nanotube/polydimethylsiloxane based conical dielectric elastomer actuators. Actuators **9**(1) (2020). https://doi.org/10.3390/act9010018
3. Rosskamp, J., Meißenhelter, H., Weller, R., Rüdel, M. O., Ganser, J., Zachmann, G.: Unreal-Haptics: plugins for advanced VR interactions in modern game engines. Front. Virtual Real. **2** (2021). https://doi.org/10.3389/frvir.2021.640470
4. Rosset, S., Shea, H.R.: Flexible and stretchable electrodes for dielectric elastomer actuators. Appl. Phys. A Mater. Sci. Process. **110**(2), 281–307 (2013). https://doi.org/10.1007/s00339-012-7402-8
5. Yang, D., et al.: Improved mechanical and electrochemical properties of XNBR dielectric elastomer actuator by poly(dopamine) functionalized graphene nano-sheets. Polymers **11**(2) (2019). https://doi.org/10.3390/polym11020218
6. Xu, T., Liu, Q., Tao, S., et al.: Study on preparation of carbon black/silicone dielectric elastomer composite. Polym. Bull. **5**, 96–101 (2021). https://doi.org/10.14028/j.cnki.1003-3726.2021.05.010
7. Zhang, R., Iravani, P., Keogh, P.S.: Modelling dielectric elastomer actuators using higher order material characteristics. J. Phys. Commun. **2**(4). https://doi.org/10.1088/2399-6528/aabb76

Resistive-Force Presentation Device Using Magneto-Rheological Fluid for Wrist-Joint Stiffness Control

Taiki Funabiki, Yoichi Yamazaki, and Masataka Imura[✉]

Kwansei Gakuin University, 2-1 Gakuen, Sanda, Hyogo 669-1337, Japan
m.imura@kwansei.ac.jp

Abstract. MR fluid has high speed responsiveness and shows a shear response in a direction perpendicular to the magnetic flux direction, when a magnetic field is applied. In this research, we propose a compact and lightweight wrist-mounted resistance force presentation device utilizing the characteristics of MR fluid. By controlling the magnetic flux density applied to the rubber tube filled with MR fluid, the resistance force is presented by increasing the rigidity of the wrist joint.

Keywords: Haptic display · Wearable device · Magnetorheological fluid

1 Introduction

Virtual reality (VR) technology is becoming increasingly popular. The major difference between VR space and real space is the lack of haptic feedback: when a user touches an object in VR space, the user you do not get the same sensation that comes with touching an object in real space. This lack of haptic feedback severely compromises the user's immersion in VR space. Presentation of haptic sense to the user is thus an essential element for practical use of VR space in medicine, entertainment, and other fields.

The aim of this study is to develop an easily handled, light-weight, highly responsive force feedback device that uses a relatively small force to present a resistance force. These features allow users to operate the device for a long time with little stress and easily experience a deep feeling of immersion.

Resistance force is generated when movement is hindered by external factors, e.g., the reaction force when touching an object, wind pressure, and resistance to movement in water. Our proposed design minimizes the increase of moment of inertia by attaching the device at a position close to the center of rotational motion and presenting the resistance force by limiting the rotational motion of the joint. To do the latter, we use magneto-rheological (MR) fluid, which can control rigidity arbitrarily.

C. Stephanidis et al. (Eds.): HCII 2022, CCIS 1581, pp. 10–17, 2022.
https://doi.org/10.1007/978-3-031-06388-6_2

2   Related Works

Force-feedback devices that have been developed to date may be roughly divided into two types: active and passive.

The active type presents force directly to a part of the user's body by means of an actuator such as a motor. The active type has the advantage of being relatively easy to implement. The active type allows users to interact with real space from the VR side independently of the user's state. Disadvantages of the active type come from the direct presentation of force by the actuator, which is likely to cause injuries, and the large actuator required to present a large force, which increases the weight.

The passive method involves force feedback by a passive force element such as a brake when the user takes an action. A passive device is intrinsically safe, because the force-presenting part is a passive element. Unfortunately, the presentation of force in a passive device depends on the user's movement, which limits the freedom of VR/real-space interaction. For example, it is possible for the user to have the sensation of touching a ball, but it is not possible for the user to have the sensation of being hit by one. Therefore, the range of expression of passive devices is narrower than that of active devices.

From the viewpoint of installation, force-feedback devices can be divided into grounded and ungrounded types.

A grounded device is one that is fixed to the work space. Typical examples are Phantom [2] and SPIDAR [8]. This implementation method is mainly used for large devices. It has the advantage of being able to exhibit stable performance precisely. However, its use is limited by the availability of a place to install the device.

Ungrounded devices are those that are not installed on the ground. Typical examples are devices that are light enough to be grasped by hand [10], devices that present multiple haptics using a drone [5], and wearable devices that users attach to their own bodies [6,9]. The advantage of the non-grounded device is that there are no restrictions on its location. Meanwhile, the force that can be presented is smaller than for the grounded type, the device is complex to install and the force is not stable.

Some force-feedback devices use the resistance acting on human joints by arbitrarily changing the joint's stiffness from the outside, thus changing the difficulty of bending the joint. There is a method using dilatancy by air aggregation for reproduction of resistance force [4,6], but there is a problem that the response is very low because air is moved.

3   Proposed Method

In both real space and VR space, work is often done by hand, and feedback to the hand is essential for such work to be accomplished smoothly. Therefore, the user's hands were chosen as the target of resistance presentation in this research.

VR equipment often places a severe burden on the user. When the device is worn, it moves in the same way that the user does, so the moment of force

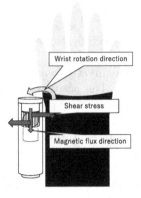

Fig. 1. Principle of resistance presentation

increases. This makes the device feel heavy. In addition, the procedure for attaching and detaching the device to the user is often complicated, making it difficult to put on unassisted.

One way to mitigate the increase in moment is to mount the device as closely as possible to the center of rotation of the motion (in this case, a human joint), thereby minimizing the moment of inertia. We chose to focus on the wrist, a place where the device can be attached fairly easily.

To present resistance, we sought a method that would be lightweight, would be able to increase joint stiffness instantaneously, and would not obstruct free movement of the joint except when presenting. MR (Magneto-Rheological) fluid is a material satisfying these three requirements.

MR fluid is a colloidal dispersion of 10 μm ferromagnetic particles in oil. When a magnetic field is applied, the particles form a chain structure along the lines of magnetic force, and the fluid exhibits a shear stress in a direction perpendicular to the chain structure. The magnitude of the shear stress corresponds to the strength of the applied magnetic-flux density; generally, its maximum value is several tens of kPa. MR fluid response-time is a few milliseconds; this is much shorter than a human's reaction time, allowing real-time control of rigidity [3].

The principle of resistance presentation is shown in the Fig. 1. A device equipped with a rubber tube filled with MR fluid (hereafter referred to as an MR tube) is attached to the wrist. Applying the strong magnetic field to the MR tube increases the viscosity of the MR fluid, and the induced shear stress resists movement of the wrist.

4 Device Development

The device configuration and prototype device are shown in the Fig. 2, the device in use is shown in the Fig. 3.

To adjust the viscosity of the MR fluid, it is necessary to control the magnetic flux density applied. The obvious method of doing this would be to use an

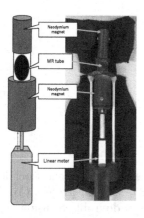

Fig. 2. Device configuration and prototype device

Fig. 3. Device in use

electromagnet. However, this is not feasible if the device is to be light-weight and wearable, because a huge electromagnet would be required to produce the necessary flux density. We use two high-field permanent magnets, one above and one below the MR tube. Fixing the upper magnet and moving the lower one up and down with a linear actuator strengthens or attenuates the magnetic flux density in the tube as desired.

Since the proposed device uses a permanent magnet instead of an electromagnet, a magnetic field is present even when sense of resistance is not required. To reduce the magnetic flux density in the deactivated state, a spring is inserted between the fixed upper magnet and the MR tube. This spring contracts when the lower magnet is brought near the MR tube by the linear actuator, and the magnetic flux density applied to the MR fluid increases. In the deactivated state, the extension of the spring increases the distance from the MR tube to the magnet and decreases the magnetic flux density.

Rather than a pure MR fluid, we used an MRα fluid [7], that is a mixture of MR fluid and non-magnetic material. The inclusion of non-magnetic material increases the hardness of the MR fluid when solidified and reduces the weight of the fluid per unit volume. In the present case, polystyrene spheres with a particle size of 0.5 mm were mixed in as a non-magnetic material. The mixing ratio was determined so that the volume ratio of MR fluid to polystyrene was 1:1.

We used the MR fluid (MRF-140CG, LORD Corporation) [1]. It exhibits a shear stress of 0–60 kPa as the applied magnetic flux density varied from 0–1 T. The MRα fluid was enclosed in a highly oil-resistant fluororubber tube with an outer diameter of 22 mm and an inner diameter of 20 mm.

To control the magnetic flux density, we used two neodymium 40 permanent magnets. The upper magnet had a diameter of 16 mm and a height of 20 mm and the lower magnet a diameter of 20 mm and a height of 30 mm. The magnet and motor cases were each made by PLA with a 3D printer.

Table 1. Result of Experiment 1

Range [mm]	Magnetic flux [mT]
0	630
10	353
20	124
30	65

A wrist fixing band was used to secure the resistance-presentation device to the user's wrist. We used a wrist holder (KA085, Medical Project Co., Ltd) as a restraint to secure the device to the wrist. It is desirable to use a rubber fixing-band that can be adjusted to fit the user's wrist. However, if rubber with high elasticity is used, it will bite into the wrist as the wrist moves, and a sense of restraint occurs. This feeling of restraint could be reduced by using rubber that is not highly stretchable. In practice, we found that the undesirable sense of restraint was strong enough when the fixed orthosis was used as it was, so the unnecessary fixing band was removed.

5   Experiments

5.1   Experiment 1: Measurement of Magnetic Flux

An experiment was conducted to confirm whether the magnetic flux density could be controlled by the prototype mechanism.

We measured the magnetic flux density under the MR tube of the prototype device with a teslameter (BST-200, Beijing Ever Good Electronic) having a range of 0–2000 mT, and a sensitivity of 0.1 mT. We conducted measurements when the distances between the MR tube and the lower magnet were 30 mm, 20 mm, 10 mm, and 0 mm.

The results are shown in the Table 1. The maximum value of the magnetic flux density was about 9.7 times the minimum value. This confirmed that the magnetic flux density could be controlled by the proposed mechanism, and that the amount of change is sufficient for our purposes.

5.2   Experiment 2: Measurement of Bending Stiffness

We measured the hardness of bending the prototype's MR tube, which is the source of resistance to wrist motion. As shown in the Fig. 4, we fixed one side of the device, applied a load to the other, and measured the resulting deformation. The bending stiffness K was calculated according to

$$K = \frac{P}{\delta},\tag{1}$$

where P is the load and δ is the device displacement. The distances between the MR fluid and the lower magnet were the same as in the experiment 1.

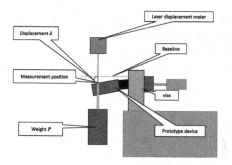

Fig. 4. Arrangement of Experiment 2

Table 2. Result of Experiment 2

Range [mm]	Displacement [mm]	Bending stiffness [N/mm]
30	18.67	1.07
20	18.46	1.08
10	17.95	1.11
0	17.53	1.14

To apply a torque of approximately 1 Nm, a 2 kg weight was attached at a position 50 mm from one end of the MR tube. A laser displacement sensor (ZX2-LD100, OMRON) was used to measure the deformation of the MR tube. The measurement range was 35 mm and the accuracy was 5 μm.

The results are shown in the Table 2 and Fig. 5. The bending stiffness was found to increase with the applied magnetic flux density, as expected. However, the difference in bending stiffness was small. This is because the fluororubber used for sealing does not expand or contract much, and is difficult to bend even when the magnetic field is not strong. By making the material stretchable, for example by wrinkling it like a bellows, the bending stiffness due to the fluororubber could be reduced.

5.3 Experiment 3: Subjective Evaluation

An experiment was conducted to investigate whether it is possible to distinguish between the activated and deactivated states.

The subjects were five males in their twenties. We measured the wrist circumference, forearm circumference, and forearm length of each subject. The subjects were asked to operate the device, with the device in the activated state or deactivated state. Thirty trials were performed in random order, fifteen for each state. In the activated and deactivated states, the distances between the MR fluid and the lower magnet were 0 mm and 30 mm, respectively. During the trial, the state of the device was not visible to the subjects. Sound was played through headphones, so that the state could not be determined from the driving sound of the device. The subjects were asked to move their hand freely and then asked in which state they believed the device to be.

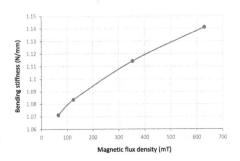

Fig. 5. Result of Experiment 2

Table 3. Result of Experiment 3

Subject	Perimeter of wrist [cm]	Perimeter of forearm [cm]	Length of forearm [cm]	Correct answer rate [%]
A	22	25	30	73.3
B	22	24	28	73.3
C	22	30	30	86.7
D	26	30	33	63.3
E	25	27	30	66.7

The results are shown in the Table 3. All the subjects achieved a correct answer rate that exceeded the chance level. The result showed that the two states could be identified with reasonable accuracy. However, an average accuracy rate of about 72.7% is still low for a practical resistance-presentation device, so further development for increasing resistance force will be necessary. We found that the correct answer rate was independent to the size of the user's arm.

After the experiment, we asked the subjects for their impressions of the force and restraint presentation in the experiment. Wrist movement direction had not been limited, and the subjects had been instructed to move their wrists freely. They reported that it was easy to perceive if they rotated their wrist joints round. And there was also an opinion that the bands for fixing the device to the wrist were annoyed and restrained smooth moving of the subjects' hand.

6   Conclusion

In this research, to develop a lightweight and easy-to-use force-feedback device, we focused on joint-stiffness control. Since MR fluid can rapidly and controllably change its stiffness in response to magnetic flux density, we proposed using an MR-fluid tube and a movable neodymium magnet in a highly responsive, lightweight resistance-presentation device attached to the wrist joint. We experimentally confirmed the performance and controllability of the magnetic flux density control mechanism of the prototype device. In addition, we conducted experiments confirming that the bending stiffness of the MR tube, which causes a sense of resistance, could be controlled by the application of magnetic flux density. The subjective evaluation revealed that users could correctly perceive the resistive state of the device with a probability significantly higher than chance.

References

1. LORD TECHNICAL DATA. http://www.lord.com
2. SensAble Technologies. http://www.sensable.com/
3. Fujita, T., Shimada, K.: Characteristics and applications of magnetorheological fluids. J. Magn. Soc. Jpn. **27**(3), 91–100 (2003)
4. Hauser, S., Robertson, M., Ijspeert, A., Paik, J.: JammJoint:: a variable stiffness device based on granular jamming for wearable joint support. IEEE Robot. Autom. Lett. **2**(2), 849–855 (2017)
5. Hoppe, M., et al.: VRHapticDrones: providing haptics in virtual reality through quadcopters. In: Proceedings of the 17th International Conference on Mobile and Ubiquitous Multimedia, pp. 7–18 (2018)
6. Mitsuda, T., Kuge, S., Wakabayashi, M., Kawamura, S.: Haptic displays implemented by controllable passive elements. In: Proceedings 2002 IEEE International Conference on Robotics and Automation. vol. 4, pp. 4223–4228 (2002)
7. Nishida, T., Okatani, Y., Tadakuma, K.: Development of universal robot gripper using MRα fluid. Int. J. Human. Robot. **13**(4), 1–12 (2016)
8. Sato, M.: SPIDAR and virtual reality. In: Proceedings of the 5th Biannual World Automation Congress, vol. 13, pp. 17–23. TSI Press, Albuquerque (2002)
9. Taniguchi, Y., Tsumugiwa, T., Yokogawa, R.: Development of force haptic device equipped with 3-DOF parallel mechanism. Trans. Jpn. Soc. Mech. Eng. C **78**(793), 3228–3238 (2012)
10. Yano, H., Yoshie, M., Iwata, H.: Development of a non-grounded haptic interface using the gyro effect. In: Proceedings of 11th Symposium on Haptic Interfaces for Virtual Environment and Teleoperator Systems, pp. 32–39 (2003)

Implementation of Remote Control of a Robot Arm by Hand Gestures

Seiji Hayashi[1]($\boxtimes$) and He Muxin[2]

[1] Department of Electronics and Computer Systems, Faculty of Engineering,
Takushoku University, Tokyo, Japan
`shayashi@es.takushoku-u.ac.jp`
[2] Mechanical and Electronic Systems Course, Graduate School of Engineering,
Takushoku University, Tokyo, Japan

Abstract. Recently, the coronavirus pandemic has led to a new normal lifestyle, and reducing contact with humans by 70% is necessary in order for preventing infection. Therefore, in order to reduce the chances of contact between humans to the greatest degree possible, we propose a prototype method for remotely controlling a robot arm using human hand gestures in a non-contact manner. By multithread processing of involving hand gesture recognition using a Kinect device, and conversion between the camera coordinate system and the robot coordinate system, smooth operation of the robot arm is realized by asynchronous communication using exclusive control (mutex class in C++) and queue buffering (queue class on C++).

Keywords: Robot arm maneuver · Remote control · Kinect · Multithread

1 Introduction

Recently, the coronavirus pandemic has led to a new normal lifestyle, and reducing contact with humans by 70% is important in order for preventing infection. However, in order to carry out economic activities, people have to be in close contact with each other in the workplace and in reception work, and the risk of infection tends to increase. Therefore, in the present research, we propose a prototype method for remotely controlling a robot arm using human hand gestures. By acting on behalf of humans, we attempt to reduce the chances of contact between humans as much as possible. In a previous study, in order to remotely operate a robot by hand gestures, the fluctuation component was calculated by acquiring the values of multiple motion sensors attached to the fingers and was reflected in the operation of the robot arm [1,2]. However, in a situation such as the coronavirus pandemic, there is a risk that the operator also increases infection cases by attaching and detaching sensors. For this reason, Microsoft Kinect is extremely effective as a device that can recognize gestures in a non-contact manner without the need to attach the sensor directly to the human body [3–6]. In the prototype system of this research, smooth robot arm operation is realized

C. Stephanidis et al. (Eds.): HCII 2022, CCIS 1581, pp. 18–25, 2022.
https://doi.org/10.1007/978-3-031-06388-6_3

by asynchronous communication using exclusive control and queue buffering. This multithread processing system involves 1) hand gesture recognition using a Kinect device, 2) conversion between the camera coordinate system and the robot coordinate system, and 3) operation of the robot arm.

2 Kinect V2 and SCARA Robot VS-ASR

2.1 Kinect V2 Coordinate System and Joint Position

Microsoft Kinect V2 [7–9] is equipped with an RGB camera, a 3D depth sensor for measuring the distance to the target object, and an infrared sensor. It is possible to acquire human skeleton information (25 skeleton data per person). Each joint is defined in the Joint class, and the type, tracking status, and position of the joint can be acquired.

The Kinect V2 coordinate system can be divided into three systems: a color coordinate system, a depth coordinate system, and a camera coordinate system. The color image uses the color coordinate system, and the depth image uses the depth coordinate system. Both coordinate systems are two-dimensional coordinate systems. The origin is the upper left of the screen. The positive X direction is to the right, and the positive Y direction is downward. The units are pixels. The camera coordinate system is a three-dimensional space coordinate system with the sensor as the origin and is the coordinate system necessary for tracking a human skeleton in the present study. Figure 1 shows a concrete example showing the relationship among these three coordinate systems. Since the resolutions of the color image and the depth image are different, it is necessary to correctly align the images to either coordinate system. We use CoordinateMapper as the conversion utility.

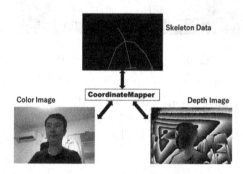

Fig. 1. Relationship among three coordinate systems in Kinect

In Kinect V2, the hand state can be detected by the hand state property. Figure 2 shows the state of each hand when the right or left hand is traceable. The open state is indicated by a green circle, and the closed state is indicated by a red circle. The lasso state is indicated by a blue circle [10].

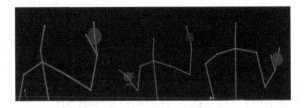

Fig. 2. Hand state recognition results (Color figure online)

2.2 SCARA Robot VS-ASR

The robot used in the present study is a pen type Selective Compliance Assembly Robot Arm (SCARA) robot VS-ASR [11] manufactured by V-stone Co., Ltd. (Fig. 3). The SCARA robot has an arm that moves in the horizontal direction, but since the robot has a Z-axis motor at its tip, the robot can be pushed up and down.

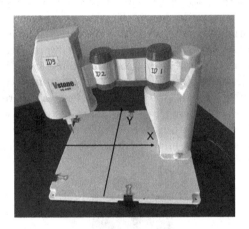

Fig. 3. External view of VS-ASR

The VS-ASR is connected to a PC via USB, and programming in the C language is possible by using the Kinect V2 SDK. The joint length of the robot arm is 80 mm, and it is possible to work on a stage with a length of 210 mm and a width of 230 mm.

3   System Development

In the present study, we considered tracking the palm of the right hand as a hand gesture and created a prototype program that operates the robot arm according to the movement distance. The system development environment in this research is shown in Table 1. The CP2110-USB-to-UART bridge of Silicon Laboratory is used for communication with the robot.

Table 1. System development environment

Operating system	Windows10
Integrated development environment	Visual Studio 2019 C++
Kinect SDK	Kinect for Windows SDK 2.0
Communication library	CP2110-USB to URAT
Motion editor	SCARA Programmer

3.1 Multithreading

The program developed in this study is multithreaded, allowing multiple processes to be performed in parallel. The reason for using multithreading is that the processing speed of the robot arm is much slower than that of the Kinect, and multiple threads are required to adjust the work. Figure 4 shows the correspondence between the threads. The process of (1) is mainly to collect and process the coordinates of the skeleton through the Kinect, and processing is performed for each video frame. The coordinates obtained from (1) are sent to (2), conversion to the robot coordinate system is performed using CoordinateMapper, and the operation command is issued to the robot arm. In (3), the robot arm is operated according to the instruction from (2). The above process is performed asynchronously using mutex class [12] and queue class [13]. The frame rate obtained from various Kinect sensors is much higher than the movement speed of the robot arm. Therefore, communication from (2) to (3) is appropriately controlled according to the operating status of each thread so that buffer overflow does not occur in the arm operation process in (3) in Fig. 4. Figure 5 shows the flowchart of this system. In Fig. 5, (1), (2), and (3) have a one-to-one correspondence with (1), (2), and (3) in Fig. 4.

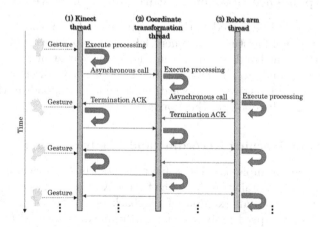

Fig. 4. Multithreaded process configuration

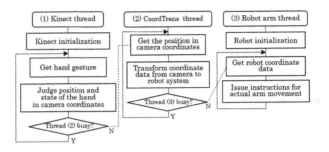

Fig. 5. Flowchart of the system

3.2 Teaching Recording and Playback Function

Figure 6 shows a flowchart of the recording and playback program. When the hand gesture changes from Open to Closed, the text file required for recording is generated. When the Closed hand gesture is maintained for 0.5 seconds, recording of the robot coordinates sent to the robot arm starts, and when the hand gesture changes from Closed to Open, recording is stopped and the file is closed. When the hand is stationary during teaching, approximately the same coordinate values are recorded. Regarding the playback function, when the gesture changes from Open to Lasso, the robot's teaching data is read into an array from the recorded JSON file. After that, the movements of the robot arm can be reproduced in the order of teaching by sequentially transmitting to the robot arm.

4   Execution Results and Considerations

4.1 Correspondence Between Gesture and Arm Movement

The robot arm could be moved in the two-dimensional X–Y coordinate system according to the hand gesture (movement left, right, up and down) that tracks the palm of the right hand. As shown in Fig. 7, movement of the palm to the right (left) corresponds to the positive direction (negative direction) of the X axis of the robot, and upward (downward) movement corresponds to the positive direction (negative direction) of the Y axis.

4.2 Results of Teaching Recording and Playback Functions

Figure 8 shows an example of a JSON file generated by the teaching record.

The teaching file contains one line each for the X-axis and Y-axis in the JSON format. Figure 9 shows an example of playback operation using the teaching data. The operating speed limit is equal to the maximum speed of the robot, although it depends on the performance of the PC. Therefore, it is easy to expect an improvement in performance by using a robot that operates faster than the robot used in this project.

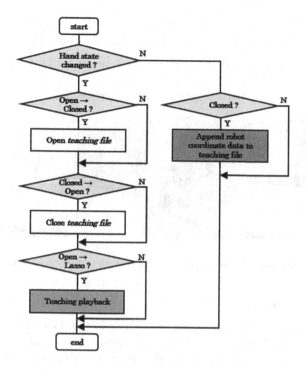

Fig. 6. Flowchart of the program to record and play

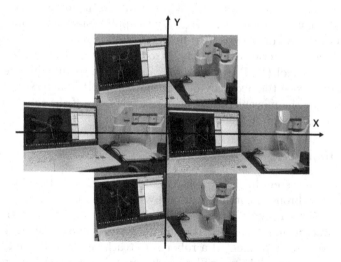

Fig. 7. Examples of hand gestures and scalar robot movements

```
[ { "x-coordinate": "-17.090189", "y-coordinate": "-8.136154" },
  { "x-coordinate": "-17.455139", "y-coordinate": "-7.944824" },
  { "x-coordinate": "-21.954224", "y-coordinate": "-0.013176" },
              ...
  { "x-coordinate": "-73.681732", "y-coordinate": "0.320969" } ]
```

Fig. 8. Example of recorded teaching data

Fig. 9. Example during playback operation using teaching data

4.3   Considerations

From the results of the program operation, the robot arm could be moved in the two-dimensional X–Y coordinate system according to the hand gesture (movement left, right, up and down) by tracking the palm of the right hand. Furthermore, we were able to implement the teaching recording and playback functions of the robot arm. However, the following improvements are required: a) In order to reduce unnecessary movements of the robot due to the influence of hand fluctuations and minute shaking, it is necessary to apply a smoothing process to the movements of the robot. However, if fine operation is required, this smoothing process need not be performed. b) By introducing interpolation processing by point-to-point control (PTP control), we can attempt to simplify the teaching method and improve the accuracy of arm movement. It is necessary to set the time required for the movement and playback functions of the robot arm to the optimum interval based on the operating environment.

5   Conclusion

In the prototype system in the present research, smooth robot arm operation is realized by asynchronous communication by multithread processing of 1) hand gesture recognition using a Kinect device, 2) conversion between the camera coordinate system and the robot coordinate system, and 3) operation of the robot arm. We also implemented a robot arm teaching recording and playback function. As a future task, we will consider applying a smoothing process to the movement of the robot in order to reduce unnecessary movement due to the influence of minute shaking of the hand. We also plan to introduce interpolation processing by PTP control, in order to simplify the teaching method and improve the accuracy of arm movement. In addition, to perform complex actions, new gestures will be added to control the robot arm.

References

1. Sato, E., Yamazaki, C., Okumura, Y.: Prototype of arm robot controlled by myo-electric potential. http://www.st.nanzan-u.ac.jp/info/gr-thesis/2017/okumura/pdf/14sc064.pdf. Accessed 26 Oct 2021
2. Noda, T., Watanabe, K., Minamizawa, K., et al.: Flexibility control of robot arm using myoelectric potential information. In: Robotics and Mechatronics Lecture Summary, pp. 1A2-E02 1–4 (2007)
3. Igarashi, H., Hayashi, S.: A study on information provision by touch-less interface in a hospital room. In: The 2018 IEICE Engineering Sciences Society/NOLTA Society Conference, A-15-10, p. 127 (2018)
4. Igarashi, H., Hayashi, S: Examination of gamification for rehabilitation using face state recognition. In: The 2019 IEICE Engineering Sciences Society/NOLTA Society Conference, A-15-10, p. 108 (2019)
5. Hayashi, S., Igarashi, H.: Touchless information provision and facial expression training using Kinect. In: Stephanidis, C., Antona, M., Ntoa, S. (eds.) HCII 2021. CCIS, vol. 1420, pp. 90–97. Springer, Cham (2021). https://doi.org/10.1007/978-3-030-78642-7_13
6. Muxin, H., Hayashi, S.: A study on controlling scalar robots using gestures. The 12th University Consortium Hachioji Student Presentation, Q214 (2020)
7. Kinect for Windows Homepage. https://developer.microsoft.com/en-us/windows/kinect/. Accessed 26 Oct 2021
8. Nakamura, K.: Using Kinect to make gesture-input-compatible home appliances. Nikkei Electronics, Nikkei BP, No.1065, pp. 121–131 (2011)
9. Chiba, S.: Kinect as a next-gen interface. J. Robot. Soc. Jpn. **32**(3), 231–235 (2014)
10. Nakamura, K., Sugiura, T., Takada, T., Ueda, T.: Kinect for Windows SDK Programming Kinect for Windows v2 Sensor Handlling Version. Shuwa System Corporation (2015)
11. Vstone Co., Ltd: Academic SCARA Robot. https://www.vstone.co.jp/products/scara_robot/index.html. Accessed 26 Oct 2021
12. Microsoft Documentation: Mutex. https://docs.microsoft.com/en-us/cpp/standard-library/mutex-class-stl?view=msvc-160. Accessed 26 Oct 2021
13. Microsoft Documentation: Queue. https://docs.microsoft.com/en-us/cpp/standard-library/queue-class?view=msvc-160. Accessed 26 Oct 2021

Character Input Interface Design for Effective Use of Motion Sensors on Smartwatches

Kaito Hino$^{(\boxtimes)}$, Tota Mizuno, Yu Matsumoto, Kazuyuki Mito, and Naoaki Itakura

The University of Electro-Communications, 1-5-1 Chofugaoka, Chofu, Tokyo, Japan
h2130099@edu.cc.uec.ac.jp

Abstract. In recent years, the opportunity to operate smartwatches has increased owing to the increase in the number of people using smartwatches. The main input methods for smartwatches are touch and voice; however, there is/are these input methods present a few problems. In this study, we focus on gesture input, which involves detection via hand and arm movements. It can be discriminated by the accelerometer and gyroscope in a smartwatch. Previously, we attempted to discriminate finger movements; however, each finger movement was difficult to distinguish. This implies that discriminating gestures using motion sensors is challenging. Therefore, we herein propose side-tap, dial-rotation, and band-rotation operations, which can be effectively performed in a motion sensor. The purposes of these operations are to tap the side of the device, twist the dial, and twist the wrist, respectively. The characteristic waveforms of these operations can be obtained using the accelerometer and gyroscope in the smartwatch. In addition, the proposed operation offers a sufficient number of selections for the character input. The waveforms of the proposed operations are analyzed, and a discrimination algorithm is developed and evaluated. First, each motion is performed 10 times consecutively; subsequently, each motion is randomly performed 10 times. The results show that the average discrimination rate is 97.5%. Therefore, the proposed motion is useful as a new input method for smartwatches. In the future, to use the proposed motion as a character input, an appropriate keyboard design is necessitated. Therefore, we develop a keyboard design that enables users to input characters intuitively using the proposed motion.

Keywords: Interface · Smartwatch · Gesture · Character input

1 Introduction

Owing to the technological developments in recent years, various types of smart devices have become widespread. According to the "Trend Survey for Communication Areas" by the Ministry of Internal Affairs and Communications, as of 2019, the maximum ownership rate of mobile terminals is 96.1% [1]. Among mobile terminals, wristwatch-type smartwatches are garnering significant attention. According to the Moving Mobile & Mobility Forward survey, the domestic sales volume in 2019 increased by 32.1% compared with the previous year; hence, the market size of smartwatches is expanding [2].

C. Stephanidis et al. (Eds.): HCII 2022, CCIS 1581, pp. 26–33, 2022.
https://doi.org/10.1007/978-3-031-06388-6_4

Therefore, the demand for smartwatches is expected to further increase in the future, which necessitates the development of functions that are more user friendly.

Currently, two typical input interfaces exist for smartwatches: touch and voice inputs. Touch input is an intuitive input method because the input target displayed on the screen is directly touched. However, touch inputs exhibit certain problems. For example, in a device with a narrow screen area, such as a smartwatch, the size of the input target becomes extremely small, which is identified when an adjacent button has been pressed, thereby resulting in an erroneous input. This problem is known as the fat finger problem [3]. In addition, because the input targets are not physically separated, the screen at the time of input must be observed to confirm the input targets. Voice input is applied by speaking the input content into a microphone. Because this method does not require touching the screen of the device for input, the problems associated with a touch input can be avoided. However, voice input is difficult to use, such as in libraries and hospitals where voice commands cannot be used, or in noisy areas such as crowds and underpasses; hence, its usage is limited to certain environments. Furthermore, reluctance in using such inputs has been reported [4]. Hence, various input interfaces are being investigated to solve these problems.

The current mainstream input method is the touch method. Therefore, touch input, which is familiar to many users, is used in smartwatches. In previous studies, touch inputs for smartwatches with small screens have been actively investigated. Various input methods have been proposed, such as slide-in [5], single strokes [6], a method that renders the key top transparent to provide a two-layer structure comprising a flick keyboard and a text area [7], and an input method that allows a QWERTY keyboard to be traced [8]. However, none of these approaches can solve the fat finger problem.

Therefore, to solve the problems posed by conventional input methods, gesture input is actively being investigated. Gesture input is applied using body movements without touching the screen. In this method, an input can be applied regardless of the screen size and surrounding environment, unlike a voice input.

In a previous study [9], a gesture input based on the bending and stretching of each finger was examined. Although the bending and stretching movements of the thumb and index finger sides and those of the finger and little finger sides can be discriminated, the movements of an entire finger could not be discriminated. In a previous study [10], researchers examined whether a motion pattern can be determined using the vibration waveform obtained from the keystroke motion of the fingertip. The results revealed that the rotation of the wrist can be discriminated, but not the number of keystrokes. In other previous studies [9, 10], difficulty in distinguishing vibrations owing to finger movements when using a smartwatch was demonstrated. Therefore, six types of inputs were proposed [11], including tapping outside the touch screen and performing wrist movement. It was discovered that the input operation can be recognized. However, the discrimination rate was lower for certain movements.

Based on the results of previous studies, we focus on the motions of tapping outside the touch screen, twisting the terminal, and turning the wrist to obtain characteristic waveforms using an acceleration/gyro sensor. We propose nine types of movements for selecting characters with few movements and examine whether the proposed movements are useful as input.

2 Proposed Method

Herein, we propose the side-tap, dial-rotation, and band-rotation operations, as shown in Fig. 1. Considering movements effectively utilize a motion sensor, the x- and y-axes of the acceleration can be used for tapping, the x-axis of the angular velocity can be used for wrist movements, and the z-axis of the angular velocity can be used for twisting the dial. In addition, because a smartwatch is small and lightweight, the device can be moved by tapping, whereas it can be held with the thumb and index finger. Based on these findings, we investigated the following nine types of operations, which can be easily applied and can secure the number of selections for the character input (three types of side-tap operations, four types of dial-rotation operations on the band, and two types of rotation operations).

- LB: Tap the bottom left
- RB: Tap the bottom right
- RT: Tap the upper right
- L_tw: Twist the device clockwise
- R_tw: Twist the device counterclockwise
- Up: A series of movements from the outside to the inside of the wrist

L_tw, R_tw, and Up comprise two types each; additionally, we determined whether the time from twisting to returning was short or long.

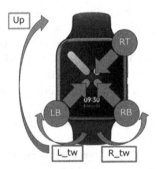

Fig. 1. Proposed action

3 Waveform Analysis

3.1 Measurement of Waveform Data

An acceleration sensor and a gyro sensor, which were built into the smartwatch, were used to determine the operation. The sampling frequency of the acceleration/gyro sensor was set to 100 Hz. In addition, because the data obtained by the accelerometer included the gravitational acceleration, the gravitational acceleration was removed using a difference filter. When the proposed operation was applied, characteristic waveforms appeared on the x- and y-axes of the acceleration in the side-tap operation, the z-axis of the angular velocity in the dial-rotation operation, and the x-axis of the angular velocity in the band-rotation operation.

3.2 Waveform Characteristics of Each Operation

As shown in Fig. 2, when each operation was performed, a waveform characteristic of the x-axis acceleration, y-axis acceleration, x-axis angular velocity, or z-axis angular velocity can be obtained. First, the waveforms obtained via the side-tap, dial-rotation, and band-rotation operations were different. It was discovered that the time from the first peak to the second peak of the side-tap operation waveform was 10 to 50 ms, whereas those of the dial- and band-rotation operations were 150 ms or higher. Side-tap operations LB, RB, and RT show characteristic waveforms on the x- and y-axes of the acceleration. LB shows a positive-to-negative waveform on both the x- and y-axes, RB shows a negative-to-positive waveform on the x-axis and a positive-to-negative waveform on the y-axis, and RT shows a negative-to-positive waveform on both the x- and y-axes. In the dial-rotation operations, L_tw and R_tw, a characteristic waveform appeared on the z-axis of the angular velocity. L_tw shows a negative-to-positive waveform, and R_tw shows a positive-to-negative waveform. In the Up band rotation operation, a negative-to-positive waveform appeared on the x-axis of the angular velocity. In addition, when the time from twisting to returning was long, the dial and band rotation operations show a waveform with a long period from the first to the second peak.

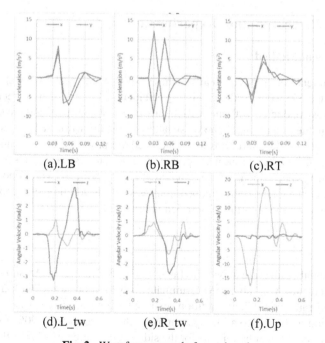

Fig. 2. Waveform example for each action

3.3 Operation Discrimination Algorithm

The algorithm was constructed based on the fact that the characteristic waveforms can be obtained during an operation. The time from the first peak to the second peak was used to distinguish among the side-tap, dial-rotation, and band-rotation operations. If the difference in peak time is 100 ms or less, then a side-tap operation is implied; if it exceeds 100 ms, then a dial-rotation or band-rotation operation is implied. The values of acceleration from the x- and y-axes were used to discriminate the three types of side-tap operations (LB, RB, and RT). For LB and RT, the waveforms of the acceleration in the x- and y-axes were in phase, whereas that of RB was out of phase. Therefore, when the integral value of the product of acceleration from the x- and y-axes is positive, LB or RT is implied, whereas when it is negative, RB is implied. When LB or RT is implied, if the first peak of the waveform on the x- and y-axes of acceleration is positive, then LB is implied; if it is negative, then RT is implied. The dial-rotation operation (L_tw, R_tw) is determined by setting a threshold value for the added value of the z-axis of the angular velocity. If the added value of the z-axis of the angular velocity is positive and exceeds the threshold value, then R_tw is implied; if it is negative and exceeds the threshold value, then L_tw is implied. The band-rotation operation (Up) is determined by setting a threshold value for the added value of the x-axis of the angular velocity. In addition, In the dial-rotation and band-rotation operations, when the time from the first peak to the second peak of the waveform of the x-axis or z-axis of the angular velocity is 500 ms or higher, then a long operation is implied.

4 Motion Discrimination Experiment

4.1 Experiment Method

For the experiment, four types of smartwatches (OPPO Watch, Galaxy Watch 4, SUNTO 7, and TicWatch S2) were used, and eight participants in their 20s were recruited. The experiment was conducted with the participants in the seated state, and the smartwatch was attached to the arm on which the wristwatch is typically worn. All participants wore the smartwatches on their left arms and conducted the proposed movements with their right hand. First, each operation was applied 10 times successively; subsequently, and each operation was performed 10 times randomly. The experiments were conducted using four models, and the total number of operations was 720. In addition, discrimination was performed based on the algorithm described in Sect. 3.3.

4.2 Results

The experimental results are shown in Table 1, Fig. 3 and Fig. 4. As shown in Table 1, most participants were able to discriminate with high accuracy, with a maximum discrimination rates of 90%. In addition, extremely high accuracy was indicated for the dial-rotation and band-rotation operations, with an accuracy of 90% for the latter half. However, the discrimination rate for the side-tap operation was lower than those of the other operations. The discrimination rate for RT was particularly low. As shown in Fig. 3, all terminals indicated a discrimination rate of 90% or higher, with TicWatch S2 exhibiting the highest discrimination rate. The discrimination rates for the side-tap, dial-rotation, and band-rotation operations varied by device. However, multiple comparisons showed no significant differences between terminals for most operations. Comparisons between group were made by analysis of variance (ANOVA), and when significant were examined by Bonferroni-Dunn multiple comparisons post hoc test. Differences were considered significant when $P < 0.05$. As shown in Fig. 4, the learning effect was not indicated. Multiple comparisons were performed, and the results showed no significant differences between rounds for all movements. Multiple comparisons were made in the same way as between terminals.

The newly introduced dial-rotation and band-rotation operations were discriminated with high accuracy, regardless of the amount of time spent from twist to return.

Table 1. Discrimination rate for each participant [%]

Participant \ Motion	LB	RB	RT	L_tw	R_tw	Up	Ltw Long	Rtw Long	Up Long	Side Tap	Dial Rotation	Band Rotation	All
A	85.0	93.8	75.0	98.8	95.0	96.3	98.8	100	88.8	84.6	98.1	92.5	92.4
B	97.5	96.3	86.3	95.0	97.5	95.0	93.8	95.0	100	93.3	95.3	97.5	95.1
C	92.5	93.8	77.5	98.8	98.8	98.8	98.8	100	98.8	87.9	99.1	98.8	95.3
D	88.8	93.8	61.3	96.3	95.0	100	96.3	87.5	98.8	81.3	93.8	99.4	90.8
E	88.8	76.3	63.8	85.0	88.8	97.5	96.3	90.0	97.5	76.3	90.0	97.5	87.1
F	93.8	95.0	80.0	97.5	93.8	96.3	98.8	93.8	97.5	89.6	95.9	96.9	94.0
G	87.5	83.8	56.3	96.3	95.0	100	90.0	92.5	100	75.8	93.4	100	89.0
H	98.8	96.3	85.0	97.5	100	96.3	100	100	98.8	93.3	99.4	97.5	96.9
Average	91.6	91.1	73.1	95.6	95.5	97.5	96.6	94.8	97.5	85.3	95.6	97.5	92.6

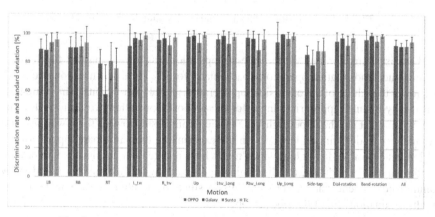

Fig. 3. Discrimination rate and standard deviation for each terminal

4.3 Consideration

The experimental results show that the proposed algorithm was able to discriminate the side-tap, dial-rotation, and band-rotation operations. Although the discrimination rate varied by participant, the accuracy was approximately 90% for most participants, which suggests the universality of this input method. The fact that the discrimination rate varied by the device model suggests that the discrimination rate may be affected by the device. The side-tap operation of the OPPO Watch indicated a lower discrimination rate than the other models. This may be because its body size was the smallest among the round models, and that the edge of the band interfered with the tap position. In addition, as no learning effect was indicated, the operation proposed herein does not require practice.

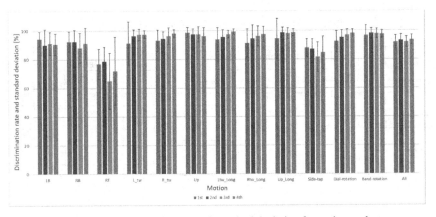

Fig. 4. Discrimination rate and standard deviation for each round

The discrimination rate for the side-tap operation was lower than that for the dial-rotation and band-rotation operations, particularly for RT. The discrimination rate of RT was lower than those of the other side-tap operations for all participants, which suggests that it may be an inappropriate input for the proposed operation. To perform RT, the participant must tap the upper right side of the terminal side toward the lower left with the index or middle finger; however, in the experiment, the participant tapped toward the left instead of the lower left, which might have resulted in misclassification or non-discrimination. In addition, the discrimination algorithm for LB and RT shared many common components and was prone to misclassification. Excluding RT would improve the discrimination rate of the side-tap operations.

5   Summary

In this study, we focused on gesture input as a new input method for smartwatches. We proposed side-tap, dial-rotation, and band-rotation operations, created a discrimination algorithm based on the characteristic waveform of each motion, and conducted a discrimination experiment. As indicated by the experimental results, the proposed operation can be discriminated with high accuracy, and the usefulness of the smartwatch as a new input method was demonstrated.

In future studies, we intend to improve the discrimination algorithm and investigate a character input approach that incorporates the operation proposed herein. Hence, we will identify the appropriate action to be performed for the input, as well as develop an appropriate keyboard design. Subsequently, we will conduct an evaluation experiment by inputting the characters to develop a new input method for smartwatches.

References

1. Ministry of Internal Affairs and Communications: Reiwa 1st Year Communication Usage Trend Survey Report (Household Edition) Ownership of Information and Communication Equipment (2019). https://www.soumu.go.jp/johotsusintokei/statistics/pdf/HR201900_001. pdf
2. MMRI: Trends/forecasts of smartwatch market size and actual usage (2020). https://www.m2ri.jp/release/detail.html?id=456
3. Siek, K.A., Rogers, Y., Connelly, K.H.: Fat finger worries: how older and younger users physically interact with PDAs. In: Costabile, M.F., Paternò, F. (eds.) INTERACT 2005. LNCS, vol. 3585, pp. 267–280. Springer, Heidelberg (2005). https://doi.org/10.1007/11555261_24
4. KDDI: Half of the information search "troublesome" by inputting characters "Voice search in public is" embarrassing "More than 70%, voice operation of home appliances, etc., 40% "I want to use" if there are no people at home (2017). http://news.kddi.com/kddi/corporate/newsrelease/2017/10/05/besshi2726.html
5. Akita, K., Tanaka, T., Sagawa. Y.: Character input method for smart watches by slide-in. In: IPSJ Interaction 2018, pp. 276–281 (2018)
6. Saito, K., Oku, H.: HARI keyboard: ultra-small touch panel devices for Japanese input keyboard. In: IPSJ Interaction 2016, 2C55, pp. 701–702 (2016)
7. Gordon, M., Ouyang, T., Zhai, S.: WatchWriter: tap and gesture typing on a smartwatch miniature keyboard with statistical decoding. In: CHI 2016, San Jose, CA, USA (2016)
8. Toriyama, R., Miyashita, H.: InvisibleFlick: Japanese input keyboard with transparent key tops on small touch screen terminals. IPSJ SIG Technical Report, vol. 2019-HCI-182, No. 27, pp. 1–8 (2019)
9. Sugawara, K., Akehi, K., Farahani, M.A., Mito, K., Mizuno, T., Itakura. N.: Gesture input using forearm movement. In: IEEE IM Society, Tokyo/Japan Sections Joint Chapter Student Meeting, IEEE_IM-S18-23 (2018)
10. Inayama, C., Farahani, M.A., Mito, K., Mizuno, T., Itakura, N.: Gesture input for smart watches using finger keystrokes. In: IEEE IM Society, Tokyo/Japan Sections Joint Chapter Student Meeting, IEEE_IM-S19-25 (2019)
11. Hino, K., Mizuno, T., Matsumoto, Y., Mito, K., Itakura. N.: Investigation of new input method for smart watches using motion sensors. In: 2021 Annual Conference on Electronics, Information and Systems Institute of Electrical Engineers of Japan, TC8-2 (2021)

A Pilot Study on the Use of Gaze Stops to Support the Search for Important Parts

Fumiya Inoue[1][✉] and Makio Ishihara[2]

[1] Graduate School of Fukuoka Institute of Technology, Fukuoka, Japan
mfm21102@bene.fit.ac.jp
[2] Fukuoka Institute of Technology, Fukuoka, Japan
m-ishihara@fit.ac.jp

Abstract. With the increasing number of opportunities to search for a desired content from a large amount of information, it is required to improve the efficiency of information search. We propose a support method for information search with eye movements. For information search, the gaze moves quickly during the search, and the gaze stops when it is judged whether the content is the desired content or something close to it. From this, it is thought that by coloring spots where a certain fixation happens, it would help users read back quickly, and it would be easier for the gaze to go to similar contents. A experiment is conducted on nine subjects and it is found that the total distance of eye movements and elapsed time to complete information search are shortened.

Keywords: Eye movements · Information acquisition · Reading comprehension

1 Introduction

In recent years, with the spread of information terminals such as smartphones and tablets, there are increasing opportunities to search for a desired content from a large amount of information. Along with this, efficient information search is required. In the field of research, properties of eye movements during reading sentences have been discussed so far [1,2], and there are not so many discussions that deal with support of information search in real time. In this research, we discuss a system that supports information search in real time by eye tracking technologies. During a user searches for a desired piece of information, quick movements of back and forth of gazing happen iteratively for him/her to organize information of sentences and determine whether the gazing content is the desired one or close to it. Our basic idea of supporting information search is to help users to organize information of sentences by making spots where gazing stops, conspicuous such as coloring, so that reading back and forth is encouraged to happen smoothly and they could find the desired content quickly.

C. Stephanidis et al. (Eds.): HCII 2022, CCIS 1581, pp. 34–38, 2022.
https://doi.org/10.1007/978-3-031-06388-6_5

2   Related Work

Eye movements in reading are classfied into two types: fixation and saccade. A fixation is a state in which the eye is kept at a point for a certain period of time, and a saccade is a state in which the eye is moving from one point to another at a high speed. As regards reading comprehension, fixation happens to capture a certain amount of characters and saccade does to move the eye to the next fixation point, and understanding of sentences is achived while repeating fixation and saccade [2]. McConkie et al. [1] analyzed data of eye movements during reading comprehension to identify factors that affect the position of the reader's initial eye fixation for a word. This study focuses on support of information search and relies on an idea that a period of duration the user spends for determining whether the gazing content is the desired one or not would become longer if it is closer. Based on this idea, when a series of fixations is kept at a spot within a given radius for a given time span, the spot is colored to make it conspicuous so that the user could read back and forth easily between those candidates for the desired content, resulting in quick access to it.

3   Experiment

3.1   Purpose

The searching speed is supposed to be improved by coloring spots where gazing for a certain period of time happens because of its contributions to organizing information of sentences. To confirm this, a comparative experiment is conducted with or without the coloring to investigate its impact on performance of information search.

3.2   Method and Tasks

Gaze data is obtained from a screen-based eye tracker of Tobii Pro Spectrum. The size of a screen attached on the tracker is 23.8 in. and the resolution is 1920 by 1080. Subjects sit in front of the screen and read several documents shown on the screen. A screenshot of a document with some colored spots is shown in Fig. 1. Subjects are asked to perform a finding task of the three main points of the given document. Six different documents which consist of about 600 characters in Japanese are prepared. Three of them are used for coloring condition and the remaining three for no-coloring condition (control condition). These documents do not include pictures, charts and diagrams because those visual stimuli are expected to add other aspects to propenties of eye movements and they could hinden subjects from concentrating on the finding task. Table 1 summarizes properties of the documents.

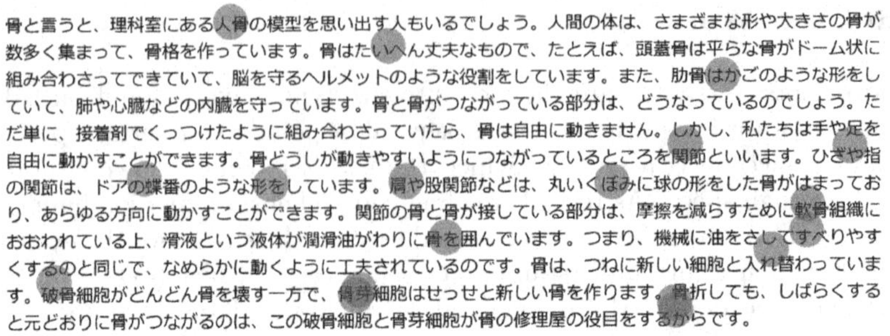

骨と言うと、理科室にある人骨の模型を思い出す人もいるでしょう。人間の体は、さまざまな形や大きさの骨が数多く集まって、骨格を作っています。骨はたいへん丈夫なもので、たとえば、頭蓋骨は平らな骨がドーム状に組み合わさってできていて、脳を守るヘルメットのような役割をしています。また、肋骨はかごのような形をしていて、肺や心臓などの内臓を守っています。骨と骨がつながっている部分は、どうなっているのでしょう。ただ単に、接着剤でくっつけたように組み合わさっていたら、骨は自由に動きません。しかし、私たちは手や足を自由に動かすことができます。骨どうしが動きやすいようにつながっているところを関節といいます。ひざや指の関節は、ドアの蝶番のような形をしています。肩や股関節などは、丸いくぼみに球の形をした骨がはまっており、あらゆる方向に動かすことができます。関節の骨と骨が接している部分は、摩擦を減らすために軟骨組織におおわれている上、滑液という液体が潤滑油がわりに骨を囲んでいます。つまり、機械に油をさしてすべりやすくするのと同じで、なめらかに動くように工夫されているのです。骨は、つねに新しい細胞と入れ替わっています。破骨細胞がどんどん骨を壊す一方で、骨芽細胞はせっせと新しい骨を作ります。骨折しても、しばらくすると元どおりに骨がつながるのは、この破骨細胞と骨芽細胞が骨の修理屋の役目をするからです。

Fig. 1. A screenshot of one of documents used in the experiment

Table 1. Summary of six documents used in the experiment

Text no.	1	2	3	4	5	6
Hiragana	337	346	386	334	337	358
Katakana	38	75	10	43	74	56
Kanji	159	129	159	159	117	127
Punctuation	39	43	38	40	44	38
Total	573	593	593	576	572	579

3.3 Procedure

There are nine subjects with the ages of 21 to 23. They perform calibration of the eye tracker at first and then move to finding tasks. Each subject performs a single finding task for each of six documents (3 for coloring + 3 for no-coloring) and the sequence of documents is balanced to remove order effects. A first document is shown on the screen and the subject starts a first finding task by hitting any key. When he/she finishes the task, he/she hits any key again to move to the next task.

$$6 \text{ subjects} \times 6 \text{ documents} \times 1 \text{ finding task} = 36 \text{ trials} \tag{1}$$

4 Results

The results obtained from the experiment are shown in Fig. 2, 3, 4, 5 and 6. Figures 2, and 3 show the results obtained from two subjects. The horizontal axis is the elapsed time in millisecond and the vertical one does the coordinates' value of the screen. Figure 2 shows the eye movement on each axis for the condition of no coloring at each subject and Fig. 3 shows it for coloring. From these figures, there is a certain difference in eye movements between coloring condition and no coloring one. Figure 4 shows the elapsed time to complete a finding task in millisecond on average. The graph shows that the elapsed time is shortened for 7 of 9 subjects for the coloring condition. It would indicate that reading comprehension is performed efficiently. So, it is expected that the gaze would be navigated efficiently to the desired information for coloring condition. Figure 5 shows the total distance of eye movements in pixel and Fig. 6 shows the number of gaze stops. From those graphs, there would be a certain difference in total distance between the conditions.

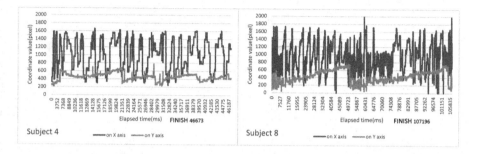

Fig. 2. Results from two subjects for no coloring

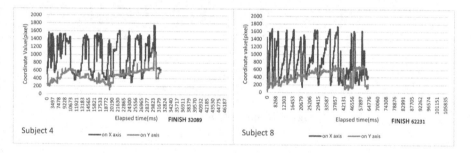

Fig. 3. Results from the same subjects for coloring

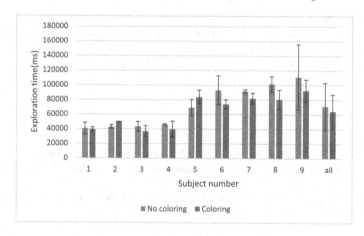

Fig. 4. Results of elapsed time

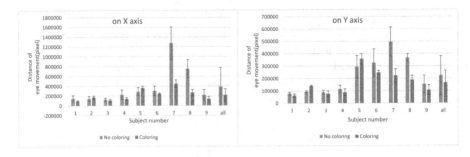

Fig. 5. Results of total distance

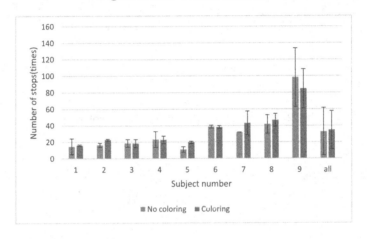

Fig. 6. Results of gaze stops

5   Conclusion

For reading comprehension, this study shows that coloring documents with marks shorten both the total distance of eye movements and the elapsed time to find out the main point of the documents, and it is a possible course of action to support reading comprehension. Our future tasks include increasing the number of subjects for reliability and devising better methods.

References

1. McConkie, G.W., Kerr, P.W., Reddix, M.D., Zola, D.: Eye movement control during reading: I. The location of initial eye fixations on words. Vis. Res. **28**(10), 1107–1118 (1998)
2. Rayner, K.: Eye movements in reading and information processing: 20 years of research. Psychol. Bull. **124**, 372–410 (1998)

VR Human Body Treatment Game 'BodyCureBot' Using Hand Tracking

Da Yeon Lee[1] ⓘ, Du Ri Kim[1] ⓘ, Edward Lee[2] ⓘ, and Jung Jo Na[1](✉) ⓘ

[1] Duksung Women's University, 33, Samyang-ro 144-gil, Dobong-gu, Seoul, Republic of Korea
jungjona@duksung.ac.kr
[2] Notre Dame Academy, Palisades Park, NJ, USA

Abstract. Virtual reality content is gaining popularity as a next-generation medium, however because the 180-degree contents previously used cannot be used in their current state, new VR content is required. Due to the current paucity of VR content, content production is happening in a range of fields, and discussions concerning viability continue. This article will detail the whole process of designing, manufacturing, and constructing a hand-tracking-based virtual reality game. It is built on the Unity game engine and was made using Autodesk's 3ds MAX, Blender, C#, and JSON. Additionally, it is a real-time interactive game that the user manipulates with his or her hands. The game 'BodyCureBot' is designed in such a way that a user wearing a head-mounted display explores and cures the human body's lungs, heart, and blood vessels. The player takes on the role of a nanorobot and inspects the diseased human body, treating the afflicted place as a game. The production of game content using hand tracking technology will deliver new experiences for game customers looking for variety. This paper proposes and applies various types of user interfaces that can be used in the VR environment. Additionally, educational benefits may be predicted when users are presented with medical knowledge and given the opportunity to understand it. 'BodyCureBot,' which was created to increase user immersion and deliver new material, wants to make realistic graphic content in the future to enable investigation of a broader range of human organs. The addition of multiplayer functionality via the identification of multiple gestures will result in increased content diversity as a consequence of user collaboration.

Keywords: Virtual reality · VR content · Hand tracking · Educational

1 Introduction

Korea is fairly competitive globally in terms of terminals, solutions, and networks critical to the growth of the emerging VR sector but lags behind in terms of platforms and content (Choi 2020) [2]. At the moment, investment and demand in the virtual reality industry are growing, but the existing VR content is insufficient. Additionally, relatively few virtual reality games use hand tracking, and the bulk of content experiences are short. To solve this content shortage and provide customers with a new experience, we designed a narrative game using VR hand tracking and then used hand tracking to increase the

C. Stephanidis et al. (Eds.): HCII 2022, CCIS 1581, pp. 39–45, 2022.
https://doi.org/10.1007/978-3-031-06388-6_6

player's sense of immersion by utilizing hand gestures rather than a VR controller. To assist the user in learning while following the story, medical information is included in the character's dialogues, allowing the user to naturally acquire (medical) knowledge. Following that, the user may play the game and reinforce learning by adding a quiz based on the prior dialogue.

2 Project Design

2.1 Game Summary

In the near future, nanorobots will be able to repair humans. Many nanorobots change one day as a result of a system abnormality, and the main character (player), one of the unaffected nanorobots, returns to the headquarters. Returning to the headquarters, the player sees a robot with a damaged body but an intact mind, and progresses through seven scenarios.

2.2 Functions Required to Progress the Game

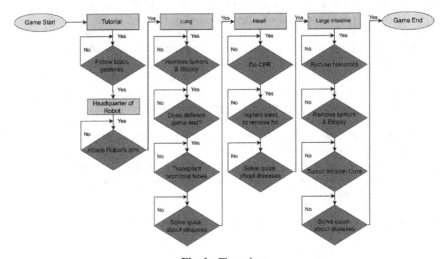

Fig. 1. Flow chart

In order to organize the functions and requirements necessary for the progress of the game, a (Fig. 1) flow chart of the game's major functions were created.

2.3 Large Intestine in Game Content Overview

Three distinct body organs were featured in the game. Among them, we described large intestine disorders and the stages and functions of the game that users face in the large intestine.

Introduction of Large Intestine Disorders. Colorectal cancer is a malignant tumor that develops in the colon and rectum [3]. It is termed colon cancer if it occurs in the colon, rectal cancer if it occurs in the rectum, and colon cancer or colorectal cancer if it occurs in both [3]. According to statistics provided in 2021 by the Korean Ministry of Health and Welfare's Central Cancer Registry, there were 254,718 new cancer cases in Korea in 2019 [3]. Among them, Colorectal cancer (C18–C20) was the fourth most common, accounting for 29,030 instances in both men and women, or 11.4% of the total [3]. Despite the fact that it is a disease with a high incidence rate, the survival rate improves when it is diagnosed early by screening [3]. Colorectal cancer was chosen as the game's large intestine ailment. Thus, the general public and patients acquire pertinent information and may hope to have a better understanding of colorectal cancer and its prevention through the game (Fig. 2).

Description of the User's Execution Steps

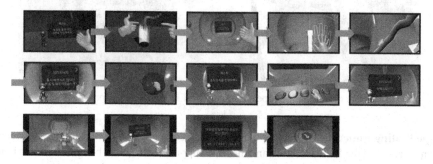

Fig. 2. Progression of the large intestine

1   After passing through the portal, flip the dialogue panel adjacent to the front nanorobot over to continue the story and acquire the quest.
2   Pass via the portal into the large intestine.
3   After the story progresses, obtain the quest by passing the dialogue panel in the front.
4   If you place your hand on the front-loading bar for three seconds, a rope forms at the front.
5   Pull the rope in front of you to rescue the nanorobot.
6   Return to the rear and flip over the dialogue panel to continue the story and obtain the quest.
7   Grab the five tumors in the front with your hands.
8   After the story progresses, obtain the quest by passing the dialogue panel in the front.
9   Conduct a tumor inspection to determine the extent of the excised tumor.
10 After the story progresses, obtain the quest by passing the dialogue panel in the front.

11 To treat the tumor, throw a water balloon at the target NPC.
12 After the story progresses, obtain the quest by passing the dialogue panel in the front.
13 Solve quizzes about diseases of the large intestine.
14 After obtaining the third key, proceed to the portal.

2.4 Functions Implemented Within the Large Intestine

Various functions were applied to the game, such as gesture recognition, Grab, flipping the dialogue panel, defense, CPR, intravascular flight, stent expansion, and rope pulling. Among the functions implemented in the large intestine, pulling the rope, pressing the button, sensing the movement of the player's head, and drawing functions are described (Figs. 3 and 4).

Fig. 3. Image of pulling the rope   **Fig. 4.** Image of pressing button

Rope Pulling Function. Referring to the existing code [1], a rope was created between the nanorobot in the large intestine and the rope support. The nanorobot gets pulled when it grasps and tugs on the linked thread. A trigger is put in a specific location to guarantee that the line, line support, and robot are all removed as the robot passes (Table 1).

Table 1. Part of code to Add GrabDetector to capsule [1]

```
//add OVRGrabbable, AjustGrabbable, GrabDetector and Collider component
segments[i].AddComponent<OVRGrabbable>();
segments[i].AddComponent<AdjustGrabbable>();
GameObject grabDetector = new GameObject("GrabDetector");
grabDetector.transform.parent = segments[i].transform;
CapsuleCollider grabsphere = grabDetector.AddComponent<CapsuleCollider>();
grabsphere.transform.position = sphere.transform.position;
grabsphere.transform.rotation = sphere.transform.rotation;
grabsphere.transform.rotation = Quaternion.Euler(0, 0, 0);
grabsphere.isTrigger = true;
grabsphere.radius = radius * 5f;
grabsphere.height = sphere.height * 1.3f;
grabDetector.AddComponent<GrabDetector>();
```

Establish a Capsule and a GrabDetector as a child to explain the rope generating idea in its simplest form. Capture the Capsule with the script, then the Capsule can be grabbed. Create several capsules and connect them using a Configurable joint. Connect Configurable joints additionally in multiples of two, four, eight, sixteen, and thirty-two. The connecting Capsules are covered with mesh, giving them the appearance of a single line.

Button Press Function. When the player solves the quiz, a button function is added to the view object so that he can pick the view he believes is the correct answer. As soon as the player presses the view button, the correct answer to the problem is displayed in the dialogue panel.

If you look at the principle of how the button works, a Box Collider with trigger properties is added to the view object to detect the player's hand. Through the OnTriggerEnter function, after checking if the object entered into the trigger matches the player's hand, the value of the view selected by the player is sent to the quiz manager.

Fig. 5. Image of detecting the player's head movement

Fig. 6. Image of drawing

The Capability to Detect the Player's Head Movement. In addition to using their hands, we introduced a feature that allows the user to enter the quiz answer by moving their head. Instructed the player to move their head up and down if the quiz sentence was accurate, and left and right if the quiz sentence was incorrect, through the dialog panel. It was implemented to recognize the player's head movement every frame. When the player moves their head up, down or left and right, the answer is immediately dis-played in the dialog panel so that the player can check the correct answer.

In order to detect the movement of the player's head, the value of the direction vector that the player is looking at must be obtained first. And then, the rate of change in the x-axis and the y-axis is calculated using the value of direction vector saved one frame ago. If the rate of change in the x-axis is greater than a value that we set, it is recognized to move their head left and right. If the rate of change in the y-axis is greater than the value, it is recognized to move their head up and down. If the amount of change in both the x-axis and the y-axis is greater than the value, the amount of change in the x-axis and the amount of change in the y-axis are compared to determine that their head is moved in the direction of the axis with more change.

Drawing Function. When taking the quiz in the large intestine, the drawing function was constructed by referencing to existing code [4] so that the player may write down the right response to the short-form question. When the player makes a pinch gesture, a line is formed in the game that corresponds to the player's hand so that the text written by the player is visible in the game (Table 2).

Table 2. Part of code that generates a line based on the position of the player's hand [4]

```
private void CheckPinchState()
{
    bool isIndexFingerPinching = ovrHand.GetFingerIsPinching(OVRHand.HandFinger.Index);
    float indexFingerPinchStrength = ovrHand.GetFingerPinchStrength(OVRHand.HandFinger.Index);
    if (ovrHand.GetFingerConfidence(OVRHand.HandFinger.Index)
        != OVRHand.TrackingConfidence.High)
    return;
    // finger pinch down
    if (isIndexFingerPinching && indexFingerPinchStrength >= minFingerPinchDownStrength)
    {
        UpdateLine();
        IsPinchingReleased = true;
        return;
    }
    // finger pinch up
    if (IsPinchingReleased)
    {
        AddNewLineRenderer();
        IsPinchingReleased = false;
    }
}
```

In terms of the drawing concept, each frame's pinch strength was monitored, and when it exceeded the threshold, a line was drawn at the player's hand location, allowing the line to be drawn constantly in the direction of the hand movement. If the pinch strength is less than the threshold, line drawing is stopped and a new line object is formed that is not connected to the previously drawn line.

3 Conclusion

Along with HMDs, virtual reality games using current controllers have been developed using Kinetic or treadmill technology. However, with the release of Oculus quest2, it has been claimed that an HMD capable of being worn wirelessly outside may be developed. The progress of these technologies demands the incorporation of a diverse range of contents within the device. As a result of the creation of the Body Cure Bot game, this article shows a controller-free HMD game. In the metaverse age, the line between virtual reality and the real world is getting increasingly blurred. As with Body Cure Bot, it provides content that enables you to have new experiences and have fun while playing virtual reality games that include a human body in the background, replicating real-world situations in virtual reality. Body Cure Bot not only provides a unique experience by tracking users' hands, but it also presents diseases that are statistically common among people and helps them learn disease prevention measures naturally through simple quizzes, thereby contributing to knowledge provision. Furthermore, the gesture recognition function based on hand tracking, as well as the player's head movement recognition and drawing function are expected to be used as reference materials for developers creating UI interfaces in a VR environment.

Benefit. When examining existing VR content, the majority is controller-centric, and developing gaming material that can be operated without a controller would provide a new level of fascination for customers already accustomed with controller-based games. This game has the benefit of lowering the entry barrier to virtual reality by allowing players who have difficulty using a controller to interact with non-controller-dependent content. Additionally, because it is a game with a body in the background, it is not stimulating, which allows it to appeal to a larger range of game players' ages. Additionally, educational effects can be obtained by providing users with medical in-formation in the dialogue and playing a quiz-style game based on the conversation.

4 Future Plans

In this paper, we propose a game that explores three human organs. Approximately eight hand gesture recognition routines were employed to accomplish this. We intend to do more research in the future to build a variety of games based on the identification of more diverse hand movements. We built a method to accept text typed in a VR game while working on the Body Cure Bot project. Following that, OCR recognition research will be conducted to develop subjective answers to be recognized. Users will be more interested in VR games as the OCR recognition capability allows them to explore numerous UI interfaces in addition to gesture approaches. Additionally, we want to delve deeper into the 3D software in order to deliver more realistic aesthetics, which has been highlighted as a disappointment with Body Cure Bot. If physical parts have an excessive sense of realism, the user may feel sense of rejection; yet, if a more realistic depiction than the one used in this research is possible, we believe that the user's absorption will improve. Additionally, a user satisfaction survey conducted via a recognition rate survey of the game's key feature, hand tracking, is deemed critical for determining the game's scalability.

References

1. Cannon, J.: TrueHandling (2020). https://github.com/cannon/TrueHandling. Accessed 2 Aug 2021
2. Choi, K.-H: A study on technology trend of VR experience contents. J. Korea Entertain. Ind. Assoc. **14**(8), 513–523 (11 p) (2020). https://doi.org/10.21184/jkeia.2020.12.14.8.513
3. National Cancer Information Center: Colorectal cancer [Internet]. Gyeonggi: National Cancer Information Center (2020). https://www.cancer.go.kr/lay1/program/S1T211C214/cancer/view.do?cancer_seq=3797. Accessed 2 Mar 2022
4. Valecillos, D.: GitHub - dilmerv/VRDraw: a drawing virtual reality experience where YES all you do is draw and run !. GitHub. <https://github.com/dilmerv/VRDraw>. Accessed 5 Mar 2022

Whole-Body Interaction and Representative Applications in Virtual Reality

Xiaolong Lou[1,2(✉)], Xinyi Li[1], Yuhaozhe Zheng[1], and Yan Shi[1]

[1] School of Humanity, Art and Digital Media, Hangzhou Dianzi University, Hangzhou, China
xlou@hdu.edu.cn
[2] State Key Laboratory of Virtual Reality Technology and Systems, Beihang University, Beijing, China

Abstract. A sufficiently qualified virtual reality (VR) application should be an immersive environment where all natural actions and behaviors, e.g., head expressive motions, torso postures, limb gestures and body signs, should be recognized and translated to interactive operations or commands. But according to our survey on the state-of-the-art applications, there is still a large gap between the actuality and the ideal. To fill this gap, we carried out a focus group discussion through which a descriptive framework of whole-body interaction (WBI) techniques was formed. The framework provides a comprehensive illustration about the natural interaction forms derived from human bodily natural actions and behaviors. We also discussed and proposed technical principles for implementing WBI techniques. Based on these, we developed experiencing prototypes and had them evaluated. An empirical user study proved the feasibility and benefits of the WBI techniques.

Keywords: Whole-body interaction · Motion-sensing interaction · Interaction paradigm · Natural user interface

1 Introduction

Benefiting from a rapid development of computer graphics rendering and motion sensing technologies in recent years, an increasing number of VR devices and applications have permeated into a wide range of domains, including remote education, entertainment and surgery training [1, 2]. A wide spread of 'metaverse' concept in particular makes the VR technology a more well-known and unique entrance to the immersive virtual world. As a most representative form of natural human-computer interaction (HCI), VR technology has an obvious advantage of naturalness and user immersion. A sufficient naturalness represents that the interaction commands are derived from and highly analogous to the operational actions that are universally accustomed by users [3]. But according to a latest survey, nowadays VR applications are often criticized for weak in naturalness and user adaptability [4]. Except for the limitations of the motion sensing techniques, another important reason lies in a lack of scientific exploration on natural interaction paradigms and design guidelines of natural user interfaces (NUIs) that can be universally exploited in a VR environment.

The original version of this chapter was revised: The grant number has been corrected in the acknowledgements section. The correction to this chapter is available at
https://doi.org/10.1007/978-3-031-06388-6_53

This research work is aimed to have a comprehensive investigation on the most fundamental and frequently used interaction commands and evaluate their naturalness in state-of-the-art applications. And then based on these propose a universal design framework of natural user interaction techniques in VR. We named this natural interaction design framework as 'whole-body interaction' (WBI) framework, which presents guidelines for designing natural forms of interaction commands and user interfaces, as shown in Fig. 1. Given the WBI framework, we then developed prototypes of the natural interaction techniques and evaluated their practical advantages in VR.

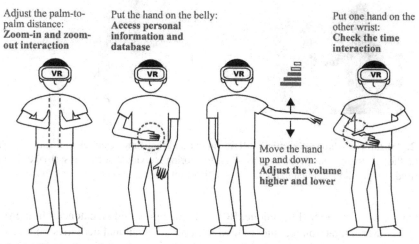

Fig. 1. An illustration about the natural interaction cases and potential applications in a VR environment.

2 Related Work

The origin of the WBI framework, or the earliest form of bodily natural interaction technique, can be dated back to the proposal by Krueger et al. [5] in more than thirty years ago. In their proposal, the silhouette of the body was employed as a tool for interacting with large displays. Such application was initially developed to perform artistic expression in a more natural way without relying on conventional input devices, which unexpectedly brought a profound and lasting effect on the natural interaction techniques development in the HCI community. More recent investigations, such as Shoemaker et al.'s [6] and Jacob et al.'s [7], further extended the forms and categories of the natural interaction applications and proposed various techniques that can be applied in specific situations, such as 'reality-based interaction' (RBI) [7], 'shadow-reaching interaction' (SRI) and 'body-centric interaction' (BCI) [6]. In the RBI technique, the physical operations and properties in the real world, such as the user's proprioception or body awareness and haptic feedback, were obeyed and simulated in user interaction. In the SRI technique and its applications, the user's shadow was purposely generated in digital form and cast on large displays. The shadow in SRI acted as a role of user representation and it was used as interactive elements on the user interface, such as a pointer for target pointing and acquisition and a file folder for storing individual documents, as shown in Fig. 2. In technical implementation, the body shadow was generated in virtual form, and the user adjusted the body orientation and the interactive distance toward the display to change the shadow size and position. The shadow can not only be used as a pointing and acquisition tool on the user interface, but can also be used as a metaphorical access to individual database.

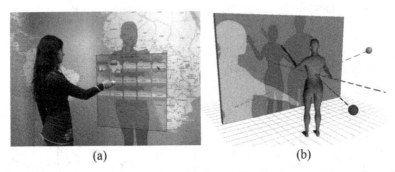

(a)   (b)

Fig. 2. 'Shadow-reaching interaction'(SRI) technique and application examples on a large display [6]: (a) the user torso shadow was used as folder for storing individual documents; (b) the shadow was used as a pointing and manipulation tool on the display.

On the basis of the SRI technique, BCI technique provided an extended framework of natural user interaction technique in which user's operational activities on and surrounding the body were detected and translated into metaphorical operations on the large display. The peripersonal space around the user and its social implications were also considered and reflected in the BCI technique. For example, the distance or the proximity from the user to the display was detected in real time and based on this aroused the display or adjusted the display content [8]. In multiple users-engaged scenario, the distance between two users was also detected and then the display interface changed the interaction modalities to adapt to the users' practical requirements, either supported individual interaction or aided collaborative interaction between two or more users. Researchers had also proposed to recognize the user's choice of the operating hand and the handedness characteristic and based on this developed a hand-adaptive interaction technique, so as to make the hand natural interaction more immersive, labor-saving and efficient [9, 10].

3   Whole-Body Interaction Framework in VR

According to our survey on the relevant research, we have learnt that earlier research mainly focused on and applied natural interaction techniques, including the RBI, SRI and BCI techniques, to aid and improve interaction naturalness in large displays-based interactive scenarios; but in virtual interactive environments such as HMD-based augmented and virtual reality applications, interaction naturalness is still restricted to hand natural interaction or voice natural interaction. More comprehensive natural operations and behaviors such as whole body postures and gestures and their related social meaning, however, had seldom or at least not comprehensively been considered nor investigated. In this study, we had a comprehensive exploratory on human natural actions and behaviors that can be translated into interaction paradigms and commands, and based on this formed a descriptive framework of WBI. To ensure that the WBI framework is applicable to a VR environment and more importantly to verify the practical benefits of the WBI techniques, we developed technical prototypes and had them evaluated.

3.1 Focus Group and Discussion

To form a scientific and comprehensive natural interaction framework of WBI, the authors and other four invited researchers who had more than 5 years of research practice in the HCI field, carried out a focus group to discuss and sum up all possible forms of bodily natural interaction operations. Then other five experts in the HCI field were invited to review and assess the rationality of the above natural interaction forms. Given the discussion outcome of the focus group and the comments gained from field experts, a descriptive framework of WBI was formed. Technical principles and implementation means were also discussed.

3.2 Descriptive Framework of WBI

Focus group is a rapid and effective method for surveying and gathering thoughts, comments and suggestions from specialists for a specific topic. In this research, a focus group was organized to discuss and then to form a descriptive framework of WBI. There were eight members participated in the focus group, each one had a basic knowledge or experience on bodily natural interaction techniques and applications, including but not limited to Microsoft Kinect-based motion sensing interactive games and immersive applications in VR. The focus group discussion was conducted in a multimedia laboratory where a wide and circle table and eight VR head mounted devices (HMDs) were provided. Figure 3 presents a few photos showing that focus group members were performing and discussing on the bodily natural interaction techniques.

Fig. 3. Performing-and-discussion scenes in the focus group.

Firstly, all participants discussed about the forms and paradigms of bodily natural interaction techniques. All valuable viewpoints and comments were recorded and classified. Then all participants worn a VR HMD and performed natural interactive operations and behaviors through a specific designed order. When one participant was performing, other seven participants provided comments which were also recorded. After all participants completed the performing tasks, the comments were collected and filtered. *The following* Table 1 *gives a descriptive summary of the WBI framework.*

Table 1. Descriptive framework of whole-body interaction techniques in VR.

Body part	Actions and behaviors	Interactive operations and commands
Head	• Head waves from left to right; • Head nods from up to down; • Keep the head tilted (for 2–3 s);	• 'Disagree' input; • 'Agree' or 'confirm' input; • Controls the visual angle in the interactive task;
Arms	• Crosses two arms to perform a 'X' sign; • Puts one arm on the other arm, and slides from up to down; • Puts one hand on the wrist of the other arm; • Puts one hand on the head; • Waves one or two arms rapidly; • Puts one hand at a specific height in air and adjusts the height; • Raises two hands palm to palm and adjusts the distance; • Puts one or two hands on the stomach; • Stretches two arms out to perform a 'fly' sign, and tilts the torso;	• 'Close' and 'reject' input; • Changes the visual field size, or controls the playing progress of general medias; • Checks the time in the system, or set a timer or timing reminder; • Reviews the system memory, and visits the history records; • Says 'goodbye' to the system and ends the task; • Adjusts the system volume up and down; • Zooms in and zooms out; • Access to the personal database; • Triggers a flight view in an immersive environment;
Torso	• Twists the body or changes the body orientation; • Leans the torso forward; • Bends the waist;	• Aids navigation in the VR environment; • enlarges information showed to make them more readable; • Switches the visual angle to the ground;
Legs	• Bends the legs to crouch; • Performs a 'walk' posture; • Steps backward; • Cocks one leg to perform a 'single-leg-standing' posture;	• Changes the perspective to a lower height; • Travels in the VR environment; • To have a wider field of view at a farther distance; • To keep balance in the VR environment;

4   Technical Prototypes and Evaluations on the WBI Framework

In this section we present a summary introduction about the technical principles in implementing WBI interaction techniques. Given the descriptive framework of WBI and its technical principles, we developed prototypes which were then evaluated in terms of usability, user immersion, user perceived naturalness and comfort level. Figure 4 presents an illustrated classification of bodily natural actions or postures, and their related interactive operations. Then Table 2 provides technical essentials in translating bodily signals into interactive operations.

Fig. 4. A summary classification of bodily natural actions and related interactive operations.

Given the descriptive framework and the technical implementing principles, we developed prototypes and had them evaluated. We selected an Oculus Rift as the HMD device since it had a sufficiently precise motion detecting module installed internally, which enables recognizing and tracking its movements in real time. We also used an RGB-Depth camera of ASUS Xtion™ to identify and track whole body joints and based on this to recognize user actions and postures. Twelve voluntarily participants (male: 6; female: 6) aged from 19 to 45 were recruited to experience and comment the WBI prototypes. In prior to formal evaluations, participants were firstly given a detailed introduction about the study purpose and the content of the WBI framework. They were also instructed to learn and practice natural operations and actions. In formal evaluations, each participant had 10 min to perform all natural interactive operations during which he or she was encouraged to express thoughts and comments. Finally we found that all participants could adapt to the WBI techniques quickly without difficulties in learning and understanding; and six participants expressed that the WBI techniques made the interactive tasks in VR more interesting and intelligent.

Table 2. Technical principles of recognizing and translating user actions.

User actions	Technical principles of recognizing actions
• Waves the head; • Nods the head nods; • Keep the head tilted;	• Measuring waves of the HMD; • Measuring movements of the HMD; • Measuring the HMD's orientation;
• Crosses two arms: X; • Slides one arm on the other arm; • Puts one hand on the other wrist; • Puts one hand on the head; • Waves arm(s); • Adjusts the hand height in air; • Changes palm to palm distance; • Puts hand(s) on the stomach; • Stretches arms out to fly;	• Detecting and tracking arm joints through cameras; • Detecting and tracking the hand joint; • Detecting and tracking two hands' joints; • Detecting and tracking the hand and the head joints; • Detecting and tracking hand joint(s) movements; • Detecting the hand joint movement in height; • Detecting the hand joints' distance change; • Detecting the hand joint position relative to the torso; • Detecting and compares 6 joints' positions of two arm;
• Changes the body orientation; • Leans the torso forward; • Bends the waist;	• Measuring the HMD's orientation; • Measuring the HMD's motion in the forward direction; • Detecting the height changes of shoulder joints;
• Crouch: bends legs; • Performs a 'walk' posture; • Steps backward; • 'Single-leg-standing' posture;	• Detecting the height changes of the knee joints; • Detecting the changes and movements of the foot joints; • Measuring the HMD's motion in the backward direction; • Detecting the foot joints' positions;

5 Conclusion

Through a focus group discussion, we proposed a descriptive framework of WBI techniques that can be applied in and benefit general VR applications. The WBI framework provides a comprehensive illustration about the natural interaction forms that are closely related to human natural behaviors in physical operations, including head movements, torso postures, limb gestures and body signs. Considering the state-of-the-art motion detecting modules and devices that have been widely used in VR applications, we also discussed technical principles and schemes for implementing all WBI techniques. To verify the feasibility and practical advantages of the WBI techniques, we developed prototypes and had them evaluated through an empirical experiment. User comments showed that WBI techniques could be familiar to users at different ages easily, they were also commented to be appealing and intelligent.

Funding and Acknowledgments. This work was funded by the 'Natural Science Foundation of Zhejiang Province' under the grant number of LQ19F020010; the 'National Natural Science Foundation of China' (NSFC) under the grant number of 61902097; the 'State Key Laboratory of Virtual Reality Technology and Systems' under the grant number of VRLAB2020B03; and the 'Science and Technology Project of Wenzhou City' under the grant number of S20180018. The authors thank all reviewers for their insightful comments on this work.

References

1. Avis, N.J.: Review: virtual reality, scientific and technological challenges. Comput. Bull. **37**(5), 26–27 (1995)
2. Xi, N., Hamari, J.: Shopping in virtual reality: a literature review and future agenda. J. Bus. Res. **134**(1), 37–58 (2021)
3. Murillo, R.: Computational interaction techniques for 3D selection, manipulation and navigation in immersive VR. Doctoral dissertation, University of Sussex (2019)
4. Pushkar, P.K., Nair, V., Gupta, H., et al.: Survey on virtual reality. Int. J. Comput. Sci. Eng. **7**(4), 569–574 (2019)
5. Krueger, M.W., Gionfriddo, T., Hinrichsen, K.: Videoplace – an artificial reality. In: Proceedings of the 3th ACM Conference on Human Factors in Computing Systems, pp. 35–40 (1985)
6. Shoemaker, G.: Body-centric and shadow-based interaction for large wall displays. Doctoral dissertation, University of British Columbia (2011)
7. Jacob, R.J., et al.: Reality-based interaction. In: Proceedings of the 26th ACM Conference on Human Factors in Computing Systems, pp. 201–210 (2008)
8. Marquardt, N., Greenberg, S.: Informing the design of proxemic interactions. Perv. Comput. **11**(2), 14–23 (2012)
9. Lou, X., Li, X., Hansen, P., Du, P.: Hand-adaptive user interface: improved gestural interaction in virtual reality. Virtual Real. **25**(2), 367–382 (2020)
10. Lou, X., Zhao, Q., Shi, Y., Hansen, P.: Arm posture changes and influences on hand controller interaction evaluation in virtual reality. Appl. Sci. **12**(5), 2585 (2022)

Dwell-Free Typing Using an EOG Based Virtual Keyboard

Matthew Mifsud[1]([⊠]), Tracey A. Camilleri[1], and Kenneth P. Camilleri[2]

[1] Department of Systems and Control Engineering, University of Malta, Msida, Malta
matthew.mifsud@um.edu.mt
[2] Centre for Biomedical Cybernetics, Department of Systems and Control Engineering,
University of Malta, Msida, Malta

Abstract. This work presents the development of an asynchronous dwell-free virtual keyboard application which can be operated using electrooculographic (EOG) data. Unlike other EOG based eye typing applications, the developed system avoids the use of dwell-times and relieves the user from the need to perform repetitive and unnatural eye movements to move a cursor towards the desired letter or the need to perform voluntary blinks to interact with the application. Instead, the proposed application requires the user to simply glance through the vicinity of the desired letters, as one would swipe through letters when typing on a touchscreen device, after which a set of word predictions are displayed for the user to select. The proposed application obtained a top five rate of $76.00 \pm 12.61\%$ using EOG data which is comparable to the top five rate of $79.00 \pm 13.37\%$ obtained when operating the application using a vision-based eye gaze tracker.

Keywords: Electrooculography · Eye typing · Virtual keyboard

1 Introduction

Gaze controlled virtual keyboards offer individuals with mobility impairments an alternative mode of communication through which one can edit documents, send emails, and participate in online chat rooms. In recent years, such human-computer interface (HCI) typing systems have been developed using videooculography (VOG) based techniques which operate through a vision-based eye gaze tracker that estimates the pixel coordinates of the point of gaze (POG) of the user on a computer screen. Although VOG based systems offer good resolution, they can be an economically unviable option for certain individuals and their performance is affected by different lighting conditions [1]. On the other hand, EOG can offer an alternative solution to human eye gaze tracking. It is based on the human eye behaving as an electrical dipole between the cornea and the retina which respectively maintain a positive and negative potential. This corneo-retinal potential (CRP) is oriented with the line of sight of the user and ranges from 0.4 to 1.0 mV [1]. This electrical activity is monitored through the use of non-invasive surface electrodes which are placed in close proximity to the human eye.

C. Stephanidis et al. (Eds.): HCII 2022, CCIS 1581, pp. 54–62, 2022.
https://doi.org/10.1007/978-3-031-06388-6_8

In the literature, most EOG based eye typing applications are cursor-based implementations which operate directly on the saccadic activity of the user to move a cursor towards a desired letter in a step-wise manner [2–4] or perform eye movements originating from the center of the keyboard towards the periphery of the application [5]. Such implementations support four-directional or eight-directional cursor locomotion whereby cursor movement is based on the direction and amplitude of the user's saccades recorded in the electrooculogram. Finally, key selection is often executed through a voluntary blink [2–4].

On the other hand, the EOG based implementation of Barbara et al. [6] supports a dwell-based mechanism and permits the user to operate the application in an asynchronous manner. While operating this application, the user is required to fixate on each key for a stipulated period of time known as the dwell time. For example, in order to type in the word 'the', the user would need to dwell on three separate individual letters and fixate upon each letter until the set dwell time is elapsed for each letter. In such systems, the dwell-time simulates the standard click used in conventional systems however heavily limits the typing speed users can achieve.

Reducing the set dwell-time can have a positive impact on the user's text entry rate however it makes the user's input heavily susceptible to the Midas Touch problem where the user's gaze is simultaneously used for vision and to actuate a command, hence leading to more mis-selections. Alternatively, dwell-free systems employ a different technique whereby the user does not need to fixate on each letter for a stipulated period of time. Instead, such systems operate on the eye gesture of the user traversing through the desired keys without requiring the user to interface with each individual key for a stipulated period of time. Such systems offer a natural mode of interaction however, they have only been developed using VOG as an eye movement recording technique.

To this effect, the main contributions of this work include an analysis on the manifestation of EOG data recorded while typing in a dwell-free manner, the implementation of the LCSMapping algorithm [7], which is a state-of-the-art approach for dwell-free typing and its fine tuning to operate with EOG-based POG estimates, and the development of a real-time eye controlled virtual keyboard application that can be operated through EOG data in a dwell-free manner. The performance achieved using the data collected from ten participants will be compared to a VOG based alternative.

The rest of this paper is organized as follows. Section 2 describes the hardware framework used for data collection and the adopted experimental protocol. Section 3 outlines the manifestation of eye movements while typing in a dwell-free manner whilst Sect. 4 provides an overview of the adopted dwell-free typing mechanism to operate using EOG data. Finally, Sect. 5 concludes this paper.

2 Hardware Framework and Data Acquisition

Ten subjects (mean age 23.8 ± 2.32 years) participated in this study which was approved by the University Research Ethics Committee (UREC) at the University of Malta. Subjects were positioned at a distance of approximately 50 cm away from a 24-inch LCD computer screen which displayed the virtual keyboard application. Subjects' EOG data was recorded using the g.tec g.USBamp biosignal amplifier in conjunction with the conventional electrode setup as shown in Fig. 1. The latter consists of six surface electrodes connected in close proximity to the user's eyes. Specifically, the electrodes labelled '1' and '2' are placed above and below the human eye and record EOG data attributed to the vertical EOG channel, whereas electrodes '3' and '4' are connected to the outer canthi of the user's eyes and record data attributed to the horizontal EOG channel. Finally, a reference electrode 'R' is positioned behind the ear whilst a ground electrode labelled 'G' is placed at the top of the user's forehead. These electrodes detect changes in the electrical potential on the user's skin surface which shed light on the size and direction of the user's eye movements. On the other hand, VOG data was recorded using the SMI RED500 vision-based eye gaze tracker from SensoMotoric Instruments. This eye gaze tracker directly provided the estimated pixel coordinates of the user's POG on the screen. During data collection, subjects were instructed to perform different dwell-free eye gestures using the virtual keyboard design developed for this study. Subjects were instructed to input a total of twenty words in a dwell-free manner using each eye movement recording modality. These words were randomly selected from the Corpus of Contemporary American English (COCA) [8].

The virtual keyboard designed for this study is shown in Fig. 2. This consists of a writing bar together with five-word prediction sections in the second row which are designed to operate in tandem with the dwell-free typing mechanism explored in this work. Due to its widespread use, the keys were designed to support a QWERTY layout with which users are familiar, allowing them to locate the desired keys with ease and ensuring an optimal user experience. While operating the virtual keyboard, visual feedback was provided, by momentarily highlighting the closest key to the user's POG. This mechanism enabled user interaction and also mitigates the Midas touch problem since the user can avoid selecting undesired keys. Throughout the data collection procedure, participants were instructed to dwell upon the first letter for a short period of time until this is highlighted in red, traverse through the remaining desired letters in a dwell free manner and finally dwell on the last letter until this is selected. This interaction enables the user to demarcate the start and end of a dwell-free eye gesture and was used to filter the lexicon when retrieving the potential word candidates.

The vision-based eye gaze tracker used in this study provides the estimated pixel coordinates of the user's POG on the computer screen. In turn, this data was directly used to operate the virtual keyboard application and accordingly highlight the closest key to the user's POG. On the other hand, the EOG electrodes registered the change in potential while performing the eye gesture to type a word, which in turn had to be processed to estimate the gaze angles corresponding to the user's POG. In order to carry out the latter, this study adopted the work of Barbara et al. [9] which estimates the horizontal gaze angle θ_h and vertical gaze angle θ_v of the user's POG. Based on the resolution of the screen being used and the distance of the user from the screen, the gaze angles were converted to the pixel coordinates of the user's POG on the screen using a trigonometric model.

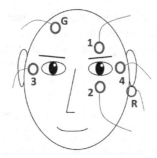

Fig. 1. EOG electrode configuration used.

3 Manifestation of Eye Movements While Dwell-Free Typing

The goal of this section is to show the nature of the EOG data while dwell-free typing, where the user is not required to fixate upon each key for a stipulated period of time but glance through the vicinity of each key in a rapid sequence instead. As the user is performing this eye gesture, he/she momentarily fixates upon the desired keys, generating what are known as quasi-fixations. These quasi-fixation periods occur naturally, as they are situated between the end of one saccade as the user's POG approaches the desired key and the start of another saccade as the user directs his/her POG towards the next key. These quasi-fixations shed light on the user's typing intent since more sample points are collected in the vicinity of the 'intended letter' candidates [7]. Figure 2 demonstrates such instances, where the intended letters have an abundance of POG estimates located within their respective key area.

When typing in a dwell-free manner, the user is also likely to select the neighboring key of the desired target thus registering a neighbour letter error [7]. There are various reasons why this happens, one of which depends on the POG estimation framework which may, in time, degrade in accuracy due to the accumulation of errors resulting from the continuous drift typical in EOG signals [6]. Moreover, neighbour letter errors also manifest themselves in the occurrence of saccadic overshoots and undershoots whereby the user's POG misses the desired target and thus falls on a neighboring key. In most cases, neighbour letter errors are followed by a corrective saccade through which the user directs his/her POG back to the desired letter. For example, while travelling from the letter 'U' (labelled as '6') towards the letter 'S' (labelled as '7') in Fig. 2, the user's POG landed on the letter *'D'* after which a corrective saccade was performed. Finally, while the user is traversing from one letter to the next, some POG estimates fall on letters in between the two desired keys. These are referred to as extra letter errors. Such instances can be noted in Fig. 2 where POG estimates on the letters *'Y'* and *'U'* were collected as the user's POG was travelling from the letter *'R'* (labelled as '3') towards the letter *'I'* (labelled as '4'). These extra letter errors occur with a low occurrence rate as they are situated within a saccadic region where the user is not maintaining a relatively fixed POG.

The next step would be to implement an algorithm which can exploit the information in the recorded eye gesture to determine the desired word that the user wanted to type, while also handling the resulting neighbour and extra letter errors. For this aim, the LCSMapping algorithm [7] will be used which will also be fine-tuned to handle EOG-based POG estimates as discussed in the next section.

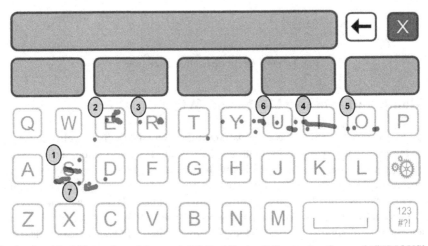

Fig. 2. Graphical illustration of the user's POG while dwell-free typing the word 'SERIOUS' on the designed virtual keyboard.

4   Adaptation of the LCSMapping Algorithm

The LCSMapping algorithm is a robust dwell-free typing algorithm developed by Liu et al. [7] which uses eye gaze tracking data obtained through a VOG based eye gaze tracker to identify the intended letter typed by the user. This algorithm regards the user's input as an '*observable transition*' which is constituted by the different letters ('*observable states*') selected by the user's eye gesture. This observable transition is then compared to each potential word in the lexicon in order to determine their resemblance. The latter is carried out by constructing a 2-D table where the first row corresponds to the observable transition whilst the first column corresponds to the considered potential transition from the dictionary [7]. The latter are then compared, and each corresponding cell is populated based on the following three conditions:

I.   Same letter condition: If the states being compared between the observable and potential transition are identical, the corresponding matrix cell is populated with the occurrence rate value of that particular state.

II. Neighbour letter condition: If the states being compared between the observable and potential transition are neighbouring letters, the corresponding matrix cell is populated with the occurrence rate value of that particular state multiplied by a neighbour weight w.

III. <u>Extra letter condition:</u> If the states being compared do not satisfy the neighbour letter or same letter condition, the cell is populated with a value of zero.

These three conditions show how the LCSMapping algorithm handles neighbouring or extra letter errors by employing the weight w or assigning a zero respectively. In this work, the goal is to use the LCSMapping algorithm using eye gaze tracking data as captured through EOG instead of VOG. Given the stream of EOG-based POG estimates, the sequence of selected letters could be determined and was translated into $<l, t>$ tuples where 'l' corresponds to the selected letter whilst 't' corresponds to the occurrence rate of that particular letter. After running the LCSMapping algorithm on this data, its performance is measured through the top five rate which corresponds to the percentage of the desired words which were ranked in the top five recommended candidates by the algorithm.

4.1 Optimal Weight Estimation

Since in this work, the LCSMapping algorithm was made to operate using EOG-based POG estimates, an optimal neighbour weight parameter w had to be identified. The latter was determined by considering the data collected from the ten participants and running the LCSMapping algorithm to determine the top five rate for different neighbor weights w ranging from 0 to 0.9 in steps of 0.1. The results shown in Fig. 3 identify the optimal neighbour weight w to be equal to 0.1. A similar procedure was carried out using the VOG data of the same subjects, in which case the optimal weight was found to be 0.2 as implemented in [7].

4.2 Results

The performance of the LCSMapping algorithm using both EOG and VOG data from the ten participants was calculated and compared. The results are tabulated in Table 1. It can be noted that the LCSMapping algorithm achieved an average top five rate of $79.00 \pm 13.37\%$ and $76.00 \pm 12.61\%$ when operated using VOG data and EOG data respectively. These results show that despite the lower accuracy of POG estimates typically obtained with EOG data as compared to that obtained with VOG data [1], the LCSMapping algorithm still yields comparable performance. This shows that the latter manages to handle neighbouring letter error mappings well even though with the recorded EOG data, these are 1.8 times more frequent than those with the recorded VOG data. The choice of the neighbour weight w is also important. For VOG data this was found to be optimal at 0.2, which means that neighbouring letters contain relevant information for the detection of the intended word. For EOG data the optimal value was found to be 0.1, half of that used for VOG data, possibly because there are much more neighbour letter errors and hence are given less weighting. This procedure drives the number of common elements between the observable transition and potential transition to a maximum hence ensuring optimal performance of the dwell-free typing algorithm.

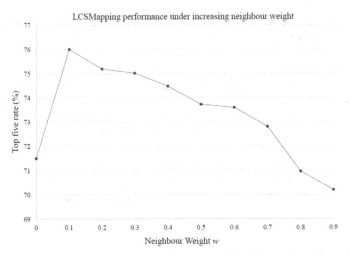

Fig. 3. LCSMapping performance under varying neighbour weight w using EOG data.

5 Conclusion

This work has presented the development of an EOG based dwell-free virtual keyboard application that relieves the user from the need to perform repetitive eye movements in order to input each character or dwell on each desired letter to select it. Instead, users can input a single word by sequentially glancing at the keys forming the desired word in a dwell-free manner. While providing a more natural mode of interaction, the proposed application also permits faster typing speeds since the use of dwell-times is only restricted to the first and last letter and for word prediction selection. In addition, the application can be operated in an asynchronous manner hence moving away from the need to perform specific actions during timed intervals or interacting with the application through saccades originating from the center of the virtual keyboard.

Subjects achieved an average top five rate of 79.00 ± 13.37% and 76.00 ± 12.61% when operating the application using VOG data and EOG data, respectively. In light of this, it can be noted that the LCSMapping algorithm [7] may be effectively tuned for EOG based dwell-free typing to compensate for the presence of selected letter errors which arise from the different levels of accuracy achieved from the two eye gaze tracking modalities. Given the small difference in the average top five rate, the proposed application makes the use of EOG signals as a viable alternative for operating an eye typing application. The achieved performance is expected to improve with increased subject familiarity with the typing application. Future work also aims to analyse the effect of the visual feedback provided in conjunction with the virtual keyboard layout used to help improve user interaction and system performance.

Table 1. Performance of the LCSMapping algorithm using VOG-based and EOG-based estimates.

Subject	Top five rate (%)	
	VOG	EOG
S1	95.00	70.00
S2	75.00	75.00
S3	80.00	55.00
S4	60.00	65.00
S5	90.00	90.00
S6	90.00	85.00
S7	55.00	95.00
S8	80.00	65.00
S9	95.00	90.00
S10	70.00	70.00
Average	79.00 ± 13.37	76.00 ± 12.61

Acknowledgements. Project R&I-2018-012-T 'EyeCon' financed by the Malta Council for Science & Technology, for and on behalf of the Foundation for Science and Technology, through the FUSION: R&I Technology Development Programme.

References

1. Heide, W., Koenig, E., Trillenberg, P., Kömpf, D., Zee, D.S.: Electrooculography: technical standards and applications. In: Deuschl, G., Eisen, A. (eds.) Recommendations for the Practice of Clinical Neurophysiology: Guidelines of the International Federation of Clinical Physiology (EEG Suppl. 52), pp. 223–240. Elsevier Science (1999)
2. Yamagishi, K., Hori, J., Miyakawa, M.: Development of EOG-based communication system controlled by eight-directional eye movements. In: EMBS Annual International Conference, New York City (2006)
3. Tangsuksant, W., Charoenpong, T., Chanwimalueang, T.: Directional eye movement detection system for virtual keyboard controller. In: The 5th 2012 Biomedical Engineering International Conference, pp. 1–5 (2012)
4. López, A., Rodríguez, I., Ferrero, F.J., Valledor, M., Rodriguez, J.C.C.: Low-Cost system based on electro-oculography. In: 2014 IEEE 11th International Multi-Conference on Systems, Signals & Devices (SSD14), pp. 1–6 (2014)
5. Nathan, D.S., Vinod, A., Thomas, K.P.: An electrooculogram based assistive communication system with improved speed and accuracy using multi-directional eye movements. In: 2012 35th International Conference on Telecommunications and Signal Processing, TSP 2012 - Proceedings, pp. 554–558 (2012)
6. Barbara, N., Camilleri, T.A., Camilleri, K.P.: EOG-based eye movement detection and gaze estimation for an asynchronous virtual keyboard. Biomed. Signal Process. Control **47**, 159–167 (2019)

7. Liu, Y., Bu-Sung, L., McKewon, M., Robust eye-based dwell-free typing. Int. J. Hum. Comput. Interact. **32** (2016)
8. Davies, M.: Word frequency data. https://www.wordfrequency.info/samples.asp. Accessed Jan 2021
9. Barbara, N.: EOG-based gaze angle estimation with varying head pose. PhD dissertation (submitted). University of Malta, Malta (2022)

Synergetic Effect of Contact Surface Area and Elbow Joint Angle on Tendon Vibration-Induced Illusory Movement

Hiroyuki Ohshima[✉] [ID] and Shigenobu Shimada

Tokyo Metropolitan Industrial Technology Research Institute (TIRI),
Sumida-ku, Tokyo 130-0015, Japan
ohshima.hiroyuki@iri-tokyo.jp

Abstract. Tendon vibration causes illusory movement in human limbs, which is a kinesthetic sensation experienced in the absence of any actual joint movement. This phenomenon can be effectively used to generate kinesthetic sensation in virtual-reality settings, which can solve various problems. However, because of the previously unknown relationship between the stimulus and perceptual characteristics, its implementation is limited. This study investigated the synergetic effect of the contact surface area and the joint angle. A vibration device was used to stimulate the biceps brachii tendons in four participants' dominant-side arms for 30 s at 100 Hz and 120 m/s^2. This device was fixed to a customized vibration fixture base, and the contact head was attached on top of the vibration device. Contact heads with different diameters (φ10, φ15, and φ20) were adopted. The shoulder was flexed at 90° on an armrest, while the elbow was flexed at 30°, both in the midsagittal plane, with palms facing upwards. After the experiment, they were asked to take two subjective evaluations of the vividness and range of extension of their elbow-joint angle. Three diameter conditions were ranked. During the illusory motion, both parameters increased with the contact surface area and the flection angle of the elbow joint. Thus, the contact surface area and joint angle had a synergistic effect on the perceptual characteristics of the illusory movement.

Keywords: Kinesthetic sensation · Sensorimotor system · VR

1 Introduction

Inducing vibrations on the tendons in human limbs evokes the illusion of motion, which is kinesthetic sensation experienced without any actual movement of the joint [1]. The underlying mechanism is that applying a vibratory stimulus to a tendon at a frequency of approximately 100 Hz excites the Group Ia [2, 3] and Group II [4] afferent nerve fibers present in skeletal muscle spindles, which causes them to communicate with the central nervous system that the muscle is stretched [5]. This appears to induce a nerve signal corresponding to the perception of joint movement. The effect of joint angles on motion illusion had not been reported before our previous work [6, 7]. Because gravitational torque depends on the joint angle, it could influence perceptual parameters such as the strength of motion illusion. We compared motion illusion for two different angles of the elbow joint using a subjective assessment of three aspects: strength of illusion, range, and velocity of extension [6], and a quantitative assessment of two other aspects: latency and duration [7]. The results showed that the three subjective aspects were affected by limb position, while the two quantitative aspects were unaffected by the joint angle. Conversely, the area of contact affects vibrotactile thresholds and is a more important stimulus parameter than the gradient or curvature of displacement [8], this is called spatial summation. Based on this, we verified the following hypothesis: the contact surface area influences perceptual parameters such as the strength of motion illusion evoked by the vibration of tendons [9]. Contact heads of different areas were tested on participants. After the experiment, participants were asked to take two subjective evaluations based on a five-point visual analog scale of the vividness and range of extension of the elbow-joint angle. Results demonstrated that both parameters increased with the contact surface area during the illusory motion. Thus, we conclude that the spatial summation affects the perceptual characteristics of illusory movement. Based on the above, this study investigated the synergetic effect of the contact surface area and the joint angle.

2   Materials and Methods

2.1   Participants

One male (aged 31) and three females (aged 44, 43, and 48) volunteered as participants in this study. In accordance with institutional requirements, they provided prior written informed consent. The Tokyo Metropolitan Industrial Technology Research Institute's ethics committee approved the experimental procedure (ES2021-14).

2.2   Apparatus and Experimental Setup

A palm-sized vibration device (WaveMaker-Mobile, Asahi Seisakusho, Japan) was fastened to a pre-existing fixing base (Fig. 1) [10]. The participants sat in front of the fixing base wearing an eye mask and earmuffs (Fig. 2). Their arm was positioned on the horizontal armrest with palms facing upwards, so that their shoulder and elbow were held still at a flexion of 90° and 30° in the midsagittal plane. The vibrator was positioned over the biceps brachii tendon, just above the elbow.

Figure 3 shows a 3D model of the contact head that was tested in this experiment. The contact heads were designed with a hole in its center for fastening a single-axis accelerometer (710-D, EMIC, Japan). Our previous studies used an accelerometer externally attached to the contact-head to record tendon vibrations [6, 7]. This setup, however, makes changing the contact surface area difficult. Hence, we developed a more convenient method for mounting an accelerometer inside a 3D-printed contact head [11], which we modified from the design of our previous studies. Figure 4 shows the setup of the vibration device, contact head, and accelerometer. The upper end of the contact head was bolted onto the vibrator, which was printed with a commercial 3D printer (Objet500 Connex3, Stratasys, USA). Figure 5 shows the contact heads of different radii (φ10, φ15, and φ20 mm) that were tested in this experiment. First, the φ10 mm (Condition

A) contact head, whose area was close to that of the biceps brachii tendon, was used. The remaining two contact heads, with diameters of φ15 (Condition B) and φ20 mm (Condition C), were then used in succession. The accelerometer was connected to a PC (VJ27M/C-M, NEC, Japan) through a vibration meter (UV-16, Rion, Japan) and a multifunction I/O device (USB-6000, National Instruments, USA). LabVIEW 2014 (National Instruments, USA) was used to record the accelerometer output.

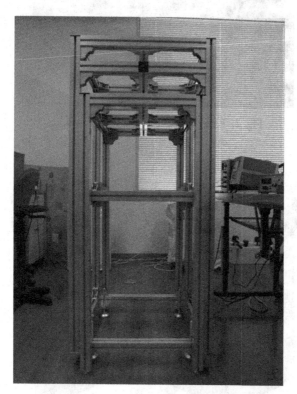

Fig. 1. Vibration device fixing base and armrest.

2.3 Procedure

Before the experiment, participants were informed that they would experience a sensation of their elbow joint extending, without any actual movement of the joint. In a preliminary experiment, we determined the appropriate anatomical location to consistently elicit the target kinesthetic sensation. The location on the participant's forearm where the stimulus was presented to them was marked on their skin with a felt-tipped marker. The right arm, which was the dominant arm for all four participants, was used.

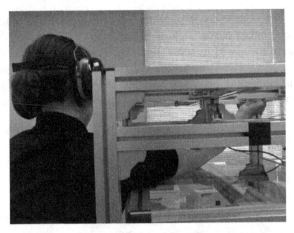

Fig. 2. Experimental setup of the elbow joint.

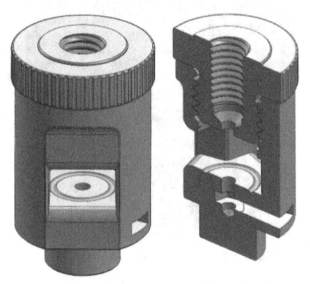

Fig. 3. 3D model of the contact head that was designed with a hole in its center for fastening a single-axis accelerometer.

The right arm biceps brachii tendon of all participants was stimulated for 30 s at 100 Hz and 120 m/s^2. The acceleration measured by the internal accelerometer was recorded at 1000 Hz and the RMS (root mean square) value of each acceleration was calculated using the following equation:

$$\text{RMS} = \sqrt{\frac{1}{n}\sum\nolimits_{i=1}^{n}(x_i)^2}, \tag{1}$$

where x_i is an acceleration sample and n is the total number of samples.

Fig. 4. The setup of the vibration device, contact head and accelerometer.

Fig. 5. Contact heads with different radii (from left to right: φ10, φ15, and φ20). The φ10 mm contact head was close to the area of the biceps brachii tendon.

The stimuli were presented in the order of φ10, φ15, and φ20 mm. After the experiment, participants were asked to take two subjective evaluations of the vividness and range of their perceived extension of their elbow-joint angle. They were asked to rank the three diameter conditions.

3 Results

All four participants described consistent sensations of motion. Table 1 shows the vividness and range of extension of the elbow-joint angle as perceived by each of the four participants. In all four participants, both parameters increased with the contact surface area.

Table 1. Subjective evaluation of vividness and range of extension of the elbow-joint angle during tendon vibration for each participant.

Participant	Vividness	Range of extension of elbow
#1	A < B < C	A < B < C
#2	A < B < C	A < B < C
#3	A < B < C	A < B < C
#4	A < B < C	A < B < C

4   Discussion and Conclusion

In our previous studies, we focused on the illusory motion in terms of joint angle [6, 7] and contact-surface area [9]. Thus, this study examined the synergetic effect of the contact surface area and the joint angle. The vividness and range of extension of the elbow-joint angle increased with the contact surface area during the illusory motion because of the effect of spatial summation [9]. In a previous study, participants' arms were positioned on a horizontal armrest with their palms facing upwards and their shoulders and elbows held still at a flexion of 90° and 0° in the midsagittal plane, respectively. In this study, the shoulder was held stationary on an armrest at a flexion of 90°, while the elbow was flexed at 30°. Because gravitational torque depends on the joint angle, it could influence perceptual parameters such as the vividness and strength of motion illusion. After the experiment, they were asked to take two subjective evaluations of the vividness and range of extension of their elbow-joint angle. The participants ranked the three diameter conditions. During the illusory motion, both parameters increased with the contact surface area. Thus, the combined results of the previous study and this study show that the perceptual characteristics of the illusory movement were affected by the contact surface area and the joint angle in a synergistic manner.

Existing virtual reality (VR) systems require the user to move their body, which poses various issues ranging from safety concerns arising from falls and collisions and economic problems that require wide spaces and large-scale equipment, to accessibility issues for users with physical disabilities. The realization of a VR system that does not require the user to move their body can make VR safer, more economical, and more accessible. However, by modulating the proprioceptive sensation, which is related to the posture and movement of the body (primarily the limbs), it is possible to generate the illusion of motion even in the absence of any actual movement. This phenomenon is called kinesthesia. Kinesthesia is just as important as the visual and auditory senses for safety, comfort, and entertainment quality in immersive VR environments. However, because the mechanisms of kinesthesia are not known in as much detail as those of the audiovisual senses, the presentation methods of kinesthesia, have lagged behind those of the visual and auditory senses. The results of this study have provided effective data for overcoming these current conditions.

However, there are still issues to be solved. Tendon thickness and location vary slightly from individual to individual. To induce the desired illusion, we must properly stimulate the user's target tendons. Additionally, the degree of subcutaneous exposure of the tendon differs when the joint is flexed and extended, as examined in this study. Therefore, it is necessary to identify the location of the targeted tendon and stimulate it appropriately according to the degree of exposure. In the current system, an expert familiar with the musculoskeletal system locates the target tendon and applies a vibrator to it. In the future work, we intend to develop a method that allows anyone to stimulate the right tendon with the right acceleration.

A systematic combination of knowledge on the relationship between vibratory stimulus and motion illusion can enable us to control kinesthesia and possibly simulate the experience of an Olympian or a Paralympian. Additionally, it can solve an important problem in motor learning, which is the transmission of first-person motor sensation, and move away from the conventional trial-and-error learning method. This is a significant step toward the development of a novel motor-learning method based on the first-person motion illusion.

Acknowledgments. This work was supported by JSPS KAKENHI Grant Numbers JP19K20105.

References

1. Goodwin, G.M., McCloskey, D.I., Matthews, P.B.: Proprioceptive illusions induced by muscle vibration: contribution by muscle spindles to perception? Science **175**(4028), 1382–1384 (1972)
2. Burke, D., Hagbarth, K.E., Lofstedt, L., Wallin, B.G.: The responses of human muscle spindle endings to vibration of non-contracting muscles. J. Physiol. **261**(3), 673–693 (1976)
3. Matthews, P.B.: Where does Sherrington's "muscular sense" originate? Muscles, joints, corollary discharges? Annu. Rev. Neurosci. **5**, 189–218 (1982)
4. Bove, M., Nardone, A., Schieppati, M.: Effects of leg muscle tendon vibration on group Ia and group II reflex responses to stance perturbation in humans. J. Physiol. **550**(Pt 2), 617–630 (2003)
5. Vallbo, A.B., Hagbarth, K.E., Torebjörk, H.E., Wallin, B.G.: Somatosensory, proprioceptive, and sympathetic activity in human peripheral nerves. Physiol. Rev. **59**(4), 919–957 (1979)
6. Ohshima, H., Shimada, S.: Does the limb position influence the motion illusion evoked by tendon vibration? In: IEEE Engineering in Medicine and Biology Society, 40th Annual International Conference, Honolulu, ThPoS-22.6 (2018)
7. Ohshima, H., Shimada, S.: The effects of the angle of an elbow joint on the latency and duration when tendon vibration evoke the motion illusion. In: IEEE Engineering in Medicine and Biology Society, 41st Annual International Conference, Berlin, WePOS-34.27 (2019)
8. Verrillo, R.T.: Effect of contactor area on the vibrotactile threshold. J. Acoust. Soc. Am. **35**(12), 1962–1966 (1963)
9. Ohshima, H., Shimada, S.: Influence of the contact surface size on the illusory movement induced by tendon vibrations. In: Stephanidis, C., Antona, M., Ntoa, S. (eds.) HCII 2021. CCIS, vol. 1499, pp. 558–563. Springer, Cham (2021). https://doi.org/10.1007/978-3-030-90179-0_72

10. Ohshima, H., Shimada, S.: Development of a system to quantify the depth of tendon stimulus for the illusion of motion achieved by a vibrator. In: IUPESM World Congress on Medical Physics & Biomedical Engineering, Prague, T10-06 (2018)
11. Ohshima, H., Ishido, H., Iwata, Y., Shimada, S.: Development of a quantification method for tendon vibration inducing motion illusion. In: Stephanidis, C., Antona, M. (eds.) HCII 2020. CCIS, vol. 1225, pp. 212–216. Springer, Cham (2020). https://doi.org/10.1007/978-3-030-50729-9_30

Fast-Response Pen-Type Interface for Reproduce a Realism Pen-on-Paper Experience

Ryota Watanabe[✉], Yoichi Yamazaki, and Masataka Imura

Kwansei Gakuin University, 2-1 Gakuen, Sanda, Hyogo 669-1337, Japan
ryota-0829@outlook.jp

Abstract. In this study, we propose a pen-type interface that uses a vibration motor to reproduces the feeling of writing on paper when writing using a stylus pen on a tablet device. Conventional pen-type interfaces have two problems. First, a delay occurs between the start of writing and the start of vibration. Second, because the frequency and amplitude of the vibration are fixed, the writing feel is not reproducible. Hence, we quantify the degree of time delay that humans can tolerate by conducting sensitivity evaluation experiments. To maintain the time delay within an acceptable range, we utilize an acceleration sensor to acquire the start of a writing action and the writing speed at the interface. This approach can reduce the system delay and ensure a fast response. Based on a subjective evaluation experiment, we confirm that the proposed method does not cause any time delays. To solve the second problem, the vibration generated in the pen when writing on paper at various speeds is measured, and the linear prediction coefficient of the autoregressive model is derived. The vibrations reproduced based on the model are transmitted to a vibrator at the interface in real time to improve the reproducibility of the writing feel. Spectrogram analysis results of the generated vibration confirm that the difference in vibration characteristics based on the writing speed can be reproduced.

Keywords: Writing feel · Auto regressive model · Vibration

1 Introduction

In recent years, the use of tablet devices has increased in various fields and industries. The adoption of information and communication technology (ICT) is accelerating in the education industry; consequently, the number of classes using tablet devices will increase. For example, the United Nations Educational, Scientific and Cultural Organization recommends ICT, because it promotes universal access to education and bridges the learning gap [1]. It has been confirmed that tablet-based applications can significantly reduce the disadvantages experienced when using curriculum-based measurements in schools [2]. In addition, drawing

C. Stephanidis et al. (Eds.): HCII 2022, CCIS 1581, pp. 71–78, 2022.
https://doi.org/10.1007/978-3-031-06388-6_10

using tablets has become mainstream not only in the education industry, but also in the animation and manga industries.

The most typical input methods for tablets are tracing with a finger or writing using a stylus pen as if it were an actual writing instrument. For people who typically write on paper, such as notebooks, using a stylus pen allows an intuitive operation. However, writing on a tablet device using a stylus pen does not transmit sufficient haptic feedback to a finger touching the stylus pen because of the slight vibration caused by friction between the pen's tip and the writing surface. This causes discomfort among users owing to the difference felt compared with the sensation of writing on paper using a writing tool.

The purpose of this study is to achieve a vibration sensation equivalent to writing on paper by reproducing the vibration of writing on paper using a vibration actuator built into a pen-type interface.

2   Related Studies

Several interfaces have been developed to improve user experience by reproducing the vibration of writing on paper, and they can be classified into two types. The first type is an interface with an internal mechanical vibration actuator. Cho et al.'s RealPen [3] reproduces the feeling of writing on paper by acquiring vibrations that occur when writing on paper using an acceleration sensor, which generates the same vibration waveform from obtained data and drives a vibration actuator. Ii presents a vibration similar to the writing vibration that occurs on paper by determining the difference between the spectrum of writing vibration on paper and the frictional vibration that occurs between the tablet device and interface, as well as by considering the transfer function from the PC to the interface [4]. However, the interfaces developed in these studies detect the writing start timing from the change in the pointer coordinates on the tablet when the user moves the pen tip, which generates and outputs vibration subsequently; therefore a delay occurs between writing and the start of vibration, causing a sense of discomfort.

The second type is haptic feedback generated during writing, based on the principle of electric vibration. The EV-Pen [5] developed by Wang et al. provides tactile feedback to the user by generating electrostatic attraction between the pen tip and the electrode layer on the tablet surface, with the silica insulating layer on the tablet surface serving as a capacitor when the user writes while driving the interface with a vibration waveform with a preset amplitude and frequency. The EV-Pen provides accurate writing with a low error rate in the steering task of tracing a predetermined path. However, the haptic feedback obtained from the EV-Pen is only a periodic vibration signal comprising a preset amplitude and frequency. Typically, when writing on paper using a pen, the haptic feedback obtained differs depending on the writing speed. However, the EV-Pen lacks reproducibility because it cannot change the vibration presented by different writing speeds. In this study, the first type of method, where mechanical vibration actuators are used, is applied to reproduces the sensation of writing on paper.

3   Fast Response Implementation

When using a pen-type interface, The user feels discomfort owing to the delay between the time of writing and the start of vibration. In this section, we explain the effect of delays on users, as well as the implementation of a system to reduce delays.

3.1   Effects of Delays

The time between writing and the onset of vibration was measured using a pen-type interface developed by Ii's [4]. The delay varied based on the writing speed; at a writing speed of 3 cm/s, the delay exceeded 0.3 s. Therefore, users felt discomfort when using the interface developed by Ii. Based on an evaluation experiment conducted by Miyazato et al. pertaining to delay [6], we investigated the amount of delay tolerable by users. Experimental collaborators were instructed to write with various lengths of delay and rate the degree of discomfort on a five-point scale. The results showed that writing with a delay exceeding approximately 0.1 s was uncomfortable to the users.

3.2   System to Reduce Delays

The authors developed a new system [7] to reduce delay. A prototype (Fig. 1) that can detect the movement of the pen nib by itself, equipped with a pressure sensor to detect the ground state of the interface pen nib and writing surface, and a gesture sensor to detect the timing of writing was built; subsequently, the delay values were measured, as shown in Table 1. It was confirmed that the writing speed was below 0.1 s, whict was the criterion for feeling discomfort, at all writing speeds. An analysis of variance at the 5-% significance level showed no significant difference in term of the increase or decrease in latency values at different writing speeds. In conclusion, the new system using the gesture sensor reduces delay, which is important for improving reproducibility.

Fig. 1. Prototype

Table 1. Average of reduced delays

Writing speed (cm/s)	Average delay (s)
1	0.064
2	0.059
3	0.061

4   Reproduction of Writing Vibration at Different Writing Speeds

When writing on paper using a pen, the vibration transmitted from the grasp to the fingers differs based on the writing speed. In general, when paper is manufactured, after the surface is smoothed via coating, it is heated by metal and elastic rolls to render it smoother and shinier. However, in terms of paper, which is typically used for drawing letters and pictures, the number of rolls used is reduced to process the paper, which results in microscopic irregularities on the surface of the paper. When the nib moves at different writing speeds while in contact with the paper, the vibration level transmitted to the finger differs, owing to the difference in the number of irregularities in contact per unit of time. Therefore, it is expected that the frequency characteristics of the vibrations produced by each increase in the writing speed will differ. In this section, we describe the construction of a system that changes the presented vibration based on the writing speed when an interface is used.

4.1   Vibration Characteristics at Different Writing Speeds

To confirm that the vibration transmitted to the fingertip varies with the writing speed, we measured the vibration produced when writing on paper at each writing speed. An acceleration sensor (ADXL337, Analog Devices) was attached to the grip of a twist-type ballpoint pen (Parker), and a straight line was written from left to right on a copy paper. The writing distance was fixed at 25.5 cm, and 10 measurements were performed for each writing speed from 1 to 10 cm/s (1 cm/s increments). A tablet device was placed under the copy paper and the writing surface, and a black dot was displayed on the screen; the black dot moved in a straight line at a specified speed. This allows users to write at a constant speed. Because the high-frequency vibration felt at the fingertip is primarily independent of directionality [8], only the acceleration component perpendicular to the pen axis was considered in this study. The sampling frequency was 5890 Hz. Figure 2 shows the results for writing speeds of 1, 5, and 10 cm/s. Figure 2 shows the waveforms and spectrograms of the writing vibrations that occur while writing on paper. As shown by the spectrograms for each writing speed, vibrations with more high-frequency components were generated as the writing speed increased. Therefore, it is more meaningful to present vibrations that match the user's writing speed.

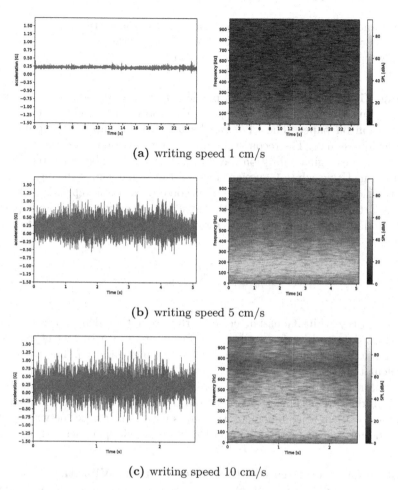

(a) writing speed 1 cm/s

(b) writing speed 5 cm/s

(c) writing speed 10 cm/s

Fig. 2. Vibration waveform and spectrogram on paper

4.2   Vibration Reproduction Method for Each Writing Speed

As indicate in Sect. 4.1, it is confirmed that the writing vibration caused by the writing speed exhibits different vibration characteristics. When writing on paper or on a tablet device, users do not maintain the same writing speed, but change their writing speed depending on the writing direction and type. Therefore, instead of periodically presenting a single vibration prepared in advance to the user, it is necessary to acquire the user's writing speed in real time, as well as generate and present a new writing vibration for each writing speed. In this study, we propose a method to model the writing vibration measured on paper at each writing speed and then present it to the user.

Writing Vibration Modeling. In particular, we propose a method to reconstruct writing vibration using linear predictive coding (LPC) based on the writing vibration on paper. The LPC can be used to estimate the current signal from previous signals. The reconstructed writing vibration reproduces the power spectrum of the original vibration waveform. Vibration can be generated for each presentation. Using white Gaussian noise as the signal source during vibration reconstruction, the waveform does not become a constant repetition of waveforms, and the user is presented with the sensation of writing without periodicity. The data $\hat{y}_n$ of the presented vibration are calculated using the following equation:

$$\hat{y}_n = e_n - \sum_{i=1}^{k} a_i y_{n-i} \tag{1}$$

where e_n is the white Gaussian noise, k the order that determines the range of previous data to be referenced, a_i the linear prediction coefficient, and y_{n-i} the i-sample past value of the reconstructed writing vibration. The value of e_n was calculated using the Box-Muller method, and k was determined using the Akaike information criterion. Using statistical model and, a Python statistical analysis library, we obtained the order from the data written data on paper, and the order $k = 27$ in this implementation. a_i is used to calculate the writing data measured on paper using the Levinson-Durbin method [9] at each writing speed.

Vibration Characteristics of Reproduced Writing Vibration. The vibration waveform and spectrogram of the reconstructed writing vibration based on the writing vibration on paper, as shown in Figure 2, are shown in Fig. 3. The reconstructed writing vibration shows that it is can reproduce the vibration characteristics of different writing speeds on paper. The results indicate that if the linear prediction coefficients are appropriately selected using the user's writing speed as a parameter, then the vibration of writing on paper can be reproduced, and the randomness of the vibration can be obtained. Furthermore, vibration can be presented to the user in real time, and hence the result above was obtained.

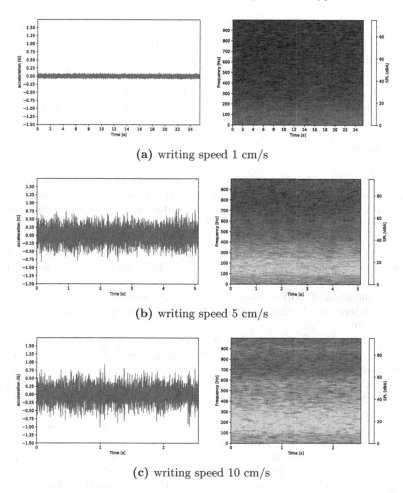

(a) writing speed 1 cm/s

(b) writing speed 5 cm/s

(c) writing speed 10 cm/s

Fig. 3. Vibration waveform and spectrogram of reconstructed writing vibration

5 Conclusion

In this study, we propose a pen-type interface that can reproduce the feel of writing on paper when writing using a stylus pen on a tablet device. We developed a system that achieves two elements: the fast response required to improve the reproducibility of the writing sensation and the real-time modification of the presented vibration in response to the writing speed. It was confirmed that the delay from the time of writing to the start of vibration can be reduced by detecting the timing of writing at the interface using a gesture sensor and a pressure sensor as a method to guarantee a high-speed response. Additionally, it was confirmed that LPC based on written vibrations on paper.

can be used to reconstruct vibrations with vibration characteristics equivalent to those of written vibrations on paper. Future prospects include the development of a system that can acquire a user's writing speed in real time and select appropriate linear prediction coefficients based on the acquired writing speed. In addition, by producing a mechanism and exterior to present the reconstructed vibration to the user and conducting comparative evaluation experiments using existing interfaces, we show that the interface developed in this study can improve the reproducibility of the writing sensation on paper.

References

1. UNESCO: ICT in education (2021). https://en.unesco.org/themes/ict-education
2. Blumenthal, S., Blumenthal, Y.: Tablet or paper and pen? Examining mode effects on German elementary school students. Computation skills with curriculum-based measurements. Int. J. Educ. Methodol. **6**(4), 669–680 (2020)
3. Cho, Y., Bianchi, A., Marquardt, N., Bianchi-Berthouze, N.: RealPen: providing realism in handwriting tasks on touch surfaces using auditory-tactile feedback. In: Proceedings of the 29th Annual Symposium on User Interface Software and Technology, pp. 195–205 (2016)
4. Ii, C.: Generation of writing sensation on a tablet based on the vibration transmission characteristics of writing instruments. Kwansei Gakuin University Graduation thesis (2019)
5. Wang, Q., Ren, X., Sarcar, S., Sun, X.: EV-Pen: leveraging electrovibration haptic feedback in pen interaction. In: Proceedings of the 2016 ACM on Interaction, Surfaces and Spaces, pp. 57–66 (2016)
6. Miyazato, T., Kishino, F.: Subjective evaluation of delayed perception between visual and tactile information. J. Inst. Telev. Eng. Japan **49**(10), 1353–1356 (1995)
7. Watanabe, R., Yamazaki, Y., Imura, M.: Development of a fast-response pen interface for improved reproducibility of writing feel. In: Information Processing Society of Japan: Interaction 2021, 2A02 (2021)
8. Bell, J., Bolanowski, S., Holmes, M.H.: The structure and function of Pacinian corpuscles. A review. Progr. Neurobiol. **42**(1), 79–128 (1994)
9. Ljung, L.: System Identification: Theory for the User. Prentice Hall, Hoboken (1999)

Proposal of Input Screen Design in Eye Glance Input Interface

Shodai Yada[✉], Yu Matsumoto, Tota Mizuno, Kazuyuki Mito, and Naoaki Itakura

The University of Electro-Communications, 1-5-1 Chofugaoka, Chofu, Tokyo, Japan
sho8.kthy@gmail.com

Abstract. Text input on smart devices with small screens has problems such as erroneous input due to the small size of each button or a small information presentation screen even if the input screen is large. To solve these problems, a previous study investigated a gaze input interface using the Eye Glance input method as an input method that does not depend on the touch panel area. Input is performed by quickly moving the line of sight back and forth from the center to the four corners of the smartphone. The purpose of this study is to propose an efficient screen design for text input using the Eye Glance input interface. Hereby, the display area is reduced by centering the input screen with a smaller size in accordance with the input operation, and at the same time, it is less likely to cause erroneous input due to unintentional eye movement. In addition, the available input options are arranged to match the input movement of the eye. Further, back taps and winks are considered for switching between input options to achieve a more intuitive input design. In the experiment, data were obtained by asking subjects to enter text using the proposed input screen design. Data analysis results showed that the interface is less prone to error and requires less time to input data, indicating its practicality. In addition, since it is possible to distinguish which eye is performing the winking, it is suggested that this could be used to create even more efficient input screen designs.

Keywords: Line-of-sight input system · Eye-gaze input · Input interface

1 Introduction

The main input method for smartphones is touch; however, the use of a small screen has been regarded as a problem from the viewpoint of operability, for example, erroneous input and keyboard screen occupancy, thus, a non-touch input method is required. One alternative to touch input is the use of eye gaze. The advantages of eye gaze input include the ability to perform quick movements at will and faithfully reflect the user's intention.

However, it is difficult to implement this method on a hand-held smartphone device because it is difficult to determine whether the user intends to input information while gazing at an object and because it requires high accuracy in locating the gazing position. As a new method for eye gaze input, the Eye Glance input interface has been proposed, which uses quick back-and-forth movement of the eyes from the center of the screen

© The Author(s), under exclusive license to Springer Nature Switzerland AG 2022
C. Stephanidis et al. (Eds.): HCII 2022, CCIS 1581, pp. 79–84, 2022.
https://doi.org/10.1007/978-3-031-06388-6_11

to the four corners in a diagonal direction as the input motion [1]. The input motion is discriminated using an optical flow waveform, which is a vector representation of the movement of an object inferred from a sequence of images.

In another previous study [2], an input screen design was proposed for an input method with fewer degrees of freedom of operation, referring to the QWERTY layout. Since this screen design has eight compartments, an increase in the degrees of freedom of operation was considered using two types of input: short input, in which the four corners are viewed only momentarily, and long input, in which the four corners are viewed for a slightly longer duration [3]. However, these interfaces are not appropriate for Eye Glance input for two major reasons. First, the screen design is horizontal. This makes Eye Glance input behavior based on the center of the screen difficult. Second, the judgment between short and long input is ambiguous, and long input increases input time. Based on the forementioned points, this study aims to improve the practicality of the Eye Glance input interface by proposing an appropriate input screen design and examining additional actions appropriate to the design.

2 Proposal Screen Design

2.1 Screen Design Overview

The screen design is a rectangle with 2×2 compartments (see Fig. 1). The layout of the options and input actions are aligned to enable intuitive input, such as moving the user's gaze back and forth from the center to the upper right for the options in the upper-right compartment. In addition, by arranging the choices in regular alphabetical and numerical orders in a clockwise direction, it is possible to shorten the time required to search for input characters. Furthermore, the regularity of the arrangement allows the user to locate the position of the input character even when only a portion of the choices are displayed. This allows for a low screen occupancy rate. The design of the input screen should be centered at the starting point of the Eye Glance input operation, and the input characters should be placed at the top of the screen to reduce the number of input errors caused by eye movement during input.

The options that can be input by Eye Glance are the colored areas outside of the screen design. Input is performed in two Eye Glance steps, with the first step displaying the characters contained in the selected option, one at a time, and the second step completing the input by selecting the characters.

The inner choices can be input by performing a switching action. Because of the 1:1 correspondence between the placement of choices and actions, two types of switching actions were considered, which are different from Eye Glance actions.

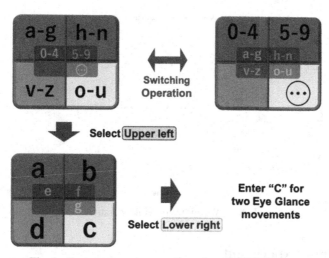

Fig. 1. Design of previous studies using QWERTY layout

2.2 Switching Operation

Two types of switching actions were considered: back tap and wink. An algorithm using the z-axis of the accelerometer was used to discriminate back tap motions. Because the accelerometer contains noise due to gravity, filtering was performed. The resulting waveforms were used to discriminate back tap movements (see Fig. 2). Optical flow similar to the Eye Glance motion was used to discriminate the wink motion. The waveform obtained by taking the optical flow from the left and right eyes separately and using the absolute value of the difference between them was used (see Fig. 3). Eye Glance and blink movements, in which both eyes are moved in the same manner, do not produce similar waveforms and can thus be distinguished from these movements.

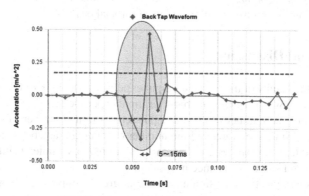

Fig. 2. Waveform of back tap operation

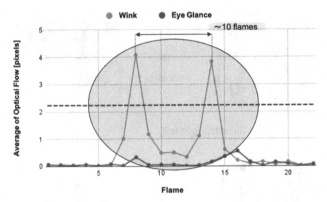

Fig. 3. Waveform of wink operation

3 Text Input Experiment

We conducted a text input experiment to confirm the operability of each interface using the proposed screen design and two types of switching behavior. The experimental equipment used was an iPhone XR with a built-in camera with a time resolution function of 30 fps. Subjects were males aged 22–24, four for switching by back tap and six for switching by wink. Subjects sat in a chair in a room and held the device in their hands while providing input.

After explaining the operation of the interface, the participants were asked to practice input freely to familiarize themselves with the interface. The subjects then typed in a sequence of random characters displayed on the screen, one at a time. The 39 characters to be input were alphabetic characters, numbers, and auxiliary keys for line feed, delete, and white space. During input, the characters were displayed on the screen for feedback. If the input character differed from the displayed character, the user was asked to continue until the input was successful. In addition to accuracy and input time data, video was also obtained from the built-in camera and used for analysis.

4 Results and Discussion

Table 1 shows the results of the character input experiments using Eye Glance and back tap, and Table 2 shows the results of character input experiments using Eye Glance and wink. The ratio of the number of correct input actions to the number of correct input actions is the discrimination rate, and the number of input characters per minute is the input speed. Table 3 also shows a comparison with previous studies using QWERTY arrays and long and short Eye Glance movements.

Table 3 shows that the discrimination rate is greatly improved compared to the previous study, and the input speed is the same as the previous study for the method using Eye Glance and wink motions, suggesting improved operability as an interface.

In addition, compared with the back tap, better results were obtained for the two switching actions proposed in this study using wink.

We analyzed the video of the experiment and classified the causes into three categories: Eye Glance, switching behavior, and human error due to screen design. In the experiment using Eye Glance and wink, 2.9% of the subjects were affected by Eye Glance, 1.7% by screen design, and 2.6% by back tap action.

The reason for the poor results obtained in the experiment when switching between the Eye Glance and back tap motion is thought to be that the shaking of the screen caused by back taps resulted in a large number of false inputs whereby the Eye Glance waveform was detected. We found that rear tap motion did not function well as an independent sensor because the acquisition of motion by the accelerometer interfered with the optical flow. Human errors due to the screen design included cases where the user forgot to switch to the inner choices, resulting in the outer choices being input, and incorrect input due to not remembering the placement of alphabets that were not currently displayed. It was found that further study is needed on screen design to minimize these errors. Furthermore, regardless of the cause of the error, there were many cases in which a character was input incorrectly in succession. A detailed analysis of the input behavior of these characters would further reduce the number of typing errors.

Table 1. Results of experiment using Eye Glance and back tap action

Input Action	Subject	Discrimination rate (%)	Input Speed(character/min)
Eye Glance + Back Tap	A	77.8	8.7
	B	87.9	11.9
	C	90.9	12.6
	D	91.6	14.9
	Average	87.1	11.6

Table 2. Results of experiment using Eye Glance and wink action

Input Action	Subject	Discrimination rate (%)	Input Speed(character/min)
Eye Glance + Wink	A	80.3	12.4
	B	89.2	12.1
	C	91.1	14.1
	D	98.2	16.3
	E	88.1	18.6
	F	100.0	18.2
	Average	92.8	15.3

Table 3. Comparison with previous studies

Input Screen Design	Input Action	Discrimination rate (%)	Input Speed (character/min)
Proposed Design	Eye Glance + Back Tap	87.1	11.6
	Eye Glance + Wink	92.8	15.3
QWERTY layout	Long and short inputs for Eye Glance operation	75	15

5 Conclusion and Future Works

This study proposed an input screen design appropriate for the Eye Glance input interface and suggested that it is useful as an interface allowing text input. In addition, a wink, which was newly proposed as an input action in this study, can be distinguished in terms of which eye is performing the action (left or right). In future work, we plan to propose an input screen design based on this interface and introduce the interface as an Input Method Editor (IME) for search engines and other applications, aiming for the practical use of the eye gaze input interface.

References

1. Saiga, Y., Matsumoto, Y., Mito, K., Mizuno, T., Itakura, N.: A proposal of eye glance input interface using smartphone built-in camera. IEEJ Trans. Fundam. Mater. **141**(12), 650–656 (2021)
2. Matsuno, S., Chida, S., Itakura, N., Mizuno, T., Mito, K.: A method of character input for the user interface with a low degree of freedom. Artif. Life Robot. **24**(2), 250–256 (2018). https://doi.org/10.1007/s10015-018-0512-4
3. Akehi, K., Marzeieh, F., Mito, K., Mizuno, T., Itakura, N.: A consideration of multiple choice of eye glance input interface by image processing. In: Annual Conference of Electronics, Information and Systems Society, TC15-3 (2018)

A Cooperative and Interactive Gesture-Based Drumming Interface with Application to the Internet of Musical Things

Azeema Yaseen[(✉)] [ID], Sutirtha Chakraborty [ID], and Joseph Timoney [ID]

Department of Computer Science, Maynooth University, Maynooth,
Co.Kildare, Ireland
{azeema.yaseen.2020,sutirtha.chakraborty.2019}@mumail.ie
Joseph.timoney@mu.ie

Abstract. The Internet of Musical Things (IoMusT) envisions a network of interconnected objects enabling multi-directional communication for novel musical interactions. The requisite demands on the interfacing technologies are significant. Challenges include users with different skills, delivering effective feedback, and signalling adverse conditions in the physical network. To this end, the design and implementation of a cooperative virtual drumming interface is investigated. It supports remote users through gestural interaction with virtual percussion objects. The GUI includes calibration mode (re-positioning objects), a performance window, community rhythm-pattern visualization, and a cooperative synchronicity display. In creative contexts, colour is often used as a metaphorical representation such as music/colour art, provides a second sensory perspective to the user, and here they are applied to highlight evolving user interactions. For evaluation a binary user cohort of students with and without prior musical experience was identified. Data was collected to measure the interactivity response and their rhythmic cohesiveness along with results on the user impressions of the collaborative aspects of this interface.

Keywords: Gesture based musical interaction · Virtual music instruments · Music-color mappings · Virtual musical collaboration · Performance synchronisation

1 Introduction

IoMusT was inspired by the fusion of ubiquitous computing and the Internet of Things (IoT) [2]. Its breadth of things includes single user devices (laptop, computer, iPad or wearables) embedded with computational abilities that have been specifically created for, or can be directed to, performing in-place or virtual musical activities. Networked Music Performance (NMP) is one of the predominant application domains of IoMusT and covers all remote musical interactions between musicians [3].

C. Stephanidis et al. (Eds.): HCII 2022, CCIS 1581, pp. 85–92, 2022.
https://doi.org/10.1007/978-3-031-06388-6_12

In the traditional performance environment sonic musical cues used in performer synchronisation are reinforced by the cues generated from the visual, physical connections in the shared composite space. However, in virtual interactions this medium becomes impaired. Thus, the virtual interface must compensate in some way.

Another compromise on the effectiveness of any virtual interactions is the inherent issue of network latency. This is a crucial obstacle as significant sound lags due to latency can completely disrupt the performers' rhythmic synchronisation. Recent papers [3,4] highlighted this challenge and proposed network adaptive metronomes to manage synchrony. Another perspective is to treat latency as a real and ever-present, albeit, unstable feature, and so to think of dealing with it by designing a new musical instrument which exploits latency as being part of the interactions [1].

An interface that could successfully integrate sonic and visual feedback that fits within IoMusT is our motivation for this work. Our approach is to investigate the development of a virtual remote-collaborative drumming interface.

2   Gesture Based Interfaces and Virtual Musical Instruments (VMIs)

Gestures refer to meaningful expressions of the human body when it moves; this may involve the hands, the arms, the head, or whole-body motions [4,5]. More recently, the handy metaphor (Handy hear and Handy see) in [6] was developed for IoMusT; in both modes it enables touchless sonic interactions to manipulate pitch, amplitude and duration of the sound. Another is "Interval Player" [7], an in-air VMI, that allows users to specify the melodic interval using their hands. The vision-based collaborative musical interface "lamascope" [8] uses image processing to produce music based on the user's body image. [9] presents a web-based interface for virtual performance of an air guitar and an upright bass; collaborative playing of two or more players is enabled. Often for gestural instruments, custom-build devices, e.g., data gloves, or body suits, or off-the shelf products, such as Kinect and Leap motion, are used to collect data. These devices may hinder movement, and have a financial and installation cost. Others use camera-based gesture recognition to avoid this and all laptop computers have a camera as standard. This leads to our use of Human Pose Estimation (HPE) as an advanced manifestation of the computer vision approach.

Pose is an arrangement of human joints and HPE is the localization of human joints from a predefined set of key-points or landmarks in a recording or sequence of live images [10]. These are shown in Fig. 1. These landmarks are tracked continuously using the Mediapipe Pose Estimation (PE) model. It was found to be accurate and so could capture user expressiveness during a musical activity. Figure 2 shows the Region of Interest (ROI) we used for the proposed interface to track, estimate and recognise users' movements during the live performance.

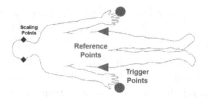

Fig. 1. Key-points extraction from human pose used as referents to determine body, limbs and fingers positions.

3   Design Description: Gestural Drumming Interface with Color Based Musical Objects

3.1   Graphical Interface for Virtual and Collaborative Drumming

The system architecture is designed based on a two-tier client server architecture to facilitate the interactive drumming performances of the remote ensemble. The performance has two levels; 1) Local-level Individual Interaction and 2) Ensemble-level Interaction. The first enables self-interaction where the participant interacts with the drum machine running locally. Here, the camera sensor is placed in front of the player for recording the gestures and detecting the actions of the musical performance. A Deep learning-based PE model [11] is used to detect the body key positions and movement of the user for acquisition of the required gestural information. The algorithm estimates the hands', arms' and lower body 3D key points for each of the video frames captured. A buffer with fifteen frames was created for each arm. To track the movements of each arm we used a queue-replacement approach. A 'speed buffer' calculates the 3D spatial displacements of the key points between two consecutive frames, so whenever an index finger enters the specified boundary on the interface and exceeds a threshold parameter, the 'hit' instance is processed. The boundary is represented as a rectangular color box (see Fig. 2(b) and (c)).

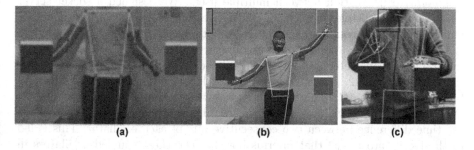

Fig. 2. Gesture recognition using computer camera and interaction with musical objects: hands within the boundary of musical object. (Color figure online)

Color Based Percussion Objects. A group of arranged percussion instruments is called a drum kit. The drum kit can comprise of any number of percussion instruments, but for this study a bass (kick) drum, a snare drum and two cymbals (hi-hat and crash) are included. Due to the variability of drum kit pitches, it was not possible to define a schematic approach for color-pitch mapping so we represented the kick and snare drums with saturated colors (red and blue) and used dark colors (dark green and firebrick) for the cymbals. The general order is observed from left (more saturated) to right (less saturated). There is configuration flexibility of the virtual drums and so re-positioning of the objects is possible (see Fig. 2(a)). When a gesture is performed, the gestural interface executes a "struck" event associated with the particular gesture and the percussion object.

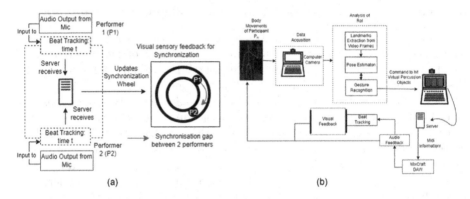

(a)   (b)

Fig. 3. (a) Representation of the beat tracking for synchronicity and its visualization, (b) the system model.

Performer's Synchronisation Wheel. For collaborative performance, participants connect to the same server and the 'hit' event initiates the virtual collaborative interaction between multiple users. We designed a socket server which handles multiple clients using multi threading. A mathematical model for multiple oscillator coupling, i.e. the Kuramoto oscillator [12,13] is applied to encourage synchronization between the virtual performers. For each participant, each object is considered as an independent oscillator. For example, for two participants P1 and P2, player P1 plays the kick(K) and snare(S), and P2 plays hi-hat(H) and crash(C). This would result in the creation of 4 oscillators OSCK, OSCS, OSCH, and OSCC. On receiving the information, the server calculates the time difference between two consecutive hits of each oscillator. This is fed to the Kuramoto model that informs how to keep these coupled oscillators in synchronization, not just in frequency, i.e. tempo, but also in phase, i.e. that the rhythmic pulse or beats happen at the same time. This is illustrated in Fig. 3(a).

Visual Feedback. Colors for a long time have been used for music visualization and there are many music-color mappings proposed between musical elements (e.g., loudness, timbre, pitch,) and color properties like hue, saturation, and brightness. A very recent survey in [9] gives a detailed overview. In our instrument colours are associated with musical objects and are also used for secondary visual feedback to the performers. Combined auditory and visual feedback supports performers during a collaboration.

We used the same color mappings used for the percussion instruments to give color-based feedback on their rhythmic patterns. Every time "auditory feedback" occurs, the color associated with that specific audio is displayed on the user's own, and on the virtual performer's interface. The complete system interface is given in Fig. 4. The interface in (a) and (b) show sample rhythmic patterns and (c) shows the information passed to the synchronization wheel.

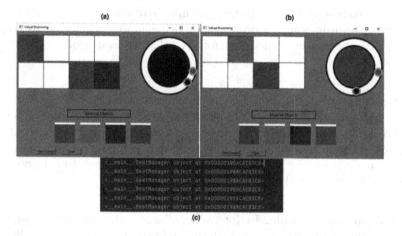

Fig. 4. The GUI of drumming interface.

4   User Experience Study

For this study, 4 participants (2 amateurs and 2 musicians) collaborated in three different settings(Musician-Amateur, Amateur-Musician and Musician-Musician) using this interface. The sessions were conducted for a time-span of approximately 2 h. To get feedback about their experience we used the think-aloud technique [14] and did not interrupt them when they were collaborating. Thus, the performance was let happen, followed by a sharing of their feedback on how they were experiencing the interface, then they played again, and following this commented further until the session ended. Each group spent 15 min on average excluding the time they took to become familiar with the interface elements. We then asked them planned open-ended questions at the end of performance.

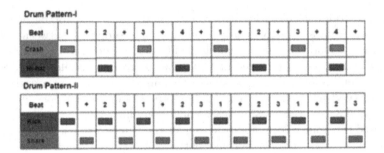

Fig. 5. Rhythmic phrases played by participants during performance.

4.1   Musical Interaction Modes

The participants were given 2 simple rhythmic patterns presented in Fig. 5 to play during the drumming performance. Participants were given time to become familiar with the interface, then they followed the two models of interactions as given below.

The 'Instrumental' Mode. An 'instrumental' interaction is based on the instrumental metaphors adopted from traditional interaction. Here, the participants tried to synchronize from the auditory feedback only. It was observed that the musicians were able to learn the patterns faster than non-musicians. The amateurs understood the "hitting drums" metaphor but took time to adapt to the sound of each musical object.

The 'Interactional' Mode. In 'Interactional' mode, they focused on using the interface at its full capability. This mode allowed participants to see the colours of percussion objects that were played by themselves and their virtual participant. Participants tried to adapt their body gestures to the visual feedback before they were able to receive the audio feedback, which was subject to a short delay. Once they found a way to balance between their gestures, with the color and auditory feedback, they tried to understand their partners' beating patterns. In the earlier stage, the synchronization wheel was not considered. When they realized the position of colors moving in the interface window, they started making gestures at different scales and they expected to achieve quick visual and audio feedback responses. Unfortunately, latency did interfere with the predictive worth of the synchronization wheel and this impacted its value.

Findings. We found that keeping the rhythmic phrases (as shown in Fig. 5) was easily achievable when the tempo ranged between 60 to 125 BPM (for simple sequences). The participants after their involvement offered similar opinions regarding gestural interactions and the drumming interface. They all agreed that the visualization of what the others were doing along with the auditory feedback in the user interface enhanced the performance. In the "Instrumental" mode the descriptions were flexible, enjoyable, and expressive. In this mode, participants were more engaged to achieve consistency. In the "Interactional" mode the descriptors were "expressive", "conversational" and "enjoyable". The synchronization wheel was only helpful when gestures were recognized quickly and the synchronization information was updated prior to the user making the gesture for next beat.

5 Conclusion and Future Work

This paper focused on musically driven efforts to adopt vision-based techniques to capture human gesture and afford non-traditional forms of sonic articulation and creative musical expressions. The intention for this new VMI interface was that it should permit live interactive performances among users from different musical backgrounds and with different levels of skills. This paper described a specially-designed collaborative VMI for drumming that incorporated auditory and visual feedback in its interface that aimed at shaping the performers' individual and joint interactions. Our experience, based on participant feedback, found that using musical interaction models that were similar to traditional models along with color-based visual stimulus can facilitate engaging and collaborative music making activities. The performances mediated by the color based visual feedback were conversational and conveyed meaningful information among the participants.

For future work, the interaction experience can be expanded by providing more coupling between sound and gestures, e.g. faster movements for high-pitched sounds and slow movements for lower pitched sounds. To achieve this, the gesture recognition model needs modification along with consideration for an enhanced color representation. This should also be easy to learn. Focus should also be placed on solving the time delay issues and their impact on the synchronization wheel. Lastly, a more comprehensive user study must be carried out.

References

1. Wilson, R.: Aesthetic and technical strategies for networked music performance. AI Soc. 1–14 (2020). https://doi.org/10.1007/s00146-020-01099-4
2. Turchet, L., Fischione, C., Essl, G., Keller, D., Barthet, M.: Internet of musical things: vision and challenges. IEEE Access **6**, 61994–62017 (2018)
3. Battello, R., Comanducci, L., Antonacci, F., Cospito, G., Sarti, A.: Experimenting with adaptive metronomes in networked music performances! J. Audio Eng. Soc. **69**(10), 737–747 (2021)
4. Battello, R., et al.: An adaptive metronome technique for mitigating the impact of latency in networked music performances. In: 2020 27th Conference of Open Innovations Association (FRUCT), pp. 10–17 (2020)
5. Mitra, S., Acharya, T.: Gesture recognition: a survey. IEEE Trans. Syst. Man Cybern. Part C (Appl. Rev.) **37**(3), 311–324 (2007)

6. Keller, D., Gomes, C., Aliel, L.: The handy metaphor: bimanual, touchless interaction for the internet of musical things. J. New Music Res. **48**(4), 385–396 (2019)
7. Lages, W., Nabiyouni, M., Tibau, J., Bowman, D.A.: Interval player: designing a virtual musical instrument using in-air gestures. In: 2015 IEEE Symposium on 3D User Interfaces (3DUI), pp. 203–204 (2015)
8. Fels, S., Mase, K.: Iamascope: a graphical musical instrument. Comput. Graph. **23**(2), 277–286 (1999)
9. Lima, H.B., Santos, C.G.D., Meiguins, B.S.: A survey of music visualization techniques. ACM Comput. Surv. (CSUR) **54**(7), 1–29 (2021)
10. Josyula, R., Ostadabbas, S.: A Review on Human Pose Estimation. arXiv preprint arXiv:2110.06877 (2021)
11. Singh, A.K., Kumbhare, V.A., Arthi, K.: Real-time human pose detection and recognition using MediaPipe. In: International Conference on Soft Computing and Signal Processing, pp. 145–154 (2021)
12. Rodrigues, F.A., Peron, T.K.D., Ji, P., Kurths, J.: The Kuramoto model in complex networks. Phys. Rep. **610**, 1–98 (2016)
13. Chakraborty, S., Timoney, J.: Robot human synchronization for musical ensemble: progress and challenges. In: 2020 5th International Conference on Robotics and Automation Engineering (ICRAE), pp. 93–99 (2020)
14. Ericsson, K.A., Simon, H.A.: How to study thinking in everyday life: contrasting think-aloud protocols with descriptions and explanations of thinking. Mind Cult. Act. **5**(3), 178–186 (1998)

More Immersed or More Manipulated? Users' Responses to Mobile Tactile Technology Adopted in a Chinese Video Platform

Lu Yifei[(✉)]

Beijing Normal University, Beijing, China
yifeilu52@gmail.com

Abstract. Through content analysis of messages posted on Sina Weibo, this paper inspected users' responses to the mobile tactile technology adopted in iQIYI, a well-known Chinese video platform that specializes in technology development. We identified this technology as a daily-use version of traditional immersive technology and analyzed users' perception, emotions and attitudes towards the stimulus under the stimulus-organism-response (S-O-R) framework. The study found that users could hardly immerse into video content through this technology. Instead, they paid more attention to the platform's strategic moves. We propose that despite the growing positive attitude towards this technology, the lack of inter-activity is a problem that needs to be addressed as immersive technology comes into everyday life. At the same time, users should be more alert to emotional manipulation when multisensory stimuli are provided. This study bridged HMC and everyday life and revealed how so-called immersive technology might be a detriment to actual immersive experience.

Keyword: Mobile · Tactile technology · Immersive experience · Chinese video platform

1 Data and Methods

Taking into account the time when iQIYI adopted tactile technology, the time when the first relevant post was published, and the time when this study began, we set the time range of our research as between August 14, 2020 and September 22, 2021, with "iQIYI" and "vibration" as shared keywords. After excluding advertisements, official propaganda, and content not directly related to the research content, 278 microblogs were finally obtained as the research samples and analyzed by means of content analysis. Seven categories of analysis units were set for the samples, according to the samples' specific contents and the sensory feedback and emotional experiences to be further investigated and interpreted: text attributes, text types, post focus, posting attitude, sensory feedback, and emotional experience.

This paper employed an S-O-R framework drawn from the study by Suh and Prophet [1], where a literature review on immersive technologies was conducted (see Fig. 1). The classification of post types was drawn from Wohn & Na [2].

C. Stephanidis et al. (Eds.): HCII 2022, CCIS 1581, pp. 93–99, 2022.
https://doi.org/10.1007/978-3-031-06388-6_13

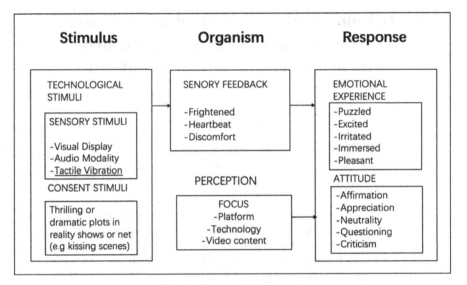

Fig. 1. Conceptual framework

2 Findings

2.1 Attributes and Types of Posts

The findings pointed to a total of 182 posts by Weibo users in 2021 about IQIYI's vibration technology, nearly double the number (n = 96) of 2020. Of those 278 posts over the two years, original (n = 272) and untagged (n = 207) posts accounted for the vast majority.

Notably, in terms of post types, the number of emotional posts was much higher than the other three categories, accounting for 46.4% of all posts, followed by opinion (r = 28.8%), attention-seeking (n = 21.9%), and pure information, which accounted for only 2.9%. This showed that most of the platform users' posts about IQIYI's vibration technology contained strong emotions. Many users also made their own value judgments or framed their own movie-viewing experiences around this technology, according to which a reasonable assessment of the dissemination effect of this technology can be made.

2.2 Post Focus and Posting Attitude

First, in terms of the target of the posts (i.e., their focus), most posts were directed at the platform (n = 139), followed by the technology (n = 75), and fewer still at the video content (n = 64). Second, in terms of the posting attitudes displayed, positive attitudes (both affirmative and appreciative) were dominant (r = 50.36%), with 45.68% of posts displaying affirmative attitudes and 4.68% of posts displaying appreciative attitudes.

By contrast, among the 32.38% of posts with negative attitudes, questioning and critical attitudes were equally likely to appear, accounting for 16.55% and 15.83%, respectively. Finally, neutral attitudes accounted for 17.27% of the posts overall. Hence, the users' attitudes towards tactile technology were found to be positive on the whole.

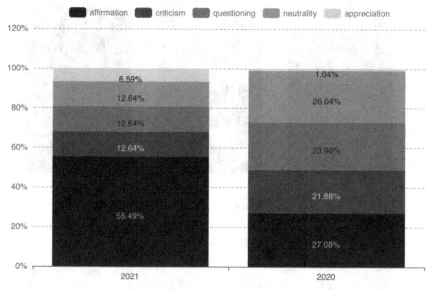

Fig. 2. Ratio of different post attitudes for different years

As Fig. 2 demonstrates, the percentage of positive attitudes was higher in 2021 compared with 2020, accounting for 62.08% of the 2021 posts overall. For the year 2020, negative attitudes accounted for 45.84% of the posts, and positive attitudes for only 28.12%. These rates suggest that in the early stages of exposure to tactile technology on the platform, users' attitudes were more inclined to be negative, gradually shifting to positive over time. There are two possible reasons for this, as described in the next paragraphs.

The first possible reason is that in 2020, iQIYI mainly used vibration technology for music clips in variety shows, and often resorted to flux technology, combining visual flashes, tactile vibration, and other sensory stimuli, with greater intensity of stimulation and a stronger sense of violation for users. In 2021, iQIYI came to apply vibration technology more to web dramas, a genre with plot settings, and with the plot padding, the degree of abruptness was expected to decrease. However, it should be noted that the role assumed by tactile technology has correspondingly transitioned from auxiliary to alternative perception, and such transformation may also cause a sense of violation among users.

The second possible reason is the positive attitude of the fan base. Reading through the microblogging texts, the coder found that the web series and its lead actors had many fan groups whose posts often showed very positive attitudes.

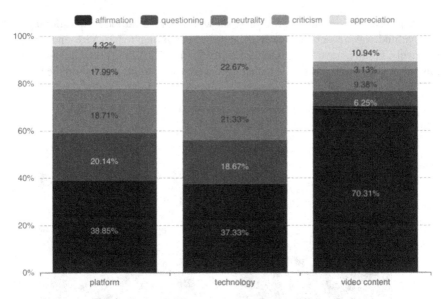

Fig. 3. Ratio of different post attitudes for different foci

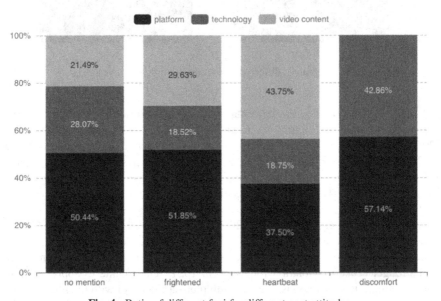

Fig. 4. Ratio of different foci for different post attitudes

In addition, as Figs. 3 and 4 demonstrate, cross-analysis of the two sub-categories found that negative attitudes dominated in posts targeting technology (r = 40.00%), while positive attitudes dominated in posts targeting video content and the platform (r = 43.17%; r = 81.25%). Among the video content, the affirmative attitude was dominant (r = 70.31%). Interestingly, except for appreciative attitudes, most posts were directed at the platform, regardless of the attitude. However, this tendency was particularly evident when the attitude was negative, meaning that the negative attitudes people displayed in their posts were mainly directed at the platform.

The divergence in positive attitude posts was not as pronounced. When people showed an affirmative attitude, it was 42.52% likely to be for the platform, 35.43% likely to be for the video content, and 22.05% likely to be for the tactile technology, while when people showed an appreciative attitude, they were more likely to be expressing their views on the video content ($r = 53.85\%$).

2.3 Sensory Feedback and Emotional Experience

Most posts did not mention their sensory feedback ($r = 82.01\%$). Of those that did, the most common sensory feedback was fright ($n = 27$), followed by heartbeat ($n = 16$) and discomfort ($n = 7$) (See Figs. 5 and 6).

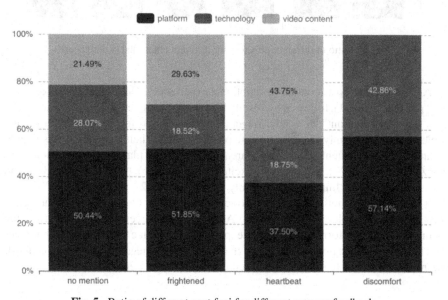

Fig. 5. Ratio of different post foci for different sensory feedback

Among these, 51.85% of the frightened feedback and 57.14% of the discomfort feedback were elicited by the platform, with the remainder of the discomfort feedback being elicited by the technology. By contrast, 43.75% of the heartbeat feedback was identified as being aroused by the video experience, meaning that the sensory experience consistent with the goal of tactile technology communication (i.e., the heartbeat), was mentioned very infrequently and not in direct relation to the technology and platform. Users preferred to combine the feeling of heartbeat with the video content, while the sensory feedback from the technology and platform was mainly negative ("frightened" and "discomfort").

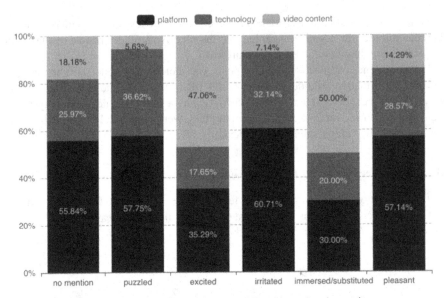

Fig. 6. Ratio of different post foci for different emotional experiences

Among the 201 posts containing emotional experiences, the most common emotion was "puzzled" (n = 71), followed by "excited" (n = 68), "irritated" (n = 28), "immersed" (n = 20), and "pleasant" (n = 14). When people expressed feeling puzzled, irritated, or pleased, it was mainly in relation to the platform, while their excitement was mainly towards the video content. The most apparent emotion in the platform-specific posts was "puzzled" (r = 29.50%), followed by "excited" (r = 17.27%), "irritated" (12.23%), and "pleasure" (5.76%). "Immersion" was only signaled by 4.32% of the posts.

It is also worth noting that the emotional experience of "puzzled" further grew to 34.67% of technology-specific posts. Although this percentage did not affect the dominance of the platform focus of posts expressing doubt (due to the small total number of technology-specific posts), it was enough for us to see the negative emotional feedback towards the tactile technology. Typical sentiments of doubt were as follows.

3   Conclusion

The main purpose of this study was to investigate users' responses to the newly adopted tactile vibration technology in the Chinese video platform iQIYI. Through our content analysis of user discussions on Sina Weibo on related topics, we arrived at the conclusions described below.

Firstly, more users posted within the emotion category in comparison with the attention-seeking, information, and opinion categories. This is consistent with previous findings [2] and suggests that emerging technologies such as tactile vibration technology have a greater potential to trigger intense emotions among users.

Secondly, the most frequent posts were platform-focused, followed by technology and video-content-focused posts. Users' corresponding attitudes showed positive characteristics overall, with attitudes becoming more positive in 2021 over 2020. However, most posts did not mention their sensory or emotional experiences; among those that did, the most frequent sensory feedback and emotional experiences were found to be "frightened" and "puzzled," respectively, while sensory and emotional experiences consistent with the communication goals of tactile technology were expressed less frequently.

The other two emotional experiences with high reference rates were "excited" and "irritated." These sensory responses collectively form the answers to the research question in this study, i.e., whether there are any other possible sensory responses towards this kind of daily immersive technology besides a sense of presence.

In sum, it would be unfair to evaluate the nature of a technology simply by the so-called immersion technology provided, considering the gross generalization of the word "immersive" and users' actual responses revealed in this study. Both platforms and technology company should reconsider whether the interaction between mobile phones and users can be endlessly amplified, in other words, whether immersion can be realized through the affordances of mobile phones without causing users' excessive cognitive load.

References

1. Suh, A., Prophet, J.: The state of immersive technology research: a literature analysis. Comput. Hum. Behav. **86**, 77–90 (2018)
2. Wohn, D.Y., Na, E.-K.: Tweeting about TV: sharing television viewing experiences via social media message streams. First Monday (2011)

Perception, Cognition, Emotion
and Psychophysiological Monitoring

Towards a GUI for Declarative Medical Image Analysis: Cognitive and Memory Load Issues

Giovanna Broccia[(✉)], Vincenzo Ciancia, Diego Latella, and Mieke Massink

Consiglio Nazionale delle Ricerche, Istituto di Scienze e Tecnologie dell'Informazione 'A. Faedo', Pisa, Italy
{giovanna.broccia,vincenzo.ciancia,diego.latella,
mieke.massink}@isti.cnr.it

Abstract. In medical imaging, (semi-)automatic image analysis techniques have been proposed to support the current time-consuming and cognitively demanding practice of manual segmentation of *regions of interest* (ROIs). The recently proposed *image query language* ImgQL, based on spatial logic and model checking, represents segmentation methods as concise, domain-oriented, human-readable procedures aimed at domain experts rather than technologists, and has been validated in several case studies. Such efforts are directed towards a *human-centred* Artificial Intelligence methodology. To this aim, we complemented the ongoing research line with a study of the Human-Computer Interaction aspects. In this work we investigate the design of a graphical user interface (GUI) prototype that supports the analysis procedure with minimal impact on the focus and the memory load of domain experts.

Keywords: User-centred design · Usability study · Cognitive evaluation · Medical image analysis · Spatial logic · Spatial model checking

1 Introduction

In the field of Medical Imaging [17], *segmentation* plays a crucial role [14]. Segmentation consist in the identification of regions of interest (ROIs) – that might correspond to tissue, organ, traces of disease, or other relevant structure – and dividing the image into meaningful segments. The current practice of manual segmentation (e.g., in Radiotherapy) is time-consuming and cognitively demanding, justifying the plethora of existing research on fully- and semi- automatic segmentation methods. In recent work (see [1–3,9]), the approach of *spatial model checking* has been proposed. Such methodology combines local image features

This work has been partially supported by the Italian MIUR-PRIN 2017 project IT-MaTTerS: Methods and Tools for Trustworthy Smart Systems.

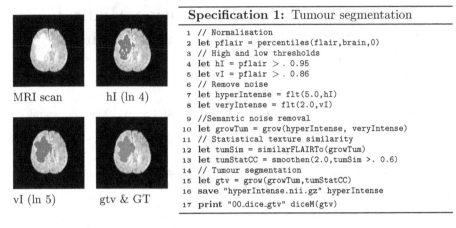

MRI scan   hI (ln 4)

vI (ln 5)   gtv & GT

Specification 1: Tumour segmentation

```
 1  // Normalisation
 2  let pflair = percentiles(flair,brain,0)
 3  // High and low thresholds
 4  let hI = pflair > . 0.95
 5  let vI = pflair > . 0.86
 6  // Remove noise
 7  let hyperIntense = flt(5.0,hI)
 8  let veryIntense = flt(2.0,vI)
 9  //Semantic noise removal
10  let growTum = grow(hyperIntense, veryIntense)
11  // Statistical texture similarity
12  let tumSim = similarFLAIRTo(growTum)
13  let tumStatCC = smoothen(2.0,tumSim >. 0.6)
14  // Tumour segmentation
15  let gtv = grow(growTum,tumStatCC)
16  save "hyperIntense.nii.gz" hyperIntense
17  print "00_dice_gtv" diceM(gtv)
```

Fig. 1. ImgQL segmentation of image `Brats17_2013_7_1`: Overlays hI, vI and gtv (pink) and ground truth (GT) (blue). (Color figure online)

(intensity, colour, texture) with spatial/topological characteristics (relative distance, contact, connectedness), exploiting a domain-specific, concise, declarative language named ImgQL ("image query language") and the efficient, parallel spatial model checker VoxLogicA[1], optimised for operating on medical images, e.g. MRI or CT scans (see [10] for a tutorial). The resulting ROIs are meant to be visualised as (semi-transparent) number-valued as well as boolean (so-called "masks") layers on top of the original images. Common similarity indexes, such as Dice-Sorensen, can be directly defined in ImgQL (see e.g. Fig. 1).

VoxLogicA has been successfully applied to BraTS 2017[2], a publicly available set of benchmark MRI images for brain tumour segmentation [3]. The obtained results are well in line with the state of the art, both in terms of accuracy and in terms of computational efficiency, while supporting explainability, easy replicability and exchange of analysis methods. So far, the approach has been used via a command line interface. This is sufficient for the technical validation of the tool, but hinders usability and broader uptake by domain experts.

The GUI design proposed in the present paper follows a user-centred approach, taking into consideration typical tasks performed by different classes of professionals in this domain [13]. In particular it aims at supporting the analysis procedures with minimal impact on the focus of attention and on the user's memory load [5,6]. The *handling of layers* is identified as one of the central tasks. The creation and visualisation of layers not only supports ROI identification but also the understanding and evaluation of the results of ImgQL queries. We analyse the effect of layers selection from the GUI on the capability of users to perform common tasks (visualise the layers identified by a logic specification, identify a new layer via a logic formula, visualise and analyse a new layer identified by a

---

[1] VoxLogicA is available at https://github.com/vincenzoml/VoxLogicA.
[2] See https://www.med.upenn.edu/sbia/brats2017/data.html.

logic formula, compare two different layers) in terms of time performance, error in the execution of tasks, and memory load, using user tests and by a theoretical evaluation of the memory load. We focus on the following research questions:

I RQ1. *What is the effect of layers selection on task performance?*
II RQ2. *Is the relation between the layers and the specification clear to users?*
III RQ3. *How does GUI vs. command line layer selection affect memory load?*

To answer RQ1 and RQ2, we performed a usability study that provided useful feedback on the efficiency and effectiveness of the layers handling mechanism. To answer RQ3 we performed a theoretical evaluation on the memory load required to complete the tasks conducted in the usability test, with and without the support of the GUI. In general, the design of GUIs for medical imaging tools is mainly inherited from the medical consoles already used in the medical domain, without a dedicated study on their usability [8]. In [12] different user interfaces for 2D and 3D imaging are reviewed and discussed, and the usability of such tools is regarded as essential for their adoption by clinicians. In [11,15] a number of tools with GUI have been evaluated regarding a set of aspects included usability, that has been assessed qualitatively as the result of the authors' experience.

For the design of the GUI three classes of users were considered: *1) Healthcare professionals.* This class consists of clinicians that generally use image segmentation. Typical tasks are manually inspecting and comparing base images and related ROIs; *2) Researchers in Medical Imaging.* Their goal is to find innovative solutions to support the work of clinicians; *3) IT professionals.* These are developers that want to create and propose tools and techniques to support the work of clinicians. Independently from the user class, image segmentation tasks are cognitively demanding, especially from a memory point of view, due to the need to manage a variety of information of very different nature such as case information, medical records, dictation systems, reporting facilities, literature search, access to databases and version control, to mention a few [18].

2   A GUI for Declarative Medical Image Analysis

Figure 2 shows the underlying architecture of `VoxLogicA` and its GUI. From the analysis of different tasks related to different classes of users, we conjecture that the GUI displaying both input and output in a single window plays a central

Fig. 2. The VoxLogicA process and architecture

role in reducing the user's memory load: having all the necessary information on display helps users to complete their tasks without having to retrieve them from their working memory at each step.

The GUI prototype has been implemented using HTML, CSS and JavaScript and it runs as a desktop application through Electron[3]. The next version of the GUI is under development, building upon the research that we present in this paper. No longer being a prototype, the next version will be based on a state-of-the-art web user interface framework, namely `vue.js` version 3, using `pinia` as its store[4].

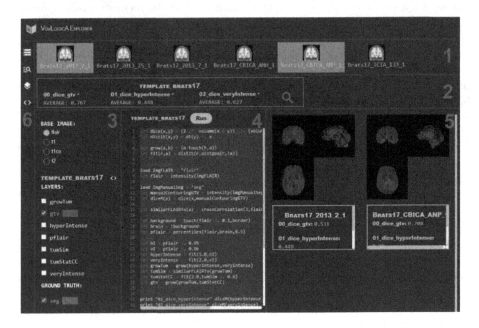

Fig. 3. VoxLogicA graphical user interface

Figure 3 shows the complete GUI prototype with all elements open (the red numbers in the figure are for reference only and are not part of the GUI). Below we describe its elements: the name of the GUI element and the corresponding number introduce each item.

Dataset Row (1). This section shows the dataset of images. To analyse one or more images more in detail, users can open/close cases by clicking on the thumbnail images. This action changes the thumbnail images background colour to yellow and opens/closes an embedded DICOM viewer for each image in the *work space* presented below.

---

[3] Electron (https://www.electronjs.org/) is an open-source software framework which allows for the development of desktop GUI applications using web technologies.

[4] See https://vuejs.org/ and https://pinia.vuejs.org/.

Indexes Row (2). A section immediately below the *dataset row* shows the similarity indexes computed over that dataset by the VoxLogicA specification shown in the *code column*. Moreover, in this section one can look for items in the *dataset row* that satisfy specific characteristics, using a dedicated search box that opens when clicking on the search icon.

Layers Column (3). The bottom-left column of the window shows the list of base images and the list of overlays saved with the VoxLogicA specification shown in the *code column*. The base image is activated by clicking on the related button: when selecting a case from the dataset row, the system will display the activated base image in the viewer referring to the chosen case in the work space. Moreover, by clicking one or more overlays they will be opened as transparent layers on top of the base image in the work space. The system automatically selects a different colour for each layer. If present, the ground truth can be shown as a layer. Its presence is indicated after the title "GROUND TRUTH".

Code Column (4). In the bottom-middle column of the window the ImgQL specification is shown through an embedded code editor. It can be edited and the modified specification can be run on the open cases shown in the workspace by clicking the button "Run"; if no cases are open, the button is not active.

Work Space (5). In the bottom-right column of the window the open cases are displayed (instantiated with the active base image), together with the active overlays, through embedded image viewers. Below each image viewer a box is shown with the information about the open case: its name and the values for the similarity indexes computed by the specification.

Icons Column (6). A column on the left side of the window shows four icons by clicking on which one can show or hide associated sections in the window.

3 GUI Evaluation

We are performing a number of usability studies on different classes of users to test specific GUI features. Each of these studies is conducted on small groups of users, following an iterative design cycle. Here we present a usability study performed on 5 users belonging to the academic research area (the group is composed of computer science students and professors recruited from a master class on spatial logic and model checking) focusing on the evaluation of the handling of the layers, in order to answer RQ1 and RQ2 (see Sect. 1). Moreover, to answer RQ3, we performed a theoretical evaluation on the memory load required to complete the tasks proposed in the usability study, comparing two variants of these tasks, one performed with the support of the GUI and one performed via command line operations.

3.1 Usability Study

The study design reproduces a realistic scenario, where users were asked to evaluate the quality of a VoxLogicA segmentation procedure with the support of the GUI. Users were asked to perform selected representative tasks and to fill out a post-study questionnaire under the supervision of a test moderator who guided and observed the participants during the test execution. The study started with a familiarisation phase during which participants freely used the VoxLogicA GUI. The central phase of the study consisted of the completion of 4 tasks, each of which composed of a variable number of basic tasks. For each basic task users provided an answer or performed an action on the GUI which were annotated by the test moderator. Each task has been developed to test a specific GUI feature. Here we focus on the following tasks:

1. Visualise and analyse results regarding the images identified in previous tasks
2. Modify the segmentation procedure by adding and saving a new layer and compare the new layer with a previous version

At the end of the central phase participants were asked to fill out a post-study questionnaire composed of 3 sections: one on personal information, one on feedback and suggestions about the GUI and one on GUI satisfaction.

Results. With the data collected through the post-study questionnaire, feedback was gathered on the GUI, as well as on its desired new features. Here we present only those aspects concerning the handling of layers.

Participants were asked to rate the comprehensibility of the opening and closing of layers on a 5-points scale ranging from 1 ("hardly comprehensible") to 5 ("very comprehensible"). The collected answers attest that this aspect is very comprehensible (4 participants rated 5 and 1 participant rated 4). Users were also asked how clear it was for them that the layers visualised in the layers column are all and only the ones computed and saved with the VoxLogicA procedure exposed in the code column. The collected answers attest that this is less well-understood: 1 user rated 2 in the 5-points scale, while the remaining users rated in equal measure 4 and 5.

Considering the users' perception on whether the GUI features are able to support them in completing the usability study they all responded that they are satisfied with the GUI features, except for one user who would find it useful to have additional support for understanding the VoxLogicA specification (such as a *reading guide* or a description of the VoxLogicA primitive operators). Regarding the collected suggestions on how to improve the GUI, we received a number of helpful proposals. Suggested were the availability of an initial guide where the basic aspects of the interface are explained and the improvement of the automatic choice of colours when multiple layers have to be displayed together (e.g. using colours with high contrast to help the visualisation, or letting the users choose the colours they prefer).

The data gathered by the test moderator on the users' performance, provides some quantitative measures on the central phase of the usability test. Here we only report the task success rate (namely the percentage of *successfully* completed tasks)[5] [16]. Although all tasks have been completed by all users, in 4 cases users had some uncertainties in completing (part of) a task, resulting in a success rate of 80%. The main issues we observed regard task 2: some users experienced difficulties in (a) adding the new layer and (b) comparing the new and old layers. Difficulties in case (a) mainly concerned the comprehension of the VoxLogicA language (ImgQL). This is also confirmed by one of the suggestions collected during the post-study questionnaire. While difficulties in case (b) concern the choice of colours automatically performed by the system. This is again confirmed by another suggestion collected during the questionnaire.

User satisfaction and perceived usability of the GUI was measured via a System Usability Scale (SUS) questionnaire provided at the end of the test [7]. Overall, based on this questionnaire, the prototype GUI was perceived as sufficiently usable and satisfying, with a mean score of 82.5. Just one participant gave a global score of 62.5, below sufficient evaluation.

3.2 Memory Load Evaluation

To answer RQ3 (see Sect. 1), we performed a theoretical evaluation of the amount of information needed by the users to complete the tasks proposed in the usability test with and without the support of the GUI (details in [4]).

When the tasks are performed without the support of the GUI users have to navigate the file system in order to find input and output images they need. This implies remembering at each step not only the names of the images but also the names of the directories, their position and whether they have been already opened or not. To this, we have to add all the information regarding the use of additional tools for open and visualise MRI scans, analysing the similarity indexes, updating the specification code and running the analysis through command line operations. With the support of the GUI, instead, all the required information is displayed, available and visible. Users do not need to navigate the file system (and thus remember names and positions) since they already have both input and output files available on the GUI. They do not need to remember how to use external tools since the GUI provides both an embedded code editor and viewers that enable a simplified task execution. Finally, users do not need to remember how to run VoxLogicA from command line since they can perform an analysis by just clicking on a button. This results in a considerable reduction of the memory load in using the proposed GUI.

4 Conclusion and Future Work

We presented a prototype of a novel GUI for various user classes in the domain of medical image segmentation. The GUI supports the use of the spatial model

---

[5] The success rate is measured as the sum of the tasks completed successfully and the tasks completed with some issue weighted 0.5, over the total number of completion attempts (i.e. the product of the number of tasks and the number of participants).

checker VoxLogicA for the design of novel medical image analysis methods. We evaluated a first GUI prototype with a usability study and a memory load evaluation. The study provides important feedback on how to improve the GUI for further analysis. The memory evaluation shows how the GUI can help users in completing their tasks successfully with a lower cognitive effort. As part of future work, we plan to carry on the usability studies on other classes of users to test further GUI features, in order to improve the tool in an iterative design cycle.

References

1. Banci Buonamici, F., Belmonte, G., Ciancia, V., Latella, D., Massink, M.: Spatial logics and model checking for medical imaging. Int. J. Softw. Tools Technol. Transfer **22**(2), 195–217 (2019). https://doi.org/10.1007/s10009-019-00511-9
2. Belmonte, G., Broccia, G., Ciancia, V., Latella, D., Massink, M.: Feasibility of spatial model checking for nevus segmentation. In: FormaliSE, pp. 1–12 (2021)
3. Belmonte, G., Ciancia, V., Latella, D., Massink, M.: VoxLogicA: a spatial model checker for declarative image analysis. In: Vojnar, T., Zhang, L. (eds.) TACAS 2019. LNCS, vol. 11427, pp. 281–298. Springer, Cham (2019). https://doi.org/10.1007/978-3-030-17462-0_16
4. Broccia, G., Ciancia, V., Latella, D., Massink, M.: A graphical user interface for medical image analysis with declarative spatial logic - cognitive and memory load evaluation. Technical report, ISTI Technical report, ISTI-2021-TR/012, pp. 1–39 (2021)
5. Broccia, G., Masci, P., Milazzo, P.: Modeling and analysis of human memory load in multitasking scenarios: late-breaking results. In: Proceedings of the ACM SIGCHI Symposium on Engineering Interactive Computing Systems, pp. 1–7 (2018)
6. Broccia, G., Milazzo, P., Ölveczky, P.C.: Formal modeling and analysis of safety-critical human multitasking. Innov. Syst. Softw. Eng. **15**(3), 169–190 (2019). https://doi.org/10.1007/s11334-019-00333-7
7. Brooke, J.: SUS: a quick and dirty' usability. Usab. Eval. Ind. **189**(3) (1996)
8. Cannella, V., Gambino, O., Pirrone, R., Vitabile, S.: GUI usability in medical imaging. In: 2009 International Conference on Complex, Intelligent and Software Intensive Systems, pp. 778–782. IEEE (2009)
9. Ciancia, V., Latella, D., Loreti, M., Massink, M.: Model checking spatial logics for closure spaces. Log. Methods Comput. Sci. **12**(4) (2016). http://lmcs.episciences.org/2067
10. Ciancia, V., Belmonte, G., Latella, D., Massink, M.: A hands-on introduction to spatial model checking using VoxLogicA. In: Laarman, A., Sokolova, A. (eds.) SPIN 2021. LNCS, vol. 12864, pp. 22–41. Springer, Cham (2021). https://doi.org/10.1007/978-3-030-84629-9_2
11. Haak, D., Page, C.E., Deserno, T.M.: A survey of DICOM viewer software to integrate clinical research and medical imaging. J. Dig. Imag. **29**(2), 206–215 (2016)
12. Iannessi, A., Marcy, P.-Y., Clatz, O., Bertrand, A.-S., Sugimoto, M.: A review of existing and potential computer user interfaces for modern radiology. Insights Imaging **9**(4), 599–609 (2018). https://doi.org/10.1007/s13244-018-0620-7
13. Ergonomics of human-system interaction - Human-centred design for interactive systems. Standard, International Organization for Standardization (2019). https://www.iso.org/standard/77520.html

14. Koundal, D., Kadyan, V., Dutta, P., Anand, V., Aggarwal, S., Gupta, S.: Computational techniques in biomedical image analysis: overview. In: Advances in Computational Techniques for Biomedical Image Analysis, pp. 3–31 (2020)
15. Liao, W., Deserno, T.M., Spitzer, K.: Evaluation of free non-diagnostic dicom software tools. In: Medical Imaging 2008: PACS and Imaging Informatics, vol. 6919, pp. 11–22. SPIE (2008)
16. Nielsen, J., Budiu, R.: Success rate: the simplest usability metric (2001). https://www.nngroup.com/articles/success-rate-the-simplest-usability-metric/
17. Ritter, F., Boskamp, T., Homeyer, A., Laue, H., Schwier, M., Link, F., Peitgen, H.O.: Medical image analysis. IEEE Pulse 2(6), 60–70 (2011)
18. Sharma, A., Wang, K., Siegel, E.: Radiologist digital workspace use and preference: a survey-based study. J. Digit. Imaging 30(6), 687–694 (2017)

Rotational Movement Perception of Spiral Patterns on Dynamic Sphere Surfaces Based on Line Angles

Guang-Dah Chen[1][(✉)] and Hsiwen Fan[2]

[1] National Taiwan University of Art, New Taipei City 22058, Taiwan
chengd@ntua.edu.tw
[2] Chiba University, Chiba 263-8522, Japan

Abstract. The research on motion perception mainly focuses on flat images, and there is lacked research on 3D aspects. This study discussed the rotational dynamic optical illusion movement perception of a sphere through the dimension of the psychology of vision in the domain of basic modeling. The modeling bodies in prior studies mainly focused on cylinders and cones; therefore, the sphere was set as the main research direction of this paper for studying the line angle optimization of spiral patterns on dynamic sphere surfaces. The study provides five different angles of samples, that angles are 5°, 10°, 15°, 20°, and 25°. This study employed the method of adjustment in experimental methods to study the induced movement effect and movement afterimage effect of spheres through dynamic modeling. The findings showed that the sample at the line angle of 5° brought a better dynamic optical illusion movement perception to the subjects when the sphere was in a rotational movement. The results of this study were expected to provide a reference for future researchers and related art design creators.

Keywords: Dynamic modeling · Sphere · Dynamic optical illusion · Induced movement · Movement afterimage

1 Introduction

This study followed the studies of Chen [1] and Chen et al. [2] to discuss the probability of rotational movement perception. The above-mentioned studies discussed changes in the induced movement and movement afterimage through the rotational movement of a cylinder, polygonal cylinder, and polygonal cone, and found that the sphere had a worse movement perception effect. As its characteristic of shape was different from the named samples, the sphere was worthy of further discussion and could be used as a sample in research to discuss its movement perception effect.

Movement perception refers to the perception of displacement of an object in space. It depends on the object's movement velocity, the distance between the moving body and the observer, the movement of the observer, and the stationary state. When an object changes its spatial position and this change can be detected, the perception of the object's movement is generated. Movement perception includes induced movement, automatic

C. Stephanidis et al. (Eds.): HCII 2022, CCIS 1581, pp. 112–120, 2022.
https://doi.org/10.1007/978-3-031-06388-6_15

movement, apparent movement, and movement afterimage. This study used a sphere with a continuous smooth body as the modeling body. As it had a continuous smooth surface and did not have a border line, a sphere was less relevant to the automatic movement and apparent movement of movement perception. As a result, the movement perception used in this study only included the induced movement and movement afterimage. According to the direction of this study, the effect of visual perception was considered, and the induced movement and movement afterimage were discussed in depth.

Induced movement refers to the movement perception generated by stationary stimuli induced by the stimuli of all actual movements [3]. Gregory [4] found that the viewer will consider environmental factors during watching. According to different influence forms, the inducement can be divided into the mutual movement between objects, the movement between oneself and the object, the differentiation of figure-ground relation, and the irregular figure being easier to generate induced movement than the regular figure [5]. This study probed into the differentiation of the figure-ground relation.

The differentiation of the figure-ground relation results from the direct relationship between the induced movement performance of forms and the figure and ground. When a continuous line rotates, an obvious figure-based rotation phenomenon will be generated, causing figure and ground to be differentiated. According to the findings of Chang [5], when the area of the ground is larger than the figure, the ground will generate the illusion of nonrotation due to the assimilation phenomenon, but the figure will be separated from the ground perception, thus generating the dynamic effect of actual rotation and causing only the induced movement of the rotating figure to be perceived.

The movement afterimage refers to the phenomenon of the naked eye perceiving the existence of an object's form for a short period of time after it suddenly disappears [6]. It is the movement perception without the actual movement stimuli which were induced by the actual movement stimuli. The movement afterimage occurs after watching the actual movement. When the eye sees a quick movement or spatial displacement of an object, object images from different time points are temporarily imaged and remain on the retina for 0.04–0.06 s, after which they are sent back to the brain through the optic nerves and perceived as the object's movement or a displacement image. If the object moves continuously or stops suddenly, the image of the object at the previous moment will not disappear immediately from the optic nerve but remain for 0.04–0.06 s, thus generating the visual illusion of existence [7].

The purpose of this study was to fabricate a spherical experimental sample using a helically continuous line pattern on the spherical surface as the basis for studying the dynamic optical illusion of the movement perception effect. The experimental results were analyzed to discuss whether the figure-ground relation generated by different line angles and different line thicknesses would influence the perception effect. This study was expected to further understand the characteristics of the rotational dynamic optical illusion and perception effect of the modeling sphere and to provide a reference for future research and creation.

In this study, a spiral line pattern was laid on the sphere surface. The pattern varied with the line angles, and the spiral movement of patterns was adjusted by the wireless variable frequency digital control system. The movement perception perceived by the subject's eye was recorded using a tachometry, and the line angle optimization result of spiral patterns on a dynamic modeling sphere surface was obtained by comprehensive analysis.

2   Experiment Method

2.1   Measurement Method

The psychophysical method can be used to obtain the relationship between the sensory system and physical stimulation through threshold measurements [8]. If a stimulation value enables the subject to detect the stimulus, the stimulation value will represent the lower absolute threshold of the sensory system; on the contrary, if the stimulation value causes the subject to fail to perceive the stimulus, the stimulation value will represent the upper absolute threshold of the sensory system. The interval threshold between the upper absolute threshold and the lower absolute threshold is called the speed threshold in this study because the stimulation value is the rotation speed.

2.2   Sample Pattern Setting

Lines were used as the basis of the sample patterns according to the experimental objective. Lines are very important in shaping art, as they can scientifically divide the space in a shape as well as simply, rapidly, and precisely segment a shape's external regions to generate ocular depth remodeling [9]. A line is characterized by its shape, thickness, and hardness, and the length, curvature, straightness, thickness, and density of a line can illustrate different artistic expressions [10]. The experimental results would be further explored according to the said characteristics of the lines, including the thickness of the lines, the density of the lines, and the space between lines.

2.3   Experiment Design

A spiral line with a thickness of 10 mm was combined with five line angles (five degrees, 10°, 15°, 20°, and 25°) in the experiment of this stage. The subjects were stimulated by varying the rotation speed stimulation value, and the researcher recorded and discussed their responses to the rotational dynamic optical illusion movement perception of spiral patterns on a dynamic sphere surface in the experiment of this stage. According to the schematic diagram of the line angle pattern samples (Fig. 1), the angle influenced the line spacing (line density) and the number of lines in a specific range. According to the requirement of the sphere sample in this experiment, the experimental samples of line angles in the first stage of the experiment were 5°, 10°, 15°, 20°, and 25°.

Line angles	5°	10°	15°	20°	25°
Sketch					

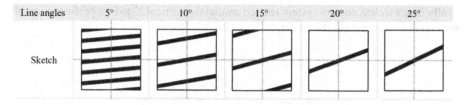

Fig. 1. Line angle pattern samples

2.4 Pattern Samples

The sample in this study was an actual three-dimensional sphere with a diameter of 200 mm. Based on the optimum viewing angle of 14°, the viewing distance was set as 800 mm, and the calculated sphere height was set at 200 mm, as shown in the schematic diagram of Stage 1.

The actual sample was fabricated by 3D printing after precise drawing and the modeling calculation by the 3D modeling software of SolidWorks 2015. Finally, the printed sphere and line pattern were further processed for the experiment.

In terms of the spiral continuous line pattern on the sphere's surface, according to the research findings of Chen [1] a 10-mm-thick black line and a 15° spiral line angle were employed as the standard for the experimental samples in this study.

According to the experimental line angle samples shown in Fig. 2, a smaller line angle indicated a larger number of lines visible to the subject and a smaller line spacing. Comparatively speaking, the larger the line angle was, the smaller the number of lines the subject could see, and the larger the line spacing. In other words, according to the division of figure and ground, the subject could perceive more figures at a smaller line angle than with a larger line angle; comparatively speaking, the subject could perceive more ground at a larger line angle than at a smaller line angle.

2.5 Subjects

A total of 20 students participated in this experiment, including ten males and ten females ranging from 22 to 25 years of age. The subjects all had training in professional design and art. The naked binocular vision or the corrected binocular vision of the participants was measured using the C-type visual acuity test scale, and the participants had a normal visual acuity of 0.9–2.0.

2.6 Experiment Equipment and Tools

The experimental environment was controlled for normal illumination and was based on a digital variable frequency wireless control system. The rotation direction of the wireless control system was adjusted according to the user or experimental conditions, and the motor speed could be controlled accurately by pressing a button. The adjustable minimum variation of this system was 1 rpm, and the rotation speed ranged from 1 rpm to 1300 rpm. The digital panel recorded the subject's stimulation value clearly and precisely to reduce errors in the experiment and enhance the reliability of the experimental results. The wireless control system rotated around the vertical X-axis to perform a spiral movement of the experimental sample.

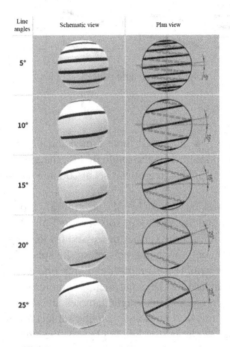

Fig. 2. Experimental line angle samples

2.7 Experiment Procedure

At the beginning of the experiment, the knowledge about movement perception was explained to the subjects, so that the subjects knew about the overall experimental process well and the target position of their focal point. The induced movement of the sample was performed at the beginning of the test, where the rotation speed stimulation value (rpm) was increased slowly until the subject detected the existence of induced movement. At this point, the lower absolute threshold of the induced movement was recorded, and the rotation speed stimulation value (rpm) was increased until the subject could no longer detect the induced movement. At this point, the upper absolute threshold of the induced movement was recorded. After a sufficient period of rest, the subject received a test for rotation speed stimulation value until the movement afterimage was perceived, and the lower absolute threshold of the movement afterimage was then recorded. In the end, the experimental data of Stage 1 ware integrated, and a sample sphere with a spiral pattern at an optimal line angle was obtained after comprehensive discussions and analyses (the sample with the widest speed threshold interval). The experimental process was as follows:

1. At the beginning of the experiment, its purpose and procedure were explained to the subjects, so that they knew that this experiment was about finding the most suitable

angle of the spiral line pattern for the optical illusion effect of a spiral sphere. An optimal sample was summarized after the experiment (the sample with the widest speed threshold interval of the movement perception). The concepts of basic dynamic optical illusions and movement perception were explained to the subjects, and further explanations were provided if the subjects had any questions.

2. The subjects engaged in several practice attempts before the formal experiment to familiarize themselves with the entire experimental process.
3. After the experiment was completed, the stimulation value (speed threshold) of the pattern perceived by the subject was recorded.

3   Results

The experimental result, from the induced movement to the movement afterimage, was analyzed. Five samples of spiral spheres at different line angles were listed in a table and arranged in an ascending order. The perception threshold in the table was divided into the lower absolute threshold (i.e., the minimum rotation speed stimulation value of which the subject could perceive the dynamic optical illusion movement perception during the rotational movement of the spiral sphere sample) and the upper absolute threshold (i.e., the maximum rotation speed stimulation value of which the subject could perceive the dynamic optical illusion movement perception during the rotational movement of the spiral sphere sample). The speed threshold in the table was the interval of the average lower absolute threshold and the average upper absolute threshold of the spiral sphere sample (i.e., the rotation speed interval value of which the subject could perceive the dynamic optical illusion movement perception during the rotational movement of the spiral sphere sample.

3.1   Induced Movement

According to Table 1, disregarding the sex of the 20 subjects, the larger the line angle of the dynamic sphere's surface spiral pattern was, the worse the effect of the induced movement's visual perception generated by the rotation speed stimulation value, and the smaller the speed threshold interval. Conversely, the smaller the line angle of the dynamic sphere's surface spiral pattern sample was, the better the effect of the induced movement's visual perception generated by the rotation speed stimulation value, and the larger the speed threshold interval. The line angle of 5° had the largest speed threshold, meaning that the spiral sphere sample with a line angle of 5° was the best spiral sphere sample compared to the spiral sphere samples with line angles of 10°, 15°, 20°, and 25°.

Table 1. Induced movement rotation speed thresholds of the spiral patterns on the sphere surface (unit: rpm)

Line angle spiral sphere sample	Perception threshold	Speed threshold	Max	Min	M	SD
5°	Upper absolute threshold	79.15	199	47	131.25	48.02
	Lower absolute threshold		83	28	52.10	15.95
10°	Upper absolute threshold	78.95	170	60	125.30	29.37
	Lower absolute threshold		79	26	46.35	15.89
15°	Upper absolute threshold	56.05	151	47	105.80	32.34
	Lower absolute threshold		91	27	49.75	18.26
20°	Upper absolute threshold	43.65	136	55	93.65	26.05
	Lower absolute threshold		88	27	50.00	17.37
25°	Upper absolute threshold	37.95	156	42	91.85	29.33
	Lower absolute threshold		94	23	53.90	21.38

3.2 Movement Afterimage

As shown in Table 2, the larger the line angle of the spiral pattern on the sample surface was, the lower the lower absolute threshold of the movement afterimage would be, and the lower absolute threshold of the overall movement afterimage decreased gradually as the line angle of the spiral pattern increased. For the induced movement and movement afterimage experiments conducted in this stage, the subjects showed a better perceptivity for the sample of the spiral pattern at a line angle of 5°, meaning there was a wider speed threshold interval for the subjects.

Table 2. Movement afterimage rotation speed thresholds of the spiral patterns on the sphere surface (unit: rpm)

Line angle spiral sphere sample	Max	Min	M	SD
5°	206	47	135.80	52.01
10°	175	52	116.70	35.20
15°	168	47	106.50	35.14
20°	157	47	97.90	34.11
25°	153	44	90.80	31.23

4 Conclusion

The line angle of 5° is the best dynamic sphere surface spiral pattern in this study. According to the experimental results, the best view point was within the viewing angle of 14°, the viewing distance was fixed at 800 mm, and the height of the sphere was 200 mm. When the line angle of the sample was 5°, the subject could generate a relatively wide speed threshold interval of induced movement and movement afterimage in the other four samples that were higher than the line angle.

The number of lines (line angle) has the greatest influence. According to the experimental results, the larger the line angle of the surface spiral pattern (the smaller the number of lines of spiral pattern is), the higher the lower absolute threshold value for the induced movement phenomenon of the sample perceived by the subject, and the lower the upper absolute threshold value for the phenomenon perceived by the subject, meaning that the induced movement phenomenon perceived by the subject only occurred in a relatively narrow speed threshold interval. The smaller the line angle of the surface spiral pattern was (the larger the number of lines of the spiral pattern was), the lower the lower absolute threshold value for the induced movement phenomenon of the sample perceived by the subject, and the higher the upper absolute threshold value for the induced movement phenomenon perceived by the subject, meaning that there was a relatively wide speed threshold interval.

References

1. Chen, G.D.: The Study of Kinetic Art Dynamic Optical Illusion on Column with Spiral Pattern. National Taiwan University of Science and Technology, Taipei (2008)
2. Chen, G.D., Lin, C.W., Fan, H.: The study of motion perception of kinetic art dynamic optical illusion on rotate pattern. In: Forum and Conference on Basic Design and Art 2014, pp. 195–203. Taiwan Society Basic Design and Art, Yunlin (2014)
3. Chen, Y.P.: Visual Psychology. Yehyeh Book, Taipei (2011)
4. Gregory, R.L.: Eye and Brain: The Psychology of Seeing. Princeton University Press, Princeton (2015)
5. Chang, C.C.: An Investigation about the Combination of Induced Motion and Reversible Figure. Kunshan University, Tainan (2007)

6. Chen, G.D.: The research on the relative to perception of movement and motion forms. National Science Council, Taipei (2003)
7. Chen, G.D., Lin, C.W., Fan, H.: The study of motion perception on the rotational motion illusion of cone. J. Sci. Technol. **24**(1), 85–101 (2015)
8. Chen, G.D., Lin, C.W., Fan, H.: Motion perception on column of rotational dynamic illusion in kinetic art. J. Des. **20**(3), 1–19 (2015)
9. Kao, Y.: Line aesthetics - the soul of plastic art expression. Popular Lit. **2015**(07), 147 (2015)
10. Wang, Y.: Talking about line teaching in art education. Art Educ. Res. **2017**(02), 53–55 (2017)

Barberpole Illusion Shaping Performance of Wagon-Wheel Phenomenon in Stroboscopic: An Investigation on Rotation Direction and Line Movement

Guang-Dah Chen[1] and Hsiwen Fan[2(✉)]

[1] National Taiwan University of Art, New Taipei City 22058, Taiwan
chengd@ntua.edu.tw
[2] Chiba University, Chiba 263-8522, Japan
tncelny@chiba-u.jp

Abstract. The probability of shaping the development of zoetrope in the wagon-wheel effect (WWE) phenomenon, shaping the performance of Barberpole illusion (BPI) on a triangular prism, pentagonal prism, heptagonal prism, and cylinder in the WWE was studied by experimentation. The shaping performance of a cylinder in the WWE has such phenomena as "clockwise and anticlockwise rotation" of the cylinder, "downward movement of line and upward movement of line" of the lines on the cylinder, "line afterimage phenomenon" of the lines on the cylinder, and failure in discrimination (no rotation or line movement phenomenon). 18 students participated in the study. The experimental results show that (1) the number of prism edges (excluding cylinder) and the number of failed discriminations increased by alternating rotations. The cylinder had the most prolonged flicker effect regarding clockwise or anticlockwise rotation performance. It was the last one having the clockwise-anticlockwise alternation compared with the other prisms. (2) All prisms have about the same number of downward and upward lines alternations. Regarding the number of alternations, the cylinder was the first to change from downward to the upward movement of lines, and the triangular prism was the last one. (3) The cylinder had the most prolonged downward movement of lines, while all the prisms were coincident in presenting the upward movement of lines. The number of prism edges positively influenced the number of failures in discriminations. (4) Different viewing distances had the same performance in the WWE of a cylinder.

Keywords: Wagon-wheel effect · Barberpole illusion · Persistence of vision

1 Introduction

Wagon-wheel effect (WWE, also known as the stroboscopic effect), it generally refers to the rotation of spokes reverse to the direction of motion. It is mostly seen in animations or movies. The eye's response to light does not disappear immediately. The effect on the retina remains for 0.1–0.4 s. This means, that when an object is moving quickly and the image seen by the human eye disappears, the human eye still maintains the image. If the rotation speed of an electric fan is synchronous to the frame frequency of the movie (24 fps), the electric fan blades look motionless. The reason is that the fan blade would be at the same position when the picture is taken. However, if the speed is a little faster, the electric fan blades appear to rotate forward. On the contrary, if the speed is a little slower, the electric fan blades appear to rotate backward [1]. If the frame rate is too low and a fast-moving object is displayed in the video, the physical movement cannot be represented accurately and the illusory motion reversal (IMR) is formed. Such a WWE is from a stroboscopic, intermittent light source, and the rotators in the movies and TV. The WWE under continuous illumination (e.g., sun) may be observed only under specific circumstances. Therefore, to achieve the bottommost persistence of vision, at least 10 fps is required. Many people describe this phenomenon as the persistence of vision, but there are differences. The persistence of vision affects the continuity of images, but the motion of objects in the picture requires the participation of cerebral interpretation [2]. The WWE in stroboscopic is the technology used by the above-mentioned artists (e.g., stroboscopic and flicker display) so that the dynamics appear, and these dynamics include clockwise rotation, anticlockwise rotation, upward movement, downward movement, and IMR variation.

To generate IMR for the experimental stimulator of WWE, the timeliness and pattern should be periodic [2–4]. Kline et al. [5–7] indicated that the IMR is a during-effect continuous stimulation to a direction of motion. The observation eventually object performs motion in a reverse direction, guiding the perception of reverse motion. Unlike prior experimental studies, this study employed three-dimensional prisms as stimulators in combination with the WWE of stroboscopic. The findings can be provided as a reference frame for creating zoetropes in the future.

Corresponding to the periodicity of patterns, this study adopted the BPI proposed by Wallach in 1935. Through parallel rotation around the cylinder axis, the spiral lines parallel to each other on the cylinder surface generate the visual effect of vertically upward movement. The visual effect corresponds to the IMR of WWE: rotation direction (clockwise and anticlockwise) and line movement (upward and downward movement of the line). Additionally, the viewing distances were almost the same in the prior experiments. None of them conformed to the viewing state corresponding to different distances in the actual exhibition of artistic or design works. As a result, this study took the viewing distance as one of the items to be investigated.

Two experiments were performed in this study. For Experiment 1 four kinds of prisms including, triangular prism, pentagonal prism, heptagonal prism, and cylinder, were developed from the shape of BPI. The rotation speed was increased from 30 rpm to 600 rpm at an interval of 30 rpm in stroboscopic. Watch prism's rotation direction and line movement direction at different rotation speeds were observed and recorded. A prism with stable performance (cylinder) was found and selected as the stimulator in Experiment 2. In Experiment 2, according to the stimulator selected in Experiment 1, the prisms were observed at the viewing distance of 1 m to 4 m. The rotation direction and line movement direction were recorded. Finally, the BPI shape fit for the WWE in stroboscopic was found.

2   Experiment Research (I)

2.1   Methods

Participants. There were 18 participants including the undergraduate students and the graduate students. These participants include nine males and nine females (M_{age} = 22.4 years old, standard deviation [SD] = 2.1). All the participants had a normal vision after correction, and none of them had color weakness or color blindness. All the participants' verbal acknowledgment and consent were obtained before the experiment.

Instruments and Stimulators. The digital variable frequency wireless control system designed and developed by this study was combined with a multifunctional disc fixer as the experimental equipment. In terms of the digital variable frequency wireless control system, the implementation size is 30 cm (Length) * 30 cm (Width) * 30 cm (Height). Vector control was used, and the operation interface was a digital control panel. The motor speed was displayed numerically, and the actual rotation speed could increase from 0 rpm to 1200 rpm. In terms of the multifunctional disc fixer, the disc diameter is 35 cm, and the surface is engraved with concentric circle graduation grooves at an interval of 1 cm. The material is aluminum alloy light metal.

In terms of the experimental environment, the experiment was performed in a dark-room to achieve an ideal state of flicker effect, and the only light source was a strobe lamp. The flicker equipment voltage is 120 V, 60 Hz (30 flashes per second) are universal fixed settings and values. The equipment was installed at 1 m above the subject and positioned vertically downward during the experiment.

The stimulators used in this study were a triangular prism, pentagonal prism, heptagonal prism, and cylinder (Fig. 1). The design of stimulators referred to the calculation and rule of graphics. The regular polygon in the circumference was worked out through the known circumcircle. The height of the prism was calculated in the golden ratio of 1:1.618. Referring to the optimal combination setting for the BPI effect of Chen et al. [8], the stimulator was designed as 25 cm high continuous parallel straight spiral lines with a surface line with a width of 10 mm at an interval of 40 mm and an angle of 15°.

Procedure. The experimental procedure is described in this section. The participants were instructed before the experiment, and further explanation was provided if the participant had any questions after reading. Afterward, the participant sat at 1 m in front of the experimental stimulator with a viewing angle between 12 to 17° [9]. The participant was acquainted with the experimental process by appropriate practices. When the formal experiment began, the digital variable frequency wireless control system equipped with the experimental stimulator was turned on. The clockwise rotation speed was increased from 30 rpm to 600 rpm at an interval of 30 rpm. Combined with the optimum flicker times suggested by Tseng et al. [10], the stroboscopic was turned on at 30 times per second for dynamic illusory motion perception response. The "nonresponse", "anti-clockwise or clockwise", "downward movement of line (DMOL) or upward movement of the line (UMOL)", and "failure in discrimination (FID)" were recorded directly, and the experiment was concluded.

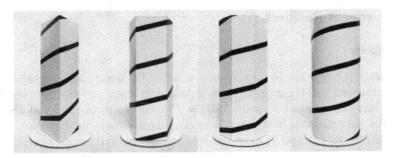

Fig. 1. Research stimulators

2.2 Results and Discussion

Excluding the cylinder, as the number of edges of the prism increased, the clockwise and anticlockwise rotation alternated more (triangular prism: 4 times, pentagonal prism: 8 times, heptagonal prism: 12 times, cylinder: 7 times), and vice versa. The heptagonal prism was the first one inducing the clockwise-anticlockwise alternation (90 rpm). The cylinder was the last one (180 rpm). The cylinder was the longest at 30 rpm–180 rpm and 480 rpm–600 rpm in the speed threshold of clockwise rotation or anticlockwise rotation, respectively. Additionally, the number of failures in discriminations increased with the number of prism edges. Contrarily, a smaller number of edges of the prism had few failures in discriminations (triangular prism: 17 times, pentagonal prism: 21 times, heptagonal prism: 24 times, cylinder: 36 times). Finally, a single-factor dependent sample ANOVA of anticlockwise, clockwise, and FID for a triangular prism, pentagonal prism, heptagonal prism, and cylinder, anticlockwise ($F = 1.094$, $p = 0.309 > 0.05$), clockwise ($F = 0.542$, $p = 0.656 > 0.05$), FID ($F = 1.691$, $p = 0.179 > 0.05$) was performed. There was no significant difference in all results.

All prisms had an insignificant difference in the number of alternations of DMOL and UMOL (triangular prism: 3 times, pentagonal prism: 3 times, heptagonal prism: 2 times, and cylinder: 2 times). The cylinder was the first to show the alternation of DMOL and UMOL (240 rpm). The triangular prism was the last one (300 rpm). The cylinder had the most prolonged effect of DMOL (30 rpm–270 rpm). All prisms had a consistent speed threshold of UMOL (390 rpm–600 rpm). Additionally, the number of failures in discriminations increased with the number of prism edges. The smaller the number of edges of the prism leads to fewer failures in discriminations (triangular prism: 55 times, pentagonal prism: 33 times, heptagonal prism: 31 times, and cylinder: 26 times).

In terms of the trend of DMOL, almost all prisms have DMOL before the rotation speed of 80 rpm. This decreased gradually after the rotation speed of 180 rpm till 300 rpm–330 rpm. However, the UMOL was observed at 360 rpm, and the DMOL was observed at about 0 times. In terms of the trend of UMOL, it approached 0 times in the beginning and increased until 180 rpm. The DMOL was observed at 300 rpm–330 rpm, and then the UMOL was observed at 330 rpm–360 rpm.

In this experiment, most subjects could not discriminate the line movement directions at about 300 rpm. This speed threshold was the intersection of the lines' upward and downward movement. Finally, the single-factor dependent sample ANOVA was performed for the DMOL, the UMOL of lines and FID of triangular prism, pentagonal prism, heptagonal prism, and cylinder, DMOL ($F = 1.105$, $p = 0.354 > 0.05$), UMOL ($F = 1.814$, $p = 0.155 > 0.05$), FID ($F = 2.467$, $p = 0.071 > 0.05$). All of the results had no significant difference.

In the experimental process, when the rotation speed was 150 rpm–210 rpm to 600 rpm, the line afterimage occurred on the prism surface. The line afterimage increased gradually as the rotation speed increased, as shown in Fig. 2. The semi-transparent line afterimage phenomenon increased from solid lines to somewhere nearly solid lines. When the speed was higher than a specific rotation speed, the afterimage of the semi-transparent line returned to the original midst of solid lines. This line afterimage phenomenon corresponded to the findings of Purves et al. [2] that the actual number of lines will exceed the original number of lines in the WWE.

Line afterimage from 150 rpm to 600 rpm (left to right)

Fig. 2. Line afterimage effect drawing of the cylinder in stroboscopic

The relationship between rotation speed and WWE is mainly established on the flicker rate and rotation speed in the persistence of vision. At a higher rotation speed, a slower frame is perceived by human eyes. This leads to the response of forward/backward rotation of prism. The upward and DMOL are the same, so this part verified the visual phenomenon of WWE. Corresponding to the research purpose, a stable and suitable display of artistic or design works was discussed. The occurrence time point of the line afterimage phenomenon was used as a boundary for the criterion of rotation speed (180 rpm) in Experiment 2.

The experiment of this stage aimed at the clockwise and anticlockwise directions and the line movement direction. The cumulative trend of "clockwise and anticlockwise directions", and "UMOL and DMOL" of the four prisms was similar to the findings of Finlay and Dodwell [11]. They pointed out that the apparent motion and flicker frequency would be symmetrized by the apparent velocity trend of clockwise and anticlockwise motions. In terms of the overall rotation speed of all prisms, the replacement trend of anticlockwise and clockwise had periodic variation [4]. However, the alternation phenomenon of "clockwise and anticlockwise directions" and "UMOL and DMOL" corresponded to the perceived discontinuity of WWE as indicated by VanRullen and Koch [12].

3   Experiment Research (II)

3.1   Methods

Participants. There were 18 participants in this experiment as Experiment Research (I). All participants' verbal acknowledgment and consent were obtained before this experiment.

Instruments and Stimulators. The experimental apparatus was the same as Experiment Research (I). The stimulator for this experiment was one cylinder.

Procedure. The experimental procedure is described in this section. The participants were instructed in reading before the experiment. Further explanation was provided if the participant had any questions after reading. The participant stood at 1 m in front of the experimental stimulator. Then the participant was acquainted with the experimental process by appropriate practice. When the formal experiment began, the digital variable frequency wireless control system equipped with the experimental stimulator was switched on. According to the result of Experiment 1, the rotation speed was increased from 30 rpm to 210 rpm at an interval of 30 rpm. This was in accordance with the optimum flicker times indicated by Tseng et al. [10]. The stroboscopic was turned on (30 times per second). For the WWE response, the "nonresponse", "anticlockwise or clockwise", "DMOL or UMOL", and "failure in discrimination (FID)" were recorded. Afterward, the participant stood at 2 m, 3 m, and 4 m before the experimental stimulator for experiments.

3.2   Results and Discussion

In this experiment, all the viewing distances had one alternation of anticlockwise to clockwise. The alternation phenomenon was generated between 150 rpm and 180 rpm. When the viewing distances were 1 m and 2 m, the clockwise phenomenon at the rotation speed of 90 rpm. When the viewing distances were 3 m and 4 m, the clockwise phenomenon occurred at the rotation speed of 30 rpm. It disappeared when the rotation speed was 60 rpm. The clockwise rotation occurred at 90 rpm and 120 rpm. Therefore, any viewing distance had a stable anticlockwise phenomenon before 150 rpm.

When the viewing distances were 1 m and 2 m and the rotation speeds were 180 rpm and 210 rpm, the discrimination failure occurred once and once, and once and twice, respectively. The FID occurred four times when the viewing distance was 3 m at a rotation speed of 150 rpm. The FID occurred two and six times respectively at 180 rpm and 210 rpm, and more than five times anticlockwise at 210 rpm. When the viewing distance was 4 m, the FID occurred four times and five times respectively at 180 rpm and 210 rpm, and more than four times of anticlockwise at 210 rpm. Therefore, the number of failures in discriminations increased with the viewing distance.

Finally, this stage performed single-factor dependent sample ANOVA on anticlockwise, clockwise, and FID for 1 m, 2 m, 3 m, and 4 m, anticlockwise ($F = 0.276$, $p = 0.842 > 0.05$), clockwise ($F = 1.075$, $p = 0.385 < 0.05$), FID ($F = 2.783$, $p = 0.071 > 0.05$). All of the results had no significant difference.

When the viewing distance was 1 m to 4 m, the number of DMOL was more significant than that of UMOL with no alternation in the line direction. Regarding line movement and FID, there was one occurrence before the rotation speed of 150 rpm. There were at most four occurrences between 150 rpm and 210 rpm. All viewing distances had shown a stable DMOL before 210 rpm. However, the DMOL decreased as the rotation speed increased.

In terms of FID, all distances had a few failures in discriminations until 180 rpm. There was a slight influence on determining the direction of line movement. In the researcher's view, this phenomenon was related to the line afterimage phenomenon. The line afterimage almost appeared at 180 rpm at any viewing distance.

Finally, this stage performed single-factor dependent sample ANOVA of DMOL, UMOL, and FID for 1 m, 2 m, 3 m, and 4 m, DMOL ($F = 1.975$, $p = 0.154 > 0.05$), UMOL ($F = 2.782$, $p = 0.071 > 0.05$), FID ($F = 0.495$, $p = 0.690 > 0.05$). All of the results had no significant difference. Therefore, the viewing distance did not influence the observation of WWE.

4 Conclusion

This study discussed the effects of different prisms at different rotation speeds and distances in stroboscopic. In Experiment 1, as the number of prism edges increased (excluding cylinder), the clockwise and anticlockwise rotation alternated more. The number of failures in discriminations increased. The cylinder had the longest speed threshold among all prisms in clockwise or anticlockwise rotation, and it was the last one having clockwise-anticlockwise alternation.

All prisms had slight differences in the number of alternating DMOL and UMOL of lines. Regarding the number of alternations, the cylinder was the first to show the alternation of DMOL to the UMOL. The triangular prism was the last one. The cylinder had the most prolonged effect of the DMOL. All prisms had a consistent speed threshold of UMOL. The number of prism edges positively influenced the number of failures in discriminations. In terms of the trend of DMOL, the overall number kept balance, decreased, increased slightly, and decreased to a low point. The trend of UMOL was opposite. When the discrimination failed, the intersection of upward and DMOL concentrated at about 300 rpm. The observation was performed at different distances in Experiment 2. Compared to the cylinder at 30 rpm to 210 rpm in Experiment 1, there was no significant difference in the clockwise and anticlockwise, DMOL, UMOL, and FID according to statistical analysis.

In comparison with prior studies [2, 5, 7] employed plane figures for experiments. To match the application of three-dimensional zoetrope, this experiment employed a three-dimensional shape as an experimental stimulator. The design of the stimulator referred to the experiment of Chen et al. [8], and the stroboscopic was used in shape, and the changes in shape were discussed.

Regarding research limitations, this study adopted different prisms, different rotation speeds, and different viewing distances to discuss the effect of shape in WWE. There are different shapes in the shaping system, and the line variation of shape will be a crucial factor influencing the visual effect. Therefore, subsequent research is suggested to apply different types of shapes (cone and sphere), colors, materials, and patterns to discuss other probability and shaping performance. Additionally, the stroboscopic is a stimulating light source, and its application requires extra attention for photosensitive viewers.

References

1. Andrews, T., Purves, D.: The wagon-wheel illusion in continuous light. Trends Cogn. Sci. **9**(6), 261–263 (2005)
2. Purves, D., Paydarfar, J.A., Andrews, T.J.: The wagon wheel illusion in movies and reality. Proc. Natl. Acad. Sci. **93**(8), 3693–3697 (1996)
3. Simpson, W.A., Shahani, U., Manahilov, V.: Illusory percepts of moving patterns due to discrete temporal sampling. Neurosci. Lett. **375**(1), 23–27 (2005)
4. VanRullen, R., Reddy, L., Koch, C.: Attention-driven discrete sampling of motion perception. Proc. Natl. Acad. Sci. **102**(14), 5291–5296 (2005)
5. Kline, K.A., Holcombe, A.O., Eagleman, D.M.: Illusory motion reversal is caused by rivalry, not by perceptual snapshots of the visual field. Vision. Res. **44**(23), 2653–2658 (2004)
6. Kline, K.A., Holcombe, A.O., Eagleman, D.M.: Illusory motion reversal does not imply discrete processing: reply to Rojas et al. Vis. Res. **6**(46), 1158–1159 (2006)
7. Kline, K.A., Eagleman, D.M.: Evidence against the temporal subsampling account of illusory motion reversal. J. Vis. **8**(4), 13 (2008)
8. Chen, G.D., Chang, C.C., Lin, P.C.: A study on the induced motion of the rotative speed and the width of line. Issue Basic Des. Art **16**, 19–22 (2007)
9. Oyama, T., Imai, S., Wake, T.: New Sensory Perception Psychology Handbook. Seishin Shobo Ltd, Tokyo (2000)
10. Tseng, C.H., Lai, Y.Z., Chang, Y.D.: How to make a stereogram. Sci. Educ. Monthly **246**, 38–44 (2002)
11. Finlay, D.J., Dodwell, P.C.: Speed of apparent motion and the wagon-wheel effect. Percept. Psychophys. **41**(1), 29–34 (1987)
12. VanRullen, R., Koch, C.: Is perception discrete or continuous? Trends Cogn. Sci. **7**(5), 207–213 (2003)

Analysis on the Effect of Living Habits and Environment to Concentration

Yukai Gu$^{(\boxtimes)}$ [ID] and Qun Jin [ID]

Graduate School of Human Sciences, Waseda University, Tokorozawa, Saitama 3591192, Japan
guyukai@fuji.waseda.jp, jin@waseda.jp

Abstract. It is believed that the living habits and living environment have a close relationship with a person's concentration. In this study, an experiment is designed to measure the degree of concentration for two subjects for 40 days. Living habits and environment data, as well as EEG (Electroencephalogram) data are collected and divided into six cases according to gender and concentration status, and then PCA (Principal Component Analysis) for each case is conducted. Furthermore, using the principal components identified by PCA, a regression model is constructed to analyze the relationship between lifestyle (living habits and environment) data and concentration indexes by EEG. The analysis results on all the data of the subjects suggested that the regression model has a certain degree of accuracy and there exists a significant relationship between concentration and the time and quality of sleep on the previous day, even if the concentration status on the following day is different.

Keywords: Electroencephalogram (EEG) · Concentration index by EEG · Principal Component Analysis (PCA) · Principal Component Regression (PCR)

1 Introduction

In recent years, people have become so busy with their work and study that their daily rhythms are often disrupted. It is common to see people skipping breakfast, not getting enough exercise, or going to bed late. It is believed that the living habits and environment have a close relationship with concentration. In this study, an experiment is designed to measure the degree of concentration. Concentration is generally measured according to the rule of 10–20 EEG system [1]. With the evolution of device manufacturing technologies, brain waves can now be measured by a portable device of brain wave meter. By collecting and analyzing the EEG data as well as the lifestyle and environment data, we try to clarify the relationship between them.

The remainder of this paper is organized as follow. Section 2 presents related work. Section 3 describes the concentration indexes by EEG and the experiment design for data collection and analysis approach. The experiment results are reported and discussed in Sect. 4. Finally, Sect. 5 provides a summary of this study and future research directions.

C. Stephanidis et al. (Eds.): HCII 2022, CCIS 1581, pp. 129–136, 2022.
https://doi.org/10.1007/978-3-031-06388-6_17

2 Related Work

2.1 Analysis of Living Habits Data and Concentration

Nonoue et al. [2] studied on living habits and subjective symptoms and academic performance of junior high school students to clarify the relationship between the living habits and subjective symptoms to physical and mental health and academic performance. In their study, 648 students from a public junior high school were asked to answer a questionnaire for two months, and the statistical analysis on their performance was conducted. The analysis results showed that adequate sleep, regular diet (breakfast, lunch, and dinner), and exercise were associated with better academic performance and a beneficial relationship with mental faculties, such as attention and concentration.

Van der Heijden et al. [3] examined the relationship of chronic sleep loss (i.e., symptoms of chronic sleep loss, such as short sleep, drowsiness, and irritability), subjective sleep quality, and sleep hygiene knowledge with academic performance and academic attention for 1378 higher education students in the Netherlands. The result showed that the chronic sleep loss was associated with the academic performance and academic attention of these higher education students.

2.2 Analysis of Environment Data and Concentration

Ichikawa [4] investigated the determinants of concentration in class considering the students' personal living environment, such as in a non-uniform thermal environment. In the study, environmental measurements and a questionnaire survey were distributed to students who take classes in a university stairwell. The questionnaire survey was conducted multiple times, including during and after class. During class, students were asked to respond to their current state of warmth, concentration, and fatigue once every 15 min. After class, the students were asked about items such as their level of interest in the class. The collected data were used to construct a multilevel model with concentration as the objective variable, and room temperature and psychological status as explanatory variables. The results of the multilevel analysis with concentration as the objective variable showed that students' concentration during classes was greatly affected by the level of interest, fatigue, and the perception of temperature. In the meantime, the effect of temperature and fatigue on concentration was different for each student, which implies that there were individual differences among students. It was reported that students with higher interest in the class may be more affected by the thermal sensation on their concentration.

Another study of Ishizawa et al. [5] showed that according to the results of their experiments on thermal environment changes and EEG measurements, there were many cases in which higher temperatures tended to decrease the level of concentration. Besides, they pointed out that individual differences and factors other than temperature may have an influence on the possibility of environmental evaluation by EEG.

Zhu et al. [6] designed an experiment, having 32 healthy young adults as subjects, who experienced 175 min of exposure to each of four air temperature levels (26, 30, 33 and 37 °C) and two relative humidity levels (50 and 70%) in a climate chamber, and who were subsequently administered a cognitive task and had their EEG signals measured.

The result showed that high humidity and high temperature increased drowsiness and made it more difficult to think clearly, which implies that they had more difficulty concentrating at high relative humidity.

2.3 Position of This Study

The study on lifestyle and concentration using questionnaires [2, 3] and the study on the relationship between living environment and concentration [4] have shown that there is a close relationship between living habits, environment, and concentration. However, the data acquisition for these studies was done using questionnaires, which means the data is highly subjective to each subject.

In recent years, it became possible to collect data with higher accuracy using a variety of sensors and devices. In this study, quantitative analysis is proposed and conducted using objective data, such as lifestyle and environment data, actually collected through the use of wearable and portable devices, rather than subjective data from questionnaire surveys.

3 Analysis of the Relationship Between Living Habits and Environment Data and Concentration Indexes by EEG

3.1 Concentration Indexes by EEG

Brain waves are generally classified into five categories according to the magnitude of frequency (δ, θ, α, β, γ): Delta (δ) 0.5–4 Hz, Theta (θ) 4–8 Hz, Alpha (α) 8–13 Hz, Beta (β) 13–32 Hz, Gamma (γ) 32–100 Hz. As shown in Table 1, the main status in which they occur are different [7].

Brain waves can be used as an indicator of a person's level of concentration. Umezawa et al. [8] pointed out that among the five brain waves, it is possible to observe the status of human thinking by measuring the power spectrum of α and β waves or the ratio of α and β waves, and further to measure the level of concentration by evaluating the value of β/α.

Table 1. Five types of brain waves and their characteristics.

EEG	Frequency	Main status
Delta δ	0.5–4 Hz	Sleeping or dreaming
Theta θ	4–8 Hz	Dreaming or in low consciousness
Alpha α	8–13 Hz	Physically and mentally relaxing
Beta β	13–32 Hz	Alerts or positive thinking
Gamma γ	32–100 Hz	Learning or solving problems

3.2 Experiment Design

In this study, wearable and portable devices are used to collect the subjects' living habits data (sleeping and physical activities) and their living environment data (temperature and humidity) during the EEG measurement experiment.

Since the movement of EEG differs depending on whether a person is in a relaxed or concentrated status, the EEG measurement experiment in this study is divided into relatively relaxed and relatively concentrated status, representing the different level of concentration. Therefore, the EEG data of the subjects is measured and collected in their comparatively concentrated and relaxed status respectively. The average power spectrum values of the five EEGs and the value of β/α are taken as indexes, which are used to conduct relevance analysis.

3.3 Analysis Methods

Regression analysis is a method of predicting an objective variable from explanatory variables. In general, a multiple regression model is expressed in Eq. (1).

$$Y = b_0 + b_1 X_1 + \ldots b_p X_p + \epsilon \tag{1}$$

where Y is the dependent variable, X_i is the independent variable, b_i is the regression coefficient, and ϵ is the error term.

When analyzing data by the multiple regression model, the more explanatory variables, the higher the coefficient of determination is likely to be. Therefore, using many explanatory variables increases the possibility of highly correlated variables among the explanatory variables and increases the possibility of multicollinearity occurring. If multicollinearity is present, it is difficult to estimate accurately from the model and is likely to produce incorrect analytical results. Variance inflation factor (VIF) defined in Eq. (2) can be used to determine the degree of multicollinearity.

$$\text{VIF} = \frac{1}{1 - R_i^2} \tag{2}$$

where R_i^2 is the coefficient of determination when the explanatory variable X_i is regressed on all other explanatory variables. Typically, if VIF is greater than 5, multicollinearity exists; if VIF is greater than 10, it indicates a high degree of multicollinearity. In such cases, adjustments should be made appropriately.

Principal Component Analysis (PCA) can be one way to solve the multicollinearity problem. In PCA, typically based on the Kaiser-Guttman [9] and parallel analysis criteria [10], the scree plot is used to determine the number of principal components.

PCR (Principal Component Regression), as a fusion of Principal Component Analysis and Regression Analysis, is a method of reducing the dimensions of data by PCA, that is, reducing variables, and then performing regression analysis. In this study, PCR is used to analyze the relationship between the living habits and concentration indexes by EEG.

4   Experiment Results and Discussion

4.1   Overview of the Experiment

Now there are many types of wearable and portable devices, each with its own unique features. In this study, we conduct an experiment using the following three devices: Muse Electroencephalograph[1], Fitbit Smartwatch[2], as well as WxBeacon2 Simple Temperature Monitor[3].

In the experiment, from August 16 to September 24, 2021, for 40 days two subjects used the Muse Electroencephalograph to measure and record their EEG data twice a day during gaming and meditation. At the same time, the data on their living habits and environment were collected by Fitbit Smartwatch and WxBeacon2 Simple Temperature Monitor. Next, the collected data were pre-processed, and 143 sets of data were divided into six cases: all subjects' game status, male subject's game status, female subject's game status, all subjects' meditation status, male subject's meditation status, and female subject's meditation status.

4.2   Analysis Results

The calculated results of VIF are shown in Table 2, which shows that the VIF is greater than 10 for the three variables of sleep duration, bedtime, and wake time. If multiple

Table 2.   Calculation results of VIF.

Variable	VIF
Time length of sleep	30.60
Time to sleep	13.59
Time to wake	10.86
Score of sleep	7.44
Time length of light sleep	6.63
Time length of wake	4.41
Time length of deep sleep	3.28
Calorie	3.07
Time of exercise	2.17
Step	1.84
Temperature	1.61
Humidity	1.49
Length of walk	1.05
Mean VIF	6.77

---

[1] https://choosemuse.com/.

[2] https:// www.fitbit.com/global/us/home.

[3] https://weathernews.jp/smart/wxbeacon2/.

regression analysis is performed using these variables as they are, issues, such as accuracy and reliability problems, may remain.

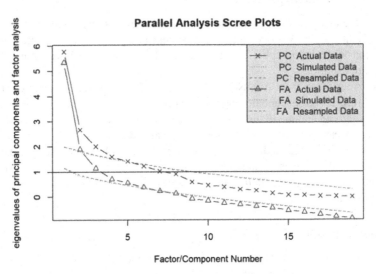

Fig. 1. Scree plot for all subjects' game status

For this reason, in this study using PCA according to gender and concentration status of the two subjects, the dimensions of the originally collected data with the explanatory variables were reduced, and then four to six principal components are obtained to solve the problem of multicollinearity. In addition, the principal components obtained for the six different cases were set as explanatory variables, and the six types of EEG data were set as objective variables, respectively. Then the multiple regression analysis was conducted. The number of principal components is six according to the results analyzed from the scree plot by all subjects' game status, as shown in Fig. 1.

According to the results of the analysis of all subjects' game status shown in Fig. 2, the six principal components were able to explain 82% of all data and were interpreted as the principal components representing "overall sleeping", "sleeping details", "exercise situation", "sleep time", "environment" and "second exercise situation".

The analysis results of PCR for all subjects' game status are shown in Table 3. From the table, the first principal component of "overall sleeping" was found to be highly significant with a test result of "***" for the regression analysis of β/α, β and α waves. Among the six regression models constructed, the coefficient of determination of the regression model obtained with β EEG data as the objective variable was the highest at 0.484, suggesting that the regression model has a certain accuracy on that the living habits and environment are relevant to the concentration indexes by EEG.

Moreover, the analysis results for all subjects at meditation showed that the principal component of "overall sleeping" was also significant in the regression analysis of beta/alpha, beta and alpha waves, indicating that sleeping is associated with concentration on the next day. On the other hand, the analysis results of PCR for the subject-specific cases show that it did not reach a high degree of precision.

```
## Principal Components Analysis
## Call: principal(r = data2[, c(-1, -2, -3, -4, -5, -6)], nfactors = 6,
##     scores = T)
## Standardized loadings (pattern matrix) based upon correlation matrix
##                          RC1   RC2   RC3   RC4   RC5   RC6   h2    u2 com
## time length of sleep    0.92 -0.08  0.03  0.33  0.05  0.06 0.97 0.033 1.3
## score of sleep          0.93  0.11 -0.01 -0.24  0.00 -0.03 0.93 0.072 1.2
## time length of wake    -0.12  0.03 -0.10  0.92  0.10  0.16 0.90 0.097 1.1
## time length of REM sleep 0.59  0.64  0.00 -0.01  0.06 -0.17 0.79 0.205 2.2
## time length of light sleep 0.52 -0.80 -0.01  0.24  0.06  0.08 0.97 0.025 2.0
## time length of deep sleep 0.08  0.81  0.10  0.18 -0.11  0.16 0.74 0.263 1.3
## time to sleep          -0.47 -0.05 -0.17 -0.70  0.07  0.39 0.89 0.110 2.6
## time to wake            0.56 -0.10 -0.25  0.11  0.23  0.59 0.80 0.199 2.8
## step                    0.28 -0.02  0.79 -0.18 -0.05  0.18 0.76 0.239 1.5
## calorie                -0.57  0.25  0.63  0.10  0.03  0.06 0.79 0.205 2.4
## length of walk         -0.07  0.07  0.20  0.00 -0.06  0.72 0.56 0.436 1.2
## time of exercise       -0.14  0.03  0.85  0.08  0.00 -0.01 0.75 0.249 1.1
## temperature             0.06  0.30  0.00  0.10 -0.83  0.03 0.79 0.212 1.3
## humidity                0.13  0.14 -0.03  0.16  0.85  0.03 0.78 0.215 1.2
##
##                          RC1   RC2   RC3   RC4   RC5   RC6
## SS loadings             3.32  1.90  1.88  1.68  1.50  1.14
## Proportion Var          0.24  0.14  0.13  0.12  0.11  0.08
## Cumulative Var          0.24  0.37  0.51  0.63  0.74  0.82
## Proportion Explained    0.29  0.17  0.16  0.15  0.13  0.10
## Cumulative Proportion   0.29  0.46  0.62  0.77  0.90  1.00
##
## Mean item complexity =  1.7
## Test of the hypothesis that 6 components are sufficient.
##
## The root mean square of the residuals (RMSR) is  0.07
##   with the empirical chi square  59.43  with prob <  2.7e-05
##
## Fit based upon off diagonal values = 0.94
```

Fig. 2. Results of PCA for all subjects' game status

Table 3. Results of PCR for all subjects' game status

	Beta/Alpha	Beta	Alpha	Gamma	Theta	Delta
x1	0.051***	0.028***	0.022***	0.019*	0.007	0.012
x2	−0.016	−0.012	−0.010	0.006	−0.003	0.006
x3	−0.048*	−0.029**	−0.023*	−0.033**	−0.019	−0.014
x4	−0.050*	−0.029**	−0.018	−0.037**	−0.011	−0.017
x5	−0.009	−0.010	−0.004	0.0001	0.009	0.019
x6	0.047	0.019	0.011	0.023	0.009	0.023
Multiple R-squared	0.417	0.484	0.364	0.265	0.130	0.101
Adjusted R-squared	0.365	0.438	0.307	0.199	0.052	0.020
Degree of freedom	67	67	67	67	67	67
p-value	1.66E−06	3.57E−08	2.34E−05	0.002	0.142	0.292

5   Conclusion

As a result, the analysis of all the data of the subjects suggested that the regression model had a certain degree of accuracy and that the relationship with the time and quality of sleep on the previous day was significant, even if the status of concentration on the following day was different. However, the analysis results for each subject were not ideal, implying that there may be insufficient experiment data. And in this experiment, only a part of living habits and environment factors were considered and used in the analysis.

For the future work, more subjects, longer duration of the experiment, and more data of lifestyle and environment factors can be considered to improve the accuracy and reliability of analysis.

References

1. Jasper, H.H.: The ten-twenty electrode system of the international federation. Electroencephalogr. Clin. Neurophysiol. **10**, 370–375 (1958)
2. Nonoue, K., Hiramatsu, K., Inamori, Y.: The relationship between lifestyle and subjective symptoms, and academic records of junior high school students in Okayama City. Jpn. J. School Health **50**, 5–17 (2008). (in Japanese)
3. Van der Heijden, K.B., et al.: Chronic sleep reduction is associated with academic achievement and study concentration in higher education students. J. Sleep Res. **27**(2), 165–174 (2018)
4. Ichikawa, Y.: Study on Determinants of Student's Concentration Level Under Non-Uniform Thermal Environment, vol. 8, pp. 1–4. Bulletin of Hosei University Graduate School. Graduate School of Design Engineering, ed. (2019). (in Japanese)
5. Ishizawa, T., Mizutani, K., Handa, M.: Studies of the air-conditioning system allowing for the difference of human body physiology and psychological condition: part 2 experiment about the effect of thermal environment on electroencephalogram. Soc. Heat. Air-Cond. Sanitary Eng. Jan. **G-33**, 1467–1470 (2010). (in Japanese)
6. Zhu, M., Liu, W., Wargocki, P.: Changes in EEG signals during the cognitive activity at varying air temperature and relative humidity. J. Eposure Sci. Environ. Epidemiol. **30**(2), 285–298 (2020)
7. Muse Homepage. https://choosemuse.com/what-it-measures/. Accessed 30 Sept 2021
8. Umezawa, K., Nakazawa, M., Kobayashi, M., Ishii, Y., Nakano, M., Hirasawa, S.: Evaluation of difficulty during visual programming learning using a simple electroencephalograph and minecraft educational edition. In: Rocha, Á., Adeli, H., Dzemyda, G., Moreira, F., Ramalho Correia, A.M. (eds.) WorldCIST 2021. AISC, vol. 1367, pp. 31–41. Springer, Cham (2021). https://doi.org/10.1007/978-3-030-72660-7_4
9. Kaiser, H.F.: The application of electronic computers to factor analysis. Educ. Psychol. Measur. **20**(1), 141–151 (1960)
10. Franklin, S.B., et al.: Parallel analysis: a method for determining significant principal components. J. Veg. Sci. **6**(1), 99–106 (1995)

Audio-Visual Shared Emotion Representation for Robust Emotion Recognition on Modality Missing Using Hemi-hyperspherical Embedding and Latent Space Unification

Seiichi Harata$^{(\boxtimes)}$ [iD], Takuto Sakuma [iD], and Shohei Kato [iD]

Department of Engineering, Graduate School of Engineering,
Nagoya Institute of Technology, Nagoya, Japan
{harata,sakuma,shohey}@katolab.nitech.ac.jp

Abstract. In Affective Computing, a mathematical representation of emotions in the computer is desirable for emotionally interactive agents. This study aims to obtain a latent representation of emotions (an emotional space) common to the modalities, focusing on that humans can recognize emotions from multiple modalities. We define the emotional space as the latent space of the multimodal DNN model and propose embedding emotional information into a Hemi-hyperspherical space. Our proposed model fuses the emotional spaces of each modality with an element-wise weighted average fashion. We train the model by combining emotion recognition and latent space unification tasks. The unification task is the loss of distance between emotional spaces from different modalities expressed simultaneously, which leads to acquiring a similar space from different modalities. Experiments using audio-visual data evaluate the robustness of emotion recognition against modalities missing. The results confirmed that the proposed method, especially in the low-dimensional Hemi-hyperspherical representations, could acquire a shared representation of emotion across modalities.

Keywords: Affective computing · Crossmodal · Emotion recognition · Representation learning · Hemi-hyperspherical representation · Emotional space

1 Introduction

In the Human-Computer Interaction with emotions, particularly in Affective Computing, understanding the partner's emotions and expressing the agent's emotions has been discussed [11]. For agents to "have" emotions, it is necessary to represent emotions mathematically in the computer. Humans communicate using various modalities such as facial expressions and voice. Also, humans can

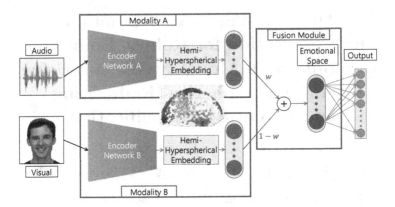

Fig. 1. Overview of the proposed model embedding the emotional information into Hemi-hyperspherical emotional space and fusing an emotional space from multimodal data.

recognize other people's emotions accurately even when some modalities are missing, such as when they are wearing a mask or their microphone is muted in an online meeting. Moreover, there is redundancy in the emotional information in each modality [3]. Deep neural networks (DNNs) are considered to capture the abstract semantic structure of input data, and researchers are working to obtain latent features as representations that are useful for downstream tasks [2]. This study aims to obtain shared latent representations of emotions (an emotional space) from different modalities using DNNs for modality-independent emotion recognition. In a author's previous work [5] showed that the latent representations embedded from different modalities are dissimilar in a trained emotion recognition model. Note that this previous work has modeled the emotional space in Euclidean space. Deep metric learning studies reported that normalizing the feature space increases the inter-class distance and makes training more stable [13,14]. Therefore, this paper extends the deep metric learning method and proposes a method to embed emotional information into a Hemi-hyperspherical representation.

2 Proposed Method

2.1 Models

Figure 1 shows an overview of the proposed model. We define an *emotional space* as the latent space preceding the final fully-connected layer of a model and attempt to acquire the representation of emotions onto this latent space. The modality A part encodes audio data into the emotional space for audio, and the modality B part encodes facial image data into the emotional space for visual.

Besides the Euclidean space, we propose representing the emotional space on a Hemi-hypersphere by the following activation function $a(\cdot)$.

$$z = a(h) = \begin{cases} [\tanh(h_1), \tanh(h_2), \ldots, \tanh(h_D)] & \text{(euclidean)}, \\ \frac{[h,1]}{\sqrt{[h,1]^T[h,1]}} & \text{(hemi-hypersphere)}, \end{cases} \quad (1)$$

where h is the output of the fully-connected layers of each encoder model, and D is the number of dimensions of the emotional space.

This method of the L2 normalization of latent representations is an extension of the method of deep metric learning [13] to incorporate the bias term of the output layer. Also, this method is considered to increase the distance of data distribution between classes in the latent space and enable efficient and effective training [14].

When fusing the emotional spaces for each modality, we referred to the modeling of human perception of different modality information in a linear additive form of fusion [4,7]. The proposed fusion method is based on an element-wise weighted average as follows:

$$z^{fused} = h\left(w \cdot z^{audio} + (1-w) \cdot z^{visual}\right) \quad (2)$$

$$h(x) = \begin{cases} x & \text{(euclidean)}, \\ \frac{x}{\sqrt{x^Tx}} & \text{(hemi-hypersphere)}, \end{cases}$$

where w is the weight of average for fusion. Compared to related works [1,9] that fuse modalities by concatenating feature vectors obtained from each modality, our method can adjust the modality of emphasis by changing the fusion weight w.

To implement of the proposed model, we used WaveNet [10] for the encoder of modality A part and ResNet-18 [6] for the encoder of modality B part.

2.2 Multitasking of Emotion Recognition and Unification

We train the proposed model on the multitasking of the emotion recognition and the unification by the following loss function. Here, $Loss_{recog}$ and $Loss_{unif}$ are the loss of the recognition and unification task, respectively.

$$Loss = Loss_{recog} + Loss_{unif}, \quad (3)$$

$$Loss_{recog} = \frac{1}{N}\sum_{i=1}^{N} -log \frac{\exp\left(f(z_i^{fused}, w_{y_i})\right)}{\sum_{c \in Label}\exp\left(f(z_i^{fused}, w_c)\right)}, \quad (4)$$

$$Loss^{unif} = \begin{cases} \frac{1}{N}\sum_{i=1}^{N}\|z_i^{audio} - z_i^{visual}\|^2 & \text{(euclidean)}. \\ \frac{1}{N}\sum_{i=1}^{N}\arccos\left((z_i^{audio})^T(z_i^{visual})\right) & \text{(hemi-hypersphere)}. \end{cases} \quad (5)$$

where N is the batch size; $Label$ is the set of emotion labels; $y_i(\in Label)$ is the target label. Here, $f(\cdot, \cdot)$ are logits of the output layer as follows:

$$f(z^{fused}, w_c) = \begin{cases} w_c^T z^{fused} & \text{(euclidean)}. \\ s \cdot a(w_c)^T z^{fused} & \text{(hemi-hypersphere)}. \end{cases}$$

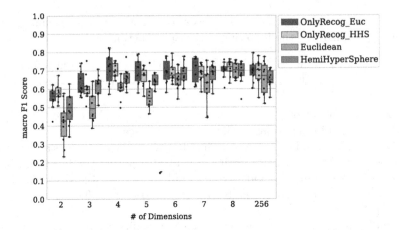

Fig. 2. Macro F1 Scores on audio-visual condition for each # of dimensions.

where $\boldsymbol{w}_c$ is the parameter of class c and s is a hyper-parameter of scaling the cosine similarity [13].

3   Experiment

This paper uses an audio-visual acting video dataset RAVDESS [8] to train and evaluation the model with seven emotion labels (Neutral, Happy, Surprise, Fear, Anger, Disgust, and Sad). We trained the model with the 2–8, 256 dimensions of emotional space. Since the results vary depending on the initial parameters, we trained the model for ten trials in each condition.

3.1   Robustness of Emotion Recognition Under Pseudo Modality Missing

This experiment evaluates the robustness of emotion recognition under the missing modality. We varied the fusion weight w in Eq. (2) and fused the emotional space of each modality using that w. For example, $w = 1$ is a condition of missing visual modality; only audio modality is provided, while $w = 0$ is missing audio modality; only visual modality is provided. Then, we input the fused space to the output layer and measured the emotion recognition performance.

Figure 2, 3, 4 shows results of $w = 0.5$ (audio-visual), $w = 1$ (audio-only), $w = 0$ (visual-only), respectively. There are significant performance drops when the emotional space is represented in Euclidean space or only trained on the recognition task, notably in the audio-only case. In contrast, the Hemi-hyperspherical representation shows better robustness in recognition performance for both audio-only and visual-only.

The results suggest that embedding emotions on a Hemi-hypersphere and training the model in multitasking recognition and unification makes it possible

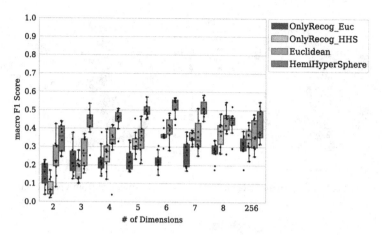

Fig. 3. Macro F1 Scores on audio only (missing visual modality) for each # of dimensions.

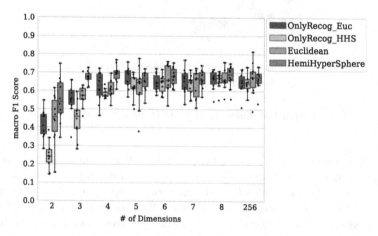

Fig. 4. Macro F1 Scores on visual only (missing audio modality) for each # of dimensions.

to derive a shared representation of emotions across audio and visual modalities. Note that the performance even in low-dimensional spaces such as four or five-dimensional space is competitive with the performance of 256-dimensional space.

3.2 Visualization of Emotional Space

Figure 5 are the visualization of train data on the two-dimensional emotional space for each modality represented on a Hemi-hypersphere. Figure 5a and Fig. 5b are projected into 2D from a 3D hemispherical surface. This visualization shows that the emotional space mapped from audio is similar to the emotional space mapped from the facial image. This result suggests that the unification

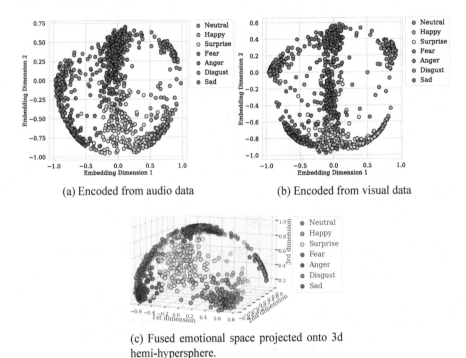

(a) Encoded from audio data   (b) Encoded from visual data

(c) Fused emotional space projected onto 3d
hemi-hypersphere.

Fig. 5. Visualization of two-dimensional Hemi-Hyperspherical Emotional Space.

task yields common latent representations from different modalities. Moreover, the same emotions are distributed close together, and different emotions are clustered apart. This indicates that the emotion recognition task lets the model acquire latent representations that semantically represent emotional information. In addition, the positional correspondence between the emotion clusters in this visualization is similar to that of Russell's circumplex model of affect [12]. Therefore, we consider that the proposed method can acquire an emotional space that supports a widely accepted model from psychology.

4   Conclusion

In this paper, to obtain a mathematical representation of emotions (an emotional space) common to modalities, we proposed embedding emotional information into a Hemi-hyperspherical representation using a deep neural network model. We trained this model on multitasking of an emotion recognition task and a unification task. The experimental results show that the proposed method can obtain a shared representation from different modalities. In future work, we will evaluate the model on different datasets and compare the proposed emotional space with other psychological models, such as Plutchik's Emotion Wheel.

Acknowledgment. This work was supported in part by the Ministry of Education, Culture, Sports, Science and Technology-Japan, Grant–in–Aid for Scientific Research under grant #JP19H01137, #JP19H04025, and #JP20H04018.

References

1. Avots, E., Sapiński, T., Bachmann, M., Kamińska, D.: Audiovisual emotion recognition in wild. Mach. Vis. Appl. **30**(5), 975–985 (2018). https://doi.org/10.1007/s00138-018-0960-9
2. Bengio, Y., Courville, A., Vincent, P.: Representation learning: a review and new perspectives. IEEE Trans. Pattern Anal. Mach. Intell. **35**(8), 1798–1828 (2013). https://doi.org/10.1109/TPAMI.2013.50
3. D'Mello, S.K., Dowell, N., Graesser, A.: Unimodal and multimodal human perception of naturalistic non-basic affective states during human-computer interactions. IEEE Trans. Affect. Comput. **4**(4), 452–465 (2013). https://doi.org/10.1109/T-AFFC.2013.19
4. Ernst, M.O., Banks, M.S.: Humans integrate visual and haptic information in a statistically optimal fashion. Nature **415**(6870), 429–433 (2002). https://doi.org/10.1038/415429a
5. Harata, S., Sakuma, T., Kato, S.: Toward mathematical representation of emotion: a deep multitask learning method based on multimodal recognition. In: Companion Publication of the 2020 International Conference on Multimodal Interaction, ICMI 2020, pp. 47–51. Companion, Association for Computing Machinery (2020). https://doi.org/10.1145/3395035.3425254
6. He, K., Zhang, X., Ren, S., Sun, J.: Deep residual learning for image recognition. In: The IEEE Conference on Computer Vision and Pattern Recognition (CVPR) (June 2016). https://doi.org/10.1109/CVPR.2016.90
7. Landy, M.S., Maloney, L.T., Johnston, E.B., Young, M.: Measurement and modeling of depth cue combination: in defense of weak fusion. Vision. Res. **35**(3), 389–412 (1995). https://doi.org/10.1016/0042-6989(94)00176-M
8. Livingstone, S.R., Russo, F.A.: The ryerson audio-visual database of emotional speech and song (RAVDESS): a dynamic, multimodal set of facial and vocal expressions in North American English. PLoS ONE **13**(5), 1–35 (2018). https://doi.org/10.1371/journal.pone.0196391
9. Nemati, S., Rohani, R., Basiri, M.E., Abdar, M., Yen, N.Y., Makarenkov, V.: A hybrid latent space data fusion method for multimodal emotion recognition. IEEE Access **7**, 172948–172964 (2019). https://doi.org/10.1109/ACCESS.2019.2955637
10. van den Oord, A., et al.: WaveNet: A Generative Model for Raw Audio. CoRR abs/1609.03499 (2016)
11. Picard, R.W.: Affective Computing. Inteligencia artificial. MIT Press (2000). https://books.google.co.jp/books?id=GaVncRTcb1gC
12. Russell, J.A.: A circumplex model of affect. J. Pers. Soc. Psychol. **39**, 1161–1178 (1980). https://doi.org/10.1037/h0077714
13. Wang, F., Xiang, X., Cheng, J., Yuille, A.L.: NormFace: L2 hypersphere embedding for face verification. In: Proceedings of the 25th ACM International Conference on Multimedia, pp. 1041–1049 (2017). https://doi.org/10.1145/3123266.3123359
14. Wang, H., et al.: CosFace: large margin cosine loss for deep face recognition. In: The IEEE Conference on Computer Vision and Pattern Recognition (CVPR), (June 2018). https://doi.org/10.1109/CVPR.2018.00552

Impact of Longer Viewing Distance to Virtual Screen upon Mouse-Manipulation Performance

Makio Ishihara[✉]

Fukuoka Institute of Technology, Fukuoka 811-0295, Japan
m-ishihara@fit.ac.jp
https://www.fit.ac.jp/~m-ishihara/Lab/

Abstract. This manuscript employs an HMD-based virtual display environment and looks carefully into impacts of long viewing distances to a virtual screen upon mouse manipulation performance by including conditions of viewing distances at smaller intervals. At the moment of writing this manuscript, the experiment is being in progress and this poster reports the latest results. The results show that the speed of mouse manipulation would increase with a certain amount of error, and physical fatigue as well as psychological one would get worse for longer viewing distances.

Keywords: Mouse manipulation · Viewing distance · Virtual display

1 Introduction

The VDT syndrome is a symptom that is caused by extensive use of eyes for long hours and pains in the neck or shoulders due to sitting at desks for long periods of time, and physiological stress that stems from monotonous and continuous work requiring no errors etc.

To deal with the VDT syndrome, international standards of ISO9241-303 specify requirements for electronic visual displays. It says for example that the viewing distance, which refers to the physical distance between the surface of the computer screen and the user's eyes, should be 30 to 40 cm for children and young people, and more than 40 cm for adults and older people. Thus, optimal viewing distances have been discussed often from the side of human ergonomics but not task performance. Previously, the authors [1,2] showed that long viewing distances to a computer screen could improve performance of mouse manipulation and calculation in terms of speed, accuracy, and psychological fatigue. In their study, three experiments of tapping, tracing (ISO9241) and kraepelin tasks were conducted for three viewing distances of 0.5 m, 32 m and 128 m from a virtual computer screen in an immersive virtual space provided by an HMD. This study aims to add more data about impacts of those long viewing distances on mouse manipulation performance and psychological fatigue by including conditions of viewing distances at small intervals.

© The Author(s), under exclusive license to Springer Nature Switzerland AG 2022
C. Stephanidis et al. (Eds.): HCII 2022, CCIS 1581, pp. 144–150, 2022.
https://doi.org/10.1007/978-3-031-06388-6_19

Fig. 1. An HMD-based virtual computer screen system.

Section 2 describes a HMD-based virtual display environment and Sect. 3 conducts an experiment. Section 4 shows the experiment results and Sect. 5 gives the concluding remarks.

2   A HMD-Based Virtual Display Environment

Figure 1 is a photo of the author's HMD-based virtual computer screen system. The user wears an HMD of HTC Vive Pro and he/she sees a virtual computer screen just before his/her eyes, which is shown in the middle of the right physical computer screen. The virtual computer screen image is a complete copy of the left physical one and all the input made on the physical screen like mouse clicks and drags goes back to the virtual one in a synchronous manner. Those two physical computer screens are connected to a high-end computer of Dell Alienware to compose a virtual space and run a virtual screen. The viewing distance can manually be adjusted between 0.5 m and 128 m.

3   Experiment on Mouse Manipulation Performance

Figure 2 shows a setting of the experiment. The left diagram shows the top view and the user sees a virtual computer screen just in front of him/her. To ensure that the computer screen is placed just in front of the user at the given viewing distance, the 3-dimensional position of the virtual computer screen is adjusted relatively to the position of the user's head in real time. The virtual computer screen is enlarged with a constant horizontal FOV of 60° depending on the viewing distance. For example, he/she perceives a large screen at a long

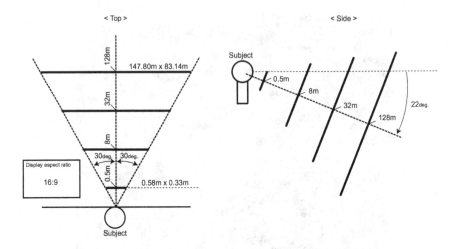

Fig. 2. Experiment setting.

distance. The right diagram shows the side view and the virtual computer screen is placed along a line at the angular position of 22° below the eye level according to ergonomics of human system interaction in ISO9241. Four constant viewing distances of 0.5 m, 8.0 m, 32.0 m and 128.0 m are given for each subject to perform the given tasks. The four constant viewing distances are referred to as Near, N-Middle, F-Middle and Far, respectively.

3.1 Tasks and Subjects

There are 11 subjects with the ages from 18 to 24 at the moment of writing this manuscript. The author is planning to hire 30 subjects in the end, so this manuscript is an interim report of the experiment. They are students from a course of computer science and engineer in the university and all are right-handed and have experience with manipulating a computer mouse. Each subject is asked to perform tapping and tracing tasks which measure accuracy and speed of mouse manipulation. For a tapping task, two rectangles are placed on the left and right of the screen separately and the subject is asked to move the mouse cursor and click on the rectangles in an alternating manner 100 times in total as quickly and precisely as possible. Figure 4 shows a schematic diagram of the tapping task. In the figure, the size and position of the rectangles are expressed as a percentage for the width or height of the screen and the value at the top is the number of counts of accepted clicks. For a tracing task, a circular path is placed in the middle of the screen and the subject is asked to move the mouse cursor along the center line of the path in a clockwise direction 100 revolutions as quickly and precisely as possible. Figure 5 shows a schematic diagram of the tracing task and the value at the top is the number of counts of accepted revolutions. The size of the circular path and cursor is expressed as a percentage for the height of the screen.

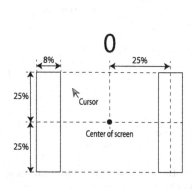

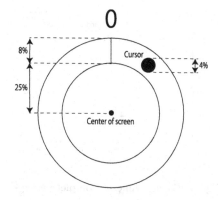

Fig. 3. Procedure of the experiment.

Fig. 4. Design of a tapping task defined by ISO9241-411.

1st:Tapping task   2nd:Tracing task

Practice	Sit still 5 min	Experiment 1st	Questionnaire	Sit still 5 min	Experiment 2nd	Questionnaire	Sit still 5 min	Experiment 3rd	Questionnaire	Sit still 5 min	Experiment 4th	Questionnaire

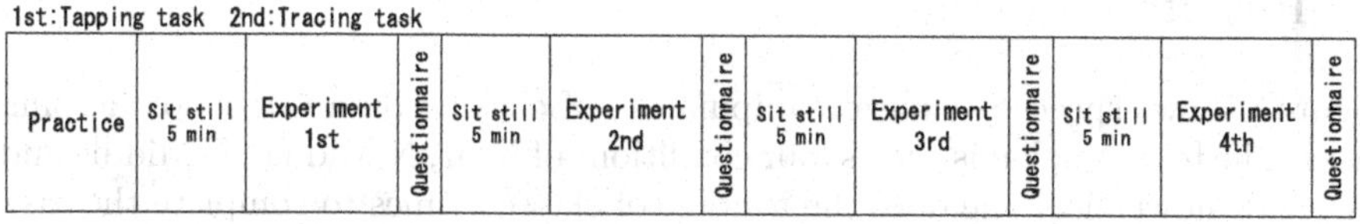

Fig. 5. Design of a tracing task defined by ISO9241-411.

3.2   Experiment Procedure

Figure 3 shows a procedure of the experiment. At the beginning of the procedure, all the subjects have check-ups for their eyesight. Each subject performs a series of tapping tasks first, which are followed by another series of tracing tasks. The subject has a practice time to become familiar with each task before it begins. After that, he/she sits still for 5 min then starts the task at one of the conditions of Near, N-Middle, F-Middle and Far, and fills out a questionnaire about his/her physical fatigue. He/she sits still for another 5 min then starts the task again at the other condition and fills out the questionnaire.

The order of conditions between Near, N-Middle, F-Middle and Far is balanced among subjects to remove order effects. Each subject performs one trial at each condition for each task, resulting in

$$11 \text{ subjects} \times 2 \text{ tasks} \times 4 \text{ conditions} \times 1 \text{ trial}$$
$$= 88 \text{ trials in total.} \tag{1}$$

As regards psychological fatigue, just before and after each task, subjects perform flicker tests. A flicker test provides a subjective indicator of psychological fatigue by asking them to see a light switching between on and off fast, and judge the timing of transition between continuous perception of the light and intermittent one. The timing is measured as the number of counts of flickering light per section and it is called Flicker Perception Threshold or FPT. The FPT holds comparatively high when the psychological fatigue is low or vice versa.

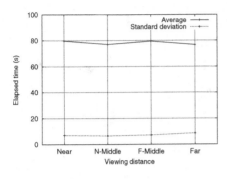
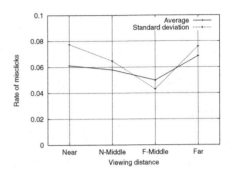

Fig. 6. Elapsed time to complete a tapping task.

Fig. 7. Rate of misclicks made during a tapping task.

4 Results

Figure 6 shows speed of mouse manipulation of clicking on a target for tapping tasks. The horizontal axis shows four conditions of Near, N-Middle, F-Middle and Far, and the vertical one does the average of elapsed times to complete the task in second across all the subjects (solid line) and its standard deviation (dashed line). From the figure, there seems to be a tendency for the speed to increase at longer viewing distances. Figure 7 shows accuracy of mouse manipulation of clicking on a target for tapping tasks. The horizontal axis is the viewing distances and the vertical one does the average of rates of misclicks across all the subjects (solid line) and its standard deviation (dashed line). From the figure, there is somewhat a tendency for the accuracy to increase at longer viewing distances in consideration of the fact that the standard deviation for Near and Far conditions is comparatively large.

Figure 8 shows speed of mouse manipulation of dragging along a round path for tracing tasks. The horizontal axis is the viewing distances and the vertical one does the average of elapsed times to complete the task in second across all the subjects (solid line) and its standard deviation (dashed line). From the figure, there seems to be more increase in speed for longer viewing distances. Figure 9 shows accuracy of mouse manipulation of dragging along a round path for tracing tasks. The horizontal axis is the viewing distances and the vertical one shows the average of gaps between the center line of the round path and a sequence of temporal positions of the mouse cursor over the task across all the subjects. From the figure, there seems to be a tendency for the mouse cursor to move inside the center line at longer viewing distances.

Figure 10 show psychological fatigue obtained from flicker tests before and after the task. The vertical axis shows the average of FPTs among all the subjects for each condition. From the figure, psychological fatigue becomes less after the task for the conditions of Near, N-Middle and F-Middle. The amount of increase of psychological fatigue holds almost the same for Far condition.

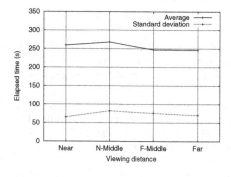

Fig. 8. Elapsed time to complete a tracing task.

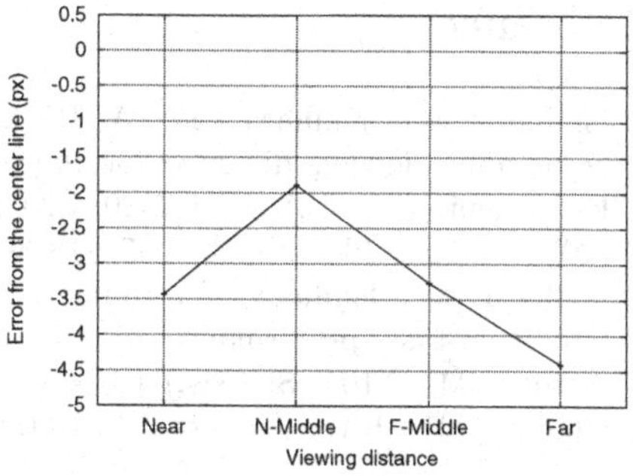

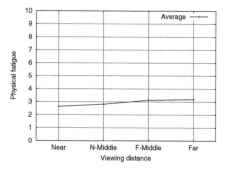

Fig. 9. Tracing errors made during a tracing task.

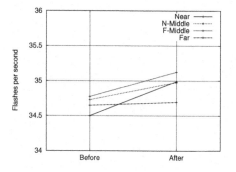

Fig. 10. Psychological fatigue.

Fig. 11. Physical fatigue.

Figure 11 shows physical fatigue. The horizontal axis is the viewing distances and the vertical one does the average of questionnaire scores among all the subjects at each condition. From the figure, physical fatigue tends to increase at longer viewing distances.

5 Conclusions

This manuscript conducted an additional experiment to add more data about impacts of long viewing distances on mouse manipulation performance and psychological fatigue. The results showed that the speed of mouse manipulation would increase with a certain amount of error, and physical fatigue as well as psychological one would get worse for longer viewing distances.

In future work, the author is going to hire more subjects to make the results more reliable and include a further task that requires a large amount of time like 10 min and 15 min to complete.

Acknowledgement. This work was supported by JSPS KAKENHI Grant Number JP20K12522.

References

1. Ishihara, M., Ishihara, Y.: A HMD-based virtual display environment with adjustable viewing distance for improving task performance. In: Chen, J.Y.C., Fragomeni, G. (eds.) HCII 2020. LNCS, vol. 12190, pp. 468–477. Springer, Cham (2020). https://doi.org/10.1007/978-3-030-49695-1_31
2. Ishihara, M., Ishihara, Y.: Impact of viewing distance to virtual screen upon Kraepelin-task performance and its psychological fatigue. In: Stephanidis, C., Antona, M., Ntoa, S. (eds.) HCII 2021. CCIS, vol. 1419, pp. 111–118. Springer, Cham (2021). https://doi.org/10.1007/978-3-030-78635-9_16

Towards a Metacognitive Accuracy Training in Military Education

Aušrius Juozapavičius[1]([⊠]) [iD], Stefan Sütterlin[2,3] [iD], and Ricardo G. Lugo[3,4] [iD]

[1] General Jonas Žemaitis Military Academy of Lithuania, Šilo 5A, 10322 Vilnius, Lithuania
ausrius.juozapavicius@lka.lt
[2] Faculty of Computer Science, Albstadt-Sigmaringen University, Albstadt, Germany
[3] Faculty of Health, Welfare and Organisation, Østfold University College, Halden, Norway
Stefan.Sutterlin@hiof.no
[4] Department of Information Security and Communication Technology, Norwegian University
of Science and Technology, Gjøvik, Norway
Ricardo.g.Lugo@ntnu.no

Abstract. Over- and under-confidence in uncertain and volatile conditions often encountered by military personnel may lead to suboptimal high impact decitions. We investigated the relation between the metacognition accuracy of cadets' performance in a technical IT subject and their observed and measured behaviour characteristics: learning outcomes, knowledge of meta-cognitive strategies, emotional states, time spent for studies, and overall satisfaction with the course and their own efforts. Growth of IT knowledge of a group of 19 cadets who received metacognition training during a three-week long IT course significantly exceeded the results of a control group. Their metacognitive accuracy changed from over-confidence to a moderate under-confidence towards the end of the course, although the relation between the accuracy and the final grade did not differ significantly from random data.

Keywords: Metacognition · Soft-skills · IT education

1 Introduction

Assessment and testing of knowledge and hard skills is an essential part of any formal education. Exam forms, exam contents and formalised curricular usually contain the teaching and testing of so-called "hard skills", i.e. competences that can be described as knowledge or skills, and can easily be assessed. This mostly works as an external motivator for individuals who may then show a tendency to focus on their grades instead of knowledge itself. Apart from knowledge, universities pride themselves in providing higher level transferable skills to their students such as critical thinking, problem solving and decision making. When looking at teaching curricula and assessment strategies of higher education institutions, it appears that these often clearly defined learning outcomes seem to be assumed to develop "naturally", because they are seldom explicitly taught and usually not directly assessed.

C. Stephanidis et al. (Eds.): HCII 2022, CCIS 1581, pp. 151–155, 2022.
https://doi.org/10.1007/978-3-031-06388-6_20

The awareness of one's own thinking is called metacognition [1]. For decision makers, metacognition, i.e. the accurate assessment of their own abilities and knowledge, is a critical transferable skill. Overconfidence may lead to overly risky decisions, while underconfidence (in extreme cases often described as "impostor syndrome") constitutes an inefficient use of human resources. Self regulation and perseverance appear to be more important predictors of academic success than IQ [2] and the underlying mechanism of these features is based on a good understanding of your own thinking. High metacognitive accuracy describes the skill to assess one's own cognitive processes such as learning and cognitive performance accurately in line with objective measures. High metacognitive accuracy thus predicts efficient learning, better decision-making and faster adaptation in volatile environments. In the military domain, this imbalance between the need for transferable "soft skills" and the lack of its systematic integration in teaching, training and assessment can be considered to be particularly important, since security-risks or inefficient use of human assets can have high costs in high-stake situations. In this pilot study following an exploratory descriptive approach we aimed to investigate the relationship between self-assessment of performance, emotional state, learning outcomes and development of metacognitive accuracy.

2 Methods

Participants ($N = 19$) were recruited officer cadets from a national military academy in their first year. Grades in their required classwork of an introductory IT course were used as outcome measures with grade "10" marking the perfect score, and grades below "5" marking failure. The course lasted for 3 weeks with 2–4 h of lectures every day, and homework assignments for the afternoons. In total there were 4 different tests of their knowledge and skills throughout the course: a pre-course knowledge test (Test 0), two tests during the course (Test 1 and Test 2), and the final test (exam). A significant amount of time was allocated to indirectly motivate the cadets via introduction of various meta-cognitive strategies [2]. The first homework assignments made them read literature on strategies of successful students, write essays about their own methods of learning they plan to use during the course, and discuss their findings about different note-taking or memorising techniques. Gradually the focus during the lectures shifted to the subject matter, but the students were encouraged to spend time on their meta-cognition: work in groups, compare their notes, review previous tests, and constantly reflect on their progress. Before the course, their trait and situational metacognition was assessed with the Metacognition Assessment Instrument (MCAI) [3]. It is a 52-item self-report with eight scales that assesses knowledge of cognition and regulation of knowledge. Items are assessed on bipolar responses (true/false) and then ratios are computed from the subscales. The test shows high reliability on all subscales (Cronbach's $\alpha = .90$). Their judgement of performance was measured before and after each test with the following items: 'How well do you think you will do on the test' (pre) and 'How well did you do on the test' (post). A metacognitive performance score was computed as the difference between the estimated and true result (the overestimation). To assess the students' situational emotional states, we used the self-assessment manikin (SAM) [4] where mood, physiological activation, and control was measured on a 9-point Likert-scale (1 to 9).

Previous research has shown the SAM to be valid for both children and adults [5]. Several additional variables have been measured after the course: the students were asked to grade their overall satisfaction with the course, estimate satisfaction with their own efforts, and specify an amount of hours they spent studying outside the classroom. The cadets were free not to participate in any activities directly unrelated to the subject matter, but they chose to answer every questionnaire except for some minor omissions in SAM towards the end of the course.

Regression analyses were performed to find relationships between the measured variables. Metacognitive awareness and judgement of performance scores were entered as the independent variables and outcome test scores were entered as the dependent variables. Alpha (α) significance levels were set to .05. JASP v16 was used for analysis.

Finally, the pre-course knowledge grades and the final grades were also compared to a control group of 81 students who had an identical course, but did not receive any meta-cognition training.

3 Results

Results show that students reported overconfidence at the beginning of the 3 week course (overestimating their grades by 1.50 points during the Test 1) and became better at predicting their coursework results during the course. During the final test (exam) they underestimated their score by 1.37 ± 0.36 points (the tests are graded on the scale of 10 with 5 points being the passing grade and 10 points the maximum). Students became more accurate in predicting their final grades ($R2 = .29$, $F = 6.95$, $p = .017$, $\beta = .539$) at the end of the course due to better metacognitive development. The metacognitive accuracy was significantly positively associated with their final grade. Namely, a larger overestimation of their exam grade corresponded to a smaller final grade ($r = -.473$, $p = .041$). This result appears to be in line with numerous other published results citing the Dunning-Kruger effect [6]. Unfortunately, the result is misleading the same way as the Dunning-Kruger effect [7]. Indeed, persons with absolute knowledge cannot overestimate it, and the plot of overestimation versus the grade always favours the least knowledgeable. In fact, the effect did not differ significantly from a set of randomly generated data. However, the score of the self-reported metacognitive awareness (MCAI) also correlated with the final grade: the correlation of the total score ($r = .389$, $p = .100$) lacked statistical accuracy, but one of the scales, the Declarative Metacognition, had a statistically significant signal ($r = .575$, $p = .010$). Our exploration failed to uncover correlations between the final grade and many other measured variables including hours spent on homework, satisfaction with the course, satisfaction with one's own efforts, overall mood, activation, and control during the course or the fluctuations of these emotional states. We only observed a tendency of the mood to decrease throughout the course together with decreasing overconfidence, but this could have been caused by other factors that we did not measure such as fatigue or disturbances in their routine (cadets usually receive many unexpected military tasks during their free study time, and the process of adaptation takes time).

Finally, Student's t-test showed that there was no significant difference between the initial (pre-course) results of the intervention group and the control group. However, the growth during the course, measured as the difference between the final and the initial grade, was significantly higher for the intervention group (t = 4.011, df = 98, p < 0.001) with a very large effect size (Cohen's d = 1.022). Namely, the group of cadets who received the meta-cognition training managed to grow their knowledge significantly more (by 3.6 grade points) than their colleagues from the control group (their average growth was 1.9 grade points).

4 Discussion

This explorative study aimed to shed light on the covert process of metacognitive accuracy development during exposure to "hard-skill" related teaching. To the best of our knowledge, this pilot is amongst the first to operationalize metacognitive skills during a military educational context on IT-related "hard-skills" both on self-report and objective level. Our preliminary results seem to indicate continuous adjustment of metacognitive skills operationalized as prediction of exam performance during the course of a 3-week teaching period. However, since high-performers are less likely to overestimate their skills than to underestimate them (and vice versa), these results have to be interpreted with caution. Further research with larger samples is needed to confirm the robustness of this effect. While this hypothesised development of metacognitive accuracy over time remains inconclusive for now, the observed tendencies and sub-test significance of a positive correlation between self-reported metacognitive accuracy and exam performance, however, suggests a relevant role of metacognitive skills for learning performance.

The resulting moderate under-confidence in the last measurement can be considered an ideal outcome given the security-sensitive high-stake situations in which graduates of military education usually face during their first deployments. The development of metacognitive skills is particularly warranted in situations that can be ascribed as being of the VUCA type. VUCA stands for volatility, uncertainty, complexity and ambiguity, i.e., situations where declarative knowledge or specific skills have rather limited effects and require a high degree of self-regulatory skills, such as metacognitive accuracy.

5 Conclusions

Results of our explorative study show a positive influence of metacognitive training on the final grade of a technical course taken by a group of cadets. Additionally, there is an indication of a correlation between the metacognitive accuracy and the final result, although a larger sample needs to be investigated to achieve a definite conclusion. We found no correlation between the final grade and hours spent on homework, satisfaction with the course, satisfaction with one's own efforts, overall mood, activation, and control during the course.

5.1 Limitations

Despite including the complete cohort of cadets available in the taught course, the sample size is moderate and thus the obtained statistical results require replication in a larger sample. That being said, the calculated confidence intervals and margins of error suggest a sufficient robustness of the obtained findings to justify the careful conclusions we propose in this chapter. Ideally, teaching, grading and performance assessment of "soft-" and "hard-skills" should be done by different persons.

5.2 Further Research

Further research should continue to improve our understanding on the role of metacognitive skill development as a "side effect" of traditional "hard-skills" teaching, and vice versa – the impact of meta-cognition teaching on acquisition of subject-related knowledge. Being a valuable skill with a high predictive value for later success, long-term competency development and personal "soft-skills" such as leadership, adaptability and resilience, the aspect of metacognitive development should not only be considered to be an essential learning outcome, but also be explicitly taught, monitored, assessed and reflected upon. Further research should also include a curriculum with the specific aim to practice and evaluate one's metacognitive accuracy in a wide range of realistic and cross-domain scenarios. We hope that this initial research contributed to uncover processes and ways of assessment.

References

1. Zimmerman, B.J.: Becoming a self-regulated learner: an overview. Theory Pract. **41**(2), 64–70 (2002)
2. Nilson, L.: Creating Self-Regulated Learners: Strategies to Strengthen Students' Self-Awareness and Learning Skills. Stylus Publishing, LLC (2013)
3. Schraw, G., Dennison, R.S.: Assessing metacogntive awareness. Contemp. Educ. Psychol. **19**(4), 460–475 (1994)
4. Bradley, M.M., Lang, P.J.: Measuring emotion: the self-assessment manikin and the semantic differential. J. Behav. Ther. Exp. Psych. **25**(1), 49–59 (1994)
5. Backs, R.W., da Silva, S.P., Han, K.: A comparison of younger and older adults' self-assessment manikin ratings of affective pictures. Exp. Aging Res. **31**(4), 421–440 (2005)
6. Kruger, J.M., Dunning, D.: Unskilled and unaware of it: how difficulties in recognizing one's own incompetence lead to inflated self-assessments. J. Pers. Soc. Psychol. **77**, 1121–1134 (1999)
7. Gignac, G.E., Zajenkowski, M.: The Dunning-Kruger effect is (mostly) a statistical artefact: Valid approaches to testing the hypothesis with individual differences data. Intelligence **80**, 101449 (2020)

Cognitive Workload Associated with Different Conceptual Modeling Approaches in Information Systems

Andreas Knoben[1]([✉])[iD], Maryam Alimardani[1][iD], Arash Saghafi[2][iD], and Amin K. Amiri[2][iD]

[1] Department of Cognitive Science and AI, Tilburg University,
5037 AB Tilburg, The Netherlands
a.j.knoben@tilburguniversity.edu
[2] Department of Management, Tilburg University,
5037 AB Tilburg, The Netherlands

Abstract. Conceptual models visually represent entities and relationships between them in an information system. Effective conceptual models should be simple while communicating sufficient information. This trade-off between model complexity and clarity is crucial to prevent failure of information system development. Past studies have found that more expressive models lead to higher performance on tasks measuring a user's deep understanding of the model and attributed this to lower experience of cognitive workload associated with these models. This study examined this hypothesis by measuring users' EEG brain activity while they completed a task with different conceptual models. 30 participants were divided into two groups: One group used a low ontologically expressive model (LOEM), and the other group used a high ontologically expressive model (HOEM). Cognitive workload during the task was quantified using EEG Engagement Index, which is a ratio of brain activity power in beta as opposed to the sum of alpha and theta frequency bands. No significant difference in cognitive workload was found between the LOEM and HOEM groups indicating equal amounts of cognitive processing required for understanding of both models. The main contribution of this study is the introduction of neurophysiological measures as an objective quantification of cognitive workload in the field of conceptual modeling and information systems.

Keywords: Information systems · Conceptual models · Entity-relationship diagram (ERD) · Cognitive workload · Brain activity · EEG Engagement Index

1 Introduction

Conceptual models are formal representations of the real world that are used for the purposes of understanding and communication between stakeholders,

ⓒ The Author(s), under exclusive license to Springer Nature Switzerland AG 2022
C. Stephanidis et al. (Eds.): HCII 2022, CCIS 1581, pp. 156–163, 2022.
https://doi.org/10.1007/978-3-031-06388-6_21

analysts, and developers of information systems [11,15]. They are used in the development of information systems with the aim to communicate the requirements of an application domain in such a way that it guides effective design of the system [8]. A widely used type of conceptual model is entity-relationship diagrams (ERDs), which communicate entities, i.e., constructs a business needs to remember in order to run the business, as well as relationships between those entities.

The use of ontology, a "branch of philosophy that deals with the order and structure of reality" [2], has been proposed to guide the creation of effective conceptual models [14]. To reduce the chance of failure in the development process of an information system, a conceptual model must faithfully represent the relevant aspects of the modeled domain, and it must be clear and understandable to "users" of the model [3]. Therefore, it has to be simple while communicating sufficient information to the user. Conceptual models that represent reality more closely are considered more ontologically expressive, but this is achieved possibly at the cost of increased complexity of the model [14].

The trade-off between "expressiveness" and "simplicity" has been studied in a number of previous papers and addressed in the meta-analysis by Saghafi and Wand (2020) [13]. It was found that models with higher ontological expressiveness significantly improved users' understanding of an application domain across different conceptual modeling grammars [13] as well as their performance on tasks that required a deeper understanding of the model, e.g., problem solving [5,8]. These findings indicated a positive influence of ontological expressiveness on user interaction with the model allowing for better performance using the system. Gemino and Wand (2005) discussed this finding from a cognitive load theory perspective, arguing that models with higher ontological expressiveness require less cognitive workload from the user as they represent the domain more clearly and the user is better able to understand and retrieve information from them [8]. However, they never provided any objective quantification of cognitive workload to support this argument.

A more direct approach to assess users' cognitive effort when they interact with and develop an understanding of a conceptual model is to measure their brain responses during the task using electroencephalography (EEG). Past neuroscientific studies indicate that changes in cognitive workload are reflected in frequency band powers of EEG signals [1,4,10,12]. A neural metric that is often employed to evaluate workload is the "EEG Engagement Index", which is defined as the ratio between beta power and the sum of theta and alpha powers extracted from an EEG signal [1,4]. This index has already been employed and verified in multiple human-technology interaction studies, however its application for user interaction with information systems remains unexplored.

This study, for the first time, investigates neurophysiological metrics of cognitive workload when two groups of users work with conceptual models of different ontological expressiveness as suggested by Gemino and Wand (2005) [8]. The research question is therefore formulated as below:

Is there a difference in cognitive workload as measured by brain activity when users retrieve information from two models with a different level of ontological expressiveness?

2   Methods

2.1   Participants

Thirty university students with a mean age of 22.13 years ($SD = 4.81$) participated in this study. They were randomly assigned to one of the two groups: One group worked with a low ontologically expressive model (the LOEM group), and the other worked with a high ontologically expressive model (the HOEM group). The study was approved by the Research Ethics Committee of the Tilburg School of Humanities and Digital Sciences (REDC 2021.144). Prior to the experiment, participants read an information letter and signed an informed consent form.

2.2   Experimental Task

Two conceptual models with different ontological expressiveness but presenting the same business domain were chosen for this study. The ERDs belonging to the selected domain, namely a machine repair facility, were taken from [9], and can be viewed in Fig. 1. The left model consists of entities with optional properties that lack certainty and hence is considered a low ontologically expressive model. The right model consists of mandatory properties that communicate unambiguous information and hence is considered as the high ontologically expressive model. Each participant was randomly assigned to one of these models and was instructed to complete missing information in a fill-in-the-blanks task using the ERD in front of them.

2.3   EEG Recording

EEG signals were recorded from 16 electrodes according to the 10–20 international system (Fp1, Fp2, F3, Fz, F4, T7, C3, Cz, C4, T8, P3, Pz, P4, PO7, PO8, and Oz). This selection allowed recording from all brain areas, i.e., left and right hemisphere and midline frontal, temporal, parietal, and occipital regions. The reference was set on the right earlobe and a ground electrode on AFz. A g.Nautilus amplifier (g.tec Medical Engineering, Austria) was used to collect the signals at the sampling rate 250 Hz.

2.4   Experiment Design

Before the day of the experiment, the participants received an email with preparation instructions for the EEG, and a video tutorial that explained ERDs. This tutorial aimed to familiarize the participants with ERDs prior to the experiment. Upon arrival on the experiment day, first, the experimental procedure was

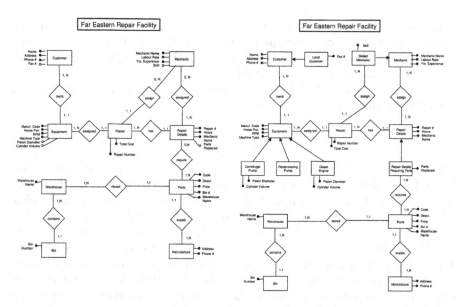

Fig. 1. The low ontologically expressive (left) and high ontologically expressive (right) models used in this study, taken from [9].

explained to the participant and informed consent was obtained. Next, participants filled in a demographic questionnaire and the EEG electrodes were placed on the participant's head. When this was done, the participant sat behind a desk with two computer screens and began the experimental tasks.

Before the main task, EEG signals in a 3-min baseline were recorded, while participants looked at a fixation cross on the screen. Then, they read a text about the domain that the ERD in the task was going to model (machinery repair), and studied the diagram itself. After that, the main task started where they answered fill-in-the-blank questions by retrieving information from the model, which was presented on a second screen. The diagram remained visible on the screen, so that the participant could refer to it while working on the task. The mean time it took for the participants to complete the task was 8.78 min ($SD = 2.06$) for the LOEM group and 10.51 min ($SD = 3.26$) for the HOEM group. Once the experiment was finished, the EEG cap was removed and the participant was briefed and thanked for their participation.

2.5   Analysis

The raw EEG data was pre-processed using MATLAB R2021b (Mathworks Inc., MA) and the EEGLAB toolbox [7]. The pre-processing steps included discarding bad channels if necessary, applying a band pass filter of 0.5 to 60 Hz, rejecting artifacts in the data temporally, and rejecting eye artifact components using

Independent Component Analysis. Then, spectral analysis was conducted on the clean data using the `spectopo` function from the EEGLAB toolbox [7] and the mean beta (13–30 Hz), alpha (8–13 Hz), and theta (4–8 Hz) powers for each channel and participant were extracted.

Using these powers, the EEG Engagement Index was calculated according to the following equation [12]:

$$E = \frac{\beta}{\alpha + \theta} \tag{1}$$

where E is the EEG Engagement Index and β, α, and θ are the mean power in the beta, alpha, and theta frequency bands, respectively [1,6,12]. For every participant, the EEG Engagement Index was baseline-corrected, i.e., the baseline EEG Engagement Index was subtracted from the task EEG Engagement Index.

The baseline-corrected EEG Engagement Indices were compared between the LOEM and HOEM groups in R (version 4.1.2). For the data of each channel, it was first determined whether it was normally distributed using a Shapiro-Wilk test. If the data was normally distributed, a Welch's independent t-test was used to compare the groups. If the normality assumption was not met, a Mann-Whitney U test was used. Because the groups were compared 16 times, the significance level was adjusted to $0.05/16 = 0.003125$ using the Bonferroni method.

3   Results

The EEG Engagement Indices for each channel are visualized in Fig. 2. Additionally, the results of the statistical test in each EEG channel are reported in Table 1. No significant differences were observed in EEG-based cognitive workload that was produced by the subjects in LOEM and HOEM groups.

4   Discussion

In this study, EEG signals were employed to obtain a neurophysiological and an objective measure of cognitive workload when two groups of participants used conceptual models with different ontological expressiveness (low versus high) to conduct an information retrieval task. Cognitive workload was quantified by the EEG Engagement Index (Eq. 1) obtained from 16 channels distributed over the scalp. Our results showed no significant difference in EEG Engagement Index between the two groups at any of the investigated brain regions.

The findings presented here are inconsistent with the hypothesis of Gemino and Wand (2005) that a high ontologically expressive model would require less workload [8]. They base their hypothesis on the argument that mandatory properties lead to a lower cognitive workload compared to optional properties, because models with mandatory properties have a clearer structure, whereas models with optional properties require extra reasoning in order to understand the domain [8]. However, our results, providing an objective quantification of

Table 1. Summary of statistical analysis comparing EEG Engagement Index between LOEM and HOEM groups at each channel. The outcome of the Welch's independent t-test (left) and Mann-Whitney U test (right) are separated.

Channel	t	df	p	Channel	W	p
T7	1.97	16.03	.07	Fp1	70	.33
C3	.73	23.78	.47	Fp2	118	.84
Cz	.49	27.44	.63	F3	124	.65
C4	.39	28.00	.70	Fz	107	.84
T8	1.02	18.59	.32	F4	106	.81
P3	−.20	23.31	.84	Oz	54	.79
Pz	.27	25.25	.79			
P4	.87	25.74	.39			
PO7	.83	24.37	.42			
PO8	1.60	19.68	.13			

cognitive workload from neural activity of participants, did not support such a hypothesis, suggesting that both groups recruited similar amounts of cognitive resources when processing optional and mandatory properties of the models.

A reason why model comparison in this study did not show a significant difference may be due to the relatively small sample size where only 15 subjects were present in each group. Particularly with individual differences present in EEG signals, future research should expand the study with a larger sample to be able to provide a reliable comparison.

Another reason could be participants' lack of experience in working with ERD models in this study. In the experiment of Gemino and Wand, participants were business students who had taken at least one course related to Management Information Systems and were thus familiar with conceptual ERD models [8]. Participants in our study were novice to this topic, and although they watched an introductory video about ERD before the task, their previous experience with conceptual models was almost non-existent. It could be speculated that such difference in background knowledge between the participants of the two studies led to different outcomes.

Finally, in this study, EEG Engagement Index was only compared during one task which required filling in missing information, whereas Gemino and Wand (2005) proposed multiple tasks in their study among which the problem-solving task was argued to illustrate deeper understanding of a model [8]. Future research should provide a more comprehensive analysis of brain activity as well as performance on the task when users interact with ERD models from various domains and conduct multiple tasks that target different levels of cognitive functioning.

In sum, the current study provides preliminary insights for future employment of neurophysiological measures in evaluation of conceptual modeling methods. Using a quantified indicator of cognitive workload borrowed from

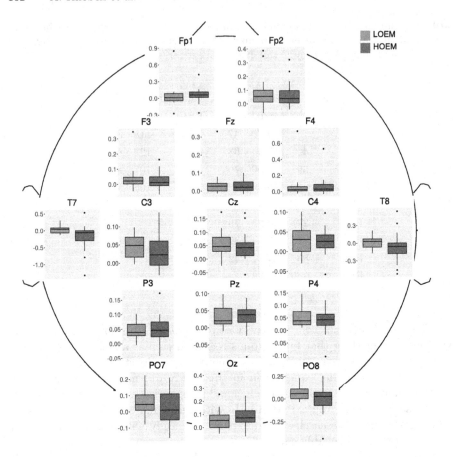

Fig. 2. Plots showing the EEG Engagement Index obtained from participants working with low ontologically expressive (LOEM group) and high ontologically expressive models (HOEM group) at all electrode locations.

neuroergonomics research, we propose that the trade-off between clarity and complexity in conceptual models can be addressed by measuring brain activity to strike an optimal balance between these two criteria from the user's perspective [5].

5   Conclusion

This study aimed to quantitatively assess user interaction with conceptual models in information systems using EEG brain activity. Cognitive workload was extracted from EEG signals when two groups of users worked with a low ontologically expressive model versus a high ontologically expressive model. Contrary to the predictions of previous research, no significant difference was found in cognitive workload as measured by brain activity in any of the EEG electrodes. This study demonstrates preliminary results for employment of neurophysiological measurements in evaluation of Management Information Systems. Future work can validate the precision and reliability of this method by employing larger groups of participants and including more complex tasks (e.g., problem-solving) to examine deeper levels of model understanding in brain responses.

References

1. Alimardani, M., van den Braak, S., Jouen, A.-L., Matsunaka, R., Hiraki, K.: Assessment of engagement and learning during child-robot interaction using EEG signals. In: Li, H., et al. (eds.) ICSR 2021. LNCS (LNAI), vol. 13086, pp. 671–682. Springer, Cham (2021). https://doi.org/10.1007/978-3-030-90525-5_59
2. Angeles, P.A.: A dictionary of philosophy (1981)
3. Bera, P., Burton-Jones, A., Wand, Y.: Research note-how semantics and pragmatics interact in understanding conceptual models. Inf. Syst. Res. **25**(2), 401–419 (2014)
4. Berka, C., et al.: EEG correlates of task engagement and mental workload in vigilance, learning, and memory tasks. Aviat. Space Environ. Med. **78**(5), B231–B244 (2007)
5. Burton-Jones, A., Meso, P.: The effects of decomposition quality and multiple forms of information on novices' understanding of a domain from a conceptual model. J. Assoc. Inf. Syst. **9**(12), 1 (2008)
6. Chiang, H.S., Hsiao, K.L., Liu, L.C.: EEG-based detection model for evaluating and improving learning attention. J. Med. Biol. Eng. **38**(6), 847–856 (2018). https://doi.org/10.1007/s40846-017-0344-z
7. Delorme, A., Makeig, S.: EEGLAB: an open source toolbox for analysis of single-trial EEG dynamics including independent component analysis. J. Neurosci. Methods **134**(1), 9–21 (2004)
8. Gemino, A., Wand, Y.: Complexity and clarity in conceptual modeling: comparison of mandatory and optional properties. Data Knowl. Eng. **55**(3), 301–326 (2005)
9. Gemino, A.C.: Empirical comparisons of system analysis modeling techniques. Ph.D. thesis, University of British Columbia (1999)
10. Khedher, A.B., Jraidi, I., Frasson, C., et al.: Tracking students' mental engagement using EEG signals during an interaction with a virtual learning environment. J. Intell. Learn. Syst. Appl. **11**(01), 1 (2019)
11. Mylopoulos, J.: Conceptual modelling and telos. Conceptual modelling, databases, and CASE: an integrated view of information system development, pp. 49–68 (1992)
12. Pope, A.T., Bogart, E.H., Bartolome, D.S.: Biocybernetic system evaluates indices of operator engagement in automated task. Biol. Psychol. **40**(1–2), 187–195 (1995)
13. Saghafi, A., Wand, Y.: A meta-analysis of ontological guidance and users' understanding of conceptual models. J. Database Manag. (JDM) **31**(4), 46–68 (2020)
14. Wand, Y., Weber, R.: On the ontological expressiveness of information systems analysis and design grammars. Inf. Syst. J. **3**(4), 217–237 (1993)
15. Wand, Y., Weber, R.: Research commentary: information systems and conceptual modeling-a research agenda. Inf. Syst. Res. **13**(4), 363–376 (2002)

Study on Cognitive Behavior and Subjective Evaluation Index of Seafarer's Alertness

Jin Liang[1(✉)], Xin Wang[1], Si Li[1,2], Chi Zhang[1], Liang Zhang[1], Yang Yu[1], Cong Peng[1], and Xiaofang Sun[1]

[1] China Institute of Marine Technology and Economy, Beijing 100081, China
liangjinpsy@126.com
[2] China Institute of Marine Human Factors Engineering, Qingdao 266400, China

Abstract. This study carried out the long-time voyage simulation experiment in the independently developed experimental cabin to explore the cognitive behavior and subjective evaluation index of seafarer's alertness during the simulated long-time voyage, and test the effectiveness of the cognitive behavior indicators for seafarer's alertness during the simulated long-time voyage. The results show that during the long voyage, the score of KSS was sensitive about seafarers' subjective alertness decline from duty during the long voyage, the mean response time, standard deviation of response time and lapse of PVT task was sensitive about seafarers' cognitive alertness decline from duty during the long voyage. The predictive effect of cognitive behavior index of alertness on the subjective alertness of long-time seafarers is better in the early voyage and worse in the middle voyage, which may be related to the rhythm disorder of seafarers in the middle and late voyage. The predictive effect after duty is better than before duty. Therefore, PVT task is more suitable for early vigilance assessment of long-time voyage seafarers and has more vigilance prediction on seafarer's alert after duty. When the seafarer's rhythm is disordered, PVT's prediction of seafarer's vigilance will be greatly inconsistent with the seafarer's subjective perception of alert.

Keywords: Long time voyage · Cognitive behavior index · Seafarer · Alertness

1 Introduction

Low cost makes shipping become one of the main ways of international trade. A long-time ocean voyage often crosses different sea areas and experiences complex and changeable marine climate. Under the rapidly changing sea conditions, how to ensure the ship complete the navigation task safely has become one of the critical issues in the field of long-distance shipping. "The seafarers should be on duty in turn during the long-term voyage to maintain high vigilance and respond to various emergencies at any time" is one of the important means to ensure the safety of voyage. With the developing of information technology and automation, the seafarer can operate the ship and ensure the ship safety through various electronic information equipment during maritime navigation, which greatly reduces the workload of the seafarer. However, long-time operation of electronic information equipment also leads to psychological burnout, decreased attention and alertness, which seriously threaten the safety of ship navigation [1–4]. So there is great significance to timely evaluate the alertness of the seafarer and give necessary intervention when the alertness of the seafarer decreases.

Some researches and products on the alertness assessment of automobile drivers, athletes and other groups have explored the reliability and sensitivity of 3 min, 5 min, 10 min psychomotor vigilance task (PVT) to alertness, fatigue and sleep loss [5–8]. Jones et al. found the 5 min PVT and 10 min PVT had similar response speed, but the 3 min PVT did not produce results comparable with the 10 min PVT for response speed, lapses or errors [5], which indicated the 5 min PVT could be a substitute for the 10 min PVT [5, 10]. However, other studies stated the 3 min PVT was able to predict fatigue and alertness [6, 7]. Differences in target populations may be a source of inconsistent results. These suggested that there might be differences in the reliability and validity of vigilance assessment for specific populations using PVT tasks. But few researches focused on the alertness assessment in the field of ships and the effectiveness of existing alertness assessment indicators under ship missions. Therefore, according to the needs of long-time voyage, this study carried out the long-time voyage simulation experiment in the independently developed experimental cabin to explore the cognitive behavior and subjective evaluation index of seafarer's alertness during the simulated long-time voyage, and test the effectiveness of the cognitive behavior indicators for seafarer's alertness during the simulated long-time voyage.

2 Methods

2.1 Participants

12 male subjects were recruited through the society in this experiment. The subjects had completed high school or college education, who were physically and mentally healthy. They all have no drug, alcohol, smoking, internet dependence and addiction, no history of inherited diseases, hepatitis b, hepatitis c, AIDS or other infectious diseases, and no history of severe allergies. They had no mental disorders, no psychological diseases, no organic and functional mental and neurological lesions, no sleep disorders or abnormalities in the two and three generations. All participants possessed normal visual acuity (or corrected visual acuity), hearing, smell and language expression ability, without color blindness, color weakness. All subjects passed the interview, systematically physical examination and psychological evaluation.

2.2 Procedure

The volunteers were required to fully implement work and life schedule of the actual seafarer during the simulated long voyage, and carry out the ship simulation task during working time. Before and after their working time, the KSS scale was used to evaluate the subjective alertness level of the seafarer, and the 5 min PVT task was used to evaluate the cognitive alertness of the seafarer. The study passed an ethical review before the experiment was conducted.

2.3 Test Tasks

Psychomotor Vigilance Task (PVT Task). The subjects were required to focus on the fixation point in the center of the screen after the start of the psychomotor vigilance task (PVT task), and press the "J" button immediately when the countdown began. The countdown would be continuing until the participant pressed the right key, and the participant's response time was recorded. Participants were asked to respond as soon as possible, but not before the number appears, otherwise an error message would appear. The experimental process is shown in Fig. 1.

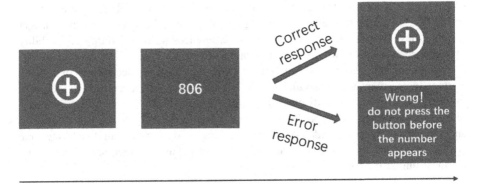

Fig. 1. Psychomotor vigilance task (PVT task)

Karolinska Sleepiness Scale (KSS). Karolinska Sleepiness Scale (KSS) only had one item asking participants represent their current awake status using 1–9 figures. 1 represented extremely sober. 9 represented sleepiness. The scores among 1–9 expressed the subjects' state from extremely sober to sleepiness. The smaller KSS score was, the higher alert participant was.

3 Results

The score of KSS scale was extracted as the subjective evaluation index of simulated seafarer alertness. The results of PVT included meant response time (mRT), fastest response time (fRT), slowest response time (sRT), the fastest 10% response time (10% fRT), slowest 10% response time (10% sRT), standard deviation of response time (SD), lapse (LA), lapse ratio (LR), the trial numbers of one test (TN) was used as the alert cognitive evaluation index [9–12]. Then the difference on the score of KSS scale was analyzed to test the sensitive of the subjective evaluation index of seafarers' alertness after duty during the long voyage, the differences on the mRT, LR, sRT, 10% sRT, LA, SD, 10% RT, fRT and TN of PVT task were analyzed to test the sensitive of the cognitive behavior evaluation index of seafarers' alertness after duty during the long voyage, the calibration correlation coefficient was calculated with the subjective alert value as the calibration standard to evaluate the effectiveness of the alert cognitive behavior index during the simulated long voyage. The results show that:

The score of KSS scale as well as the mean response time, standard deviation of response time and lapse of PVT task after duty were significantly larger than before duty (which was shown in Table 1), which meant the score of KSS was sensitive about the seafarer's subjective alertness decline from duty during the long voyage, the mean response time, standard deviation of response time and lapse of PVT task were sensitive about the seafarer's cognitive alertness decline from duty during the long voyage.

Table 1. .

Index	t	df
KSS	-2.47^*	11
mean response time (mRT)	-2.89^*	11
fastest response time (fRT)	-0.89	11
slowest response time (sRT)	-2.19	10
fastest 10% response time (10% fRT)	-0.29	10
slowest 10% response time (10% sRT)	-1.94	10
standard deviation of response time (SD)	-4.09^{**}	10
lapse (LA)	-3.75^{**}	10
lapse ratio (LR)	-3.80^{**}	10
trial numbers of one test (TN)	1.81	10

* means $p < 0.05$, ** means $p < 0.001$

The prediction effect of mRT, SD, fRT 10, 10% sRT, sRT, LA and LR of PVT task on seafarer's subjective alertness after duty were significantly better than those before duty.

Before duty, the prediction effect of cognitive behavior index on the subjective evaluation index of simulated seafarer alertness from good to bad is the mRT, 10% fRT, sRT, fRT, LR, LA, SD,10 sRT TN of PVT task, However, these index's prediction effects were poor. All index the calibration correlation were smaller than 0.2, which meant PVT task might not effectively predict seafarers' alertness changes from good to bad before duty during the long voyage.

After duty, the prediction effect of cognitive behavior index on the subjective evaluation index of simulated seafarer alertness from good to bad is the 10% sRT, mRT, LR, LA, SD, sRT, 10% fRT, fRT and TN. But only the calibration correlation coefficient of 10% sRT and mRT was larger than 0.4, Which meant 10% sRT, mRT of PVT task might predict seafarers' alertness changes from good to bad after duty during the long voyage (Fig. 2).

In time dimension, the prediction effect of PVT task mRT on the seafarer's subjective alertness after duty in the first and second stages of voyage is significantly better than that in the third stage. The prediction effect of LA and LR of PVT task in the first stage

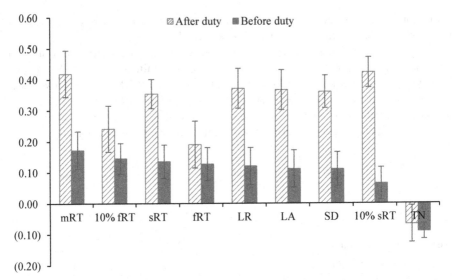

Fig. 2. The prediction effect of cognitive evaluation index on seafarer's subjective alertness before and after duty (mRT is the mean response time, fRT is the fastest response time, sRT is the slowest response time, 10% fRT the fastest 10% response time, 10% sRT is the slowest 10% response time, SD is the standard deviation of response time, LA is the lapse, LR is the lapse ratio, TN is the trial numbers of one test).

of voyage were significantly better than those in the fourth stage. The prediction of subjective alertness by PVT task TN in the fifth stage of voyage was significantly better than that in the fourth stage. The prediction of the 10% fRT on subjective alertness in the second stage of voyage is significantly better than that in the third and fourth stages, the prediction of the 10% fRT on subjective alertness in the fifth stage is significantly better than that in the third stage, the prediction of the 10% fRT after duty on subjective alertness in the second stage of voyage is significantly better than that in the third stage, and the prediction of the 10% fRT on subjective alertness before duty in the fifth stage is significantly better than that in the third stage. The prediction of the fRT on subjective alertness in the second and fifth stages was significantly better than that in the third stage, and the prediction of the fRT on subjective alertness in the second stage was significantly better than that in the third stage; The prediction of the 10% sRT on subjective alertness in the second stage was significantly better than that in the fifth stage. These results show that during the long voyage, the predictive effect of cognitive behavior index of alertness on the subjective alertness of long-time seafarers is better in the early voyage and worse in the middle voyage, which may be related to the rhythm disorder of seafarers in the middle and late voyage. Therefore, PVT task is more suitable for early vigilance assessment of long-time voyage seafarers. When the seafarer's rhythm is disordered, PVT's prediction of seafarer's vigilance will be greatly inconsistent with the seafarer's subjective perception of alert (Figs. 3 and 4).

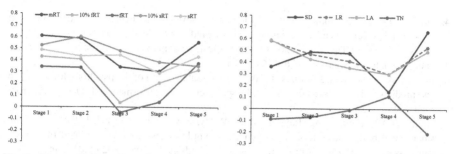

Fig. 3. The prediction effect of cognitive evaluation index on seafarer's subjective alertness after duty in time dimension

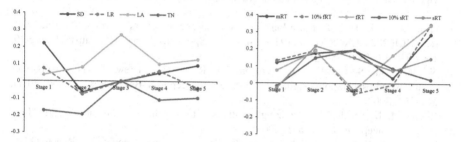

Fig. 4. The prediction effect of cognitive evaluation index on seafarer's subjective alertness before duty in time dimension

4   Conclusion

This study has shown that the score of KSS was sensitive about seafarers' subjective alertness decline from duty during the long voyage, the mean response time, standard deviation of response time and lapse of PVT task were sensitive about seafarers' cognitive alertness decline from duty during the long voyage. The predictive effect of cognitive behavior index of alertness on the subjective alertness of long-time seafarers is better in the early voyage and worse in the middle voyage, which may be related to the rhythm disorder of seafarers in the middle and late voyage. The predictive effect after duty is better than before du-ty. Therefore, PVT task is more suitable for early vigilance assessment of long-time voyage seafarers and has more vigilance prediction on seafarer's alert after duty. When the seafarer's rhythm is disordered, PVT's prediction of seafarer's vigilance will be greatly inconsistent with the seafarer's subjective perception of alert.

References

1. Barnett, M., Pekcan, C., Gatfield, D.: The Use of Linked Simulators in Project "Horizon": Research into Seafarer Fatigue (2012)
2. Goel, N., Basner, M., Rao, H., Dinges, D.F.: Circadian rhythms, sleep deprivation, and human performance. Prog. Mol. Biol. Transl. Sci. **119**, 155–190 (2013)
3. Vidacek, S., Sarić, M.: Circadian variation in alertness, readiness for work and work efficiency. Arch. Indust. Hygiene. Toxicol. **42**(1), 13–25 (1991)

4. Dinges, D.F., et al.: Summary of the Key features of seven biomathematical models of human fatigue and performance. Aviat. Space Environ. Med. **75**(3), 4–14 (2004)
5. Jones, M.J., et al.: The psychomotor vigilance test: a comparison of different test durations in elite athletes. J. Sports Sci. **36**, 1–5 (2018)
6. Basner, M., Rubinstein, J.: Fitness for duty: a 3 minute version of the psychomotor vigilance test predicts fatigue related declines in luggage screening performance. J. Occup. Environ. Med. **53**(10), 1146 (2011)
7. Grant, D.A., Honn, K.A., Layton, M.E., Riedy, S.M., Van Dongen, H.P.A.: 3-minute smartphone-based and tablet-based psychomotor vigilance tests for the assessment of reduced alertness due to sleep deprivation. Behav. Res. Methods **49**(3), 1020–1029 (2016). https://doi.org/10.3758/s13428-016-0763-8
8. Wilson, A., Dollman, J., Lushington, K., Olds, T.: Reliability of the 5-min psychomotor vigilance task in a primary school classroom setting. Behav. Res. Methods **42**(3), 754–758 (2010)
9. Liang, J., et al.: The effect of a long simulated voyage on sailors' alertness. In: Rau, P.-L. (ed.) HCII 2020. LNCS, vol. 12192, pp. 454–462. Springer, Cham (2020). https://doi.org/10.1007/978-3-030-49788-0_34
10. Nicole, L., Jay, S.M., Jillian, D., Ferguson, S.A., Roach, G.D., Drew, D.: The sensitivity of a palm-based psychomotor vigilance task to severe sleep loss. Behav. Res. Methods **40**(1), 347–352 (2008)
11. Basner, M., Dinges, D.F.: Maximizing sensitivity of the psychomotor vigilance test (PVT) to sleep loss. Sleep **34**(5), 581–591 (2005)
12. Matthews, R.W., Ferguson, S.A., Sargent, C., Zhou, X., Kosmadopoulos, A., Roach, G.D.:. Using interstimulus interval to maximise sensitivity of the psychomotor vigilance test to fatigue. Accident Anal. Prevent. **99**(PT.B), 406–410 (2017)

Using Virtual Reality to Measure Working Memory Performance and Evaluate the Effect of the Degree of Immersion on Working Memory Performance

Majdi Lusta, Cheryl Seals$^{(\boxtimes)}$, and Susan Teubner-Rhodes

Auburn University, Auburn, USA
{mal0087,sealscd,see0026}@auburn.edu

Abstract. Today Virtual Reality is widely researched and applied in non-conventional, informal educational settings, psychology, and memory-based applications. The popular definition of working memory is a system that works to provide temporary access to a select set of representations allowing for manipulation [1]. However, there is a consensus that this system has a limited capacity. This limitation of capacity explains the systematic drop in performance with an increase in task complexity. There is increasing attention to developing applications that measure working memory. However, these applications are relatively low validity. Working memory performance (WMP) is typically measured by computerizing a WMP task and calculating the participant's score, but these applications neglect aspects of the computer-user interface that may affect user's WMP (e.g., immersion, presence, satisfaction, and usability). To build a valid measuring system, all these conditions need to be considered, and their impact on participant WMP must be thoroughly understood. We plan to investigate the impact of the degree of immersion on working memory performance. First, we will evaluate the effect of the immersion on the user's feeling of being in the environment (i.e., presence), usability, and satisfaction, and then we will investigate the correlation between WMP and presence, usability, and satisfaction. This work will measure the WMP in levels of immersion that are provided through desktop VR (DVR), immersive VR (IVR), and immersive embodied VR (IEVR). We predict that these factors will impact participant WMP, with WMP increasing with higher levels of immersion.

Keywords: Virtual Reality (VR) · Working memory · Head-mounted display (HMD) · Immersive environments · User experience · N-back task · Automated operation span task (Ospan)

1 Introduction

Working memory (WM) is one of the most-studied cognitive psychology and cognitive neuroscience topics. Since Baddeley and Hitch introduced the concept

C. Stephanidis et al. (Eds.): HCII 2022, CCIS 1581, pp. 171–178, 2022.
https://doi.org/10.1007/978-3-031-06388-6_23

of working memory in [2], there has not been a unanimous agreement upon the definition of working memory. Working memory is vital for performing multifaceted tasks essential for day-to-day functioning. Tasks such as reading an article, calculating numbers, and comparing different features or prices of cars to decide the best to buy usually go through multiple steps, and results in each step need to be temporarily saved in memory to get the task done [2]. WM is the system that maintains task-relevant information while performing cognitive tasks. In different definitions, WM is a system that temporarily provides access to a set of tasks or relevant representations for manipulating [9]. The traditional definition of short memory describes it as a passive storage buffer, while the WM refers to a more active function with processing and storage units. [11]. It also serves as a place of process execution and result storage [8, 11]. Although there are some different ideas about how to conceptualize WM, there is a consensus that the WM has limited capacity, which means that only a limited amount of information can be ready for access at any given time. This capacity limitation accounts for the decline in cognitive performance with increasing task complexity [5].

Over recent years, the increased usage of VR increased the focus on user engagement and immersion. In this technology, the level of immersion is referred to as presence, which can be defined as the feeling of being there in the virtual environment [13]. Some research reported that the intensity of emotions that users experience is directly impacted by the level of presence [13]. Due to its ability to recall and intensify affective states, VR is an "affective medium" [13]. Many studies compare the impact of immersive virtual environments against non-immersive environments. For example, Coulter et al. [4] compared the effect of a fully immersive head-mounted display (HMD)-based learning and desktop-based learning in the field of medical education. The result showed that the HMD environment had a significant positive impact on knowledge gain among participants. In the field of airline safety, Chittaro et al. [3] found that learning outcomes of the HMD immersive environment were better than traditional card-based learning among passengers. Patel et al. [12] found that immersive virtual environments positively impacted participant knowledge gain in physical tasks in the same context. The researchers compared a fully immersive environment with a 2D video system that teaches participants some physical tasks. In contrast, Moreno et al. [10] found no performance difference with either using HMD or desktop-based applications for learning about botany. Juan et al. [7] also found no significant difference in immersive and desktop in their study in which students learned about the interior human body.

Researchers have been investigating the impact of immersion and presence in learning environments; the research showed that this impact is varied among environments. First, however, it is crucial to conduct empirical studies on the impact of immersion on working memory performance.

2 System Design

To induce different feelings of immersion, we varied the visual and auditory fidelity of the environment. As a result, the environment varies from an embodied and high level of visual and auditory fidelity to abstract and low fidelity (Fig. 1.0). The user will be immersed in all the environments through a virtual game that utilizes N-Back working memory tasks. In the immersive embodied VR environment (IEVR), the user's working memory performance will be scaled through a VR game that immerses the user into an embodied virtual environment. However, in the immersive non-embodied VR (IVR) environment, the game will immerse the user into a non-embodied virtual environment. Finally, in the desktop VR (DVR) environment, this game will immerse the user into a non-embodied 2D environment (Fig. 1).

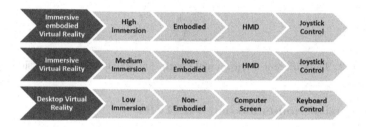

Fig. 1. The different environments with different levels of immersion.

2.1 Immersive Embodied VR (IEVR)

In this environment, we aim to measure the user's working memory performance through a VR game. This game will immerse the user into an embodied virtual game that utilizes the N-Back working memory task. The high-level flow diagram for the Immersive embodied VR Working Memory scale is presented in Fig. 1. The game familiarizes players with either little or no VR experience with the virtual environment through exploration and tutorials. However, the game provides the highest level of immersion, as it provides an immersive embodied virtual reality metaphor that includes sounds, avatar hands, and head-tracking ability. The player views a first-person perspective and controls through the controllers that come with the HMD. Furthermore, the player goes through three levels of the N-Back task, where the difficulty increases in each level. For performance assessment, each achievement is given upon completion of a quest. The user's working memory performance is based on his score (correct answer and response time) (Fig. 2).

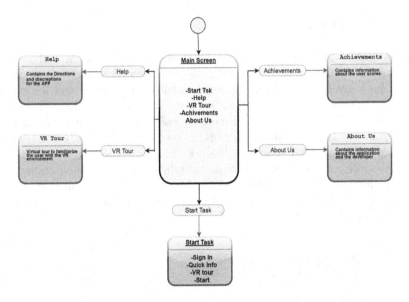

Fig. 2. The different environments with different levels of immersion.

2.2   Immersive Non-embodied VR (IVR)

This environment provides a lower level of immersion as the game will immerse the user into a non-embodied (no avatar hands) virtual reality game. This environment also provides a lower level of design fidelity (less realistic design). In addition, no sound is provided in this environment. Otherwise, it has the same features as the IEVR environment.

2.3   Desktop VR (DVR)

This environment provides the lowest level of immersion among the different environments. The environment immerses the user into traditional non-embodied 2D games that offer lower fidelity. The player goes through three levels of the N-Back task, where the difficulty increases in each level. After finishing the N-back task in all three environments, the participant will do the Aospan task in the DVR environment. These games follow the same approach as the previous environments for score calculation.

3   Methodology

This research uses the N-Back task (working memory task adopted from Hussey et al. 2017) [6] in different environments that create different levels of immersion and interaction and studies how these circumstances impact WMP. To assess the validity of the VR WMP measure, the Aospan task (working memory task adapted from Unsworth et al.) [14] will be used for comparison at the end of the experiment. Therefore, the participant will do the Aospan task in the DVR environment after finishing the N-back task in all other environments. We chose these two WMP tasks based on the following criteria:

1. They are transformable to the computer environment.
2. These tasks include different aspects of WM (transformation, supervision, and coordination).
3. Based on the literature review, these tasks are validated and reliable.

3.1 N-back Task

This task is adopted from Hussey et al. 2017 [6]. The participant will be asked to recognize the stimulus object that appeared "n" trials earlier. The trail starts with 500 ms of fixation followed by 500 ms of stimulus then 2 s of inter-stimulus interval. Next, the participant determines whether the displayed object is a "Target" or "Non-target" by pressing one of two keys. Each sequence of items consists of targets, lures, and fillers (6 targets, 6 lures, and 8+n fillers). Targets are the items repeated in the n position (i.e., that matches the object that occurred n trials back), while fillers are items that did not repeat. The lures, however, are objects that repeat in position n+1, n+2, n−1, and n−2. Non-targets include both lures and fillers. The user score is calculated based on the number of correct answers and the time to choose the correct answers.

3.2 Automated Operation Span

This task is adapted from Unsworth et al. 2005 [14]. This task consists of fifteen trials, each containing 3–7 items. Each item set consists of a math problem and a letter. First, participants solve a simple math equation as quickly as possible and decide whether the answer given on the next screen is true or false. After choosing an answer, a letter will appear on the screen for 800 ms. At the end of each trial, the participant is required to recall all the shown letters in the correct order. Accuracy feedback will be provided after each set. To ensure that participants were not biased in attempting to solve the math operations and remember the letters, they were encouraged to always keep their math accuracy at or above 85%. Participants are scored by the number of items recalled in the correct serial position.

3.3 Questionnaires

In each environment, the sense of being present will be evaluated using Witmer and Singer's presence questionnaire [15,16]. Here is a sample of the questionnaire questions:

1. How likely you are to use this system?
2. How involved were you in the virtual environment experience?

3. Were there moments during the virtual environment experience when you felt completely focused on the task or environment?

A questionnaire will be used to gather qualitative responses regarding participants' overall experience, system usability, and satisfaction. This data gives insight regarding the participant's satisfaction with the design and experience. For example, the participant will be asked questions such as:

1. How much were you able to control events?
2. What would you change in this system?
3. Do you think this immersive experience would help you learn better?

3.4   The Experiment

The participant will do the N-back in three different environments: DVR, IVR, and IEVR. The order will be counterbalanced across participants. The task begins with a block of 3-back sequences, followed immediately by a block of 4-back and 5-back sequences, all with lures in positions $n + 1$, $n + 2$, $n-1$, and $n-2$. Following each sequence, the subject will be provided with the accuracy and the average response time feedback. The participant will be provided with practice before the first block in each environment. After the participant has done the N-back task in the three different environments, they will be given a questionnaire (Witmer and Singer's presence questionnaire [15, 16], and usability and satisfaction questionnaire). They will then do the Aospan task in the DVR environment. In this stage, score feedback will be provided. However, no questionnaire will be given after this task. Data will be gathered after each stage. The experiment is designed as follows:

1. The participant does the N-back WMP task in DVR, IVR, and EIVR environments in counter-balanced order.
2. Recording the score considering the number of correct answers, the number of wrong answers, and reaction time.
3. The exit survey evaluates the participant experience in terms of presence, usability, and satisfaction in each environment.
4. The participant does the Aospan WMP task in DVR environment.
5. Recording the score of the Aospan task.

4   The Expected Results

In this study, we expect that increasing the level of immersion increases the feeling of being in the virtual environment (presence). In addition, a good design and a higher level of immersion improve usability and user satisfaction. We predict that increasing the level of presence, satisfaction, and usability will lead to higher WMP. As a result, the level of immersion that the test environment provides can significantly affect the user's WMP.

5   Conclusion

This research investigates the impact of immersion on a users' feeling of presence and user satisfaction when performing a working memory task. The foundational works were prior studies of human working memory capacity using the N-back task methodology. Existing computer applications that measure WM capacity neglect conditions that may affect performance, such as immersion, presence, satisfaction, and usability. As such, these applications may compromise the experimental validity of the WMP estimate. This project extends former research studies and develops a more accurate measuring system that incorporates other necessary measures (e.g., immersion, presence, satisfaction, and usability) to consider dimensions that affect human conditions and user experience. Addressing these considerations and their impact on participant WMP will provide greater insight into working memory and the effects of virtual reality. This work discusses the application's design and development plan to measure the WMP in various levels of immersion, and we predict that these factors will dramatically influence and impact participant WMP.

References

1. Baddeley, A.: Working memory. Science **255**(5044), 556–559 (1992)
2. Baddeley, A.D., Hitch, G.: Working memory. In: Psychology of Learning and Motivation, vol. 8, pp. 47–89. Elsevier (1974)
3. Chittaro, L., Buttussi, F.: Assessing knowledge retention of an immersive serious game vs. a traditional education method in aviation safety. IEEE Trans. Visual. Comput. Graph. **21**(4), 529–538 (2015)
4. Coulter, R., Saland, L., Caudell, T., Goldsmith, T.E., Alverson, D.: The effect of degree of immersion upon learning performance in virtual reality simulations for medical education. InMed. Meets Virtual Real. **15**, 155 (2007)
5. Halford, G.S., Wilson, W.H., Phillips, S.: Processing capacity defined by relational complexity: Implications for comparative, developmental, and cognitive psychology. Behav. Brain Sci. **21**(6), 803–831 (1998)
6. Hussey, E.K., Harbison, J., Teubner-Rhodes, S.E., Mishler, A., Velnoskey, K., Novick, J.M.: Memory and language improvements following cognitive control training. J. Exp. Psychol. Learn. Mem. Cogn. **43**(1), 23 (2017)
7. Juan, C., Beatrice, F., Cano, J.: An augmented reality system for learning the interior of the human body. In: 2008 Eighth IEEE International Conference on Advanced Learning Technologies, pp. 186–188. IEEE (2008)
8. LaBerge, D., Samuels, S.J.: Toward a theory of automatic information processing in reading. Cogn. Psychol. **6**(2), 293–323 (1974)
9. Miyake, A., Shah, P.: Models of Working Memory: Mechanisms of Active Maintenance and Executive Control. Cambridge University Press, Cambridge (1999)
10. Moreno, R., Mayer, R.E.: Learning science in virtual reality multimedia environments: role of methods and media. J. Educ. Psychol. **94**(3), 598 (2002)
11. Newell, A.: Production systems: models of control structures. In: Visual Information Processing, pp. 463–526. Elsevier (1973)
12. Patel, K., Bailenson, J.N., Hack-Jung, S., Diankov, R., Bajcsy, R.: The effects of fully immersive virtual reality on the learning of physical tasks. In: Proceedings of the 9th Annual International Workshop on Presence, Ohio, USA, pp. 87–94 (2006)

13. Riva, G., et al.: Affective interactions using virtual reality: the link between presence and emotions. CyberPsychol. Behav. **10**(1), 45–56 (2007)
14. Unsworth, N., Heitz, R.P., Schrock, J.C., Engle, R.W.: An automated version of the operation span task. Behav. Res. Methods **37**(3), 498–505 (2005)
15. Witmer, B.G., Jerome, C.J., Singer, M.J.: The factor structure of the presence questionnaire. Presence Teleoper. Virtual Environ. **14**(3), 298–312 (2005)
16. Witmer, B.G., Singer, M.J.: Measuring presence in virtual environments: a presence questionnaire. Presence **7**(3), 225–240 (1998)

Modern Human Brain Neuroimaging Research: Analytical Assessment and Neurophysiological Mechanisms

Sergey Lytaev[1,2]([✉]) [iD]

[1] St. Petersburg State Pediatric Medical University, St. Petersburg 194100, Russia
physiology@gpmu.org
[2] St. Petersburg Federal Research Center of the Russian Academy
of Sciences, St. Petersburg 199178, Russia

Abstract. This article aims at a comparative analysis of modern methods of neuroimaging for studying cognitive processes in clinical practice and psychophysiology, taking into account the original experience and data – event-related potentials (ERP), EEG, functional magnetic resonance imaging (fMRI) and positron emission tomography (PET). The main feature of neurophysiological diagnostics is time – spatial resolution. As a rule, these are fractions of a second (ERP), seconds (EEG), minutes (fMRI). Three groups of traditional neurophysiological research methods are used – EEG, fMRI and ERP based on the P300 component. The advantages of EEG include high temporal resolution, high gamma activity in the right temporal lobe, as an indicator of the mechanism of binding conscious information. The advantages of fMRI are high spatial resolution, increased blood flow in the right temporal lobe, hippocampus, striatum, medial prefrontal cortex, and dopamine region, nuclei adjacent to the ventral region. ERPs to some extent combine the advantages of EEG and fMRI. PET reflects the state of the brain over several days, which is associated with the life cycle of radioactive isotopes. The level of research corresponds to the entire brain. Microelectrodes, maps allow exploring individual neurons and nerve centers – nuclei.

Keywords: Event-related potentials · Brain computer interface · Positron emission tomography · fMRI

1 Introduction

What place among the methods of brain mapping do the approaches of clinical neurophysiology and applied psychophysiology take? If we represent on the abscissa the level of research from the whole brain to molecules, and along the ordinate, the time from milliseconds to several years, one can trace the inclusion of various neurophysiological mechanisms and their importance in the realization of mental functions (see Fig. 1). The main feature of neurophysiological diagnostics is time – spatial resolution. As a rule, these are fractions of a second (ERP), seconds (EEG, MEG), minutes (fMRI). Only positron emission tomography reflects the state of the brain over several days, which is

C. Stephanidis et al. (Eds.): HCII 2022, CCIS 1581, pp. 179–185, 2022.
https://doi.org/10.1007/978-3-031-06388-6_24

associated with the life cycle of radioactive isotopes. The level of research corresponds to the entire brain. Microelectrodes, maps allow exploring individual neurons and nerve centers – nuclei [8, 15, 22].

Research in time	Research level				
	Brain	**Mapping**	**Layers/ Nuclei**	**Cells**	**Synapses**
Millisec/ sec	EEG, ERPs, MEG, ECoG		Neural activity		Biophysics
Sec/ hours	fMRI, USDG, NIRS, EDA		Vascular video microscopy		
Days	PET-scan		Angiography		Molecular biology
Years	CT, MRI				

Fig. 1. Comparative characteristics of neuroimaging methods (original).

2   Brain Evoked Potentials. Event-Related Potentials

In many psychophysiological studies carried out over the past 2–3 decades in various laboratories around the world, and during neurosurgical operations, the nature of the relationship between physiological and psychological indicators of perception had much in common. Early sensory evoked potentials (EP) waves (with PL up to 100 ms) show a high correlation with the indicator of sensory sensitivity, and the late ones, including the P300 wave, with the indicator of the decision criterion. Intermediate EP components with a PL of 100–200 ms revealed a double correlation – both with the sensitivity index and the decision criterion [10, 13].

Informative data on the essence of mental processes that make up the content of the third stage of perception were obtained in studies devoted to the analysis of the functional meaning and informational significance of the wave P300, which shows the highest correlation with the decision-making criterion. It should be said that over the past 40 years a phenomenon, and even a paradigm "P300", has formed in the literature, combining not one positive oscillation with a peak latency of 300 ms, but a whole complex of waves following this period of time [4, 9, 12, 14, 19].

Last two decades practical studies of the P300 ERP component have been associated with brain-computer interface (BCI) systems, which, in addition to solving physiological and psychological problems, have medical and social significance. Modern BCI systems can use a number of electrophysiological signals – visual EPs, slow cortical potentials, alpha and beta EEG rhythm, and the P300 component of evoked potentials [9]. The P300 has a number of interesting qualities that aid in the implementation of such systems. First, the wave is constantly detected and triggered in response to precise stimuli. And secondly, the signal to register the P300 can be triggered in almost all subjects with slight differences in measurement methods, which can help simplify the interface design and improve usability [11, 16, 17].

The bioelectrical activity of the brain is converted into an electrical signal during the signal acquisition phase [9]. Then the target user's desire is extracted from the signal. For this, various electrophysiological characteristics can be used. Algorithms developed specifically for BCIs interpret the desired action and send it to an output device, which can be a display with letters or targets (P_{300} speller, alphabet), a wheelchair or neuroprosthesis (for example, a robot arm) [14]. Feedback helps maintain and improve the accuracy and speed of communication/action. Finally, the P_{300} component of the evoked potentials can be used as control signals for the BCI. In a number of studies, P_{300} BCI systems have been tested in people with disabilities [9, 14].

Persons with disabilities can use the P300-based BCI for communication [9, 14]. The P300 spelling system (speller) is proposed, which allows subjects to transmit a sequence of letters to a computer. To create a "weird" oddball paradigm, a 6×6 matrix containing letters of the alphabet and numbers is displayed on the computer screen. A person can choose a specific sign by focusing attention on it. The BCI can also be used to drive a wheelchair. With the P300 BCI system, the user can select a destination in the menu by counting the number of flashes of the destination. Further, the wheelchair moves to the selected and desired destination along a predetermined path.

In addition to the wheelchair, an important application for people with severe motor impairments is the control of neuroprosthetic devices. BCIs can be used to control limb movements, for example, a robotic arm. It has been shown that BCIs based on the activity of cortical neurons are able to control three-dimensional movements of a robot arm [14]. In the future, P300-based BCI systems are being considered for controlling combat information posts and computer virtual games.

3 Functional Magnetic Resonance Imaging

One of the most interesting technologies of modern magnetic resonance imaging, fMRI, was developed in the early 1990s and was first used in human studies [16, 20]. fMRI is able to detect changes in blood flow volume and blood oxygen saturation level, morphologically and functionally associated with the identification of working neural networks, the formation of new and reconstruction of pre-existing neural ensembles (NE). The contrasting mechanism is based on the difference in the magnetic properties of oxyhemoglobin, which carries oxygen, and deoxyhemoglobin, which is formed at the places of its consumption. During the formation of an active NE in the first seconds, local energy consumption leads to an increase in the concentration of paramagnetic deoxyhemoglobin; then follows the reaction of the vascular system, which consists in increasing the regional blood supply and blood supply to the brain tissues (by regulating the volume and speed of blood flow). This leads to a sharp increase in the flow of blood saturated with diamagnetic oxyhemoglobin.

The sensitivity of fMRI to the physiological processes described above is due to the strong influence of the concentration of paramagnetic substances on the rate of magnetic relaxation of water protons. In the presence of a paramagnet, the rate of transverse relaxation T2* increases, which causes a decrease in the magnetic resonance signal and, conversely, a decrease in the level of deoxyhemoglobin leads to an increase in the signal [7, 17, 18].

Standard fMRI, where the physiological content is cognitive and sensorimotor processes, consists of several blocks, each of which includes a resting phase and an activation phase. The periods of activation and rest should not be too short, since the delay time of the vascular response is measured in several seconds, so the recommended duration of each phase is 20–30 s. The optimal sensitivity of the method is achieved by choosing such a phase duration at which the signal (BOLD) is in a state of dynamic equilibrium [15, 20].

Functional MRI can solve two classes of problems. Firstly, related to the measurement of hemodynamic response function (HRF) and, secondly, with the localization of the response. In the first case, the HRF is measured as a set of harmonic functions with a possible subsequent Fourier transform, while in the second case, the canonical form of the HRF is used, which empirically corresponds to most of the experimental data. The canonical HRF model is best applied in cases where it is necessary to determine when, where and in what sequence the evoked neuronal activity occurred. It may include delay and dispersion as degrees of freedom, allowing adaptation to regional or group characteristics [15, 20].

4 Positron Emission Tomography

The degree of preservation of human cognitive functions ranges from normal to profound disorders. Differential diagnosis of the causes of such disorders often causes difficulties in clinical practice. This was the basis for increasing neuroimaging research in this area. As is known, the most common causes of cognitive disorders are neurodegenerative disorders. Among the latter, Alzheimer's and Parkinson's diseases are the most common, accompanied by significant changes in brain metabolism with devastating neurological, clinical, as well as economic and social consequences. Such changes are visible using positron emission tomography (PET) already at the earliest stages [1–3, 5, 6].

Most often PET studies of the brain in neurodegenerative diseases were performed using [18F] fluorodeoxyglucose (FDG), an imaging radiopharmaceutical. Such data demonstrate diagnostic and prognostic value in assessing cognitive impairment and differential diagnosis of primary neurodegenerative disorders with different etiologies of changes in cognitive functions [5, 6, 8, 12, 21].

The intercortical interaction of the associative (frontal and parietal) parts of the brain, based on the analysis of PET data on glucose metabolism, was assessed by the activity of the line of cognitive systems. Four factor's systems were established: factor 1 – dorsal system of attention (voluntary attention), factor 2 – ventral system of attention (involuntary attention), factor 3 – system of the state of operational rest, and factor 4 - visual system in the norm and in patients with cognitive impairments of varying severity and pathology genesis were studied [12].

It has been established that the factor structure of regional levels of glucose metabolism in individuals with different nosologies, but without cognitive impairment, is stable in terms of the composition of factors. These factors in accordance with the affiliation of the areas of the brain experiencing the greatest load on the factor to one or another neuroanatomical system are explained.

The 1st factor includes the 8, 6 and 7 fields of Brodmann (the precentral cortex of the frontal lobes and the upper half of the parietal lobes of both cerebral hemispheres). The

2nd factor includes 46 and 40, 39 of Brodmann fields (the anterior third of the convexital part of the frontal lobes and the lower half of the parietal lobes). The 3rd factor includes the 23, 36, 29 and 30 Brodmann fields (the posterior cingulate gyrus). The 4th factor is the 17th Brodmann field (primary visual cortex).

Factor analysis found that in patients with Parkinson's disease without the syndrome of executive dysfunction, a factor structure with all 4 factors is formed. The same factor structure was recorded in patients of the control group and in healthy young patients. The syndrome of impaired executive functions and in the group of patients with vascular dementia is also accompanied by reorganization of the ventral and dorsal attention systems, as well as the system of operational rest (see Fig. 2) [12].

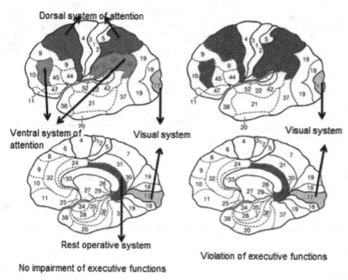

Fig. 2. Factor structure of self-organizing work of functional neuroanatomical systems for patients without impaired executive functions (left) and with syndrome of impaired executive functions, right (original).

5   Conclusion

In cognitive psychology, neurology, and psychiatry, the following areas and methods of studying perception are considered relevant (an example, the phenomenon of insight) (see Fig. 3). Three groups of traditional neurophysiological research methods are used - EEG, fMRI and ERP based on the P300 component. The advantages of EEG include high temporal resolution, high gamma activity in the right temporal lobe, as an indicator of the mechanism of binding conscious information, and the time interval of the insight effect (1310–560 ms) in terms of making an analytical decision. The advantages of fMRI are high spatial resolution, increased blood flow in the right temporal lobe, hippocampus (as a pleasure response), striatum, medial prefrontal cortex, and dopamine region, nuclei adjacent to the ventral region. ERPs to some extent combine the advantages of EEG and fMRI. ERPs have high spatial and temporal resolution, allow you to get closer to the problem of insight scaling. These results allow you to evaluate internal and external insight.

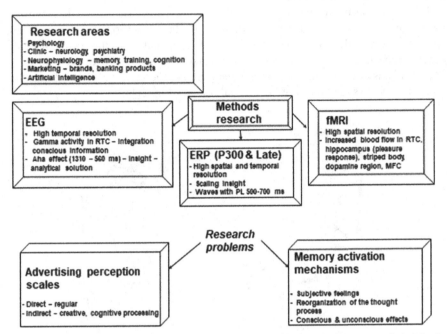

Fig. 3. The general directions, methods and problems of perception (insight) research (original).

References

1. Bridges, R.L., Cho, C.S., Beck, M.R., Gessner, B.D., Tower, S.S.: F-18 FDG PET brain imaging in symptomatic arthroprosthetic cobaltism. Eur. J. Nucl. Med. Mol. Imaging **47**(8), 1961–1970 (2019). https://doi.org/10.1007/s00259-019-04648-2
2. Buchert, R., Buhmann, C., Apostolova, I., Meyer, P.T., Gallinat, J.: Nuclear imaging in the diagnosis of clinically uncertain parkinsonian syndromes. Dtsch Arztebl Int. **116**, 747–754 (2019)
3. Campoy, A.-D.T., et al.: [18F] Nifene PET/CT imaging in mice: improved methods and preliminary studies of α4β2* Nicotinic Acetylcholinergic receptors in transgenic A53T mouse model of α-synucleinopathy and post-mortem human Parkinson's Disease. Molecules **26**, 7360 (2021)
4. Danek, A.H., Wiley, J.: What causes the insight memory advantage? Cognition **205**, 1–16 (2020)
5. Gan, J., et al.: Clinical characteristics of Lewy body dementia in Chinese memory clinics. BMC Neurol. **21**, 144 (2021)
6. Kane, J.P.M., et al.: Clinical prevalence of Lewy body dementia. Alzheimers Res. Ther. **10**, 19 (2018)
7. Kizilirmak, J.M., et al.: Learning of novel semantic relationships via sudden comprehension is associated with a hippocampus-independent network. Conscious. Cogn. **69**, 113–132 (2019)

8. Khil'ko, V., et al.: The topographic mapping of evoked bioelectrical activity and other methods for the functional neural visualization of the brain. Vestn. Ross. Akad. Med. Nauk **3**, 36–41 (1993)

9. Levi-Aharoni, H., Shriki, O., Tishby, N.: Surprise response as a probe for compressed memory states. PLoS Comput. Biol. **16**, e1007065 (2020)

10. Lytaev, S.A., Shostak, V.I.: The significance of emotional processes in man in the mechanisms of analyzing the effect of varying contrast stimulation. Zhurnal Vysshei Nervnoi Deyatelnosti Imeni I.P. Pavlova. **43**(6), 1067–1074 (1993)

11. Lytaev, S., Aleksandrov, M., Ulitin, A.: Psychophysiological and intraoperative AEPs and SEPs monitoring for perception, attention and cognition. Commun. Comp. Inf. Sci. **713**, 229–236 (2017)

12. Lytaev, S., Aleksandrov, M., Popovich, T., Lytaev, M.: Auditory evoked potentials and PET-scan: early and late mechanisms of selective attention. Adv. Intell. Syst. Comput. **775**, 169–178 (2019)

13. Lytaev, S., Aleksandrov, M., Lytaev, M.: Estimation of emotional processes in regulation of the structural afferentation of varying contrast by means of visual evoked potentials. Adv. Intell. Syst. Comput. **953**, 288–298 (2020)

14. Lytaev, S., Vatamaniuk, I.: Physiological and medico-social research trends of the wave P300 and more late components of visual event-related potentials. Brain Sci. **11**, 125 (2021)

15. Lytaev, S.: Modern neurophysiological research of the human brain in clinic and psychophysiology. In: Rojas, I., Castillo-Secilla, D., Herrera, L.J., Pomares, H. (eds.) BIOMESIP 2021. LNCS, vol. 12940, pp. 231–241. Springer, Cham (2021). https://doi.org/10.1007/978-3-030-88163-4_21

16. Oh, Y., et al.: An insight-related neural reward signal. Neuroimage **214**, 1–15 (2020)

17. Shen, W., et al.: Quantifying the roles of conscious and unconscious processing in insight-related memory effectiveness within standard and creative advertising. Psychol. Res. (2021). PMID: 34417868

18. Simola, J., Kuisma, J., Kaakinen, J.K.: Attention, memory and preference for direct and indirect print advertisements. J. Bus. Res. **111**, 249–261 (2020)

19. Salvi, C., et al.: Oculometric signature of switch into awareness? Pupil size predicts sudden insight whereas microsaccades predict problem solving via analysis. Neuroimage **116933**, 1–9 (2020)

20. Shtark, M.B., Korostishevskaya, A.M., Resakova, M.V., Savelov, A.A.: Functional magnetic resonanse imaging and neuroscience. Usp. Fiziol. Nauk **43**(1), 3–29 (2012)

21. Szeto, J.Y.Y., et al.: Dementia in long-term Parkinson's disease patients: a multicentre retrospective study. NPJ Parkinson's Dis. **6**, 2 (2020)

22. White, T.L., Gonsalves, M.A.: Dignity neuroscience: universal rights are rooted in human brain science. Ann. NY Acad. Sci. **1505**(1), 40–54 (2021)

Reaction Times and Performance Variability in Touch and Desktop Users During a Stroop Task

Gianluca Merlo$^{(\boxtimes)}$ (iD), Luna Jaforte (iD), and Davide Taibi (iD)

Istituto per le Tecnologie Didattiche, Consiglio Nazionale delle Ricerche, 90146 Palermo, PA, Italy
gianluca.merlo@itd.cnr.it

Abstract. Reaction times (RTs) are a measure of the time elapsed between the sensory stimulation and the occurrence of a response. It depends upon many factors. This paper focuses on one of the possible sources of variability introduced by the device used to gather RTs data and compares RTs performance between subjects who completed a Stroop task through desktop or mobile devices. The research hypothesizes that mobile devices users' (a) have faster RTs in incongruent trials than the desktop ones, (b) have a lower error rate, and (c) perceive the task easier. The results showed significant differences in RTs, error rate, and perception of the difficulty of the task between devices but only the last two hypotheses are supported by data. Subjects under 40 years achieved a lower error rate than older people in the incongruent and neutral trials. Moreover, participants always perceived the task easier when they complete it through mobile devices. Some implications of the results are discussed, and a second ongoing within-subjects study is described.

Keywords: Reaction time · Mobile device · Stroop task

1 Introduction

Reaction times (RTs) have been used as a psychological task since the mid-19th century [1] and it is also called response time or response latency. RTs are a simple, and presumably the most widely used, measure of behavioral response in time units (usually in milliseconds), from a presentation of a given task to its completion. There are two typical and functional procedures to estimate response latency: choice reaction time and simple reaction time. The first one is more complicated because it requires the subject to make the appropriate response to one of some stimuli. The second one concerns making a response as fast as possible in reaction to a single stimulus [1].

According to Kosinski [2], many factors impact RTs in addition to the type of stimulus, the type of RT experiment, and stimulus intensity. For example, age, gender, arousal, left/right hand, direct/peripheral vision [2, 3] have a direct influence on RTs.

Previous studies showed that RT latencies and variability increase and become more variable with age [4–9]. RTs tend to slow down with age starting from the 20s for choice

© The Author(s), under exclusive license to Springer Nature Switzerland AG 2022
C. Stephanidis et al. (Eds.): HCII 2022, CCIS 1581, pp. 186–193, 2022.
https://doi.org/10.1007/978-3-031-06388-6_25

tasks and 30s for simple [10] but, in general, the decline accelerates after the age of about 70 [11, 12]. Rabbitt, Osman, Moore, & Stollery [13] proposed that the increase in mean RTs with age is a result of increasing variability, and variability is, therefore, a more important component of cognitive aging.

The present research hypothesizes that another possible source of variability is introduced by the device used to gather RTs data. Many studies revealed that touch devices are faster [14] and more natural and convenient [15] than desktop computers. Moreover, users usually prefer touch-input devices because of a coordination factor. Touch input implicates eyes-hand direct coordination, unlike mouse which requires a greater effort of coordination: "the input is also the output device" [16]. The ordinary use of touchscreen is also associated with the cortical reorganization of the fingertips in the somatosensory cortex [17].

According to the above-mentioned theoretical background, this paper describes a research aimed to compare RTs performance between subjects who completed a Stroop task [18], one of the most widely used measures of cognitive functioning [19], through desktop or mobile devices. The Stroop task requires participants to name the color of ink in which a color name is printed while ignoring the written word. Indicating the color with which the congruent color-word stimuli were written takes less time than indicating the color of the incongruent color-word stimuli. Increased RTs during incongruent trials have been attributed to the interfering effects of the printed color name on the different colored ink.

The study hypothesizes that mobile devices users' (a) have faster RTs in incongruent trials than the desktop ones, (b) have a lower error rate, and, (c) perceive the task easier.

2   Methods

Data were collected from June 2020 to June 2021. Participants (general population aged 18 years or older) were contacted through the authors' network and posts on the most popular social networks. The compilation instructions informed the participants that the answers were anonymous and that there were no right or wrong answers. Informed consent was obtained from all subjects involved in the study. A privacy policy at the beginning of the questionnaire described to the participants the purposes and methods of treatment operated by the data controller on the personal data collected. The research was submitted to the ethics committee of the University Polyclinic "Paolo Giaccone" of Palermo and obtained a favorable opinion for its development.

2.1   Participants

The full sample comprised 397 subjects, with an overall mean of 41.24 years (SD = 11.85). Their age ranged from 18 to 74 years. Among all participants, 304 (76.57%) were female, 92 (23.17%) were male, and 1 (0.25%) other.

68.26% of the subject participated in the research through a mobile phone, while the rest (31.74%) did it through a desktop computer. A Wilcoxon signed-rank test showed that these groups did not differ in age ($Z = 19,062.50$, $p = 0.06$) or the proportion of male and female X^2 (2, N = 397) = 4.37, p = 0.10.

2.2 Stroop Task

A web-based computerized version of the Stroop color-naming task has been developed for the study. The Stroop task was coded using HTML5 and JavaScript programming. In particular, the web-based Stroop Task implemented the High-Resolution Time API that provides the time in sub-millisecond resolution, such that it is not subject to system clock skew or adjustments [20]. In order to make the Stroop Task usable from both desktop computers and mobile devices, the Bootstrap responsive frontend framework [21] has been used to design the task templates.

The Stroop Task included 21 training trials and 28 experimental trials for each type: congruent, incongruent, and neutral (displayed as a colored horizontal rectangle). Participants were instructed to focus their attention on a fixation cross at the center of the screen. Then, after 1000 ms, stimuli were presented against a white background. For all trial types, participants responded by choosing the color (red, green, blue, or yellow) of the stimulus by typing on the keyboard the letter corresponding to the color or touching a box matching the color displayed on the screen. Letters (only for desktop computers) and colors were displayed in a bar at the bottom of the screen (Fig. 1).

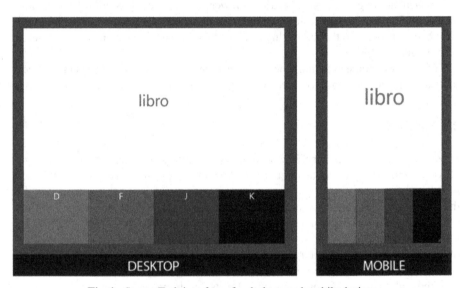

Fig. 1. Stroop Task interfaces for desktop and mobile devices

At the end of the Stroop task, a question about the difficulty was asked to participants with a response mode from 0 to 100.

2.3 Data Analysis

Starting from the results obtained to the Stroop task, mean reaction time and error rates for congruent, incongruent, and neutral trial types were calculated. The training trials are not included in the analysis. For statistical analyses, a logarithm transformation was applied to data to better approximate a normal distribution. The dependent variables of the study were the reaction time latency, the error rate, and, according to the work of Cain and colleagues [22], indexes of interference (mean RTs of incongruent trials - mean RTs of neutral trials) and facilitation (mean RTs neutral trials - mean RTs congruent trials). While the interference index refers to the additional time needed to respond when reading the word interferes with responding to the color, the facilitation index is a measure of the increased speed of reaction when color and word matched. The independent variables used in the statistical models were: age group (18–40, >40), device (desktop, mobile), and trial typology (congruent, incongruent, neutral). The age groups were chosen applying a median split transformation and this is consistent with the research of Deary and Der [6] who demonstrated that RTs tend to slow down with age 30s for simple tasks and that intraindividual variability in choice reaction time increases steadily from the mid-30s to the mid-60s. The post hoc comparisons showing significant effects related to the variability of RTs related to age and task are not reported because they are well documented in the literature. The interquartile range method was applied to detect and remove the outliers. All statistical analyses were performed with R software.

3   Results

3.1   Latency and Task Per Age Group

The distribution of response time violated both the assumption of normality and homogeneity of variances. A Shapiro-Wilk test was performed and showed that the distribution of response times departed significantly from normality ($W = 1.00$, p-value < 0.01). To analyze data according to a Task(3) × Age group (2) × Device (2) design, first, the Aligned Rank Transform (ART) procedure [23–25] was applied and then a factorial ANOVA based on the aligned-and-ranked responses was calculated. The ART techniques for analysis of variance are considered a powerful and robust nonparametric alternative when the assumption of a normal error distribution is violated [26]. The ART procedure and the post hoc pairwise comparisons were calculated with the support of the ARTool R package [27, 28]. The three-way interaction between age, task, and device was not significant, ($F_2 = 0.06$, p > 0.05). A significant interaction between the age group and the device used was found ($F_1 = 37.31$, p < 0.001). Significant main effect on reaction times for age group ($F_1 = 144.81$, p < 0.001), task ($F_2 = 39.60$, p < 0.001), and the device used to complete the Stroop task ($F_1 = 1.94$, p < 0.05) were found. The ART-C post hoc pairwise comparisons, corrected with Holm's sequential Bonferroni procedure, indicates that users under 40 years were faster in incongruent tasks when they completed the Stroop task via desktop devices (p < 0.001).

3.2   Error Rate and Task Per Age Group

The error rate distribution significantly deviates from a normal distribution ($W = 0.76$, p-value < 0.01). Applying the already mentioned ART procedure, a Task (3) × Age group (2) × Device (2) design was analyzed through a factorial ANOVA. A three-way interaction was identified between task, age group, and device ($F_2 = 3.30$, p < 0.05).

Statistically significant interactions between task and device used ($F_2 = 11.30$, p < 0.001), and age group and task ($F_2 = 11.86$, p < 0.001) were found. Simple main effects analysis showed that age group ($F_1 = 24.75$, p < 0.001), task ($F_2 = 43.44$, p < 0.001), and the device used have a statistically significant effect on error rate ($F_1 = 30.27$, p < 0.001). Post hoc pairwise comparisons, applied with the support of the ART-C align-and-rank procedure and corrected with the Holm method, revealed that subjects under 40 years have a lower error rate in the incongruent (p < 0.001) and neutral (p < 0.01) trials when they did the Stroop task from mobile.

3.3 Interference and Facilitation Indexes

Facilitation and interference indexes violated the assumption of normality ($W = 0.96$, p-value < 0.01; $W = 0.98$, p-value < 0.01). As a consequence, the ART procedure was applied to the analyzed variables. A two-way ANOVA revealed that there was not a statistically significant interaction between age group and device both for facilitation ($F_1 = 0.96$, p > 0.05) and interference ($F_1 = 0.09$, p > 0.05) indexes. Simple main effects analysis showed that the device used did have a statistically significant effect on both facilitation ($F_1 = 5.83$, p < 0.05) and interference indexes ($F_1 = 16.41$, p < 0.001). The age group had a significant main effect only on the interference index ($F_1 = 5.91$, p < 0.05). Post hoc pairwise comparisons, applied with the support of the ART-C align-and-rank procedure and corrected with the Holm method, revealed that the index of interference is greater in mobile device users in both age groups (p < 0.05).

3.4 Difficulty

The perceived difficulty distribution is positively skewed ($W = 0.94$, p-value < 0.01). After having applied the ART procedure on the analyzed variables, the interaction between the device used and age group was not significant ($F_1 = 2.21$, p > 0.05) but a simple main effect of the device used was found ($F_1 = 25.36$, p < 0.001). Post hoc pairwise comparisons revealed that mobile users perceived the task easier in both the analyzed age groups.

4 Conclusion

The study explored the variability of reaction times, error rates, and perception of difficulty comparing users who performed a Stroop task via desktop or mobile devices. The authors' hypotheses were only partially supported by the data. Although not always statistically significant, young users (<40 years) tend to be faster from desktop computers than from mobile devices, especially in incongruent tasks. This tendency is identifiable, also, in the interference index, higher in the just mentioned group of users. This result needs further investigation, and, for this reason, a second within-subject study is in progress. The within-subjects design has been chosen to expose every subject to both the mobile and desktop conditions and to control the possible bias introduced by the JavaScript library developed for the data gathering. Secondly, the second study is collecting data about the daily use and experience that subjects have with the devices.

Familiarity and ability to use the device probably influence the speed and accuracy of the task. The finding that young people are slower during incongruent tasks with mobile devices could also be due to diminished attentional capacity among heavy users of mobile devices [29]. For example, Leiva and colleagues reported that when the user's thoughts drift toward a smartphone-related activity, task completion in one app can be delayed by up to 400% when these endogenous interruptions appear [30].

In the study presented in this paper, as predicted, users made fewer errors when they completed the task via mobile devices. Age, task typology, and the device used affect the number of errors made during the color naming tasks. In particular, subjects under 40 years showed a significantly lower error rate in the incongruent and neutral trials when they did the Stroop task from mobile. A clear difference is also found in the perception of the task difficulty: users perceived the task easier when completed through mobile devices. The perception that tasks based on reaction times are easier when performed from mobile devices may increase their uptake as a cognitive screening tool for older people. RTs are widely used to evaluate cognitive performance in general [31] and even life expectancy [10], and intraindividual variability of reaction times in cognitive aging is a predictor of dementia [32] and chronic fatigue syndrome [33].

Finally, the second study will have to try to balance the proportion of males and females which is unbalanced in the present study due to convenience sampling.

References

1. Deary, I.J., Liewald, D., Nissan, J.: A free, easy-to-use, computer-based simple and four-choice reaction time programme: the deary-liewald reaction time task. Behav. Res. Methods **43**, 258–268 (2011)
2. Kosinski, R.J.: A literature review on reaction time. Clemson Univ. **10**, 337–344 (2008)
3. Chundakal, D., Kulkarni, P., Chavan, S., Prabhakar, R.: Effect of music therapy and frenkel exercise on reaction time in geriatric population-a comparative study. Ed. Adv Board. **15**, 17 (2021)
4. Lindenberger, U., Mayr, U., Kliegl, R.: Speed and intelligence in old age. Psychol. Aging **8**, 207 (1993)
5. Verhaeghen, P., Salthouse, T.A.: Meta-analyses of age–cognition relations in adulthood: estimates of linear and nonlinear age effects and structural models. Psychol. Bull. **122**, 231 (1997)
6. Ratcliff, R., Thapar, A., McKoon, G.: The effects of aging on reaction time in a signal detection task. Psychol. Aging **16**, 323 (2001)
7. Jevas, S., Yan, J.H.: The effect of aging on cognitive function: a preliminary quantitative review. Res. Q. Exerc. Sport **72**, 38–40 (2001)
8. Hultsch, D.F., MacDonald, S.W., Dixon, R.A.: Variability in reaction time performance of younger and older adults. J. Gerontol. B Psychol. Sci. Soc. Sci. **57**, P101–P115 (2002)
9. Der, G., Deary, I.J.: Age and sex differences in reaction time in adulthood: results from the United Kingdom health and lifestyle survey. Psychol. Aging **21**, 62 (2006)
10. Deary, I.J., Der, G.: Reaction time, age, and cognitive ability: longitudinal findings from age 16 to 63 years in representative population samples. Aging Neuropsychol. Cogn. **12**, 187–215 (2005)
11. Era, P., Sainio, P., Koskinen, S., Ohlgren, J., Härkänen, T., Aromaa, A.: Psychomotor speed in a random sample of 7979 subjects aged 30 years and over. Aging Clin. Exp. Res. **23**(2), 135–144 (2011). https://doi.org/10.1007/BF03351077

12. Pierson, W.R., Montoye, H.J.: Movement time, reaction time and age. J. Gerontol. **13**, 418–421 (1958)
13. Rabbitt, P., Osman, P., Moore, B., Stollery, B.: There are stable individual differences in performance variability, both from moment to moment and from day to day. Q. J. Exp. Psychol. Sect. A. **54**, 981–1003 (2001)
14. Zabramski, S., Shrestha, S., Stuerzlinger, W.: Easy vs. tricky: the shape effect in tracing, selecting, and steering with mouse, stylus, and touch. In: Proceedings of International Conference on Making Sense of Converging Media, pp. 99–103 (2013)
15. Forlines, C., Wigdor, D., Shen, C., Balakrishnan, R.: Direct-touch vs. mouse input for tabletop displays. In: Proceedings of the SIGCHI Conference on Human Factors in Computing Systems, pp. 647–656 (2007)
16. Stark, J., Burwitz, M., Braun, R., Esswein, W.: Cognitive efficient modelling using tablets. In: Enterprise Modelling and Information Systems Architectures (EMISA 2013) (2013)
17. Gindrat, A.-D., Chytiris, M., Balerna, M., Rouiller, E.M., Ghosh, A.: Use-dependent cortical processing from fingertips in touchscreen phone users. Curr. Biol. **25**, 109–116 (2015)
18. Stroop, J.R.: Studies of interference in serial verbal reactions. J. Exp. Psychol. **18**, 643 (1935)
19. MacLeod, C.M.: Half a century of research on the stroop effect: an integrative review. Psychol. Bull. **109**, 163 (1991)
20. Grigorik, I., Simonsen, J., Mann, J.: High resolution time level 2. https://www.w3.org/TR/hr-time-2/. Accessed 07 Aug 2021
21. Otto, J.M., Thornton, J., Rebert, C., Xhmikos, R., Lauke, P.H., Mazovetskiy, G.S.J.: Build fast, responsive sites with bootstrap. https://getbootstrap.com/. Accessed 07 Aug 2021
22. Cain, S.W., Silva, E.J., Chang, A.-M., Ronda, J.M., Duffy, J.F.: One night of sleep deprivation affects reaction time, but not interference or facilitation in a stroop task. Brain Cogn. **76**, 37–42 (2011)
23. Fawcett, R., Salter, K.: A monte carlo study of the f test and three tests based on ranks of treatment effects in randomized block designs. Commun. Statist. Simul. Comput. **13**, 213–225 (1984)
24. Higgins, J.J., Tashtoush, S.: An aligned rank transform test for interaction. Nonlinear World **1**, 201–211 (1994)
25. Salter, K., Fawcett, R.: The ART test of interaction: a robust and powerful rank test of interaction in factorial models. Commun. Statist. Simul. Comput. **22**, 137–153 (1993)
26. Mansouri, H., Paige, R.L., Surles, J.G.: Aligned rank transform techniques for analysis of variance and multiple comparisons. Commun. Statist. Theory Methods **33**, 2217–2232 (2004)
27. Wobbrock, J.O., Findlater, L., Gergle, D., Higgins, J.J.: The aligned rank transform for non-parametric factorial analyses using only ANOVA procedures. In: Proceedings of the SIGCHI Conference on Human Factors in Computing Systems, pp. 143–146 (2011)
28. Elkin, L.A., Kay, M., Higgins, J.J., Wobbrock, J.O.: An aligned rank transform procedure for multifactor contrast tests. In: The 34th Annual ACM Symposium on User Interface Software and Technology, pp. 754–768 (2021)
29. Egan, T.: The eight-second attention span. The New York Times, 22 (2016)
30. Leiva, L., Böhmer, M., Gehring, S., Krüger, A.: Back to the app: the costs of mobile application interruptions. In: Proceedings of the 14th International Conference on Human-Computer Interaction with Mobile Devices and Services, pp. 291–294 (2012)
31. Collardeau, M., Brisswalter, J., Audiffren, M.: Effects of a prolonged run on simple reaction time of well trained runners. Percept. Mot. Skills **93**, 679–689 (2001)

32. Hultsch, D.F., MacDonald, S.W., Hunter, M.A., Levy-Bencheton, J., Strauss, E.: Intraindividual variability in cognitive performance in older adults: comparison of adults with mild dementia, adults with arthritis, and healthy adults. Neuropsychology **14**, 588 (2000)
33. Fuentes, K., Hunter, M.A., Strauss, E., Hultsch, D.F.: Intraindividual variability in cognitive performance in persons with chronic fatigue syndrome. Clin. Neuropsychol. **15**, 210–227 (2001)

Analysis of Influence of Preference on Emotions in Relation to Physiological Indexes

Takahiro Oami, Yuri Nakagawa, Narumon Jadram, Tipporn Laohakangvalvit[✉],
Peeraya Sripian, and Midori Sugaya

Shibaura Institute of Technology, 3-7-5 Toyosu, Koto City, Tokyo 135-8548, Japan
{al18028,ma21067,ma21101,tipporn,peeraya,doly}@shibaura-it.ac.jp

Abstract. In recent years, research has been conducted to evaluate human emotions. Emotions have been evaluated using various methods such as subjective evaluation and physiological indexes. However, the relationship between these evaluation methods has not been clarified. Previous research by Ueno et al. analyzed correlation between in-vehicle conditions and subjective evaluation using adjective pairs as well as physiological indexes using electroencephalograph (EEG) and heart rate variability (HRV). However, the relationship between the subjective evaluation and the physiological indexes itself has not been scrutinized yet. In addition, the physiological indexes were reported to have large individual difference. Therefore, this study take into account preferences to clarify the relationship between the subjective evaluation and the physiological indexes, focusing on music genres as emotional stimuli. As a result, preferences were strongly correlated with arousal level measured by EEG, suggesting that human preferences may influence human emotions.

Keywords: Preference · Emotion · Electroencephalograph (EEG) · Heart Rate Variability (HRV)

1 Introduction

In recent years, various systems have been improved by taking human emotions into account, for example, communication robots to improve user-friendliness [1] and in-vehicle entertainment to improve driver's comfort [2]. To realize those systems, an evaluation of human emotional responses is required.

There are several methods for evaluating human emotional responses, including subjective evaluation and measurement of physiological signals. The widely used subjective evaluation method, Self-Assessment Manikin (SAM) scale [3], lets the user select an item closest to his/her feelings from the nine levels of Valence (pleas-ant-unpleasant) and Arousal (arousal-inactivate). Since it can be used non-verbally, it is valid across languages and cultures, which enables an intuitive evaluation. On the other hand, Osgood's Semantic Differential (SD) method [4], allows the user to rate his/her impression toward property-based adjective pairs. This method has an advantage of using terminology

© The Author(s), under exclusive license to Springer Nature Switzerland AG 2022
C. Stephanidis et al. (Eds.): HCII 2022, CCIS 1581, pp. 194–201, 2022.
https://doi.org/10.1007/978-3-031-06388-6_26

(adjective pairs) that is commonly understood in daily life. Thus, it allows us to evaluate impressions more specifically.

On the other hand, an emotion estimation method using physiological signals has recently been proposed as an objective method of evaluating emotions [5]. This method is considered highly objective because it can be used to obtain unconscious responses from human body and is free from social bias due to human subjectivity. Since both the subjective and objective methods have various advantages, they are usually used in combination for emotion estimation. However, some studies reported that the results between those two methods can be different [6]. For example, a person is judged as being relaxed according to the heart rate variability (parasympathetic dominant in the autonomic nervous system), but in contrast, he evaluates his current emotion as being sleepy in a questionnaire. Therefore, the relationship between subjective and physiological response is still unclear, making it difficult to determine which one is correct and should be used for emotion estimation. Therefore, it is necessary to clarify such relationship in order to establish a method to evaluate human emotional responses more accurately.

Previous study by Ueno et al. [2] evaluated comfort of five in-vehicle spatial patterns (physical space) and mapped emotional states using a combination of physiological indexes and SD scale onto an arousal-valence space called "Emotion Map", which was proposed based on Russell's circumplex model of affects [7]. However, the study only analyzed the relationship between physical space vs. subjective evaluation, and physical space vs. physiological indexes separately. Thus, the relationship between subjective evaluation and physiological indexes has not been clarified yet.

According to studies by Yoshinaga et al. [8] and Doi et al. [9], people's preferences influence both physiological responses and subjective evaluation. Preference is a representative of human subjectivity and attributed to positive actions and decisions, which is regarded as an index in affective evaluation [8]. Therefore, our study aims to clarify the relationship between physiological and subjective responses by taking into account people's preferences in emotion estimation.

2 Experiment Method

In this study, we conducted an experiment to estimate emotions and preferences toward several genres of music as stimuli. To estimate emotions, we used questionnaire as subjective evaluation method to evaluate preference on music genres and emotions, and two types of physiological indexes (i.e., EEG and HRV) during music listening as objective evaluation method.

2.1 Emotional Stimuli

According to Ueno et al. [5], 10 music genres (i.e., J-POP, K-POP, Hip-Hop, Rock, Reggae, Jazz, Classic, Electro Dance Music (EDM), Metal, and Japanese traditional Enka), were effectively used to evoke emotions. Out of those music genres, we selected 4 of them (J-POP, K-POP, Hip-Hop, and Classic) to be used as emotional stimuli in our experiment. These music have never been heard before by the participants.

2.2 Subjective Evaluation by Questionnaire

We evaluated the preference on music genres using a questionnaire. The participants were asked to rank the 4 music genres from most (1st rank) to least (4th rank) preferred music genres by filling each music genre in the blank in corresponding to their preference ranking as shown in Fig. 1. (Note that we also used SD scale to evaluate the 4 music genres. However, this paper only focuses on the analysis of preference.)

Rank	Music genre
1st rank	
2nd rank	
3rd rank	
4th rank	

Fig. 1. Questionnaire for preference on music genres

2.3 Objective Evaluation by Physiological Indexes

We used EEG and HRV as physiological indexes to estimate emotions on arousal-valence space model using the method proposed by Ikeda et al. [3] as follows:

To estimate the arousal level, we used an EEG index that is a difference between Attention and Meditation values. The Attention and Meditation are the parameters obtained from an original algorithm of an EEG sensor, MindWave Mobile 2 (NeuroSky Inc.).

To evaluate the valence (pleasantness) level, we used two HRV indexes that are pNN50 and RMSSD. The index was calculated using time-domain analysis from the data obtained from a pulse sensor (Switch Science, World Famous Electronics llc.). The pNN50 is defined as the proportion of NN50 divided by the total number of NN intervals, in which NN50 is the consecutive beat-to-beat interval that differ by 50 ms or more. In this study, we set the total number of NN intervals to 30. The RMSSD is the root mean square of the difference between successive RRIs. Both HRV indexes are the indexes related to the parasympathetic nervous system.

2.4 Experimental Procedure

The experiment was conducted by the following procedure.

1. Participant sat in front of the PC display and answered the questionnaire to rank their preference on music genres.
2. EEG and heart rate sensors were attached to the participants and the data recording was started.
3. Participant was asked to stay in a resting state for 1 min to stabilize the physiological sensors.
4. Participant listened to one music for 1.5 min.
5. Steps 3 and 4 were repeated until the participant listened to all four music genres.

3 Experimental Results

3.1 Participants

We recruited 6 participants for our experiment. They are 6 healthy males in their 20 s. The collected experimental data from all participants was used for the analysis explained in the next sections.

3.2 Evaluation of Music Influence on Emotions

We evaluated the influence of music on emotions estimated by physiological indexes to confirm that the emotions are effectively evoked by the selected musics. We performed one-way analysis of variance (ANOVA) and Tukey's post-hoc analysis to compare the means of physiological indexes (pNN50, RMSSD, and Attention-Meditation) among five conditions: resting state and 4 music genres.

The ANOVA results for pNN50, RMSSD, and Attention-Meditation are shown in Figs. 1, 2, and 3 respectively. For the pNN50, there was no significant difference in means of pNN50 between any pairs of conditions (Fig. 2). For the RMSSD, here were significant differences in means of RMSSD between the resting state and each of the 4 music genres, but no significant difference between any pairs of music genres (Fig. 3). For the Attention-Meditation, there were significant differences in means of Attention-Meditation between most of the pairs of conditions except for J-POP and K-POP (Fig. 4). In the figures, $\bigcirc$ denotes significant difference with $p < 0.05$ and $\times$ denotes no significant difference.

Based on the above results, we confirmed the possibility of the four music genres to evoke emotions as estimated by physiological indexes especially Attention-Meditation measured by the EEG sensor.

	Rest	Classic	J-POP	K-POP	Hip-Hop
Rest		×	×	×	×
Classic			×	×	×
J-POP				×	×
K-POP					×
Hip-Hop					

Fig. 2. ANOVA results for pNN50 (HRV index)

	Rest	Classic	J-POP	K-POP	Hip-Hop
Rest		○	○	○	○
Classic			×	×	×
J-POP				×	×
K-POP					×
Hip-Hop					

Fig. 3. ANOVA results for RMSSD (HRV index)

	Rest	Classic	J-POP	K-POP	Hip-Hop
Rest		○	○	○	○
Classic			○	○	○
J-POP				×	○
K-POP					○
Hip-Hop					

Fig. 4. ANOVA results for Attention-Meditation (EEG index)

3.3 Correlation Analysis Between Physiological Indexes and Preference

We performed Pearson's product moment correlation analysis to clarify the relationship between the preference ranking from questionnaire result and the physiological indexes. The correlation coefficients between preference ranking and each of the physiological indexes for each participant are shown in Table 1. We performed the correlation analysis for each participant separately due to the individual differences of preference.

The results show that there is a significantly strong negative correlation between Attention-Meditation and preference ranking ($p < 0.05$) for participant B. Also, some moderate to strong correlations between preference ranking and all physiological indexes for all participants were also obtained, however, without statistical significance possibly due to a small number of data. If the number of data is increased, there is possibility to obtain the statistical significance.

Table 1. Correlation coefficients between preference ranking and physiological indexes

Participant	pNN50	RMSSD	Attention-Meditation
A	0.713	0.839	−0.817
B	−0.881	−0.802	−0.977
C	−0.333	−0.223	0.206
D	−0.462	−0.600	0.349
E	0.023	0.053	0.603
F	0.216	0.627	0.390

Figure 5 visualizes the correlation between them for participant B whose correlation between preference ranking and Attention-Meditation is significant, and participant C whose the same correlation is not significant.

In addition, we analyzed the relationship between EEG index (i.e., Attention-Meditation) and HRV indexes (i.e., pNN50 and RMSSD) using time-series analysis. The time-series plots between Attention-Meditation and pNN50 and between Attention-Meditation and RMSSD of participant B are shown in Figs. 6 and 7 respectively. The blue background in the figure shows the periods in which each of the 4 music genres as emotional stimuli were presented during the experiment.

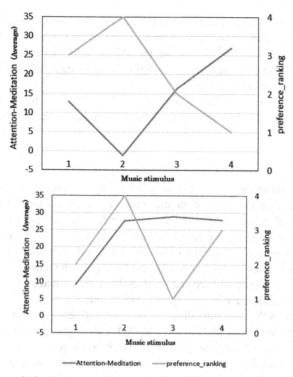

Fig. 5. Plots of correlation between preference ranking and Attention-Meditation for participant B (upper) and participant C (lower).

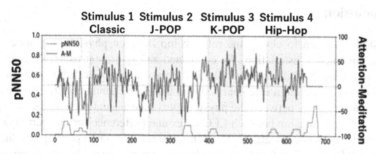

Fig. 6. Time-series plot between Attention-Meditation and pNN50 of participant B

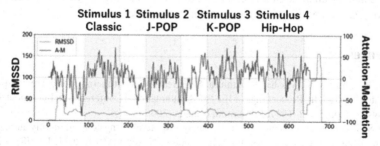

Fig. 7. Time-series plot between Attention-Meditation and RMSSD of participant B

As shown in Fig. 7, the Attention-Meditation values tended to increase during the stimuli periods, indicating that more arousing state while listening to the music than while not listening to it. On the other hand, the pNN50 values were zero during most of the experiment period, indicating that the HRV was not strongly affected by the stimuli. However, it slightly increased during the music stimuli 3 (K-Pop) and 4 (Hip-Hop), which are the music genres with low preference based on the preference ranking. This result indicates a comfortable state while listening to those music with low preference.

4 Discussion

From the correlation analysis, a significantly strong negative correlation between preference ranking and Attention-Meditation (index to estimate arousal level) was obtained for one participant, and strong correlations without significance for other participants. Also, we obtained moderate to strong correlations without significance between preference ranking and HRV indexes. Although no significant correlation between human preference and HRV could not be confirmed, the results suggest the tendency of relationship between human preference and arousal level, and that individual preference is a factor that may cause the difference in the experimental results,

In addition, the ANOVA results show a significant difference in Attention-Meditation among stimuli, but not for the pNN50 and RMSSD. This might cause by the similarity of tones among the music although the genres are different. Therefore, these results suggest that human preference is likely to influence the arousal level in human's internal state and cognition.

5 Conclusion

In this study, we aim to clarify the relationship between physiological indexes and preference in emotion estimation. We conducted an experiment using 4 music genres as emotional stimuli while the physiological data was being collected as well as the preference ranking on the music genres. From the experimental results, we performed the correlation analysis between the physiological indexes and preference. As a result, we suggest the relationship between EEG index and preference for one participant. We considered that the same correlation cannot be obtained from other participants due to the individual preference. Our future work will continue to analyze the physiological data and subjective evaluation data in detail, as well as increasing the number of emotional stimuli that are more likely to produce differences in preference.

References

1. Wada, K., Shibata, T., Musha, T., Kimura, S.: Effects of robot therapy for demented patients evaluated by EEG. In: Proceedings of IEEE/RSJ International Conference on Intelligent Robots and Systems, pp. 1552–1557, Edmonton, Canada (2005)
2. Ueno, S., Zhang, R., Laohakangvalvit, T., Sugaya, M.: Evaluating comfort in fully autonomous vehicle using biological emotion map. In: Stanton, N. (ed.) AHFE 2021. LNNS, vol. 270, pp. 323–330. Springer, Cham (2021). https://doi.org/10.1007/978-3-030-80012-3_38

3. Bradley, M.M., Lang, P.J.: Measuring emotion: the self-assessment manikin and the semantic differential. J. Behav. Ther. Exp. Psych. **25**(1), 49–59 (1994)
4. Osgood, C.E.: Semantic differential technique in the comparative study of cultures. Am. Anthropol. **66**(3), 171–200 (1964)
5. Ikeda, Y., Horie, R., Sugaya, M.: Estimate emotion with biological information for robot interaction. In: Proceedings of 21st International Conference on Knowledge-Based and Intelligent Information & Engineering Systems (KES-2017), pp. 6–8, Marseille, France (2017)
6. Yang, H., Lee, C.: Annotation matters: a comprehensive study on recognizing intended, self-reported, and observed emotion labels using physiology. In: Proceedings of 8th International Conference on Affective Computing and Intelligent Interaction (ACII), pp. 1–7, Cambridge, UK (2019)
7. Russell, J.A.: A circumplex model of affect. J. Pers. Soc. Psychol. **39**(6), 1161–1178 (1980)
8. Yoshinaga, N., Fujita, M., Tanaka, Y.L.: Fundamental research about individual variation in illuminance preference during hypnagogic stage and biological responsiveness: influence on physiological function and subjective evaluation. Japanese J. Nursing Art Sci. **10**(2), 23–29 (2011). (In Japanese)
9. Doi, S., Kamesawa, K., Wada, T., Kobayashi, E., Karaki M., Mori, N.: Basic study on individual preference for scents and the arousal level for brain activity using MNIRS. In: Proceedings of IEEE/ICME International Conference on Complex Medical Engineering, pp. 119–124, Gold Coast, Australia (2010)

EEG-Based Robot Alert System for Improving User Concentration

Kiruthika Raja[✉], Tipporn Laohakangvalvit, Peeraya Sripian, and Midori Sugaya

College of Engineering, Shibaura Institute of Technology, 3-7-5, Toyosu, Koto-ku,
Tokyo 135-8548, Japan
{am20007,tipporn,peeraya,doly}@shibaura-it.ac.jp

Abstract. Brain-computer Interfaces (BCIs) and robots hold great potential for enhancing focus in tasks and acting as educational agents. In this research, we propose to create a robot alert system that helps improve user's concentration by alerting the user when their concentration drops. The user's concentration is detected by their brain activity using a commercially available electroencephalograph (EEG) sensor. This paper presents our design and development of the proposed EEG-based robot alert system using voice and facial expressions. To investigate the possibility of improving user's concentration, we evaluated the developed system by carrying out an experiment to improve user's concentration while learning. This was evaluated by monitoring the user's concentration using EEG while watching an educational video with and without our proposed robot alert system. The experimental results show the user's concentration levels to increase after the alert, thereby suggesting that our EEG-based robot alert system successfully improved the user's concentration. Our alert system contributes to improving user's concentration in situations that require cognitive thinking such as e-learning and driving.

Keywords: Brain-computer interface · Robot · Affective interaction · Social robot · Concentration

1 Introduction

Due to the advancements in fields of robotics, robots have become increasingly accessible and visible in our day-to-day life even in the field of education (Qu et al. [1], Toh et al. [2]). With the demand for distance learning increasing due to the expansion of the COVID-19 pandemic, students completing classes in the online learning environment are at a risk in facing setbacks due to various factors.

The most common reason behind this set back is the student's distraction, which interferes with their ability to concentrate in the online class [3]. Davison et al. reported the positive effect that praise delivered by social robots have on the growth of children's mindset [4]. Park et al. suggests that robots who offer remarks, feedbacks and praise may promote a growing mindset to improve academic achievements [5]. Similar researches leads us to speculate that having a robot alongside a student can help regain their concentration and improve the student's learning and attention span. This kind of robot not only provides to be helpful in situation of e-learning but also any other task that requires cognitive thinking.

Therefore, our research focuses on creating a robot alert system that alerts the user when their concentration drops to encourage and increase the user's concentration. The goal of our research is to design an effective robot alert system and conduct a preliminary experiment to verify the possibility of using the proposed robot for e-learning.

2 Background

A person's concentration or attention can be interpreted by their neural activity. A review of related literature reveals different methods and tests used to measure attention and concentration. These range from psychometric tests designed to measure cognitive function to invasive methods such as electrocorticography (ECoG) and noninvasive methods such as magnetoencephalography (MEG), electroencephalography (EEG) and fMRI [6].

EEG is a non-invasive method widely used to study brain activity occurring at the surface of the brain. It depicts electrical activity as waveforms of varying frequencies and amplitude: delta wave (1–3 Hz), theta wave (4–7 Hz), alpha wave (8–12 Hz), beta wave (13–30 Hz), and gamma wave (31–50 Hz).

Previous research by Szafir et al. used techniques from brain-computer interfaces (BCI) and educational psychology to design agents that monitor student's attention in real time using EEG measurements and recapture the decreasing attention levels using verbal and nonverbal cues [7]. Equation 1 was used to calculate user engagement (E) from neural activity with alpha, beta, and theta waves [8].

$$E = \beta(\alpha + \theta) \tag{1}$$

Research by Shiraiwa et al. used an index shown in Eq. 2 to calculate user's concentration and alert the user when their concentration drops [9].

$$1 < \frac{\text{Low beta}}{\text{Low alpha}} \text{ or } 1 < \frac{\text{High alpha}}{\text{Low alpha}} \tag{2}$$

In this research, we use the approach of obtaining attention from a commercially available EEG sensor (Mindwave Mobile 2; NeuroSky Inc.) [8]. This EEG sensor perceives brainwaves and transforms them into Attention and Meditation values using manufacturer's original algorithm (eSense). These two values have been used to develop various apps that aim at estimating attention and focus. The Attention and Meditation data is scaled between 1 and 100. As shown in Table 1, the Attention scale is divided into 5 ranges: The neutral state is set to be between 40 and 60, 60 to 80 is slightly high and 80 to 100 is very high. Likewise, 20 to 40 is slightly low and 0 to 20 is very low. Sethi et al. used this EEG-based attention feedback to help improve focus in e-learning [10]. Genaro et al. have assessed the usability of Attention parameter to detect attention levels [11].

Table 1. Overview of NeuroSky Mindwave values and their attention level

Range of values	Attention level
1–20	Strongly lowered
20–40	Reduced
40–60	Neutral
60–80	Slightly elevated
80–100	Elevated

3 Designing Our Robot Alert System

The goal of the Robot Alert System is to help increase the user's concentration. We investigated various basic features of facial expression and voice to determine what features in specific are suitable for our goal. We also surveyed various concentration indexes to use for our robot. Figure 1 Shows the overview of our robot alert system.

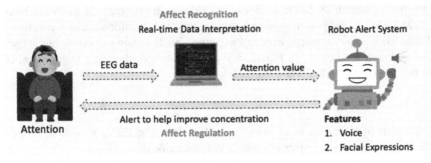

Fig. 1. Overview of our robot alert system.

3.1 Robot Voice

Pitch, pitch range, volume, and speech rate are four fundamental voice characteristics that indicate personality. These factors make a social robot more appealing and increase user's engagement [12]. Thus, it is important to consider these factors while designing our robot alert system to obtain the best results for improving user's concentration.

Impression studies investigating the effect of voice reported that more mature voices result in higher dominance and assertiveness [13]. In addition, a higher pitch is better rated as voice appeal [14]. Hayati et al. suggests that attention and focus are given to natural rather than slow speech rates [14]. Other research proposed an agent using a non-monotonous tone and have the agent raising the volume of its voice at times to help re-engage student's attention [7]. Our design incorporates all the mentioned factors to design our robot voice. According to the concentration level, our robot gives positive affirmation messages to increase user's engagement level (Table 2).

Table 2. Robot alert messages according to the user's condition of concentration

Condition	Message
Concentration drop	Your concentration appears to be dropping
Cont. concentration drop	Pay Attention! Your concentration is dropping
Better concentration	That's better, keep going!
High concentration	You're doing great, keep going!

3.2 Robot Facial Expression

Similar to designing robot voice, it is also essential to consider robot facial expressions such that they increase user engagement. Studies reported that increasing eye contact and serious and mature facial expressions helps improve user's concentration [7, 13]. Increased eye contact indicates a higher level of dominance as well as affiliation and immediacy. Instructor's head nodding has also been shown to positively affect student's reactions [15].

In addition to these factors, the display of happy expressions when concentration is high acts as a reward to the user further encouraging them to maintain their level of concentration. We used a total of 10 facial expressions as shown in Fig. 2, which were selected to be displayed based on the concentration level.

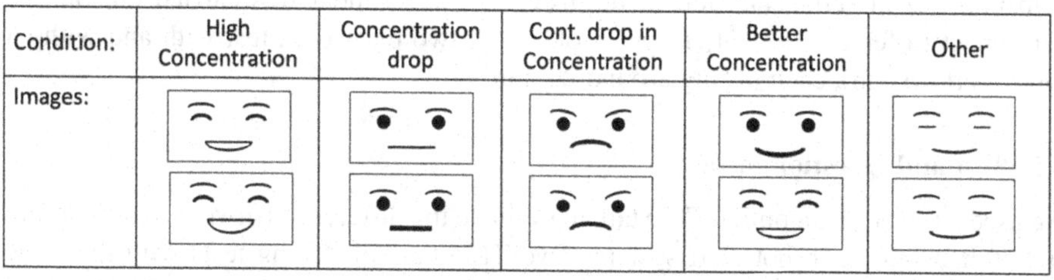

Condition:	High Concentration	Concentration drop	Cont. drop in Concentration	Better Concentration	Other
Images:					

Fig. 2. Images of the robot facial expressions and their respective condition.

3.3 Selecting a Concentration Index

Our robot alert system needs to alert the user by judging the user's concentration by their neural activity. Previous studies used various concentration indexes as discussed in Sect. 2. To select the appropriate concentration index for our robot alert system, we gathered EEG data from one participant during two scenarios: (1) taking online classes and (2) doing homework, while wearing the EEG sensor (Mindwave Mobile 2). The collected data was analyzed by three different concentration indexes, and as a result, we decided to use Attention parameter provided by the NeuroSky original algorithm.

3.4 Generating Alerts and Selecting a Threshold

To avoid the robot alert system from continuously alerting users, we need to set a threshold for each alert. The alert threshold can be set in two ways 1) relative threshold that keeps changing the Attention value or 2) fixed threshold. We use a fixed threshold to send out alerts to user. The eSense's Attention parameter at 40 is set as a neutral state as shown in Table 1. Attention value greater than 40 is defined as high attention, and that of lower than 40 is defined as low attention. Table 3 shows the alert conditions and their corresponding alert threshold.

Table 3. Robot alert condition and its respective threshold.

Alert condition	Alert threshold
Concentration drop	Low attention (Attention < 40) for 30 s
Cont. concentration drop	Low attention (Attention < 40) for 60 more seconds
Better concentration	High attention (Attention > 40) for 30 s
High concentration	Hight attention (Attention > 40) for 180 s

4   Experiment Method

The goal of the experiment is to evaluate whether the robot alert system can efficiently help improve the concentration of the user. The experiment was carried out on one participant (a female student, 19 years old) with two parts (i.e., test with and without robot alert system), each lasting around 20 min.

4.1 Test and Questionnaire

We used a test from an online TED talk to evaluate the difference between scores before and after using our robot alert system. Two TED talk's listening tests with the same level of hardness were selected for this purpose. After the listening test, 34 questions related to the selected TED talks were answered using the following answering styles: true/false, multiple choice and short answer.

In addition, we used a questionnaire to check how the user felt about the robot, which consists of the following items:

- Did you find it to help improve your concentration?
- Did you find it annoying or helpful?
- Would you use the robot alert system again?

4.2 Biological Information

For the evaluation of the robot alert system along with the test and questionnaire, the EEG data was collected using NeuroSky's Mindwave Mobile 2 during the experiment, The data was then used to calculate the Attention parameter and analyzed to compare the effects that the alert system has on the user.

4.3 Experiment Procedure

The experiment is conducted in two folds, with and without the robot alert system. For each of them, the procedure is as follows:

1. The participant is required to always wear the EEG sensor.
2. The participant is given some time before hand to read the question presented on the paper after which they are presented with the first TED talk video and without the robot alert system.
3. Once the test is complete, some more time is given to complete the test.
4. Steps 2 and 3 are repeated with the second TED talk video and the robot alert system.

5 Experimental Results

5.1 Test and Questionnaire

We obtained the test scores as follows:

- Test score without Robot Alert system = 78%
- Test score with Robot Alert System = 89%

5.2 Biological Information

The Attention values obtained during the experiment is plotted in time-series as shown in Fig. 3. With the alert system, we can observe the Attention values over the threshold at 40 and some Attention values reaching the peak at 100. Figure 4 illustrates the average increase in the user's attention with the help of a robot alert system clearly.

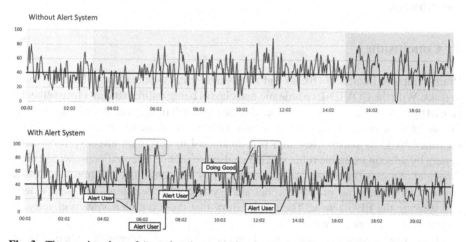

Fig. 3. Time-series plots of Attention data with the alert system (top graph) and without the alert system (bottom graph) where 100 is the highest and 0 is the lowest attention level.

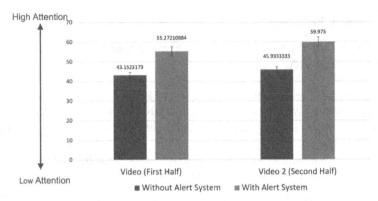

Fig. 4. Average Attention values during the first and second half of the TED talk using the alert system (blue) and without the alert system (orange). (Color figure online)

6 Discussion

By comparing the Attention values obtained from the EEG sensor during the experiment with and without robot alert systems, we obtained the following findings:

- With the help of the robot alert system (Fig. 4), the user achieved the maximum Attention value of 100 after the robot alerts the user.
- The user's concentration measured by Attention with the help of the robot alert system was increased from 43.2 to 55.3 and 45.9 to 60.0 (Fig. 5). The results from the test scores also show an improvement of 11%.

Therefore, we confirm that our robot alert system successfully improved the user's concentration.

7 Conclusion

Brain-computer Interfaces (BCIs) and robots hold great potential for enhancing focus in tasks. With the COVID-19 pandemic and classes being online, students face setbacks caused by lack of concentration. The goal of this research is to create a robot alert system that alerts the user when their concentration drops and increase the user's concentration measured by EEG sensor. Research was conducted to design an effective robot alert system by selecting suitable robot voice, facial expression, concentration index and alert threshold. An experiment was conducted to verify the possibility of improving user's concentration using our proposed robot alert system while watching TED talk videos and wearing the EEG sensor. The results show that the robot alert system effectively improved user's concentration.

The current research has only carried out one preliminary experiment for a particular user and used only one concentration index. Our future work will continue to investigate other concentration indexes and employ different concentration and alert thresholds, with more robot features and users.

References

1. Qu, J.R., Fok, P.K.: Cultivating students' computational thinking through student–robot interactions in robotics education. Int. J. Technol. Des. Educ. 1–20 (2021). https://doi.org/10.1007/s10798-021-09677-3
2. Toh, E.L.P., Causo, A., Tzuo, P.W., Chen, I.M., Yeo, S.H.: A review on the use of robots in education and young children. Educ. Technol. Soc. 19(2), 148–163 (2016)
3. Meigan, R., Teresa, S.: The distracted online student: strategies to capture attention and promote connection. Teach. Learn. Nurs. 16(4), 389–392 (2016)
4. Davison, D.P., Wijnen, F.M., Charisi, V.: Words of encouragement: how praise delivered by a social robot changes children's mindset for learning. J. Multimodal User Interf. 15, 61–76 (2021)
5. Park, HW., Rosenberg-Kima, R., Rosenberg., Gordon, G., Breazeal, C.: Growing growth mindset with a social robot peer. In: Proceedings of the international conference on human-robot interaction (HRI 2017), pp 137–145. ACM Press, New York (2017)
6. Astrand, E., Wardak, C., Ben Hamed, S.: Selective visual attention to drive cognitive brain-machine interfaces: from concepts to neurofeedback and rehabilitation applications. Front Syst. Neurosci. 8, 144 (2014)
7. Szafir, D., Mutlu, B.: Pay attention! designing adaptive agents that monitor and improve user engagement. In: Proceedings of the SIGCHI Conference on Human Factors in Computing Systems, pp. 11–20 (2012)
8. Pope, A.T., Bogart, E.H., Bartolome, D.S.: Biocybernetic system evaluates indices of operator engagement in automated task. Biologic. Psychol. 40(1–2), 187–195 (1995)
9. IPSJ Proceedings. https://www.interaction-ipsj.org/proceedings/2021/data/pdf/2A19.pdf
10. Chaitanya, S., Harsh, D., Chirag, D., Mohit, D., Divyashikha, S.: EEG-based attention feedback to improve focus in E-learning. In: Proceedings of the 2018 2nd International Conference on Computer Science and Artificial Intelligence, pp. 321–326. New York, USA (2018)
11. Rebolledo-Mendez, G., et al.: Assessing NeuroSky's usability to detect attention levels in an assessment exercise. In: Jacko, J.A. (ed.) Human-Computer Interaction. New Trends: 13th International Conference, HCI International 2009, San Diego, CA, USA, July 19-24, 2009, Proceedings, Part I, pp. 149–158. Springer, Heidelberg (2009). https://doi.org/10.1007/978-3-642-02574-7_17
12. Niculescu, A., van Dijk, B., Nijholt, A., Li, H., See, S.L.: Making social robots more attractive: the effects of voice pitch, humor and empathy. Int. J. Soc. Robot. 5(2), 171–191 (2012). https://doi.org/10.1007/s12369-012-0171-x
13. Zuckerman, M., Miyake, K., Elkin, C.S.: Effects of attractiveness and maturity of face and voice on interpersonal impressions. J. Res. Pers. 29(2), 253–272 (1995)
14. Hayati, A.: The effect of speech rate on listening comprehension of EFL learners. Creat. Educ. 1(2), 101–114 (2010)
15. Harris, M., Rosenthal, R.: No more teachers' dirty looks: effects of teacher nonverbal behavior on student outcomes. Applications of nonverbal communication. In: Perry, R.P., Smart, J.C. (eds.) The Scholarship of Teaching and Learning in Higher Education: An Evidence-Based Perspective, pp. 157–192. Springer, Dordrecht (2007). https://doi.org/10.4324/9781410612786-18

Fast Detection and Classification of Drivers' Responses to Stressful Events and Cognitive Workload

Fabien Rogister[1]($\boxtimes$), Marie-Anne Pungu Mwange[1], Luka Rukonić[1,2], Olivier Delbeke[1], and Richard Virlouvet[1]

[1] Connected and Sharing Solutions, AISIN Europe, Braine-L'Alleud, Belgium
fabien.rogister@aisin-europe.com
[2] Institute for Language and Communication, Université catholique de Louvain, Louvain-la-Neuve, Belgium

Abstract. We apply machine learning techniques to detect moments of stress and cognitive load during simulator driving experiences. The use of the electrical skin conductance, or more precisely the electrodermal activity (EDA), is particularly interesting for assessing drivers' states because it is easily measurable; it is also involuntary and uncontrollable. Detection of responses to external stimuli can be performed on a scale of seconds with an accuracy of 86%. Moreover, we observe that responses to stress events and cognitive efforts can be differentiated with an accuracy of 80% over sub-minute time intervals. We compare our results to others reported in the literature. Automatic and fast detection of responses to stressful events and high cognitive workload can be used to assess drivers' user experience (UX) and their interaction with their vehicle.

Keywords: Machine learning · Driver state recognition · User experience · Electrodermal activity

1 Introduction

While aiming to make the driving experience more enjoyable and safer, it is highly desirable to automatically detect, avoid or alleviate stressful or cognitively demanding situations. Continuous monitoring of driver state is necessary to reach this goal.

Many studies are based on the analysis of physiological signals such as respiration, temperature, electromyograms, electrocardiograms (ECGs), and electrodermal activity (EDA), i.e. the variation in skin conductance. Their objectives are similar: the detection of the driver's state and its automation using machine learning techniques. These techniques have been applied to physiological signals measured on drivers, both in real driving (see [1, 2] and references therein) and on a simulator (see [3, 4] and references therein) to detect reactions to stressful events with high accuracy. However, they combine several physiological signals and the classification between several stress states relies on the analysis of long signal intervals, thus preventing the detection of driver states on short time scales.

C. Stephanidis et al. (Eds.): HCII 2022, CCIS 1581, pp. 210–217, 2022.
https://doi.org/10.1007/978-3-031-06388-6_28

In this study carried out in a simulated environment, our objective was to automatically detect on the shortest possible time scale, the physiological responses of drivers to external stimuli, and to determine those which are induced either by stress events or by cognitive load. To this end, we first considered the characteristics extracted from the electrodermal activity and from signals derived from the electrocardiogram, namely the heart rate and its variability. We nevertheless realized that the analysis of the EDA alone allowed a rapid detection and classification of driver states with an accuracy of 80%.

In this paper, we briefly present our driving simulator and the experimental scenarios we used to train and test our models. We investigate qualitatively the physiological responses to stimuli of participants to our experiments. We examine their electrodermal activity, heart rate, and heart rate variability. We show that, in our opinion, these last two signals are not relevant for fast detection of the responses to stress and cognitive tasks. We present the two successive steps of our method to automatically classify drivers' states.

2 Simulator and Electrophysiological Signals Measurement

The simulator is based on a customized version of CARLA [5], an open-source simulation environment based on Unreal engine. The setup consists of three large 50-inch-curved screens, an adaptable car seat and a Fanatec® set of a steering wheel, a gear shifter and pedals. Two cameras and a microphone were also used to record the experiment. A small auxiliary screen displayed a simplified navigation map.

Drivers' physiological signals were recorded at 2000 samples per second with a BIOPAC® MP36R connected to participants with adhesive electrodes. Two electrodes were positioned on the sole of the left foot for the EDA measurement; ECG electrodes were positioned close to the left medial malleolus and on the right wrist. The sole of the left foot for the EDA measurement was chosen to avoid motion artifacts, the simulator replicating an automatic transmission car.

3 Detection of Physiological Responses to External Stimuli

We have designed a first scenario in which we alternate periods of normal driving with stressful situations and situations requiring cognitive effort. A preliminary analysis of how these signals were varying with the succession of events allowed us to understand that the signals derived from the ECG, the heart rate and its variability, were not relevant on short time scales. We, therefore, decided to use EDA alone. In this section, we briefly present this scenario and our preliminary observations. We then explain the algorithmic steps we have implemented for the automatic detection of skin conductance responses to stimuli.

3.1 First Scenario and Preliminary Observations

The first scenario was completed by seven participants. They started in a town and after a few hundred meters they continued on a highway with a speed of 90 kph.

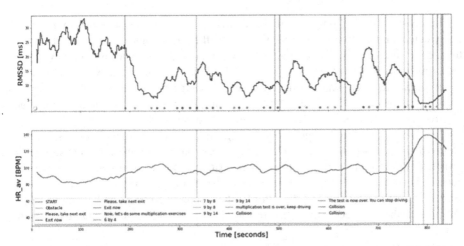

Fig. 1. RMSSD and heart rate (HR) of participant 7 enrolled in the first experiment. RMSSD is calculated over a 20 s window sliding by steps of one second. HR is averaged over 20 s. The vertical lines correspond to events (obstacle avoidance, interaction with the vocal assistant, mathematical exercises, etc.). The small dots correspond to turns on the highway. During the cognitive exercises, we observe an important increase in the heart rate while its variability decreases.

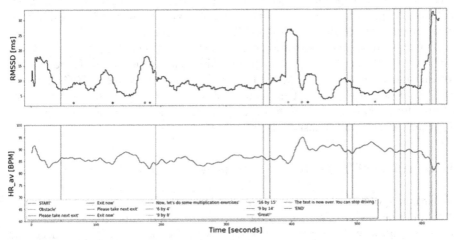

Fig. 2. RMSSD and heart rate (HR) of participant 2 enrolled in the first experiment. There is no observable increase in the heart rate and decrease in its variability concomitant with stressful events and cognitive tasks.

During the drive, which lasted approximately 12 min, they had to avoid an obstacle, then they were instructed by a voice assistant to take an exit and then come back on the highway. Later, they were instructed by the voice assistant to take another exit and then come back again on the highway. They were submitted to a few multiplication exercises in the last part of the scenario.

A qualitative analysis of heart rate and its variability, which are both derived from the ECG, and the EDA signal of the seven participants in this first experiment has been carried out. It is well known that heart rate increases, and its variability decreases in presence of stressful stimuli, but we have observed this trend in few situations only (Fig. 1 provides an example); this behavior is indeed not observed in five out of seven recordings (Fig. 2 provides an example where this trend is not observed). This is a noticeable difference with other studies based on ECG derived signals [1–4]. We explain this discrepancy by the fact that, in our experiments, stressful stimuli and periods of relative calm alternate on short timescales while, to the best of our knowledge, most studies consider a succession of longer sequences with very distinctive levels of stress.

EDA refers to variation in skin conductivity. It is linked to the sympathetic nervous system and is an indication of physiological and psychological arousal. It can be used as an indicator of cognitive and emotional states. Figure 3 presents an EDA signal, which consists of a succession of peaks, the skin conductance responses (SCRs). These responses can be spontaneous, but most are generated by stimuli. Both are unconscious and uncontrollable. The figure shows that most SCRs are following well-defined stressful events (such as sharp turns on the road, the avoidance of an obstacle or the interaction with the voice assistant) or are generated in a repetitive way during the cognitive tasks at the end of the scenario. We, therefore, focus in the following on EDA signals only for stress and cognitive load detection without paying more attention to ECGs.

3.2 First Classification Algorithm

Artifacts in raw EDA were removed with a median filter with a local window of one second. As the process is time-consuming, the signal was first decimated by a factor of 10 after applying an order 8 Chebyshev type I anti-aliasing filter. After removing artifacts, the signal was resampled using Fourier method. A clean EDA and its fast-changing component (namely the phasic component) were then calculated using the Python NeuroKit2 library [6]. Phasic was obtained by high-pass filtering the EDA. Figure 3 displays an EDA signal and its phasic component. The energy of the phasic signal, its mean absolute value, its mean absolute derivative, its maximum absolute derivative, its mean derivative and its mean absolute derivative are calculated for every 5-s-long intervals. The last two features are observed to be the most important to achieve an accurate classification. Each of the 5-s-long intervals are also labeled by one of the researchers as 0' in the absence of SCR, or conversely as 1' in the presence of response. For this task, he is assisted by the BIOPAC Acqknowledge software and functions from NeuroKit2 library. It must be pointed out that a small percentage of responses detected by both tools is questionable and we think this is an important source of errors in the subsequent supervised classification. Five different classifiers have been trained and tested by using the leave-one-out validation method: a k-Nearest Neighbors (k-NN) classifier, a Random Forest (FR) classifier, a Support Vector Machine (SVM) classifier with linear kernel, a Support Vector Machine classifier with a Radial Basis Function (RBF), and a four-layer artificial neural network (ANN) classifier. Accuracy, sensitivity and specificity obtained after hyper-parameter tuning are of the same order, SVM with RBF and ANN performing slightly better. In the case of the ANN, they are 86%, 84%

and 87%, respectively. Figure 4 shows the result of the first classification, where intervals
without any SCR are in green, while intervals with SCRs are in grey.

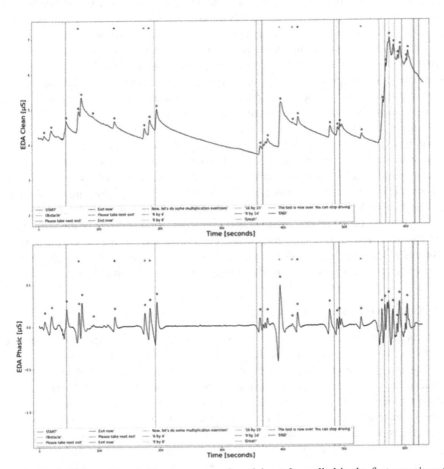

Fig. 3. Clean EDA and its phasic component of participant 2 enrolled in the first experiment.
Red dots correspond to SCR peaks. The vertical lines and the other dots have same meaning as in
Fig. 1. (Color figure online)

4 Classification of Physiological Responses to Stressful Events and Cognitive Tasks

The time duration devoted to the cognitive effort is very short in the first scenario and
data collected were not sufficient to train and test a second classifier whose task would
be to separate responses to cognitive effort from those relating to stressful events. Data
collected during two other experiments have been used for this purpose. We describe
below the scenarios, then the method used for the second classification process.

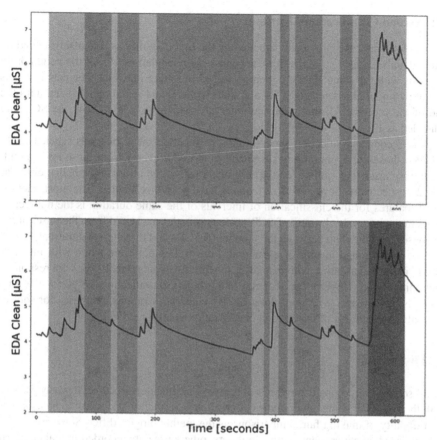

Fig. 4. Top: Result of the first classification. Intervals classified as without SCRs are in green, intervals classified as with SCRs are in grey. Bottom: Result of the second classification. Intervals corresponding to responses to stressful events are yellow. Intervals corresponding to responses to cognitive tasks are in red. (Color figure online)

4.1 Second and Third Scenarios

In the second scenario, participants were sitting in a real stationary car. They were instructed to first think about a song, then sing it in front of an experimenter while being video recorded. After relaxing, they had to add the number 3333 to seemingly randomly generated 4-digit numbers. After a second relaxing time, they achieved a "Stroop color-naming task" [7]. 7 participants took part in this experiment.

In the third scenario, the participants were driving on a highway, sharing the road with other cars controlled by the simulator. They were successively submitted to an "auditory Stroop task" [7], they had to count backwards by steps of 3 then 7, and finally they had to spell words backwards.

4.2 Second Classification Algorithm

The 5 s long intervals previously labelled by the first classifier as 0' but surrounded by intervals labeled as 1' (thus with SCR peaks) are relabeled as 1'. All the neighboring intervals with the same label are then coalesced in longer intervals. The new intervals that are without any detected SCRs are relabeled as 0 and remain unchanged until the end of the process. All the other new intervals, which include at least one SCR, are relabeled as 1''.

The second classification process aims to separate these intervals labeled as 1'' between those corresponding to responses to stressful events from those corresponding to responses to cognitive load. These intervals will be ultimately labelled either as 1 or 2, respectively. Several sets of features have been investigated. The most relevant set of features for the classification of intervals of the same duration is the number of SCRs in the intervals, the sum of SCR peak amplitudes measured from the onset of the responses, and the ratio between the number of SCRs and the interval duration.

The training and testing of a Random Forest classifier were made with intervals clearly identified as either with responses to stressful events (label 1) or with responses to cognitive tasks (label 2). The accuracy of this binary classification is 80% for 40 s long intervals. It increases with their duration. By contrast, it rapidly decreases for shorter intervals. An example of this second classification is presented in Fig. 4.

5 Discussion

In this section, we compare the results of the two classification processes described above with the results of some other studies [1–4]; it is nevertheless necessary to be aware of the difficulty of making fair comparisons as the methodologies differ. Some works are indeed based on experiments with simulators, others use data recorded in real cars. All use resting periods as a baseline measurement, contrary to our work.

We can compare the results obtained with our first classifier with a study aiming at a binary classification between stress and no stress [1]. This study is based on scenarios alternating relatively short periods of driving with and without obstacles to avoid. There, the best accuracy is 88% with Long Short-Term Memory networks with 15 s long intervals. This is overall comparable to the results of our first classifier.

The studies aiming at the classification of different levels of stress (namely absence of stress, low stress, high stress) consider long, uninterrupted, and very distinctive periods of driving (city streets, highways) in addition to resting periods [2, 4]. In [2], an overall accuracy of 97% is obtained but with 5-min intervals and features extracted from multiple physiological signals (skin conductance, respiration, heart rate, electromyogram). Only features extracted from skin conductance, heart rate and respiration on 100 s intervals are considered in [4]. The overall accuracy for the three states classification is around 90% but it must be pointed out that this value is pulled up by the nearly 100% correct detection of the resting periods. Therefore, the binary classification accuracy between low stress and high stress is likely close to 80%. That study shares the same limitations as those of [2] as it uses the same database.

6   Conclusion

We have not only shown that it is possible to reliably detect physiological responses to stressful events and cognitive tasks but also that it is possible to separate them over sub-minute time intervals.

The tool we have developed here can allow the improvement of drivers' experience as we can monitor their emotional state. We already applied it to assess the physiological adaptation of drivers to our simulator [8]. This research takes place in a project that deals with semi-automated cars.

Acknowledgement. We acknowledge the support by the project VIADUCT under the reference 7982 funded by Service Public de Wallonie (SPW), Belgium.

References

1. Zontone, P., Affanni, A., Bernardini, R., Del Linz, L., Piras, A., Rinaldo, R.: Supervised learning techniques for stress detection in car drivers. Adv. Sci. Technol. Eng. Syst. J. **5**(6), 22–29 (2020)
2. Healey, J.A., Picard, R.W.: Detecting stress during real-world driving tasks using physiological sensors. IEEE Trans. Intell. Transp. Syst. **6**(2), 156–166 (2005)
3. Meteier, Q., et al.: Classification of drivers' workload using physiological signals in conditional automation. Front. Psychol. **12**, 596038 (2021)
4. Chen, L.-L., Zhao, Y., Ye, P.-F., Zhang, J., Zou, J.-Z.: Detecting driving stress in physiological signals based on multimodal feature analysis and kernel classifiers. Expert Syst. Appl. **85**, 279–291 (2017)
5. Dosovitskiy, A., Ros, G., Codevilla, F., Lopez, A., Koltun, V.: CARLA: an open urban driving simulator. In: 2017 Conference on Robot Learning (CoRL), pp. 1–16 (2017)
6. NeuroKit2 Homepage. https://neurokit2.readthedocs.io/
7. Knight, S., Heinrich, A.: Different measures of auditory and visual stroop interference and their relationship to speech intelligibility in noise. Front. Psychol. **8**(230) 2017
8. Pungu Mwange, M.-A., Rogister, F., Rukonić, L.: Measuring driving simulator adaptation using EDA. In: Proceedings of the 13th International Conference on Applied Human Factors and Ergonomics (AHFE) (2022)

Prediction of Visibility of Two Colors Schemes Using the Convolutional Neural Networks

Shodai Sasaki[1] and Yoshihisa Shinozawa[2(✉)]

[1] Graduate School of Science and Technology, Keio University, Yokohama, Japan
[2] Faculty of Science and Technology, Keio University, Yokohama, Japan
shino@ae.keio.ac.jp

Abstract. In this study, we propose a method to predict the visibility of images composed of different color schemes using Convolutional Neural Networks (CNN), which introduces the Multi-Stage Color Model (MSC Model), a human color vision model. Using the MSC model, a method has been proposed to predict the visibility of color schemes on a computer by reproducing the way humans see colors. In this study, the response values of multiple cell layers by the MSC model are used as input values to the CNN. In constructing the CNN, we propose a CNN with an improved structure to extract the features for the visibility between images, and attempt to improve the prediction accuracy of visibility. The CNN is trained on the color scheme visibility data collected in a pairwise comparison experiment, and the trained CNN is used to predict visibility for unknown color schemes. The results show that the construction of a CNN with the MSC model improves the accuracy of color scheme visibility.

Keywords: Multi-Stage Color Model · Color scheme · Convolutional Neural Networks

1 Introduction

Humans can acquire a lot of valuable information from visual information such as text, graphics, and images. Today, the medium for receiving such information is diversifying through various interfaces such as smartphones and web browsers. In designing such an interface, the size, color, and layout of the object are important. Color combinations (color schemes) have a particularly large impact on visibility. However, there are no fixed indicators or criteria for determining a color scheme that is visible to all humans. Therefore, by reproducing the process of human color vision on a computer and clarifying the visibility of color schemes, we think it will be possible to design with visibility in mind.

As prior methods for color scheme visibility, there are studies that collect visibility data through experiments [1], and studies that predict the visibility of unknown color schemes after building a visibility prediction model to reduce the time and effort of data collection [2]. In particular, in a previous study [2], a model was devised that consists of a reproduction part of the color vision process composed of the Multi-Stage Color model

C. Stephanidis et al. (Eds.): HCII 2022, CCIS 1581, pp. 218–226, 2022.
https://doi.org/10.1007/978-3-031-06388-6_29

(MSC model) [3], which is a human color vision model, and a visibility prediction part that predicts the visibility of the color scheme based on the responses of the reproduction part. In this study, we attempt to improve the visibility prediction part of the previous study [2] by using a convolutional neural network (CNN) to improve the accuracy of color scheme visibility prediction. In particular, to improve the visibility prediction part, we propose a CNN model with an improved structure to extract features that contribute to visibility between images. The effectiveness of the proposed method is then verified on the data from the pairwise comparison experiments collected in the previous study [3].

2 Visibility Prediction Methods

2.1 Data Collection Through Pairwise Comparison Experiments

In this study, we use data from a pairwise comparison experiment collected in a previous study [1] as an index of the visibility of images consisting of two color schemes (background color and text color). The data collection method in the previous study [1] is to display two pairs of images (called pairwise comparison images) of horizontally written text with different luminance values on the same background color in the same system color to 20 subjects (users with normal color perception in their 20s to 30s) on a web browser, and ask them to select the image (right image or left image) they judged to be easier to see (see Fig. 1). Under experimental conditions, lighting is placed approximately 180 cm directly above the display (approximately 400 lx). Subjects are measured from a viewpoint approximately 50 cm from the display, and the pairwise comparison image is placed approximately in the center of the browser.

The color scheme used in the experiment is based on 10 saturated color systems (red, green, blue, cyan, magenta, yellow, and four systems from the web safe colors #ff**99, #**9900, #99cc**, #**66**, denoted WSC1, WSC2, WSC3, and WSC4), with the luminance value changed in four steps (66, 99, cc, ff for the ** element) for the background color (40 colors). The text color is changed from the same 10 saturated colors to five different luminance values (33, 66, 99, cc, and ff for the ** elements). The number of pairwise comparison experiments is 4,000 in total, since 10 colors are compared by combining text colors of the same system color with 5 different luminance values ($_5C_2 = 10$ pattern) on the same background color (40 color combinations). For the data collected by the above pairwise comparison experiment (a total of 4,000 pairwise comparison images), the percentage (visibility value) of subjects who answer that the right image is easier to see out of 20 subjects is determined. Then, the right area is judged to be easier to see for pairwise comparison images with visibility values of 0.5 or higher, while the left area is judged to be easier to see for pairwise images with visibility values of less than 0.5.

2.2 Outline of the Proposed Method

The proposed method consists of a reproduction part of the color vision process and a visibility prediction part (Fig. 1). The reproduction part of the color vision process uses a model from a previous study [2] based on the Multi-Stage Color Model (MSC model) [3], which is one of the color vision models.

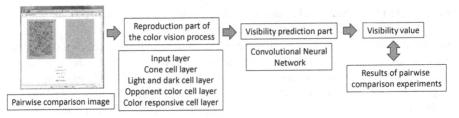

Fig. 1. Outline of the proposed method.

2.3 Reproduction Part of the Color Vision Process

Input Layer

Let $f(x, y) = (R, G, B)$ be the RGB values at coordinate (x, y) $(x = 1, 2, \cdots, X, y = 1, 2, \cdots, Y)$ in the pairwise comparison image (Fig. 1). The input layer consists of three cell layers (L, M, S input layer), and the size of each cell layer is $X \times Y$. RGB values are input to each input layer, and after converting from RGB values to XYZ values, the XYZ values are converted to LMS values using Eq. (1).

$$\begin{pmatrix} L \\ M \\ S \end{pmatrix} = \begin{pmatrix} 0.155 & 0.543 & -0.0329 \\ -0.155 & 0.457 & 0.0329 \\ 0.0 & 0.0 & 0.016 \end{pmatrix} \begin{pmatrix} X \\ Y \\ Z \end{pmatrix} \tag{1}$$

Each input layer outputs e values. M input layer outputs M values. S input layer outputs S values. Let $f_L(x, y)$ denote the L values output from L input layer, $f_M(x, y)$ the M values output from M input layer, and $f_S(x, y)$ the S values output from S input layer.

Cone Cell Layer

Based on the LMS values from the input layer, the response values of the cone cell layer are calculated. The response values $L(x, y)$ at the coordinate (x, y) in the L cone cell layer, $M(x, y)$ in the M cone cell layer, and $S(x, y)$ in the S cone cell layer are calculated from Eq. (2) to (4), respectively.

$$L(x, y) = \sum_{j=-K/2}^{K/2} \sum_{i=-K/2}^{K/2} f_L(x + i, y + j) F(i, j) \tag{2}$$

$$M(x, y) = \sum_{j=-K/2}^{K/2} \sum_{i=-K/2}^{K/2} f_M(x + i, y + j) F(i, j) \tag{3}$$

$$S(x, y) = \sum_{j=-K/2}^{K/2} \sum_{i=-K/2}^{K/2} f_s(x + i, y + j) F(i, j) \tag{4}$$

The F in the equations represents the Gaussian filter (Eq. 5). K is the size of the Gaussian filter.

$$F(i, j) = \frac{1}{2\pi\sigma^2} exp(-\frac{i^2 + j^2}{2\sigma^2}) \tag{5}$$

Light and Dark Cell Layer
Based on the LMS values from the input layer, the response values of the light and dark cell layers are calculated. The response value for the coordinate (x, y) in the light and dark cell layer $\lambda(x, y)$ is calculated from Eq. (6). For the brightness, only the response values of the L and M cone cell layers are considered to be affected.

$$\lambda(x, y) = \sum_{j=-K/2}^{K/2} \sum_{i=-K/2}^{K/2} (f_L(x + i, y + j) + f_M(x + i, y + j))F(i, j) \quad (6)$$

Opponent Color Cell Layer
Based on the response values of the cone cell layer, the response values of the three opponent color cell layers (L_0, M_0, S_0 cell layers) are calculated. The response value $L_0(x, y)$ at coordinate (x, y) in the L_0 cell layer, the response value $M_0(x, y)$ in the M_0 cell layer, and the response value $S_0(x, y)$ in the S_0 cell layer are calculated from Eq. (7) to (9).

$$L_0(x, y) = \sum_{j=-K/2}^{K/2} \sum_{i=-K/2}^{K/2} (f_L(x + i, y + j), f_M(x + i, y + j), f_S(x + i, y + j))P_{L_0}F(i, j)$$
$$(7)$$

$$M_0(x, y) = \sum_{j=-K/2}^{K/2} \sum_{i=-K/2}^{K/2} (f_L(x + i, y + j), f_M(x + i, y + j), f_S(x + i, y + j))P_{M_0}F(i, j)$$
$$(8)$$

$$S_0(x, y) = \sum_{j=-K/2}^{K/2} \sum_{i=-K/2}^{K/2} (f_L(x + i, y + j), f_M(x + i, y + j), f_S(x + i, y + j))P_{S_0}F(i, j)$$
$$(9)$$

Based on the MSC model, the ratio of excitatory cells in the center to inhibitory cells in the periphery is 1:1 in the opponent color cells. The ratio of L-cones, M-cones, and S-cones in the inhibitory cells is 10:5:1. In the case of the L_0 cell layer, it is assumed that the central part is composed of L-cones and the surrounding area is composed of L-cones, M-cones, and S-cones, and the ratio of the number of cells is set to the above. At coordinate (x, y) in the L_0 cell layer, $P_{L_0}(x, y) = (1, 0, 0)^T$ if excitatory L-cones are located, $P_{L_0}(x, y) = (0, 1, 0)^T$ if M-cones, and $P_{L_0}(x, y) = (0, 0, 1)^T$ if S-cones. On the other hand, $P_{L_0}(x, y) = (-1, 0, 0)^T$ when the inhibitory L-cone is located, $P_{L_0}(x, y) = (0, -1, 0)^T$ when the M-cone is located, and $P_{L_0}(x, y) = (0, 0, -1)^T$ when the S-cone is located. Similarly, $P_{M_0}(x, y)$ for M_0 cell layer and $P_{S_0}(x, y)$ for S_0 cell layer.

Color Responsive Cell Layer
Based on the response values of the opponent color cell layer, the response values of the color responsive cell layer are calculated. In the MSC model, the basic combination of $L_0 - M_0$ and $M_0 - L_0$ responses in the color responsive cells, to which the S_0 response is added or subtracted, yields response values corresponding to red, yellow, green and blue perception. The number of cells is taken into account when calculating the addition and subtraction. In the MSC model, the ratio of Lo, Mo and So is 10:5:2. The reaction values $R(x, y)$ for the coordinate (x, y) in the R cell layer, $B(x, y)$ for the B cell layer, $G(x, y)$ for the G cell layer, and $Y(x, y)$ for the Y cell layer are obtained from Eq. (10) to (13), respectively.

$$R(x,y) = \sum_{j=-K/2}^{K/2} \sum_{i=-K/2}^{K/2} (f_L(x+i,y+j), f_M(x+i,y+j), f_s(x+i,y+j))(10,-5,2)^T F(i,j)$$
(10)

$$B(x,y) = \sum_{j=-K/2}^{K/2} \sum_{i=-K/2}^{K/2} (f_L(x+i,y+j), f_M(x+i,y+j), f_s(x+i,y+j))(-10,5,2)^T F(i,j)$$
(11)

$$G(x,y) = \sum_{j=-K/2}^{K/2} \sum_{i=-K/2}^{K/2} (f_L(x+i,y+j), f_M(x+i,y+j), f_s(x+i,y+j))(-10,5,-2)^T F(i,j)$$
(12)

$$Y(x,y) = \sum_{j=-K/2}^{K/2} \sum_{i=-K/2}^{K/2} (f_L(x+i,y+j), f_M(x+i,y+j), f_s(x+i,y+j))(10,-5,-2)^T F(i,j)$$
(13)

2.4 Visibility Prediction Method by a CNN Model

In this study, we use a regression-type convolutional neural network to predict the visibility values of a pairwise comparison image for the response values of these cell layers. Furthermore, we propose a CNN model with an improved structure to extract visibility features between images. The structure of the CNN used for the visibility prediction part is shown in Fig. 2.

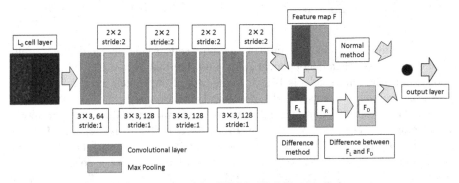

Fig. 2. Structure of the CNN for Visibility Prediction.

Figure 2 shows an example with the response values of the L_0 cell layer as input. The size of the cell layer, which is the input to the CNN, is $X \times Y$. As shown in Fig. 2, the structure of a CNN consists of several convolutional layers, a pooling layer, and an output layer (with one neuron). The CNN can be divided into two parts: the part that generates feature maps by convolution and pooling, and the part that predicts visibility values from the feature maps.

In the former processing part, the convolution layer and the pooling layer are basically arranged alternately, and the size of the filter used is set to 3×3. The feature map generated from the convolution layer is used to calculate the output value using the ReLU function. In the pooling layer, max-pooling is performed with a size of 2×2. The number of filters and strides in each convolution layer and the number of strides in the pooling layer are shown in Fig. 2. Padding is assumed to be zero padding.

The latter part is a procedure that calculates output values from the obtained feature maps, and uses two different methods. One is a method in which the feature map F and the output layer are fully connected (called normal method). The feature map F obtained from a pairwise comparison image can be divided into a feature map representing features in the left region F_L and a feature map representing features in the right region F_R with the center as a border. As a visibility factor, we consider it important to use the difference in features between the right and left regions. Therefore, the difference F_D between the feature maps of the right and left regions is obtained, and this is used as a new feature map, which is connected with the output layer (called difference method). If the size of the feature map F in Fig. 2 is $X_F \times Y_F$, k channels, the feature map F_D of the difference method has size $(\frac{X_F}{2}) \times Y_F$, k channels.

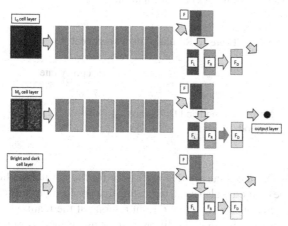

Fig. 3. Structure of the CNN when using response values from multiple cell layers.

Next, we discuss the case where the response values of multiple cell layers are used as input values to the CNN. In Fig. 3, L0 cell layer, M_0 cell layer, and the light and dark cell layer are used as input. As shown in Fig. 3, feature maps are created for the response values of each cell layer using a separate network consisting of a convolutional layer and a pooling layer. The feature maps obtained from each network are integrated and then connected to the output layer (with one neuron). In the normal method, if each feature map F has size $X_F \times Y_F$ and k channels, the feature map after integration has size $X_F \times Y_F$ and $k \times 3$ channels. On the other hand, in the case of the difference method, the integrated feature map has size $(X_F/2) \times Y_F$, $k \times 3$ channels. The integrated feature map and the output layer are fully connected.

When training a CNN model, we use 1,200 pairwise comparison images with background colors of red, green, and blue for training and 2,800 pairwise comparison images with background colors of cyan, magenta, yellow, WSC1, WSC2, WSC3, and WSC4 for evaluation. The teacher signal is the visibility value, the percentage of judges who judged the right area to be easy to see in a pairwise comparison experiment, described in Sect. 2.1. Therefore, the activation function used in the output layer of the CNN is a sigmoid function. The loss function is the sum of error squares, and the parameters are modified using stochastic gradient descent.

3 Evaluation

We evaluate the proposed method through evaluation experiments. To evaluate the structure of CNN models, we compare the difference method with the normal method (Experiment 1). In this case, we do not use the response values from the reproduction part of the color vision process as input values to the CNN, but use the pairwise comparison images (RGB values) for comparison (other training conditions are kept the same). The results are shown in Table 1. The accuracy rate in the Table 1 indicates the percentage (in percent) of the predictions that matched the experimental results for the pairwise comparison images (2,800 images) for evaluation.

Table 1. Results of the Experiment 1.

	Accuracy rate
Normal method	87.68%
Normal method and Difference method	90.79%

Table 1 shows that the accuracy rate is 87.68% for the normal method and 90.79% when the difference method is also used, indicating that the accuracy rate can be improved when the difference between the left and right regions of the feature map is also used. Next, the CNN is trained using eight different response values from the reproduction part of the color vision process as input values (Experiment 2). The results are shown in Table 2.

Table 2. Results of the Experiment 2.

	Accuracy rate
Pairwise comparison image (RGB)	90.79%
Light and dark cell layer	93.46%
L_0 cell layer	89.0%
M_0 cell layer	91.43%
S_0 cell layer	63.75%
R(G) cell layer	77.71%
B(Y) cell layer	60.29%

From Table 2, it can be seen that the prediction accuracy is improved when using the response values for the light and dark cell layer (93.46%) and the M_0 cell layer (91.43%), compared to when using the pairwise comparison images as input values (90.79%). Next, the CNN is trained using the response values of multiple cell layers as shown in Fig. 3 (Experiment 3). The results are shown in Table 3.

Table 3. Results of the Experiment 3.

	Accuracy rate
Light and dark cell layer	93.46%
Light and dark cell layer, L_0 cell layer	93.71%
Light and dark cell layer, M_0 cell layer	94.29%
L_0 cell layer, M_0 cell layer	91.43%
Light and dark cell layer, L_0 cell layer, M_0 cell layer	94.61%
All cell layers	94.07%

From Table 3, we obtain a 94.61% accuracy rate when using the response values for the light and dark cell layer, the L_0 cell layer, and the M_0 cell layer. It can be shown that the use of response values from multiple cell layers improves prediction accuracy. However, the prediction accuracy is lower when the response values of all cell layers are used (94.07%) than when the response values of the light and dark cell layer, L_0 cell layer, and M_0 cell layer are used (94.61%). We believe that the addition of response values from the S_0 cell layer and $B(Y)$ cell layer, which have low prediction accuracy, have an effect.

4 Conclusion

In this study, we proposed a method for predicting the visibility of images with unknown color schemes. In the proposed method, the response values of multiple cell layers of the MSC model are used as input values to the CNN, and filters are trained to improve the feature extraction used in visibility prediction. In addition, we proposed a CNN with an improved structure to extract features that contribute to visibility between images, and attempted to improve the prediction accuracy. An evaluation experiment was conducted on the data collected in the pairwise comparison experiment. The results showed that the proposed method was effective, with a 94.61% correct response rate when predictions were made using the response values of the light and dark cell layer, L_0 cell layer, and M_0 cell layer. In the future, we plan to test the effectiveness of the proposed model by collecting visibility data on general images using multiple colors, and to establish a more generalized prediction method.

References

1. Oikawa, T., Shinozawa, Y.: Prediction of visibility for background and character colors on the web browser. Trans. Hum. Interf. Soc. **14**(2), 75–86 (2012). (in Japanese)
2. Yoshioka, T., Shinozawa, Y.: Prediction of visibility of images composed of background and character colors with the Multi-Stage Color Model. Trans. Hum. Interf. Soc. **19**(1), 129–140 (2017). (in Japanese)
3. De Valois, R.L., De Valois, K.K.: A multi-stage color model. Vision. Res. **33**(8), 1053–1065 (1993)

Beyond Skin-Deep Investigations of Epidermal Activity to Predict Mental Workload Using Multiple Phasic Components: Implications for Real-Time Analysis Using Affordable Wearables

Simran Sian$^{(\boxtimes)}$ ⓘ, Anya D. Pejemsky ⓘ, Kathleen Van Benthem ⓘ,
and Chris M. Herdman ⓘ

Carleton University, Ottawa, ON K1S 5B6, Canada
SimSian@cmail.carleton.ca

Abstract. Epidermal Activity (EDA) has proved difficult for use in predicting workload states in complex tasks. Furthermore, a reliance on a single phasic component of the EDA may mask the true effects of workload on EDA. We hypothesized that decomposing a single time series into multiple principal components would identify a variety of phasic components reflecting the effects of task workload. In a 30-min simulated flight, pilots flew in two workload conditions which varied by task complexity. Mixed-factor ANOVA was used to analyze workload (within-subjects) and age (between-group) effects on the phasic components. The largest phasic component showed a marginal effect of workload, where higher workload was associated with larger EDA. Likewise, the smallest phasic component showed a significant main effect of workload, where higher workload was associated with larger EDA. Additionally, there was a significant effect of age, such that older pilots demonstrated larger EDA as compared to younger pilots. Results show that it is advantageous to decompose EDA time series data into multiple components of phasic data when predicting workload. Further work should be done to increase our understanding of using principal components of EDA in predicting workload during complex tasks.

Keywords: Epidermal activity · Mental workload · General aviation

1 Background

General aviation pilots are usually the sole operators of aircraft, which requires them to fully attend to and address a variety of flight information from multiple sources. General aviation pilots rely on all sensory modalities to maintain safe flight which can tax cognitive workload in the visual, auditory, and sensorimotor domains. Unsurprisingly, the accident rate in general aviation is significantly greater that of scheduled airline operations [1], and this rate tends to increase almost threefold when pilots surpass 65 years, as compared to 30-year-old pilots [2]. Real time monitoring of pilot mental workload would alert novice and experienced pilots to potentially dangerous situations.

© The Author(s), under exclusive license to Springer Nature Switzerland AG 2022
C. Stephanidis et al. (Eds.): HCII 2022, CCIS 1581, pp. 227–233, 2022.
https://doi.org/10.1007/978-3-031-06388-6_30

2 Literature Review

Epidermal activity (EDA) shows promise as an index of mental states and offers the benefits of being non-invasive, passive, and economical. The literature on the relationship of EDA and cognitive workload is varied. High cognitive workload has been shown to result in high skin conductivity (i.e., EDA) [3]. Yet, for complex tasks in naturalistic settings, EDA has mixed findings in predicting moderate versus high mental workload. Some studies found EDA and cognitive load to have significant negative relationships [4], while other studies have found significant positive relationships with cognitive load [3]. Furthermore, the influence of age on EDA is inconclusive [5]. Some studies have found age-related effects on EDA, such that older individuals have decreased skin conductance levels [5, 6]. While other research reports that older adults show similar emotion-related skin conductance responses, as compared to younger adults [7].

EDA data is typically decomposed into two components: a tonic (i.e., gradual change) and a single phasic (i.e., oscillatory) components. This dual component approach may mask potential effects of workload on EDA [8] due to a lack of granularity in the phasic component. In the present work we hypothesized that using Singular Spectrum Analysis (SSA) [9] to decompose a single time series into ten or more principal components (PCs) would identify both the non-useful tonic data [8] and also elicit multiple phasic components. We hypothesized that this fine-grained approach to phasic EDA could increase the opportunity of finding EDA components that were sensitive to the effects of cognitive workload during flight.

3 Methods

3.1 Flight Simulation

Pilots flew a 30-min simulated flight in two workload conditions which varied by flight-task complexity. The flight environment was a level-6 Cessna 172 flight simulator constructed from an actual fuselage. The flight control unit consisted of realistic instruments and controls and included calibrated rudder pedals, a yoke, throttle, and radio stack. Visuals were projected onto a large, curved screen. Pilots flew at two aerodromes where task load (e.g., aircraft control, landing, and communication) requirements were high. Between the aerodromes the flight tasks were less demanding, where the pilots flew at higher altitudes, had minimal communication requirements, and made fewer heading changes.

3.2 Biometric Data Collection, Processing and Analysis

EDA was measured on the supine surface of the left wrist and recorded at 4 Hz using a commercial off-the-shelf Empatica E4 wristband. The E4 uses proprietary algorithms to clean data of artifacts before accessing the data from a cloud-based service. The data was processed to insert labels denoting the low and high workload phases of flight and removed noisy artifacts from the start of each file. Singular Spectrum Analysis [9] was used to decompose the single time series data into 30 PCs. The decomposition used the trajectory approach (cf. Broomhead and King [10]). The goal of SSA is to mathematically decompose single time series data into multiple PCs that are interpretable, and separate tonic, phasic and even noise artifacts from the original source [11]. Components 11 to 30 were not used in the present analysis because they were small in magnitude and, similar to Aladağ et al. [12], we found the use of less than 10 components may be adequate to decompose EDA data. In this method, PC #1 was considered the tonic PC due to its reflection of the longer and slower change over the entire time series. The PCs 2–10 reflected almost all phasic data from the original EDA. The PCs were reconstructed to confirm the minimal loss of information using this SSA process. The nine PCs were loaded into a software normally used to analyze EEG but found appropriate to analyze EDA data (EEGLAB 2021.1, [13]). The processing steps included segmentation into six- second lengths, detrending, and removal of outlier segments. Data was exported in a format that provided average EDA values for each workload condition for each PC. The PCs were analyzed using repeated measures analysis of variance (SPSS v 27) with workload as a within-subject variable and age group as a between-group variable (ages 50+ were the older age group, $n = 23$ in each age group).

3.3 Sample Characteristics

The present investigation is part of a larger research agenda studying the effects of aging and experience on pilot performance. While 51 pilots flew the flight scenarios, 46 pilots had adequate EDA data from both workload conditions. Pilot age ranged from 18 to 71 years. Pilot experience ranged from student to highly experienced airline pilots. Written informed consent was obtained and this experiment was reviewed by the university research ethics board.

4 Results

4.1 Raw EDA Data Decomposition

The SSA algorithms decomposed the original single stream of data into components that were ordered by magnitude. Thus, PC #2 had larger EDA values in comparison to PC#3, etc. The decomposition was not based on peripheral information pertaining to workload states or other potential moderators of the data, such as participant age. As described above, the tonic component (PC #1) had the largest in magnitude compared to the remaining PCs (2–9). PC #1 was not used in the present analysis due to its tendency to steadily increase from the beginning to end of the flight, which was likely an index of overall warmth of the pilot under the overhead light in the simulator cockpit (see Fig. 1, left image). The remaining nine PCs show typical phasic characteristics of EDA, without the steady increase in values across the 30-min in the simulator as is shown by the raw data (see Fig. 1 [left]).

4.2 Workload and Age Effects on EDA

Two of the nine phasic components showed an effect of workload and/or age factors; PCs 3–8 had $ps > .05$ for all main or interaction effects. The largest phasic PC showed

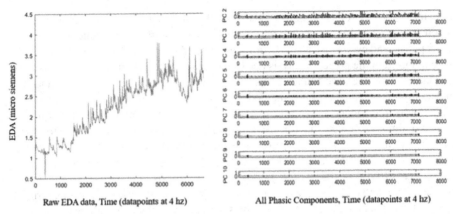

Fig. 1. Raw EDA (left) and phasic PCs (right) from a single participant. Note the increasing tonic trend across the full time course (left).

a marginal effect of workload, where higher workload was associated with larger EDA, $F(1,41) = 3.52$, $p = .068$, $\eta p^2 = .079$. This result was mainly driven by an interaction with age group, $F(1,41) = 3.47$, $p = .07$, $\eta p^2 = .078$, where the effect of workload is seen only in the older age group (see Fig. 2, left panel).

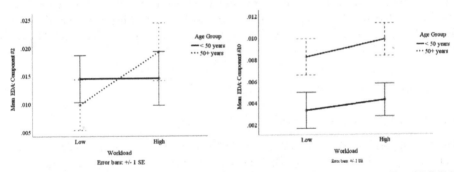

Fig. 2. Effects of workload and age group on EDA for the phasic PC #2 (left panel) and PC #10 (right panel).

The smallest phasic PC (#10) showed a significant main effect of workload, where higher workload was associated with larger EDA, $F(1,44) = 4.68$, $p = .036$, $\eta p^2 = .096$ (see Fig. 2, right panel). Also, a significant main effect of age was seen where older pilots demonstrated larger EDA than the younger pilots, $F(1,44) = 5.88$, $p = .019$, $\eta p^2 = 118$.

4.3   Ad Hoc Investigation of Spectral Power in Relevant Components

In the present work there were no a priori hypotheses regarding which phasic PC might show any effects of workload or age. Given that components were ordered by magnitude, it was surprising that both the largest and smallest PCs revealed effects of workload and/or age. An ad hoc analysis was conducted to investigate the unique and inherent spectral features (i.e., spectral signatures) of PCs #2 and #10. The spectral information was extracted at both low and delta frequencies for all the phasic PCs. The absolute power at a low frequency band (average of .1 to .9 Hz) and at the delta range (average of 1 to 4 Hz) were extracted using the Darbeliai plugin for EEGLAB [13].

There were clear trends in the power values at the low and delta frequency bands across all phasic PCs. The power at less than 1 Hz (see Fig. 3, left panel) was greatest in PC #2 and then dropped significantly for PCs 3–10, with little difference in power noted between the smallest PCs. In contrast, at the delta range the power was greatest for the smallest component (#10) and increase incrementally across PCs 2–9 (see Fig. 3, right panel). The ad hoc analysis indicated that the spectral features of the phasic components varied systematically across the PCs.

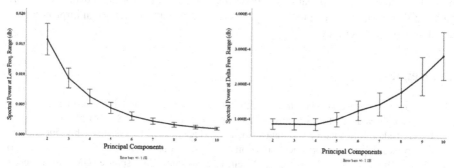

Fig. 3. Spectral power at low and delta frequencies for all PCs.

5 Discussion

In decomposing the EDA data into 10 PCs using SSA, we showed that the PCs 2–9 displayed typical features of phasic data (i.e., the range of the EDA values were within 0 to 1.5μS. for the entire time series). Each successive component showed incrementally smaller values, which confirmed that no more than 9 PCs were required to reconstruct most of the phasic structure of the data. This finding is similar to Aladağ et al. [12], who found that seven components provided adequate decomposition of their EDA data. Interestingly, both the largest and the smallest phasic components showed sensitivity to workload manipulations. For PC #2, only the older group presented the characteristic increase in EDA in the high workload condition. Although studies have shown that EDA responses in older adults are typically attenuated, not all indices of skin activity necessarily decrease in older age [5]. The strong low frequency band feature in the largest phasic PC may be tied to the neural networks that also affect heart rate when workload increases, which also operate at low and very low frequencies. For PC #10, stronger workload and age effects were noted, with higher values associated with the high workload condition and with the older pilots. Although PC #10 was relatively much smaller in EDA values, it showed a stronger sensitivity to workload and age, as compared to PC #2. The ad hoc spectral analysis showed that PC #10 had the largest power for the delta band frequency, as compared to the remaining phasic components. Delta band power for other biometric indices, such as electroencephalography, show that increases in delta power may indicate attentional activity, where the brain uses delta rhythm to block out less-relevant information from the periphery during periods of high workload [14]. Our finding regarding the pattern of changes in low and delta power across the PCs may lead to further insights into how some PCs of EDA may reflect mental states [15].

6   Conclusion

In this work, changes in cognitive demands during flight affected two phasic components of EDA such that higher workload was associated with higher EDA. The novel methods and findings in this work are useful for future research on real time monitoring of pilot mental workload. The implications of early detection of high workload using accessible and non-disruptive wearable technology may be an important strategy in improving the accident rate in general aviation.

References

1. Northcutt, M.: General aviation accident rate: how general aviation differs from commercial airline flight and how to correct the discrepancy. J. AIR L. COM. **78**, 381 (2013)
2. Li, G., Baker, S.P., Qiang, Y., Grabowski, J.G., McCarthy, M.L.: Driving-while-intoxicated history as a risk marker for general aviation pilots. Acc. Anal. Prevent. **37**(1), 179–184 (2005)
3. Shi, Y., Ruiz, N., Taib, R., Choi, E., Chen, F.: Galvanic skin response (GSR) as an index of cognitive load. In: Conference on Human Factors in Computing Systems - Proceedings, pp. 2651–2656 (2007). https://doi.org/10.1145/1240866.1241057
4. Ikehara, C.S., Crosby, M.E.: Assessing cognitive load with physiological sensors. In: Proceedings of the Annual Hawaii International Conference on System Sciences, vol. 295 (2005). https://doi.org/10.1109/HICSS.2005.103
5. Bari, D.S., Yacoob Aldosky, H.Y., Martinsen, Ø.G.: Simultaneous measurement of electrodermal activity components correlated with age-related differences. J. Biol. Phys. **46**(2), 177–188 (2020). https://doi.org/10.1007/S10867-020-09547-4/TABLES/4
6. Gavazzeni, J., Wiens, S., Fischer, H.: Age effects to negative arousal differ for self-report and electrodermal activity. Psychophysiol. **45**(1), 148–151 (2008). https://doi.org/10.1111/J.1469-8986.2007.00596.X
7. Aupée, A.M.: Effect of Normal Aging on Emotional Processing and Impact of Emotion on Memory : Psychophysiological and Cognitive Findings. Thesis, Lund University (2006). http://lup.lub.lu.se/record/546007
8. Posada-Quintero, H.F., Chon, K.H.: Phasic component of electrodermal activity is more correlated to brain activity than tonic component. In: 2019 IEEE EMBS International Conference on Biomedical Health Informatics (BHI), pp. 1–4 (2019). https://doi.org/10.1109/BHI.2019.8834567
9. Groth, A., Ghil, M.: Monte Carlo Singular Spectrum Analysis (SSA) revisited: detecting oscillator clusters in multivariate datasets. J. Clim. **28**, 7873–7893 (2015)
10. Broomhead, D.S., King, G.P.: Extracting qualitative dynamics from experimental data. Physica D **20**, 217–236 (1986)

11. Hassani, H.: Singular spectrum analysis: methodology and comparison. J. Data Sci. **5**, 239–257 (2007)

12. Aladağ, S., Ayşegül, G., Nazan, D., Hatice, Ö.: The Role of sports participation in hemispheric dominance: assessment by electrodermal activity signals. IU-JEEE **17**(1), 3113–3119 (2017)

13. Delorme, A., Makeig, S.: EEGLAB: an open-source toolbox for analysis of single-trial EEG dynamics. J. Neurosci. Methods **134**, 9–21 (2004)

14. Harmony, T.: The functional significance of delta oscillations in cognitive processing. Front. Integr. Neurosci. **7**(December), 83 (2013). https://doi.org/10.3389/fnint.2013.00083

15. Vautard, R., Yiou, P., Ghil, M.: Singular-spectrum analysis: A toolkit for short, noisy chaotic signals. Phys. D **58**(1–4), 95–126 (1992)

The Effect of Exercise on Visual Fatigue Based on Eye Movement

Guilei Sun[✉], Yanhua Meng, and Luyao Wang

School of Safety Engineering, China University of Labor Relations, Beijing 100048, China
sunguilei@culr.edu.cn

Abstract. The wide application of visualization equipment makes people's visual fatigue more and more serious. Correspondingly, the recovery of visual fatigue is a very important topic in the current society. An experiment was carried on the recovery of visual fatigue. 30 subjects in a state of visual fatigue were measured by Tobii Glasses X-30 for 5 min exercise or overlooking. Questionnaire was used to obtain subjects' subjective sensation of visual fatigue. The results showed that both table tennis exercise and overlooking had a good effect on visual fatigue recovery. Questionnaire indicated that table tennis exercise had a little better recovery effect on the visual fatigue than overlooking far away because table tennis exercise caused much more eye movement. Overlooking far away focused more on the rest of eyes so that the physiological parameters caused by visual fatigue can be easy recovered.

Keywords: Eye movement · Number of blinks · Pupil diameter · Visual fatigue recovery · Overlooking

1 Introduction

The problem of visual fatigue has been widely concerned around the world. If visual fatigue can't recover for a long time, it will cause serious adverse consequences for the body. Many kinds of visual fatigue analysis were researched, and eye movement analysis was the more commonly used objective analysis method. Through the analysis of the eye movement data, it can be judged and summarized the visual responses and laws of the subjects in the experiment, thus revealing the basic cognitive processes, comprehension processes and visual processing processes [1]. Through the study of driving simulation with eye tracker, Wang [2] found that the hierarchical ordered discrete selection model can realize the consideration of individual differences and enable the driver to accurately identify different fatigue levels. Chen et al. [3] found that the physiological data of human body is correlated with the degree of visual fatigue, the degree of fatigue is positively correlated with blood oxygen saturation and negatively correlated with heart rate. Zhao [4] showed that the combined classification of ECG and pulse can accurately measure visual fatigue. Shi [5] concluded that there is a significant positive correlation between the degree of visual fatigue and pupil diameter through the fatigue eye movement experiment. Zhang et al. [6] obtained through the eye tracker experiment that when

C. Stephanidis et al. (Eds.): HCII 2022, CCIS 1581, pp. 234–240, 2022.
https://doi.org/10.1007/978-3-031-06388-6_31

watching 3D videos, the blink frequency was reduced compared with ordinary videos, and the speed, frequency and amplitude of saccade were improved. And after watching for 40 min, it will gradually approach the degree of watching ordinary videos. Sun et al. [7, 8] used eye tracker, questionnaire survey and flash fusion instrument to study the fatigue caused by the 3D display, the result showed that the pupil diameter of the left and right eyes is not synchronized with Red Blue 3D glasses and 3D visual fatigue lead to a decrease in respiratory frequency.

At present, more and more scholars have studied the visual fatigue based on the relevant parameters obtained by the eye tracker, such as eye blink, gaze, pupil diameter and saccade. However, there is little research on visual fatigue recovery, especially on recovery method.

2 Experiments

2.1 Subjects

30 college students without eye diseases and with corrected vision of 1.0 or above were selected, including 15 males and 15 females, with an average age of 21.2 years old. Before the experiment, all subjects signed informed consent.

2.2 Design of the Subjective Fatigue Survey Questionnaire

The purpose of the questionnaire was to obtain the subjective feelings of the subjects before and after the experiment. The quantification of visual fatigue is divided into 10 grades in the questionnaire, ranging from 1 level to 10 level, in which 1 means completely no fatigue and 10 means severe fatigue. Fatigue level was determined by the subjects themselves before and after the experiment.

2.3 Experimental Methods

30 subjects were in a visual fatigue state (above 5 points) through watching 60 min VR video. Then, the subjects were divided into two groups: one for 5-min overlooking (named group of overlooking the distance, GOD) and the other for 5 min playing table tennis (named group of table tennis, GTT). The real-time eye movement parameters of the subjects were measured through TOBII GLASSES X 30, and the subjective feelings of visual fatigue were obtained through questionnaire.

3 Data Analysis

3.1 Questionnaire Analysis

Apparently improved means equal to, or more than 3 levels reduced while a certain degree improvement is less than 3 levels. As shown in Table 1, the results of the questionnaire showed that the number of subjects significantly improved in the GTT is more than GOD, which means that the subjects had better subjective feelings after the exercise in reducing visual fatigue than overlooking far away. The reason is that table tennis exercise caused much more eye movement which alleviate visual fatigue.

Table 1. Results of the survey questionnaire

	GTT	GOD
All subjects	15	15
Number of apparently improved	9	0
Number of a certain degree improvement	3	12
Number of not obvious improvement	3	3

3.2   Analysis of Eye Movement Data

3.2.1   Eye Blink Times

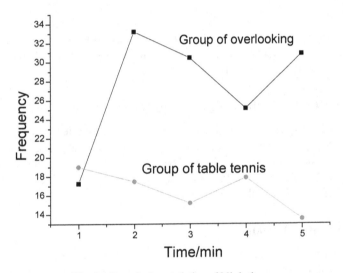

Fig. 1. Descriptive statistics of blink times

Differential analysis indicates that the eye blink times between GTT and GOD showed no significant difference, therefore, the data of two groups can be used for analyzing. Descriptive statistics of the eye blink times for GTT and GOD in the first minute (1st min), the second minute (2nd min), the third minute (3rd min), the fourth minute (4th min) and the fifth minute (5th min) are shown in Fig. 1.

The average blink times of GTT showed a downward trend while the blink number of group of overlooking increased significantly in the 5 min experiment. However, GTT were less than the blink times at the beginning and GOD were higher than the beginning. Further, the data were tested for normality. Since the sample size was 15 which was a small sample test, the Shapiro-Wilke test was selected, and the test results are shown in Table 2.

Table 2. Blink times Shapiro-Wilke normality test

	Mean value of GTT blink times		Mean value of GOD blink times	
	Statistics	Sig.	Statistics	Sig.
1st min	0.891	0.069	0.879	0.046
2nd min	0.881	0.049	0.880	0.048
3rd min	0.894	0.077	0.946	0.466
4th min	0.916	0.167	0.799	0.004
5th min	0.888	0.062	0.840	0.012

The results showed that GTT was less than 0.05 only at the 2nd min, which did not meet the normal distribution, the Wilkerson signed-rank test was required in non-parametric variables, and the paired t test was used for the remaining groups. The Shapiro-Wilke test indicates that the 1st min, the 2nd min, the 4th min and the 5th min were less than 0.05, which does not conform to the normal distribution rule. Therefore, Wilcokson signed rank test should be used for the difference analysis of the blinking times. The test results are show in Table 3 (Table 4).

Table 3. Test of difference for GTT in eyeblink times

min-min	Average value	Standard deviation	Sig.	Method of calibration
2nd-1st	2.937	20.134	0.572	Shapiro-Wilke test
3rd-1st	3.800	20.288	0.480	Paired t test
4th-1st	1.133	19.430	0.825	Paired t test
5th-1st	5.467	20.266	0.314	Paired t test

Table 4. Test of difference for GOD in eyeblink times.

min-min	2nd-1st	3rd-1st	4th-1st	5th-1st
Z	−1.875	−2.074	−0.880	−2.160
Asymptotic significance (double-tail)	0.061	0.038	0.379	0.031

The test results showed that the blink times of GOD at the 3rd and the 5th min was statistically different compared with the 1st min data, and the number of blinking would increase in subjects. Although the number of blink times showed a downward trend, the change of blink times still did not show a statistical difference, and the GTT did not show a significant difference in the number of blink times in visual fatigue.

The number of blinking in GTT is on a downward trend and group of overlooking shows an upward trend, which may be caused by the subjects who need to focus on table tennis, so the number of blinking is less. However, in the group of overlooking far away, the visual fatigue gradually recovers, the eyes rest and the eye muscles are fully relaxed.

Differential Analysis of the Pupil Diameter. Descriptive statistics of mean pupil diameter at each minute for GTT and GOD are shown in Fig. 2.

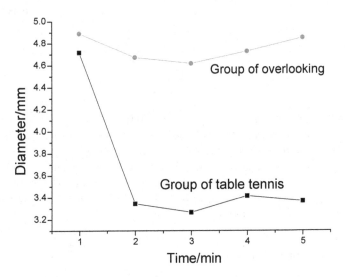

Fig. 2. Descriptive statistics of mean pupil diameter

It can be seen from the description statistical results that the subjects had only a slight decrease in mean pupil diameter of GOD, while the mean pupil diameter of the GTT had a significant decrease. The data were normally tested, and the test results are shown in Table 5.

Table 5. Mean pupil diameter by Shapiro-Wilke normality test.

	GTT		GOD	
	Statistics	Sig.	Statistics	Sig.
1st min	0.930	0.270	0.964	0.764
2nd min	0.970	0.864	0.956	0.622
3rd min	0.934	0.318	0.944	0.434
4th min	0.938	0.359	0.913	0.149
5th min	0.932	0.289	0.903	0.106

Shapiro-Wilke normality test was used for the mean pupil diameters of GTT and GOD. The results of sig. were all seems greater than 0.05. With paired t-test, the results were shown in Table 6 and Table 7.

Table 6. Difference test of in mean pupil diameter for GTT.

min-min	Average value	Standard deviation	Standard error mean value	Difference value: 95% confidence interval		t	Sig.
				Lower limit	Superior limit		
2nd-1st	0.21933	0.80650	0.20824	−0.22729	0.66596	1.053	0.310
3rd-1st	0.27467	0.91899	0.23728	−0.23425	0.78359	1.158	0.266
4th-1st	0.16200	10.00435	0.25932	−0.39419	0.71819	0.625	0.542
5th-1st	0.04000	0.94892	0.24501	−0.48550	0.56550	0.163	0.873

The difference test results showed that the slight drop did not have significant difference compared with the 1st min, and the mean pupil diameter could change in subjects with visual fatigue during exercise.

The description of the statistical results showed that the 15 subjects of GOD had a significant decrease in mean pupil diameter during the 2nd min to the 5th min compared to the 1st min, and whether this difference was statistically significant or not, differential analysis is required.

Table 7. Group of overlooking test of difference in mean pupil diameter.

min-min	Average value	Standard deviation	Standard error mean value	Difference value: 95% confidence interval		t	Conspicuousness
				Lower limit	Superior limit		
2nd-1st	1.37267	0.93211	0.24067	0.85648	1.88885	5.704	0.000
3rd-1st	1.45133	0.97660	0.25216	0.91051	1.99215	5.756	0.000
4th-1st	1.30133	1.01707	0.26261	0.73810	1.86457	4.955	0.000
5th-1st	1.34800	1.05006	0.27112	0.76649	1.92951	4.972	0.000

The difference test results showed that the mean pupil diameter of each minute decreased significantly compared with that of the 1st min. This conclusion was statistically significant, indicating that the mean pupil diameter of the visual fatigue person could decrease significantly in the distance, which was because the eyes had a full rest when looking in the distance.

4 Conclusions

1. There was a trend towards decreases in the group of playing table tennis while there was a significantly increase in the group of overlooking the distance.

2. Overlooking the distance can make the visual fatigue of the eye muscles to resume the active state, has a positive impact on the recovery of visual fatigue.
3. The pupil diameter playing the table tennis group becomes smaller because of the fixation while overlooking the distance does not need fixation.
4. The questionnaire survey shows that eye movement will make the subjects have a better subjective feeling.

Acknowledgements. The presented work has been supported by General project of China University of Labor Relations (22XYJS006).

References

1. Morita, K., Maeda, N., Kawaoka, T., et al.: Effects of the time interval between clamping and linear stapling for resection of porcine small intestine. Surg. Endosc. **22**(3), 750–756 (2008)
2. Wang, X., Li, F.: Eye Indicators and drowsy level analysis based on driving simulator. J. Tongji Univ. (Nat. Scie. Ed.), **43**(02), 226–231 + 264 (2015)
3. Chen, Y., Tu, Y., Wang, L., Shen, L., He, Y.: Study on physiological indicators during visual fatigue state. Electron. Dev. **38**(06), 1245–1248 (2015)
4. Zhao, Z.: Study on the identification method of visual fatigue state based on ECG pulse signal. Lanzhou University of Technology (2010)
5. Zhang, L., Ren, J., Xu, L., Zhang, J., Zhao, J.: Visual comfort and fatigue measured by eye movement analysis when watching three-dimensional displays. Ophthalmol. China **23**(01), 37–42 (2014)
6. Shi, X., Wang, S.: Evaluation of visual fatigue based on eye motion parameters. Technol. Inf. **21**, 172–173 (2012)
7. Sun, G.: Research on respiratory signals for visual fatigue caused by 3D display. In: Long, S., Dhillon, B.S. (eds.) MMESE 2020. LNEE, vol. 645, pp. 663–672. Springer, Singapore (2020). https://doi.org/10.1007/978-981-15-6978-4_76
8. Sun, G., Lin, Y., Ran, L., Meng, Y.: Effect of red blue 3D videos on visual fatigue. In: Harris, D., Li, W.-C. (eds.) HCII 2021, LNAI, vol. 12457, pp. 427–437. Springer, Cham (2021). https://doi.org/10.1007/978-3-030-77932-0_33

The Effect of Social Media Interruptions on Office Workers' Mental Workload Using Physiological Measures

Elmira Zahmat Doost[1]($\boxtimes$) and Wei Zhang[1,2]

[1] Department of Industrial Engineering, Tsinghua University, Beijing 100084, China
zahmatde10@mails.tsinghua.edu.cn, zhangwei@tsinghua.edu.cn
[2] State Key Laboratory of Automobile Safety, Beijing, China

Abstract. Recently, the availability of physiological measures to estimate cognitive activity builds new opportunities to help people understand themselves and their work or for systems to adapt. However, office employees often have to deal with a significant mental workload (MWL) due to the increasing proliferation of mobile technology interruptions. This study investigated the impact of social media (SM) interruptions on MWL and physiological reactions with 30 office workers. Each participant executed four simulated computer tasks. The simulated tasks included reading and writing tasks performed during two conditions (single vs. interrupted). The results identified that MWL was significantly higher during interrupted tasks than single tasks. Moreover, the effect of SM interruption on perceived MWL and physiological responses during the reading task is higher than in writing, but participants during interrupted condition did the writing task with less accuracy than the reading task. These findings provide practical and theoretical implications for both employers and employees on how to manage SM information interruptions in the workplace and may lead future studies into cognitive activity monitoring in real environments.

Keywords: Social media · Interruptions · Office workers · Physiological measurement

1 Introduction

Interruptions while performing a task are a necessary part of work environments. With the rapid development of mobile technology and smart devices, social media such as wikis, blogs, instant messaging (IM), and social networking sites (SNSs) have dramatically increased the number of interruptions [1]. Although the widespread use of social media (SM) provides convenience, it also has some negative outcomes, such as frequent interruptions, particularly at work [2, 3]. The negative effects of frequent interruptions (personal inquiries, calls, emails, etc.) are increased mental workload (MWL), recovery effort, increased error rate, time loss, and elicit feelings of stress and anxiety as well [4]. Time loss encompasses not only the duration of the interruption but also the time required to resume the primary task following the interruption. Human brains need about twenty-three minutes to continue their task after getting interrupted [5]. Research has found that individuals at work are interrupted four times per hour on average, and online distractions are the most common [6]. Office workers face a variety of interruptions, such as emails, co-workers' inquiries, or instant messages [7]. Despite the existing research evidence, the effect of SM interruptions on office workers' MWL has not yet been investigated. Thus, to develop the understanding of MWL in the office environment, simulated office-like tasks (i.e., writing and reading) with mobile SM interruptions were characterized.

According to distraction theory, interruptions can be defined as externally generated, unpredictable events that disrupt the flow of cognitive focus on the ongoing task [8, 9]. In addition, interruptions cause an attention switch and use the same sensory channel as those used by the primary task [9]. Due to limited cognitive resources that are not well allocated across multiple tasks, interruptions mainly caused increased MWL, reduced efficiency, and deteriorated psychological symptoms such as feelings of "time pressure" and overloaded responsibility [10].

MWL has been used as an essential factor to evaluate human performance in complex systems. Moray (1988) also found that optimizing the MWL allocation could decrease human errors and improve operators' satisfaction [11]. Mental workload can be defined as the amount of mental effort required for an individual to complete a specific task [12]. To measure MWL, earlier studies developed assessment by performance measures, subjective ratings, and measurement of physiological processes [13–15]. In comparison with subjective and performance measures, physiological indices possess better performance in terms of sensitivity, potential diagnostic, and non-intrusiveness [16, 17]. Although MWL is multidimensional and hard to assess directly [18], former researchers have proposed that using merged indices (subjective rating, task performance, and physiological responses) can arrive at satisfying precision [22]. In this work, we also applied a combination of subjective rating, task performance, and physiological signals to evaluate MWL.

2   Method

2.1   Study Population

To estimate a suitable sample size, an a-priori power analysis was invoked by G*Power (version 3.1.9.6) [27] and the 'Cohen (1988)' effect size option. The analysis showed that 28 participants would be needed. However, two extra participants were recruited because of experimental dropout and deletions. Therefore, thirty participants were recruited from the university employments (n = 30; sixteen females and fourteen males; age = 44.8 ± 14.8 years). All selected participants were healthy individuals and were excluded if they had a history of neurological or mental illness or organic disease, such as heart-related and skin conditions. Each participant signed a consent form and received 150 RMB (~23 US dollars) as a financial incentive. The experiment protocol was approved by the Institutional Review Board of the Industrial Engineering Department, Tsinghua University.

2.2 Apparatus

Subjects were seated in front of an Acer P229HQL screen with 1920×1080 resolution. The experiment was controlled by PsychoPy 3.0. For interruption condition, we employed an online tool on http://www.wjx.cn, a professional online survey platform in China, to disturb participants' attention from the primary task by their cell phones. Participants sat in a quiet place with standard lighting, about 55 cm from the screen, with no chin rest. Electromyography was used to evaluate the MWL fluctuations due to SM interruptions over office-like tasks, including reading and writing. For physiological signal acquisition, non-invasive wearable electrocardiography (ECG) and electrodermal activity (EDA) sensors were used (Fig. 1(a)). The analysis and signal recording were accomplished on the ErgoLAB® cloud platform (Kingfar Technology Co., Ltd, Beijing, China) for human-machine-environment examinations, which obtains the subjects' physiological change data in the factual state without restriction and interference. The EDA raw data were captured from the finger extensors set on the index fingers and left-hand middle, and ECG indications were read from the ear clip sensor and index.

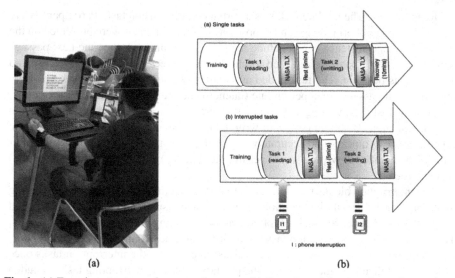

Fig. 1. (a) Experiment setup and sensors placement (b) Overview of the experimental procedure

2.3 Procedure

Participants were reminded to have a good rest the night before the experiment and prevent caffeinated drinks. While participants reached the lab, the experimenter gave an overview of the experiment and described the primary and interrupted tasks, and users performed several practice tasks.

The experiment used 2 primary tasks (writing and reading) $\times$ 2 conditions (single vs. interrupted) mixed design, and users completed a total of 4 tasks with a 10 min rest between two sections. Figure 1(b) presents a sequence comprising start of the primary task in single and interrupted conditions; (a) single condition: the participant was instructed to finish two main tasks as quickly as possible while keeping accuracy on the tasks. The user was also required to fill in the NASA-TLX questionnaire instantly after completing each task. Once the questionnaire was finished, a fixation cross was revealed on the monitor for 5 min as a baseline condition before each further task. (b) interrupted condition: participants started interrupted tasks after 10 min recovery. The procedure for the disrupted circumstance was like that of the single condition. The distinction was that each main task was halted with three SM interruptions with an uncertain time distance in between. Disrupted tasks were exhibited on subjects' cellphones, and they should complete the interruption tasks immediately and then continue the primary tasks. To diminish learning effects, the order of the primary and interruption tasks were randomized.

2.4   Task and Conditions

As shown in Fig. 1(b), the reading and writing tasks were designed to require corresponding levels of MWL with the addition of SM interruptions to overload participants' MWL.

Reading task: The reading task was a verbal comprehension task. Participants were required to read a short passage and choose one of four sentences were presented on the screen (only one sentence can conclude the passage accurately), then the next passage will appear. Participants were asked to choose the correct conclusion as quickly and accurately as possible. The task ended automatically after 5 min. The outcomes were the number of passages read per minute (latency) and the wrong answers (error rate).

Writing Task: The writing task included several sentences that were presented on the screen, and subjects should copy and write them in the answer box. Participants were asked to write as quickly and accurately as possible. The task ended automatically after 5 min. The number of written words per minute (latency) and wrong words (error rate) was recorded.

The interruption blocks were designed to distract an individual's attention and bring the primary task to a halt, interruption's handling, and resumption. Participants scanned the prepared QR code with their cellphones at the beginning of the interrupted condition. They received three interruption tasks with different time distances (t_1, t_2, and t_3) during each primary task. Participants were asked to complete the interruption tasks once they received them and then resumed the primary task. The interrupting tasks included watching short videos and receiving text messages that required to reply.

2.5   Measurements and Data Analysis

This study investigated the impact of the independent variable (SM interruptions) on the dependent variables (i.e., subjective perceptions of workload, task performance, and physiological measures). Behavioral data were assessed using the number of words read and written per minute and the error rate of the primary tasks. The NASA-TLX workload questionnaire [21] gathered subjective MWL information. Participants' physiological indices (EDA and ECG) were also recorded. First, physiological signals were pre-processed by ErgloLAB. Data cleaned with wavelet denoising and high-pass, low-pass, and root-mean-square (RMS) filtering. The signal under each task level was divided into five-time nodes (1 min, 2 min, 3 min, and 5 min during the experiment). The quality of recordings data was checked, and poor signals were excluded from the analysis. Then, a two-way repeated-measures analysis of variance (ANOVA) was used to examine the effects of SM interruption on subjective ratings, task performance, and physiological parameters. To make sure all ANOVA assumptions were met, residual normality and constant variance were applied. The variables with non-normal distribution were transformed using Z-score standardization (standardization of x is ($X_{current}$ − $X_{average}$)/(SD $_{of\ raw\ data}$) [23]. If Mauchy's test of sphericity was significant ($p < 0.05$), the Greenhouse-Geisser correction was used to adjust degrees of freedom. A paired t-test was used to evaluate the pairwise comparisons. The data analysis was done using SPSS version 25.0 (IBM Corporation, Armonk, NY, USA). Statistical significance for all tests was set at $p < 0.05$.

3 Results

3.1 Self-reported Mental Workload Levels

Figure 2 presented the mean TLX overall workload for different reading and writing tasks in single and interrupted conditions. The results of the NASA-TLX questionnaire indicate that the participants perceive a higher workload during interrupted tasks than the single tasks. A two-way ANOVA with repeated measures showed a significant effect of SM interruption on overall MWL with ($F(1, 29) = 1134.63$, $p < 0.05$, $\eta^2 = 0.975$). Additionally, paired t-tests showed that differences between single and interrupted conditions for reading tasks are more than writing ($t_{writing}(29) = -20.99$, Δmean $= -21.76$, $p < 0.05$ and $t_{reading}(29) = -26.61$, Δmean $= -28.06$, $p < 0.05$).

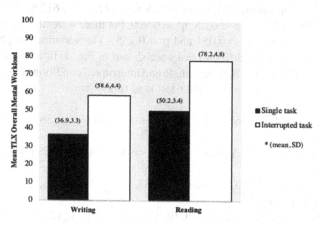

Fig. 2. Comparisons of TLX overall

3.2 Task Performance (TP)

The ANOVA test showed that there was a main effect of and SM interruption on latency and error rate with $F(1, 29) = 27.14$, $\eta^2 = 0.484$, $p < 0.05$ and $F(1, 29) = 1177.67$, η^2

= 0.976, p < 0.05, respectively. Figure 3 shows that the participants were more accurate and responded faster in the single condition than in the SM interrupting condition. Additionally, paired t-tests showed that there are significant differences between single and interrupted tasks performance but the effect of interruptions on writing is more than reading (error rate: $t_{writing}(29) = -43.36$, Δmean $= -8.23$, p < 0.05 and $t_{reading}(29) = -12.00$, Δmean $= -2.03$, p < 0.05; latency: $t_{writing}(29) = 4.63$, Δmean $= 17.5$, p < 0.05 and $t_{reading}(29) = 13.85$, Δmean $= 2.33$, p < 0.05).

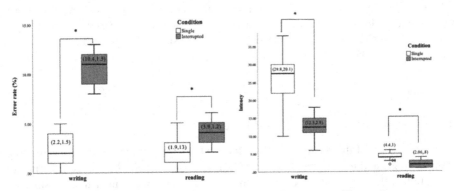

Fig. 3. The comparison of task performance (error rate and latency)

3.3 Physiological Results

The ANOVA results of physiological signals showed that there were significant main effects of SM interruption on LF/HF and SDNN with $F(1, 26) = 612.84$, p < 0.05, $\eta^2 = 0.959$ and $F(1, 26) = 26569$, p < 0.05, $\eta^2 = 0.909$, but there were no significant effects on HR and SC responses (p = 0.054 and p = 0.155). The variations of physiological signals with time under the different tasks are shown in Fig. 4. In addition, the paired t-test showed that differences between single and interrupted conditions for reading tasks are more than writing. The result of the t-test is as follows:

HR: $t_{writing}(26) = -.459$, Δmean $= -1.33$, p = 0.65 and $t_{reading}(26) = -8.37$, Δmean $= -2.43$, p < 0.05;
SDNN: $t_{writing}(26) = 12.44$, Δmean $= 3.59$, p < 0.05 and $t_{reading}(29) = 13.15$, Δmean $= -3.65$, p < 0.05;
LF/HF: $t_{writing}(29) = -29.89$, Δmean $= -2.83$, p < 0.05 and $t_{reading}(29) = - 18.47$, Δmean $= -2.48$, p < 0.05;
SC: $t_{writing}(29) = -8.923$, Δmean $= -1.10$, p < 0.05 and $t_{reading}(29) = -11.55$, Δmean $= -1.19$, p < 0 .05.

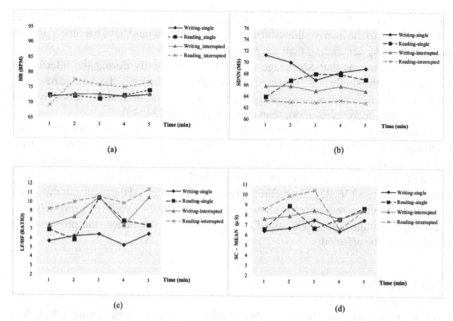

Fig. 4. The comparison of physiological signals evoked by tasks in different conditions

4 Discussion

The aim of this work was to assess SM interruptions' impacts over office-type tasks on MWL. This paper reports outcomes relevant to MWL acquired from 30 office employments when doing the simulated-computer tasks (writing and reading). MWL data was measured by physiological responses (EDA and ECG), the NASA TLX method, and task performance data including latency and error rate. The results demonstrated subjective rating (NASA-TLX), physiological responses (LF/HF and SDNN), and task performance changed with SM interruptions.

The main finding of this study was that indices from ECG (LF/HF and SDNN) had a significant increment as SM interruptions occurred which was consistent with the results of previous studies [24–26, 28, 29]. Contrary to expectations, there were no main effects of task levels for SC mean and HR mean. There were no significant differences for AVHR and SC among the tasks, which was not consistent with the results of previous studies [22]. One explanation for this pattern of results could be that task demands increasing is not accompanied by changes in HRV as long as the manipulation affects only structural or computational structures in the human information processing system [30, 31]. In this view, the task difficulty levels seem not to differ by SM interruptions significantly in this respect.

In addition, the effect of SM interruption on perceived MWL and physiological responses during the reading task is higher than in writing, but participants during interrupted condition did the writing task with less accuracy than the reading task. If we consider this in relation to spare capacity [32], as the interrupted writing task was subjectively rated as requiring more MWL, there might not have enough cognitive resources available to take on the interrupted task concurrently with the primary task. This means that responding to the interruptions during the writing task would have become a primary task that was less demanding than the reading tasks [33].

This result means that SM usage increased brain activity during the interruption compared with the single task. This could be explained by the limited cognitive resources that are not well allocated across multiple tasks and interruptions mainly caused by more mental effort to accomplish more than one task at a time [34, 35].

It should be noted that participants were asked to conduct varied tasks in a limited amount of time in this experiment, which could cause stress. Further, suppose a given cognitive activity requires extensive application of resources and that activity has to be carried out for an uninterrupted period of time. In that case, it is likely that the activity would induce stress [36, 37]. Therefore, stress may have affected the results of this study. In addition, previous research has shown that stress controls a variety of physiological processes, particularly the ECG and EDA indexes [36, 37]; hence, the physiological responses may be affected.

5   Conclusion

This study is an important observation toward elucidating the role of mobile SM in office workers' MWL. Our findings show that SM interruptions reduce primary task performance and increase MWL. These results help us understand the effect of interruption on MWL levels during office tasks and could further aid in improving the working habits and lives and may pose the greatest load on the office workers. Also, previous research about the effect of SM has been conducted the subjective measurements, but this study took place in a laboratory environment and used behavioral and physiological methods to find the variations. Therefore, this study's inferences promote the prevailing understanding of the "dark side" of SM usage in the office surrounding, which may impact enterprise efficiency and employees' health. Additionally, this study provides practical and theoretical implications for both employers and employees on how to manage SM information interruptions in the workplace.

References

1. Yu, L., Cao, X., Liu, Z., Wang, J.: Excessive social media use at work: exploring the effects of social media overload on job performance. Inf. Technol. People **31**(6), 1091–1112 (2018)
2. Gupta, A., Li, H., Sharda, R.: Should i send this message? Understanding the impact of interruptions, social hierarchy and perceived task complexity on user performance and perceived workload. Decis. Support Syst. **55**, 135–145 (2013)
3. Addas, S., Pinsonneault, A.: Theorizing the multilevel effects of interruptions and the role of communication technology. J. Assoc. Inf. Syst. **19**(11), 1097–1129 (2018)
4. Baethge, A., Rigotti, T., Roe, R.A.: Just more of the same, or different? An integrative theoretical framework for the study of cumulative interruptions at work. Eur. J. Work Organ. Psychol. **24**(2), 308–323 (2015)
5. Mark, S.Y., Karel, A.B., Christopher, D.W., Peter, A.: State of science: mental workload in ergonomics. Ergonomics **58**(1), 1–17 (2015)

6. Mark, G., Iqbal, S., Czerwinski, M.: How blocking distractions affects workplace focus and productivity. In: Proceedings of the 2017 ACM International Joint Conference on Pervasive and Ubiquitous Computing and Proceedings of the 2017 ACM International Symposium on Wearable Computers, pp. 928–934 (2017)

7. Schaule, F., Johanssen, J., Bruegge, B., Loftness, V.: Employing consumer wearables to detect office workers' cognitive load for interruption management. In: Proceedings of the ACM on Interactive, Mobile, Wearable and Ubiquitous Technologies, vol. 2, no. 1, pp. 1–20 (2018)

8. Corragio, L.: Deleterious effects of intermittent interruptions on the task performance of knowledge workers. In: 18th International Conference on Information Systems (1990)

9. Speier, C., Vessey, I., Valacich, J.S.: The effects of interruptions, task complexity, and information presentation on computer-supported decision-making performance. Decis. Sci. **34**, 771–797 (2003)

10. Carayon, P., et al.: Evaluation of nurse interaction with bar code medication administration technology in the work environment. J. Patient Saf. **3**(1), 34–42 (2007)

11. Moray, N., Huey, B.: Human Factors Research and Nuclear Safety. National Academies Press (1988)

12. Gao, Q., Wang, Y., Song, F., Li, Z., Dong, X.: Mental workload measurement for emergency operating procedures in digital nuclear power plants. Ergonomics **56**(7), 1070–1085 (2013)

13. Casali, J.G., Wierwille, W.W.: On the measurement of pilot perceptual workload: a comparison of assessment techniques addressing sensitivity and intrusion issues. Ergonomics **27**(10), 1033–1050 (1984)

14. Charles, R., Nixon, J.: Measuring mental workload using physiological measures: a systematic review. Appl. Ergon. **74**, 221–232 (2019)

15. Matthews, G., Reinerman-Jones, L.E., Barber, D.J., Abich, J., IV.: The psychometrics of mental workload: multiple measures are sensitive but divergent. Hum. Factors **57**(1), 125–143 (2015)

16. Parasuraman, R., Rizzo, M.: Neuroergonomics: The Brain at Work. Oxford University Press, New York (2007)

17. Zhao, G., Liu, Y., Shi, Y.: Real-time assessment of the cross-task mental workload using physiological measures during anomaly detection. IEEE Trans. Hum. Mach. Syst. **48**(2), 149–160 (2018)

18. Hancock, P., Matthews, G.: Workload and performance: associations, insensitivities, and dissociations. Hum. Factors J. Hum. Factors Ergon. Soc. **61**(3), 374–392 (2019)

19. Ding, Y., Cao, Y., Duffy, V., Wang, Y., Zhang, X.: Measurement and identification of mental workload during simulated computer tasks with multimodal methods and machine learning. Ergonomics **63**(7), 896–908 (2020)

20. Faul, F., Erdfelder, E., Buchner, A., Lang, A.-G.: Statistical power analyses using G*Power 3.1: tests for correlation and regression analyses. Behav. Res. Methods **41**(4), 1149–1160 (2009). https://doi.org/10.3758/BRM.41.4.1149

21. Hart, S.G.: NASA-task load index (NASA-TLX); 20 years later. In: Proceedings of the Human Factors and Ergonomics Society Annual Meeting, vol. 50(9), pp. 904–908 (2006)

22. Guyon, I., Elisseeff, A.: An introduction to feature extraction. In: Guyon, I., Nikravesh, M., Gunn, S., Zadeh, L.A. (eds.) feature extraction, pp. 1–25. Springer, Heidelberg (2006). https://doi.org/10.1007/978-3-540-35488-8_1

23. Fairclough, S., Venables, L., Tattersall, A.: The influence of task demand and learning on the psychophysiological response. Int. J. Psychophysiol. **56**(2), 171–184 (2005)

24. Finsen, L., Søgaard, K., Jensen, C., Borg, V., Christensen, H.: Muscle activity and cardiovascular response during computer-mouse work with and without memory demands. Ergonomics **44**(14), 1312–1329 (2001)

25. Fournier, L., Wilson, G., Swain, C.: Electrophysiological, behavioral, and subjective indexes of workload when performing multiple tasks: manipulations of task difficulty and training. Int. J. Psychophysiol. **31**(2), 129–145 (1999)
26. Orlandi, L., Brooks, B.: Measuring mental workload and physiological reactions in marine pilots: Building bridges towards redlines of performance. Appl. Ergon. **69**, 74–92 (2018)
27. De Rivecourt, M., Kuperus, M., Post, W., Mulder, L.: Cardiovascular and eye activity measures as indices for momentary changes in mental effort during simulated flight. Ergonomics **51**(9), 1295–1319 (2008)
28. Jorna, P.G.: Spectral analysis of heart rate and psychological state: a review of its validity as a workload index. Biol. Psychol **34**, 237–257 (1992)
29. Mulder, L., de Waard, D., Brookhuis, K.: Estimating mental effort using heart rate and heart rate variability. In: Stanton, N., Hedge, A., Brookhuis, K. (eds.) Taylor and Francis, London (2004)
30. Sharples, S., Megaw, T.: The definition and measurement of human workload. In: Evaluation of Human Work, pp. 516–544 (2015)
31. Midha, S., Maior, H., Wilson, M., Sharples, S.: Measuring mental workload variations in office work tasks using fNIRS. Int. J. Hum Comput Stud. **147**, 102580 (2021)
32. Alm, H., Nilsson, L.: The effects of a mobile telephone task on driver behaviour in a car following situation. Accid. Anal. Prev. **27**(5), 707–715 (1995)
33. Card, S., Moran, T., Newell, A.: The Psychology of Human-Computer Interaction, pp. 1–43 (1983)
34. Hancock, P.: A dynamic model of stress and sustained attention. Hum. Factors J. Hum. Factors Ergon. Soc. **31**(5), 519–537 (1989)
35. Warm, J., Parasuraman, R., Matthews, G.: Vigilance requires hard mental work and is stressful. Hum. Factors **37**(2), 111–121 (2008)
36. Healey, J., Picard, R.: Detecting stress during real-world driving tasks using physiological sensors. IEEE Trans. Intell. Transp. Syst. **6**(2), 156–166 (2005)
37. Sun, F.-T., Kuo, C., Cheng, H.-T., Buthpitiya, S., Collins, P., Griss, M.: Activity-aware mental stress detection using physiological sensors. In: Gris, M., Yang, G. (eds.) MobiCASE 2010. LNICSSITE, vol. 76, pp. 211–230. Springer, Heidelberg (2012). https://doi.org/10.1007/978-3-642-29336-8_12

Psychological Mechanism of Civil Aviation Staff's Unsafe Behavior

Chunyang Zhang[✉] and Yuan Zhang

Aviation Safety Institute, China Academy of Civil Aviation Science and Technology, Beijing 100028, China
381323884@qq.com, Zhangyuan@mail.castc.org.cn

Abstract. In the aviation field, the concept of systems management has been widely recognized, and the human factor analysis of aviation accident/unsafe behavior has been more focused on finding system vulnerabilities. However, the analysis of unsafe behavior from the perspective of individual psychology is relatively low. In order to promote the safety of civil aviation and to reduce unsafe behaviors such as errors and violations caused by civil aviation personnel, the current study concluded the psychological factors associated with the unsafe behavior of civil aviation practitioners. The study was based on the core principles of safety psychology and the human factors analysis and classification system (HFACS). The psychological factors influencing the unsafe behaviors of civil aviation employees included risk perception, safe attention, memory, negative emotions, job burnout, self-control, safety attitude, safety motivation, and personality traits. Combined with the social cognition theoretical framework and the psychological factors associated with the unsafe behavior of civil aviation personnel, a model was formed. The model provides theoretical and practical reference during the analysis of psychological factors such as errors and violations caused by civil aviation personnel.

Keywords: Safety psychology · Unsafe behavior · Psychological factor · Civil aviation

1 Introduction

Human factors are the main cause of aviation accidents in recent years. However, they are often overlooked as the solution to the problem is not considered to be related to them. In particular, most models of aviation human error analysis, such as the SHEL and REASON models are often based on a system perspective and inevitably focus more on the role of the system of organization and management [1]. The concept of system management has also been recognized by most professionals, which could guarantee the current aviation safety.

However, the analysis of the internal psychological process of people who make mistakes and violations is not systematic and comprehensive. This limits the possibility of reducing human errors and violations at an individual level. Mental activity is undoubtedly the most important part of individual human factors. The effects of human

C. Stephanidis et al. (Eds.): HCII 2022, CCIS 1581, pp. 251–256, 2022.
https://doi.org/10.1007/978-3-031-06388-6_33

perception, memory, attention, decision-making, emotion, fatigue, and stress on safety behavior have been gradually discovered in the field of coal mines and transportation [2, 3]. However, few studies systematically analyzed the cause of unsafe behavior from the perspective of individual psychology, especially in the field of civil aviation. Therefore, based on the HFACS human factor analysis framework and the core principle of safety psychology, the current study explored the near-end, mid-end and remote-end psychological factors that could affect the unsafe behavior of civil aviation personnel.

2 Psychological Factors and the Unsafe Behavior of Civil Aviation Workers

HFACS model is an important method for investigating and analyzing human factors in-flight accidents. According to the HFACS model, individual unsafe behavior can be divided into errors and violations [4]. Therefore, based on the HFACS model, the causes of accidents and associated human symptoms can be systematically analyzed. However, the psychological reasons behind individual violations and errors are relatively rough.

Safety psychology is based on the principles of safety science and psychology, which guides safety management through the study of human safety psychological phenomena and behavioral process characteristics [5]. According to the core principles of safety psychology, psychological processes (perception, emotion), motivation, attitude, and personality were all important influencing factors of unsafe behaviors [6].

2.1 Psychological Process Factors and Unsafe Behavior

The near-end psychological factors such as cognitive and emotional processes can directly affect the unsafe behavior of civil aviation personnel. Individual cognitive processes include risk perception, safety attention and memory. Risk perception refers to the ability of individuals to identify potential dangers in the external environment while making corresponding preparedness behaviors. Aviation safety practitioners with good risk perception can better identify possible risks based on their ability, resulting in fewer unsafe behaviors [7]. Safety attention can also affect the safety behavior of personnel. Once employees' safety attention decreases, their perception of safety and risk would also be weakened, resulting in more decision-making and skill-based errors [8]. Meanwhile, unsafe behaviors may also occur if civil aviation staff have memory deviation due to old age, lack of sleep, mood fluctuation, disease and stress [9].

The impact of emotions in unsafe behaviors has been widely recognized. During the violation and error, the role of negative emotions such as fear, anger, impatience, anxiety, and boredom has been verified for the subway construction workers, motorists and airport security personnel [10]. In addition, the accumulation of negative emotions for a long time (burnout) could affect the degree of work involvement, while resulting in errors and violations [11].

2.2 Motivation, Attitudes and the Unsafe Behavior

Mid-end psychological factors such as self-control, safety motivation and safety attitudes can affect the cognition and emotional processes of an individual while having an impact on their unsafe behaviors.

People with a high level of self-control are generally able to follow the rules and have fewer violations on the job. For example, workers who can control their impulsive behavior and negative emotion in time can be more emotionally stable. Moreover, the same worker can also abide by the rules and regulations of a company while committing fewer errors and violations [12].

Safety motivation refers to an individual's willingness to perform work safely, while safety attitude refers to an individual's stable and generalized tendency to respond the safety in the process of work. Employees with strong safety motivation and attitudes tend to abide by safety rules. For example, those who are just to evade punishment and do not truly agree with the value of safe operation are usually unable to perform safe operations continuously, which results in daily violations [13].

2.3 Personality and the Unsafe Behavior

Personality, as a remote psychological factor, is quite stable in the time dimension. Personality indirectly affects unsafe behaviors of civil aviation personnel through cognitive processes, attitudes and emotional factors.

Personality traits have a wide range of effects on individual behavior, even in the field of security. The accident proneness theory illustrates that personality plays a leading role in accidents and hence, certain stable internal personal tendencies are closely related to unsafe behavior [14]. The Big Five personality theory with broad applicability demonstrates that there are five personality traits, namely openness, agreeableness, conscientiousness, neuroticism and extraversion. Meta-analysis results show that agreeableness and conscientiousness can negatively predict unsafe behavior, while extraversion and neuroticism can positively predict unsafe behavior. However, openness and unsafe behavior have a minor relationship [15]. Specifically, individuals who are helpful, confident, responsible and value the interpersonal relationships in their personalities have fewer violations in their daily work. On the contrary, emotionally unstable commits more errors and risky decisions. For example, overly selfish airport workers displayed lower safety performance, while the active and social air traffic controllers committed more skill-based errors [16, 17].

3   Psychological Mechanism of Unsafe Behavior of Civil Aviation Employees

The social cognitive theory suggests that human behavior is affected by the external environment and internal cognition. Therefore, individual unsafe behavior is not only affected by the external working environment but also closely related to internal cognition (memory, motivation, attitude, belief) [18]. The existing cognitive models of human error in the field of security often focus on sorting out cognitive processes (identification, observation, interpretation, evaluation) and the reason behind unsafe behaviors [19]. However, the cognitive process is affected by various factors, such as emotion, attitude, motivation and personality. To accurately determine the psychological factors behind the unsafe behavior of civil aviation practitioners, it is more scientific and practical to establish a comprehensive framework of analysis.

The cognitive structure within an individual is divided into different levels based on its stability. Emotional systems and cognitive processing are superficial structures that influence behavior and are more likely to change. Deeper attitudes, motivations and self-control are formed as individuals grow up and are relatively difficult to change. These factors usually affect behavior through superficial emotional and cognitive processes. Personality, as a "remote" predictor of behavior, indirectly affects unsafe behavior through factors such as cognitive processes, attitudes, motivation, self-control and emotions.

Therefore, the current study summarized the psychological factors affecting the unsafe behavior of civil aviation personnel, including risk perception, safe attention, memory, negative emotions, job burnout, self-control, safety attitude, safety motivation, and personality traits. Moreover, the study proposed a psychological factor influence model on the unsafe behaviors of civil aviation personnel based on the cognitive structure of individuals (Fig. 1).

As per the model, superficial psychological processes such as risk perception, safe attention, memory, negative emotions and job burnout can directly affect the unsafe behaviors of civil aviation personnel. Correspondingly, personality, safety attitude, self-control and safety motivation also have an indirect influence on unsafe behaviors.

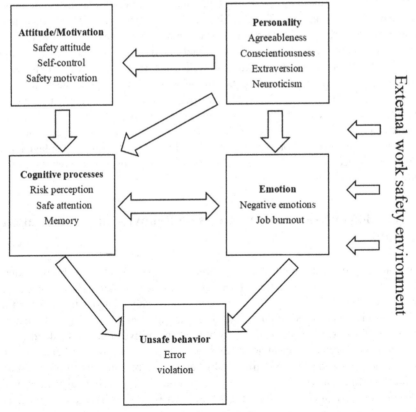

Fig. 1. Psychological mechanism model of unsafe behavior of civil aviation staff.

We have also further sorted out the attention-worthy areas for future research and practice. First, lack of attention to the violations and errors committed by other civil aviation professionals except for pilots, such as air traffic controllers, maintenance personnel, ground support personnel and management personnel cannot be ignored. Second, the existing research mainly adopted the self-assessment questionnaire survey method. In the future, it can be further explored in combination with physiological indicators and experimental methods. Third, research on intervention programs for civil aviation practitioners' unsafe behaviors is required. Considering the diverse psychological factors associated with unsafe behaviors, there is still a lack of systematic intervention programs, which restricts the development of psychological research to practical applications.

References

1. Sun, R., Zhao, Q.: Study on ECAR model for human error analysis of aviation accident/incident. China Saf. Sci. J. **22**(2), 18–22 (2012)
2. Cheng, A., Liu, K., Tulliani, N.: Relationship between driving-violation behaviours and risk perception in motorcycle accidents. Hong Kong J. Occup. Ther. **25**(C), 32–38 (2015)
3. Yi, Y.: Influence of self-control ability on miner's habitual peccancy. Safety in Coal Mines **50**(4), 253–256 (2019)
4. Wiegmann, D.A., Shappell, S.A.: A Human Error Approach to Aviation Accident Analysis. Ashgate Publishing Limited, Farnham (2003)
5. Zhang, Y., You, B., Shi, S., et al.: Research on safety psychology methodology. China Saf. Sci. J. **31**(5), 181–188 (2021)
6. Li, S., Wang, W., Wu, C.: Research on core principles of safety psychology. China Saf. Sci. J. **25**(9), 8–13 (2015)
7. Liu, R.: Research on internal and external factors and mechanism affecting pilot's flight unsafe behaviors. Civil Aviation University of China, China (2020)
8. Madigan, R., Golightly, D., Madders, R.: Application of human factors analysis and classification system (HFACS) to UK rail safety of the line incidents. Accid. Anal. Prev. **97**, 122–131 (2016)
9. Wang, Y., Zhang, X., Song, Z.: Study on relationship between memory and safety performance of pilots. J. Saf. Sci. Technol. **14**(1), 160–165 (2018)
10. Feng, J.: The influence of emotional labor of airport security personnel on human error. Co-Operative Econ. Sci. **7**, 130–133 (2020)
11. Da, Y.: Research on job burnout, self-efficacy and relation with human errors of flight dispatcher. Wuhan University of Technology, Wuhan (2013)
12. Sani, S., Tabibi, Z., Fadardi, J.S., et al.: Aggression, emotional self-regulation, attentional bias, and cognitive inhibition predict risky driving behavior. Accid. Anal. Prev. **109**, 78–88 (2017)
13. Wang, X.: On the relationship between the psychological empowerment and violation behavior of the airport security staff members. J. Saf. Environ. **17**(5), 1849–1853 (2017)
14. Hansen, C.P.: Personality characteristics of the accident involved employee. J. Bus. Psychol. **2**(4), 346–365 (1988). https://doi.org/10.1007/BF01013766
15. Beus, J.M., Dhanani, L.Y., Mccord, M.A.: A meta-analysis of personality and workplace safety: addressing unanswered questions. J. Appl. Psychol. **100**(2), 481–498 (2015)
16. Xu, Y., Luo, F.: Influence mechanism of machiavelliansm on airport staff's safety performance. Saf. Environ. Eng. **116**(2), 184–190 (2018)

17. Hedayati, S., Sadeghi-Firoozabadi, V., Bagher, M., et al.: Evaluating differences in cognitive functions and personality traits among air traffic controllers with and without error history. Saf. Sci. **139**, 105208 (2021)
18. Locke, E.A.: Social foundations of thought and action: A social cognitive theory. Acad. Manag. Rev. **12**(1), 169–171 (1987)
19. Li, X., Tan, L., Gao, L., et al.: Research progress of human error theory in industry safety engineering. J. China Acad. Electron. Inf. Technol. **15**(7), 612–619 (2020)

Human Motion Modelling
and Monitoring

Digital Self-monitoring to Improve Perceptions Regarding Physical Activity: A Case of Quantifying Self with University Students

Farhat-ul-Ain, Kristjan Port, and Vladimir Tomberg$^{(\boxtimes)}$

Tallinn University, Tallinn, Estonia
vtomberg@tlu.ee

Abstract. Purpose: Self-monitoring is one of the most effective behavior change techniques to enhance awareness and task motivation. Wearable devices provide a unique opportunity for individuals to self-monitoring compared to traditional record-keeping methods. Furthermore, digital self-monitoring helps to engage with the technologies/intelligent systems to track, collect, monitor, and display information about daily activities. This study aimed to implement a quantified self-approach for university students to explore changes in students' attitudes and perceptions after self-monitoring of physical activity. Method: 70 university students were recruited in the study. The study was divided into four stages i. Preparation stage: participants filled out pre-survey and were instructed to use a step counter or any other fitness tracker over three weeks. ii. Collection stage: participants monitored themselves regularly for three weeks. iii. Integration stage: The collected data was analyzed and transformed for users to reflect on. iv. Reflection stage: participants reflected on the findings in a post-survey. Results: 47% of study participants reported that self-monitoring raised awareness related to physical activity in study participants. 54% of study participants felt the urge to increase physical activity after self-monitoring. Before and after self-monitoring, there was no change in the perception of being more physically active. Conclusion: The study suggested that self-quantification can raise awareness related to physical activity. Longitudinal studies can be designed to explore how self-quantification approaches would be utilized for long-term self-reflection.

Keywords: Quantifying self · Personal informatics · Self-tracking · Lifelogging · Activity tracking · Self-perception

1 Introduction

Understanding various aspects of an individual's everyday life motivates us to record behaviors, activities, and emotions [1, 2]. Advancement in self-tracking devices (e.g., smartwatches, fitness bracelets) has made it possible to quantify and monitor daily activities remarkably easily, referred to as personal informatics or self-quantification [3]. Self-quantification enables individuals to engage with the technologies/intelligent systems that help track, collect, monitor, and display information about their daily activities

C. Stephanidis et al. (Eds.): HCII 2022, CCIS 1581, pp. 259–266, 2022.
https://doi.org/10.1007/978-3-031-06388-6_34

to enhance self-sensing or self-awareness [4, 5]. Further, it helps people to record and evaluate both subjective (e.g., emotion, situation) and objective aspects (e.g., intensity, frequency) of the observed behaviors [6]. Self-tracking devices to monitor health and well-being enable individuals to self-reflect. It helps in health preservation, referred to as the self-improvement hypothesis of personal informatics [7–9]. Digital Self-monitoring can enhance people's self-awareness, which positively affects people's task motivation [3, 10].

1.1 Theoretical Underpinnings of Self-improvement Hypothesis

Many behavior change theories, such as control theory and self-regulation, theory Trans-theoretical Model of Change (TTM) [12], propose that self-monitoring enhances self-evaluation and goal setting, which, after receiving feedback, increases an individual's responsibility, independence, and person's active role in goal setting [11]. Transtheoretical Model of Change (TTM) [12] explains that an individual's transition to a state of intention (contemplation stage) from a state of no intention to change behavior (precontemplation stage) is triggered by awareness, knowledge (e.g., possible outcomes of the behavior) and environmental cues [13, 14]. Contemplation leads to other stages, i.e., preparation, action, and maintenance, and individuals can lapse to any stage. Similarly, models of personal informatics such as the *"stage-based model of personal informatics systems"* (Fig. 1) and *"lived informatic model"* explain how people use personal informatics tools to monitor their behaviors [15, 16].

The stage-based model [15] explains that individuals initially think about collecting data and determining how to collect and record information (Preparation). Then they collect data using trackers about themselves (Collection Stage). Further, they integrate data for reflection (Integration) and then reflect and explore data (Reflection stage). In the reflection stage, people identify their future goals and figure out the potential possibilities to achieve them. Lastly, based on reflection, people in the 'action stage' either inform behavior or perform certain activities to match their goals. Similarly, Epstein e al. [16] integrated both the TTM model and staged-based model of personal information [15] to develop a "lived informatics model." It includes the process of deciding to track and selecting tools, tracking and acting as an ongoing process of collection, integration, and reflection, and lapsing of tracking that may later be resumed.

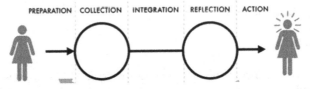

Fig. 1. Five stages of personal informatics adapted for the study

1.2 Related Works

Prior work has demonstrated the effectiveness of using self-tracking devices to promote goal-directed activities and users' physical activity motivation. Digital Self-monitoring is also proven helpful in promoting physical activity when used in behavior change interventions such as improvement in moderate to vigorous activities and goal-directed activities [3, 9, 17, 18]. Further, fitness tracking improves task motivation, user's motivation and anticipated motivation to be physically active [10, 20, 21]. Further, motivation to indulge in physical activity decreases with the unavailability of the tracking devices [24] have shown that motivation for physical activity decreases when fitness trackers are not available. Maitland et al. [22] also have found that fitness tracking apps (with information sharing feature) lead to increased motivation for physical activities (e.g., walking).

1.3 Study Aim

For the present study, we used the Documentary tracking approach of "quantified self", i.e., detailing activities to collect data for reflection, instead of changing them [23] and adapted the Li et al. [15] model of personal informatics. We explored changes in students' attitudes/perception of their daily activity level after self-monitoring. The main research question was whether university students intend to do more physical activity if they find activity tracking results less satisfying after reflection?

2 Method

The study was divided into five stages adapted from Li et al.'s [15]. The project team used Google Drive to collaborate, compile, and share the necessary project documentation. Overall, the study lasted for 8 weeks.

1. Preparation Stage: Each willing participant filled out the pre-survey questionnaire before starting data collection. The objective was to gather demographic information about the participants. The participants' identity was remained anonymous throughout the study.
2. Collection Stage (2 weeks): Participants self-monitored themselves for three weeks using activity trackers. The activity diary was filled out by each participant every day with the number of steps made and other information related to the number of steps.
3. Integration Stage: Collected data was analyzed and transformed for users to reflect on.
4. Reflection Stage: Participants reviewed their results for reflection. The post-survey questionnaire was filled out for reflection.
5. Action Stage: Participants decide how to use their newfound understanding of themselves.

Lastly, the study findings were summarized to present the overall change in participants' perceptions and attitudes after self-monitoring. The details about participants' characteristics and changes in attitude and perceptions are mentioned in the result section.

3   Results

Seventy university students participated in the current study. The average age of study participants was 26.7. Most of the study participants were female (97%) and regular university students (47%). The average number of steps taken by study participants per person were 7867 (two weeks). Results of the pre-survey indicated that approximately 80% of the study participants were already tracking their physical activities. Pre-survey results indicated that physically active is important for 94% participants, However, 54% of participants do not consider their lifestyle as active. It was found that students tend to take slightly more steps during the weekdays (8152 steps) rather than on the weekend (7758 steps). 47% of study participants raised awareness related to physical activity after self-monitoring (Fig. 2).

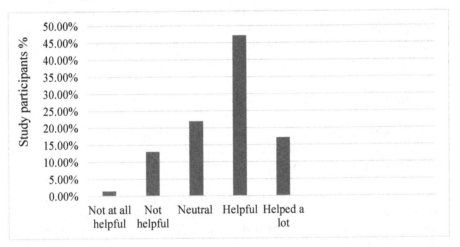

Fig. 2. The extent to which self-monitoring helped to raise awareness in study participants (post-survey)

The post-survey results indicated that 54% of study participants felt an urge to increase physical activity after self-monitoring (Fig. 3).

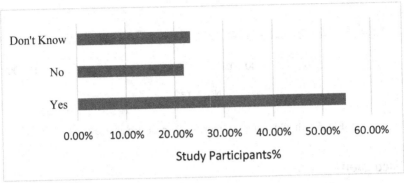

Fig. 3. Did this research urge you to move more? (Post-survey question)

Results of both pre-post surveys indicated that approximately 63% of participants did think that they moved enough (Fig. 4). However, there was no change in the perceived level of physical activity after reflection.

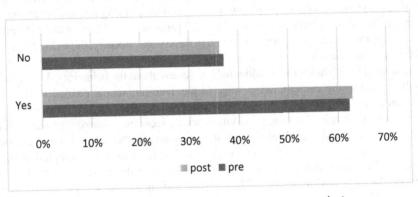

Fig. 4. Do you move enough? (Pre-post survey question)

Results of both pre-post surveys indicated that almost 83% of the participants felt that they should move more. However, there is no change after reflection in study participants (Fig. 5).

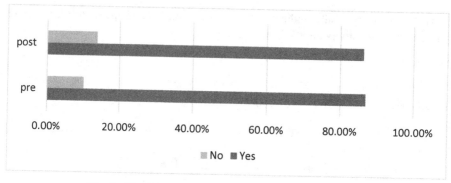

Fig. 5. Should you move more? (Pre-post survey question)

4 Discussion

This study aimed to explore changes in the perception of physical activity after self-monitoring. The results indicated that self-monitoring raised awareness about physical activity, and participants felt the urge to move more after reflection. Studies have demonstrated that regular self-tracking promotes short-term and long-term self-reflection [15]. The short-term reflection happens after data collection and helps individuals improve self-knowledge and awareness. The current study supports the idea of short-term reflection as approximately 47% of participants found self-monitoring helpful. According to the "Stage-based model of personal informatics" proposed by Li Dey et al. [15], reflective learning through tracking devices occurs in three steps. Initially, the individuals plan and prepare for data collection, followed by data collection, and, lastly, reflect on the data obtained, which helps raise individual awareness about the behaviors. This is more closely related to the contemplation stage in the Transtheoretical change model. The increased awareness promotes change in behavior and attitude [20, 25]. Previous studies also suggest that tracking physical activity from devices can promote physical activity [22]. The current study result also suggests no change in the need for more physical activity after self-reflection. According to the TTM, individuals in contemplation phase remains ambivalent about changing behaviors and it takes three to six months to starts preparing for the behavior change [12]. The increased duration of self-monitoring could have resulted in change of perception related to physical activity i.e., need to do more physical activity.

The current study highlighted the role of self-quantification in raising awareness regarding physical activity. Further experiments and longitudinal studies can be designed to explore how self-quantification approaches would be utilized for long-term self-reflection.

References

1. Ayobi, A., Sonne, T., Marshall, P., Cox, A.L.: Flexible and mindful self-tracking: design implications from paper bullet journals. In: Conference on Human Factors in Computing Systems – Proceedings (2018). https://doi.org/10.1145/3173574.3173602

2. Choe, E.K., Lee, N.B., Lee, B., Pratt, W., Kientz, J.A.: Understanding quantified-selfers' practices in collecting and exploring personal data. In: Conference on Human Factors in Computing Systems - Proceedings, pp. 1143–1152 (2014). https://doi.org/10.1145/2556288. 2557372
3. Jarrahi, M.H., Gafinowitz, N., Shin, G.: Activity trackers, prior motivation, and perceived informational and motivational affordances. Pers. Ubiquit. Comput. **22**(2), 433–448 (2017). https://doi.org/10.1007/s00779-017-1099-9
4. Swan, M.: The quantified self: fundamental disruption in big data science and biological discovery. Big Data **1**, 85–99 (2013). https://doi.org/10.1089/big.2012.0002
5. Wang, Y., Weber, I., Mitra, P.: Quantified self meets social media: sharing of weight updates on Twitter. In: DH 2016 - Proceedings of the 2016 Digital Health Conference, pp. 93–97 (2016). https://doi.org/10.1145/2896338.2896363
6. Shin, D.H., Biocca, F.: Health experience model of personal informatics: the case of a quantified self. Comput. Hum. Behav. **69**, 62–74 (2017). https://doi.org/10.1016/j.chb.2016. 12.019
7. Kersten-van Dijk, E.T., Westerink, J.H.D.M., Beute, F., IJsselsteijn, W.A.: Personal informatics, self-insight, and behavior change: a critical review of current literature. Hum.-Comput. Interact. **32**, 268–296 (2017). https://doi.org/10.1080/07370024.2016.1276456
8. Khorakhun, C., Bhatti, S.N.: mHealth through quantified-self: a user study. In: 2015 17th International Conference on E-Health Networking, Application and Services, HealthCom 2015, pp. 329–335 (2015). https://doi.org/10.1109/HealthCom.2015.7454520
9. Li, I., Medynskiy, Y., Froehlich, J., Larsen, J.: Personal informatics in practice: improving quality of life through data. In: Conference on Human Factors in Computing Systems - Proceedings, pp. 2799–2802 (2012). https://doi.org/10.1145/2212776.2212724
10. Randriambelonoro, M., Chen, Y., Pu, P.: Can fitness trackers help diabetic and obese users make and sustain lifestyle changes? Computer **50**(3), 20–29 (2017). https://doi.org/10.1109/ MC.2017.92
11. Michie, S., Abraham, C., Whittington, C., McAteer, J., Gupta, S.: Effective techniques in healthy eating and physical activity interventions: a meta-regression. Health Psychol. (2009). https://doi.org/10.1037/a0016136
12. Prochaska, J.O., Velicer, W.F.: The transtheoretical model of health behavior change. Am. J. Health Promot. **12**(1), 38–48 (1997). https://doi.org/10.4278/0890-1171-12.1.38
13. Klein, M., Mogles, N., van Wissen, A.: Why won't you do what's good for you? Using intelligent support for behavior change. In: Salah, A.A., Lepri, B. (eds.) HBU 2011. LNCS, vol. 7065, pp. 104–115. Springer, Heidelberg (2011). https://doi.org/10.1007/978-3-642-25446- 8_12
14. De Vries, H., et al.: The European smoking prevention framework approach (EFSA): an example of integral prevention. Health Educ. Res. **18**(5), 611–626 (2003). https://doi.org/10. 1093/her/cyg031
15. Li,I., Dey, A., Forlizzi, J.: A stage-based model of personal informatics systems. In: Conference on Human Factors in Computing Systems - Proceedings, pp. 557–566 (2010). https:// doi.org/10.1145/1753326.1753409
16. Epstein, D.A., Ping, A., Fogarty, J., Munson, S.A.: A lived informatics model of personal informatics. In: UbiComp 2015 - Proceedings of the 2015 ACM International Joint Conference on Pervasive and Ubiquitous Computing, pp. 731–742 (2015). https://doi.org/10.1145/275 0858.2804250
17. Butryn, M.L., Arigo, D., Raggio, G.A., Colasanti, M., Forman, E.M.: Enhancing physical activity promotion in midlife women with technology-based self-monitoring and social connectivity: a pilot study. J. Health Psychol. **21**(8), 1548–1555 (2016). https://doi.org/10.1177/ 1359105314558895

18. Jakicic, J.M., et al.: Effect of wearable technology combined with a lifestyle intervention on long-term weight loss: the IDEA randomized clinical trial. JAMA J. Am. Med. Assoc. **316**(11), 1161–1171 (2016). https://doi.org/10.1001/jama.2016.12858

19. Kolt, G.S., Schofield, G.M., Kerse, N., Garrett, N., Ashton, T., Patel, A.: Healthy steps trial: Pedometer-based advice and physical activity for low-active older adults. Ann. Fam. Med. **10**(3), 206–212 (2012). https://doi.org/10.1370/afm.1345

20. Fritz, T., Huang, E.M., Murphy, G.C., Zimmermann, T.: Persuasive technology in the real world: a study of long-term use of activity sensing devices for fitness. In: Conference on Human Factors in Computing Systems - Proceedings, pp. 487–496 (2014). https://doi.org/10.1145/2556288.2557383

21. Preusse, K.C., Mitzner, T.L., Fausset, C.B., Rogers, W.A.: Older adults' acceptance of activity trackers. J. Appl. Gerontol. **36**(2), 127–155 (2017). https://doi.org/10.1177/073346481562 4151

22. Maitland, J., et al.: Increasing the awareness of daily activity levels with pervasive computing. In: 2006 Pervasive Health Conference and Workshops, PervasiveHealth (2006). https://doi.org/10.1109/PCTHEALTH.2006.361667

23. Rooksby, J., Rost, M., Morrison, A., Chalmers, M.: Personal tracking as lived informatics. In: Conference on Human Factors in Computing Systems - Proceedings, pp. 1163–1172 (2014). https://doi.org/10.1145/2556288.2557039

24. Attig, C., Franke, T.: I track, therefore i walk – exploring the motivational costs of wearing activity trackers in actual users. Int. J. Hum. Comput. Stud. **127**, 211–224 (2019). https://doi.org/10.1016/j.ijhcs.2018.04.007

25. Compernolle, S., et al.: Effectiveness of interventions using self-monitoring to reduce sedentary behavior in adults: a systematic review and meta-analysis. Int. J. Behav. Nutr. Phys. Act. **16**, 63 (2019). https://doi.org/10.1186/s12966-019-0824-3

Additive Manufacturing of Flexible Sensors for Human-Computer Interaction

Charisma Clarke⬤, Kyle Steel⬤, and Edwar Romero-Ramirez$^{(\boxtimes)}$ ⬤

Florida Polytechnic University, Lakeland, FL 33805, USA
eromeroramirez@floridapoly.edu

Abstract. High-performance wearable strain gauges have always been of interest for human-computer interaction. Many sensors have been developed using traditional manufacturing techniques or processes that are costly to replicate. This work showcases the use of commercially available filaments using additive manufacturing technology to create a sensor that can be used to monitor human motion with little user discomfort. A sensor was designed and tested, and it was found to have good sensitivity and reliability. The sensor uses the piezoresistive effect with changes up to 50% when conforming to small-sized objects. The sensor was tested on a glove and found to detect finger motion while grabbing objects or typing on a keyboard.

Keywords: Monitoring · Flexible sensor · Additive manufacturing

1 Introduction

Human-computer interaction requires arrays of sensors that can capture as much information as possible. There are two main approaches for this process, contact and contactless. Contactless systems are based on vision or radar systems for overall positioning or motion detection and are less intrusive but are limited by physical obstruction of the field of vision. Contact-based systems might be cumbersome to use but provide information not easily attainable by contactless methods. Smart gloves, for instance, have been used for a number of applications, such as gesture recognition and machine interaction [1–4]. Traditional approaches have used finger, wrist, or forearm locations for tactile feedback, whereas capacitive, strain, or vision sensing have been the standard technologies employed [5]. Other miniaturized wearable inertial sensors have also been used to identify some tasks, such as accelerometers, gyroscopes, magnetic sensors, or combinations on those in inertial measurement units (IMU) [4, 5].

Force-sensitive sensors are of particular interest since they made it possible to quantify the forces being applied for higher interactivity and better control. This is typically done by employing strain gauges that measure the strain or deformation by an externally applied load. Traditional strain gauges use piezoresistive (change in electrical resistance) or piezoelectric (change in electrical charge) materials producing a difference when a deformation due to a force is encountered. Most applications use rigid or brittle materials for strain gauges in mechanical systems and are not suitable for large deformations

C. Stephanidis et al. (Eds.): HCII 2022, CCIS 1581, pp. 267–273, 2022.
https://doi.org/10.1007/978-3-031-06388-6_35

such as the stretch of the fingers [2]. Recent developments have used polymer-based materials for flexible strain sensors using carbon nanotubes, silver nanowires, or carbon black as the sensing elements [6–8] for wearable applications. In addition, the rapid advance in additive manufacturing technology (equipment and materials) have made it possible to develop flexible and soft sensors employing commercial filaments [9, 10]. Devices in contact with the skin need to consider mechanical flexibility to conform to the body while minimizing discomfort on a wide range of motion. Stretchability is another important parameter, not just for the mechanical structure but the sensor itself, to avoid constraining the range of motion at the joints.

Additive manufacturing is now the precursor of rapid prototyping, a manufacturing technique that allows building a three-dimensional mechanical component by stacking multiple two-dimensional layers together for prototyping purposes at small-to-medium volumes. This technique enables the development of complex structures at a fraction of the cost of what was previously available by the succession of multiple manufacturing processes. Parts are designed using computer-aided design software and then converted into slices, where the machine, typically known as a 3D printer, deposits the material until the component is finalized. The deposition process follows multiples technologies, where fused filament fabrication is one of the most popular ones. Material is fed into the machine as a continuous filament where it melts and is deposited following instructions similar to a computerized numerical control found in milling machines. Flexible and conductive filaments allow designing parts other than rigid structural components while new machines add multi-material handling capabilities. It also makes it possible to develop custom prosthetics solutions that conform to the human body at levels not available before, even to the extent of finding custom soft robotic and biomedical applications [10].

This work focuses on developing an additively manufactured flexible strain gauge that demonstrates the detection of hand gestures.

2 Methodology

A strain gauge is a type of sensor that employs a sensing element deformed under strain when a load applied changes its properties, such as its electrical resistance. A typical strain gauge uses a long conductor patterned onto a nonconducting substrate. On metallic conductors, when the applied strain elongates the sensing element, the electrical resistance is increased since the cross-section becomes smaller. When a polymer material with conductive additives, such as metallic nanowires, carbon nanotubes, graphene, or carbon black, is used, the electrical resistance reduces when the same load is applied (decreasing the cross-section) since the conductive particles get closer to each other, increasing the path for the electric current to flow.

The design for the strain gauge follows the topology of the resistive foil-type, where a long conducting element (1 mm linewidth) is deposited onto a flexible substrate (20 mm × 50 mm), as shown in Fig. 1. Thermoplastic polyurethane (TPU) was used for the backing material due to its flexibility and ease of use on a regular desktop 3D printer. In contrast, a conductive TPU infused with carbon black was used as the sensing element material. TPU filament, 1.75 ± 0.05 mm diameter (SainSmart) and conductive TPU (PI-ETPU, Palmiga Innovation), both with a Shore hardness of 95 A were acquired for this task. A Prusa Mk3S+ was used for the manufacturing of the custom strain gauge using the default 0.4 mm nozzle. The flexible strain gauge is constituted of a support material (color white in the picture) with the conductive filament deposited on top (color black in the image). A layer thickness of 0.2 mm was selected to evaluate the effect of single- and double-layer stacks (single- and double-layer strain gauges were manufactured). Figure 1 also shows some staining from the conductive filament onto the nonconductive backing material.

Fig. 1. Strain gauge design and prototype.

3   Results and Discussion

Samples were tested by bending them against known diameter cylinders to evaluate their ability to conform to different body shapes and measurement results, as shown in Fig. 2. Two different thicknesses sensors were tested: single layer (0.2 mm conductive layer) and double layer (0.4 mm thick layer). Due to the nature of the composite conductive material, conductivity increases with increased strain (smaller electrical resistance). This can be appreciated by the lower resistance at the smaller diameters of 1-in and 2-in (25 mm and 50 mm), indicating the possibility of detecting smaller feature sizes. There was no significant change in electrical resistance between the readings at 3-in (75 mm), 4-in (100 mm), and flat orientations. The resistance was reduced by 25% by decreasing the bending diameter from 3 inches to 2 inches, while the reduction was up to 50% when reaching 1 inch for both tested samples. This test presents the sensors with a sensitivity that is identical for both samples regardless of the thickness of the conductive layer.

The second set of tests was run with the double-layer sensor to evaluate its repeatability under loading conditions. The sensor was clamped on a cantilever, and the resistance was measured while increasing the load in 10 g increments, as shown in Fig. 3. The same loading conditions were repeated five times where the sample deviation was found to be less than 4% with respect to the average electrical resistance value. This test shows the good repeatability of the additively manufactured sensor.

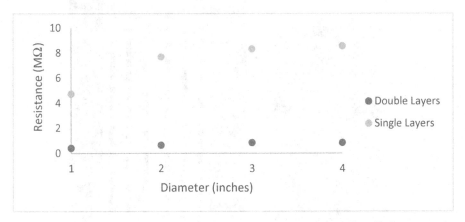

Fig. 2. Strain gauge resistance changes when wrapped around a cylinder.

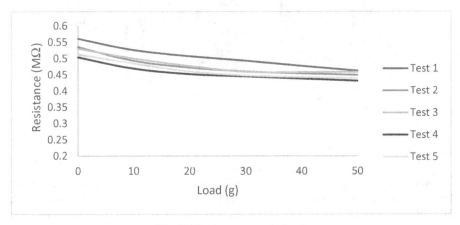

Fig. 3. Strain gauge under load

Once the sensitivity and repeatability of the sensor were demonstrated, another test was performed to evaluate the performance of the 3D printed strain gauge to detect finger motion. This time, a microcontroller (Arduino UNO) was used to record the change in resistance using a voltage divider while the sensor was attached to a glove, as shown in Fig. 4. Snippets of two tests are shown in Fig. 5 (grabbing an object) and in Fig. 6 (typing on the keyboard). The baseline reference voltage remained low (near 3.6 V) when the sensor was extended in the resting position and peaked (near 3.8 V) when the finger was curled.

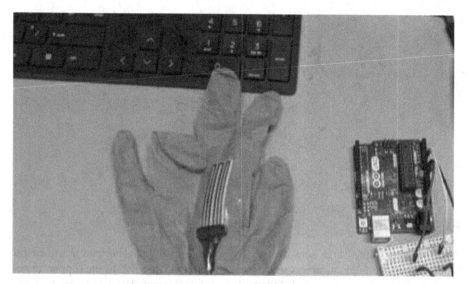

Fig. 4. Strain gauge attached to a glove.

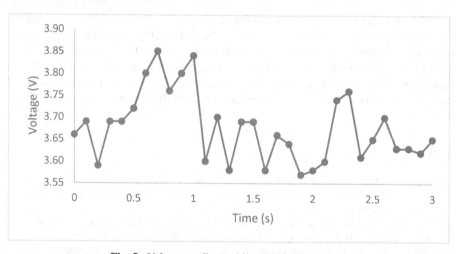

Fig. 5. Voltage readings while grabbing an object.

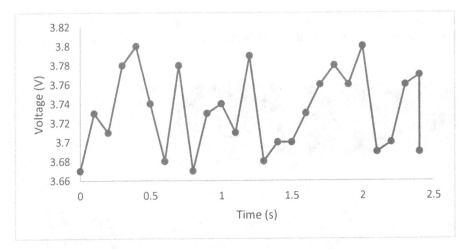

Fig. 6. Voltage readings while typing on a keyboard.

4 Conclusion

A stretchable strain gauge sensor made by additive manufacturing and designed for human-computer interaction was tested experimentally using TPU as the support material with conductive carbon black TPU as the sensing element. The sensor was found to have excellent sensitivity while bending at smaller curvatures with good repeatability. The preliminary sensor was tested while it was attached to a glove to evaluate the feasibility of detection finger motion, and it was found adequate for this task. This shows that the low-cost 3D printing technology machines can be successfully employed in conjunction with commercially available filaments to develop applications that were cost-prohibitive in the past. This can make it possible to expand the use of human-computer interaction to many applications since the technology is maturing at a fast pace. Future research might explore applications to detect body motion other than fingers or extend it for sensory feedback.

References

1. Lin, J.W., et al.: BackHand: sensing hand gestures via back of the hand. In: UIST 2015: Proceedings of the 28th Annual ACM Symposium on User Interface Software & Technology, November 2015, pp. 557–564 (2015)
2. Dong, W., Yang, L., Fortino, G.: Stretchable human machine interface based on smart glove embedded with PDMS-CB strain sensors. IEEE Sens. **20**(14), 8073–8081 (2020)
3. Guo, X., et al.: Biomimetic flexible strain sensor with high linearity using double conducting layers. Compos. Sci. Technol. **213**, 108908 (2021)
4. Espinoza, A., Restrepo, B., Romero-Ramirez, E.: Technology-enhanced monitoring of physical activity. In: Stephanidis, C., Antona, M., Ntoa, S. (eds.) HCII 2020. CCIS, vol. 1294, pp. 436–441. Springer, Cham (2020). https://doi.org/10.1007/978-3-030-60703-6_56
5. Byun, S.W., Lee, S.P.: Implementation of hand gesture recognition based on flexible sensor array for mobile devices. In: IEEE International Conference on Consumer Electronics (ICCE) 2019, Las Vegas, 11–13 January 2019 (2019)

6. Christ, J., Aliheidari, N., Ameli, A., Potschke, P.: 3D printed highly elastic strain sensors of multiwalled carbon nanotube/thermoplastic polyurethane nanocomposites. Mater. Des. **131**, 394–401 (2017)

7. Wang, R., Xu, W., Shen, W., Huang, J., Song, W.: A highly stretchable and transparent silver nanowire/thermoplastic polyurethane film strain sensor for human motion monitoring. Inorg. Chem. Front. **6**, 3119–3124 (2019)

8. Moheimani, R., Aliahmad, N., Aliheidari, N., Agarwal, M., Dalir, H.: Thermoplastic polyurethane flexible capacitive proximity sensor reinforced by CNTs for applications in the creative industries. Sci. Rep. **11**, 1104 (2021)

9. Guo, S.Z., Qiu, K., Meng, F., Park, S.H., McAlpine, M.: 3D Printed Stretchable Tactile Sensors. Adv. Mater. **29**, 1701218 (2017)

10. Wolterink, G., Sander, R., Beijnum, B.J., Vetink, P., Krijnen, G.: A 3D-printed soft fingertip sensor for providing information about normal and shear components of interaction forces. Sensors **21**, 4271 (2021)

Integrating Electromyography Sensors in Tangible Augmented Reality

Kelly Fischer[✉] and Young-Mi Choi

School of Industrial Design, Georgia Institute of Technology, Atlanta, GA 30332, USA
{kfischer30,christina.choi}@gatech.edu

Abstract. The study proposes incorporating electromyography sensors with tangible augmented reality during the completion of a series of low stress motion-based tasks. Specifically, 3 tasks were completed by the users in a laboratory setting while equipped with an EMG armband and their subsequent signal output recorded for those tasks. The same tasks were then completed with the utilization of a simple tangible augmented reality system, and the subsequent signal outputs recorded once more. These signal outputs are gathered by an armband consisting of 8 surface electrodes which can record the EMG signals generated from the muscles in the forearm for each task performed by the user. The tangible augmented reality system incorporates both physical and digital interactions to best mimic the real-life tasks performed by users.

Keywords: Electromyography · Tangible augmented reality · Muscular activation

1 Introduction

Electromyography (EMG) is the detection and recording of electrical signals generated by muscle fibers. The size and properties of the fibers varies as does the conduction velocities of the axons, morphology of nerve muscle junctions, and the physiological properties of the muscle fibers. Augmented reality is an experience where the users' interactions are enhanced through sensory modalities and often computer-generated input. The utilization of augmented reality for guiding user motions and the incorporation of sensors as an assessment tool are areas of growing application and interest [1, 7]. There exists discord between the current relationship of exercise recommendation in the realm of physical therapy and muscle strengthening with the extent to which these conscious efforts affect muscle activation over time [6]. In this work, the EMG signals output by users when completing tasks in a tangible augmented reality (TAR) setting are measured. The purpose of this study is to determine the impact of the change in visualization and interaction methods on muscle activation in the user while performing low stress motion-based tasks. These tasks include removing the cap from a pen, lifting a teacup from a table, and removing the lid from a disposable coffee cup. Such actions were chosen to be easily reproducible while including familiar, everyday objects. The tasks require

© The Author(s), under exclusive license to Springer Nature Switzerland AG 2022
C. Stephanidis et al. (Eds.): HCII 2022, CCIS 1581, pp. 274–280, 2022.
https://doi.org/10.1007/978-3-031-06388-6_36

minimal instruction from the researcher for the users to understand and complete the actions.

To read the EMG signals from the user, surface electrodes are used. When the users move, electrical signals generated by the muscles can be recorded from the surface of the skin. This form of EMG is called surface electromyography (sEMG). sEMG is an alternative to embedding needle electrodes directly into the muscles which is called intramuscular electromyography (imEMG). When recording sEMG signals, noise from various sources can contaminate the readings which makes the analysis and classification of these signals more challenging. Previous works have explored the detection, processing, and classification analysis in electromyography for standardizing practices and following signal evaluation [3]. However, sEMG comes with the advantages of being easier to set up and incorporate with other devices as well as being non-intrusive.

2 Methods

2.1 Participants

Basic information of the users is gathered via a pre-study questionnaire, including age, gender, race, dominant arm, and any motor limitations or injuries with their dominant arm. Users with serious injury or current disability that prevents full, uninhibited motion of the dominant arm and fine motor control of the dominant hand were not measured in this study to decrease unknown influences in EMG signal readings.

2.2 Materials

Myo Armband. To generate the data that will be analyzed, a user wears the EMG sensor on their dominant arm. The sensor is the Myo gesture control armband by Thalmic Labs. The Myo does not require any skin preparation such as removing arm hair or applying conductive gel. Consisting of 8 electrodes, the band goes around the upper forearm (see Fig. 1). These electrodes create an 8-channel EMG reading which is sampled at 200 Hz per channel.

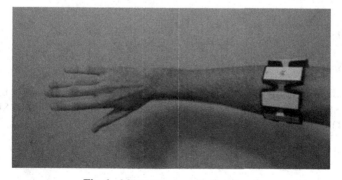

Fig. 1. Myo gesture control armband

Tangible Augmented Reality System. The users were asked to perform the same tasks while physically interacting with the objects directly and visually receiving feedback from an AR interface of the objects. The system simulated 3D models of the objects through the display to show their motions as they completed the tasks.

2.3 Usability

The System Usability Scale (SUS) was used to measure the usability of the TAR system. SUS is an industry-based tool for measuring system usability, or the ease of use of an application. It consists of a 10-item questionnaire with 5 response options, ranging from "strongly disagree" to "strongly agree". The calculated scores from each questionnaire range from 0–100 and represent system usability, with the acceptable SUS score being 68. A paper-based SUS questionnaire was administered after the TAR task recordings.

2.4 Procedures

The user is fitted with the armband and receives instruction for the tasks prior to each recording. To aid in the recordings, the user was provided a countdown to know when to perform the task. The recording also automatically cuts off after 1.5 s, eliminating the need to later trim around the time when the task was completed. The tasks measured in this study include:

- removing the cap from a pen
- lifting a teacup from a table
- removing the lid from a disposable coffee cup

Each user undergoes 3 real-life task recordings and 3 TAR task recordings per session which are stored in a comma separated value (CSV) file with the raw EMG values. For the purposes of this work, the EMG signals underwent full-wave rectification prior to analysis [8]. This is due to the inclusion of negative and positive values in the raw EMG signals and the attempt to compare the intensity of EMG output from this study.

3 Results

3.1 SUS Scores

Please The SUS score for the TAR system was 68.2, an acceptable score for usability as a supplemental device to the study. There are statistically no outliers in the SUS scores (see Table 1).

Table 1. SUS scores

Average SUS score	68.22
Standard deviation	3.56
IQR	4

3.2 EMG Output

The purpose of the work was to determine the impact on EMG output from users while performing tasks in tangible augmented reality versus real-life. In the analysis of the EMG signals, the data collecting in the CSV files were then rectified for analysis. This full-wave rectification converted the negative values from the signal to positive values and thus prevents the calculation of the signal's mean output to come out to zero. The main method of EMG signal modeling used in comparison for this study was integrated EMG (iEMG), which can be summarized as the area under the curve of the rectified EMG signal [2] (see Fig. 2). In the equation below N is the length of the segment, i is the segment increment, and x_i is the value of the signal amplitude. Focus values from the EMG signal recordings included maximum, minimum, mean, range, and iEMG.

$$iEMG = \sum_{i=1}^{N} |x_i| \tag{1}$$

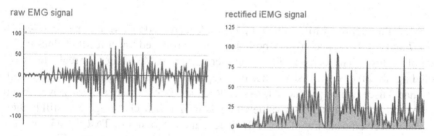

Fig. 2. Recorded user EMG signal (raw on the left, rectified on the right)

Recorded EMG values of the users were compared between individual users, individual real-life tasks, individual TAR tasks, all real-life tasks averages, and all TAR task averages. Of the 48 tasks performed in real-life and TAR, 38 produced higher maximum EMG values in TAR, 41 produced higher mean EMG values in TAR, and 39 produced higher iEMG values in TAR. While maximum and mean values for the tasks both display generally higher values in TAR, it can be questioned whether a singular value (in the case for maximum) or the average of an oscillating signal (in the case for mean) can be appropriately reflective of EMG intensity. While iEMG does not contain a unit of measurement, its value encompasses the duration of time while reducing the influence of the signal's alternating characteristic. The difference between the average iEMG values for real-life and TAR tasks per user were observed as well (see Fig. 3).

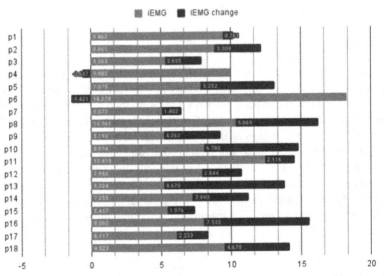

Fig. 3. Average real-life task iEMG values and difference with TAR task iEMG values (iEMG change) per user

While the average iEMG value for p4 and p6 decreased in TAR compared to real-life (−.637 and −1.421 respectively), both users only produced lower iEMG values in TAR for 1 of the tasks. This is likely due to the averaging of iEMG values for real-life vs TAR including all three of the tasks rather than repetitions of the same task. However, all 3 tasks had 3 users which produced lower TAR values, though there was only overlap with p2 who only had 1 higher TAR value while their TAR iEMG average was still higher.

The perceived usability of the TAR system and the values of TAR iEMG output for users can also be observed. We calculated the change from the real-life iEMG average to the TAR iEMG average per user as a percentage increase or decrease (see Fig. 4).

While inclusive of decreasing TAR iEMG averages for 2 users, Fig. 4 reflects a moderately significant trend between the higher SUS score of a user and a lower % change of average iEMG in TAR. Such observation may be attributed to the perceived comfort of a user when experiencing interactions with a novel system with an overcompensation of EMG output due to the shift in visual cues and feedback from the norm.

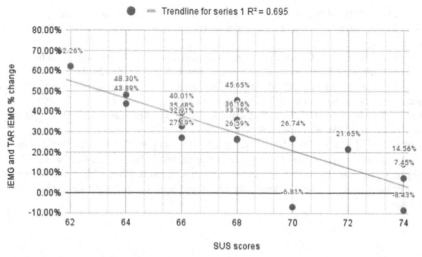

Fig. 4. Percent difference of iEMG to TAR iEMG averages and SUS score per user

4 Conclusion

This study and its findings are aimed at determining what impact utilizing a tangible augmented reality system has on EMG output of users performing motion-based tasks. The tasks performed by the users required minimal instruction and mental effort, and the satisfactory SUS score largely removes poor TAR system usability as an influence on the recorded EMG signals.

While the user data appears to indicate some level of increase in EMG output when using the TAR system, there are still limitations when accurately collecting and interpreting sEMG signals. The TAR system solely utilized changes to the users' visual interactions and can be improved to include a wider range of adjusted sensory input and feedback mechanisms for further study. Though limited in result capabilities, this study indicates an opportunity to explore areas to identify influences in muscular activation, as well as potential development of methods to incite specific levels of activation in users through augmented simulation [4, 5]. Specifically, there exists the potential for the application of electromyography in the medical and physical therapy fields as a method of assessment, tracking, and creating a personalized and immersive standard for rehabilitation.

References

1. Chen, P.J., Penn, I.W., Wei, S.H., Chuang, L.R., Sung, W.H.: Augmented reality-assisted training with selected Tai-Chi movements improves balance control and increases lower limb muscle strength in older adults: a prospective randomized trial. J. Exerc. Sci. Fit. **18**(3), 142–147 (2020)
2. Christopher, S., MdRasedul, I.: A Comprehensive study on EMG feature extraction and classifiers. Op. Acc. J. Biomed. Eng. Bio. Sci. **1**(1) (2018)

3. Chowdhury, R.H., Reaz, M.B., Ali, M.A., Bakar, A.A., Chellappan, K., Chang, T.G.: Surface electromyography signal processing and classification techniques. Sensors (Basel) **13**(9), 12431–12466 (2013)
4. Jones, C.L., Kamper, D.G.: Involuntary neuromuscular coupling between the thumb and finger of stroke survivors during dynamic movement. Front. Neurol. **9**, 84 (2018)
5. Kim, J.H., Ari, H., Madasu, C., Hwang, J.: Evaluation of the biomechanical stress in the neck and shoulders during augmented reality interactions. App. Ergon. **88**, 103175 (2020)
6. Kristof, R., Moldovan, C., Ciupe, V., Maniu, I., Banda, M.: Applications based on electromyography sensors. ITM Web Conf. **29**, 02007 (2007)
7. Limbu, B.H., Jarodzka, H., Klemke, R., Specht, M.: Can you ink while you blink? Assessing mental effort in a sensor-based calligraphy trainer. Sensors (Basel) **19**(14), 3244 (2019)
8. Negro, F., Keenan, K., Farina, D.: Power spectrum of the rectified EMG: when and why is rectification beneficial when identifying neural connectivity. J. Neural Eng. **12**(3), 036008 (2015)

Yerkes' Neuropsychological Test Using Leap Motion

A. Belem Juárez Mendez[1], Erika Hernández-Rubio[2],
C. Ricardo Hernández-Hernández[1], J. Angel Molina-García[1],
Amilcar Meneses-Viveros[3(✉)], and Oscar Zamora Arévalo[4]

[1] ESCOM, Instituto Politécnico Nacional, Mexico City, Mexico
`abjuarezm@ipn.mx`
[2] SEPI-ESCOM, Instituto Politécnico Nacional, Mexico City, Mexico
`ehernandezru@ipn.mx`
[3] Departamento de Computación, CINVESTAV-IPN, Mexico City, Mexico
`ameneses@cs.cinvestav.mx`
[4] Posgrado - Faculta de Psicología, Universidad Nacional Autónoma de México,
Mexico City, Mexico

Abstract. The use of eHealth tools allow more people to have access to health services. In particular, neuropsychological treatments can benefit from the use of this type of tools. These tests can be applied using computer devices such as desktops, tablets or smartphones. Yerkes' test allows an oculomotor evaluation and is related to spatial intelligence. Due to the oculomotor skills that the user must perform in the test, it is necessary to use a device, such as Leap Motion, to capture the hand movement. In this work, the design of the virtual reality Yerkes' tests for a desktop application using Unity and Leap Motion for interaction is presented. Finally, the definition of user gestures is included to perform some main tasks through Leap Motion.

Keywords: eHealth · Leap motion · Virtual reality · Yerke's tests

1 Introduction

The use of eHealth tools allow more people to have access to health services through information systems, or computer and mobile device applications, to name a few [7,8]. This is very important in countries like Mexico where there is a health gap where the growth of the health sector is less than the growth of people who require these services [5]. In particular, neuropsychology treatments can benefit from the use of this type of tools, through systems and applications to help specialists to monitor the remote treatment of people who have difficulties moving to hospitals, or health clinics, to carry out this type the neuropsychological tests [2,5,7,8]. These tests can be applied using computer devices such as desktops, tablets or smartphones [1,3,4,6,9]. The Yerkes' test is responsible for evaluating oculomotor impairment and measuring the spatial ability of

C. Stephanidis et al. (Eds.): HCII 2022, CCIS 1581, pp. 281–286, 2022.
https://doi.org/10.1007/978-3-031-06388-6_37

patients through exercises to form 3D figures from a set of cubes that serve as basic objects [11]. The Yerkes' cubes test requires the use of virtual reality [6,9]. Interaction is important so that the user can take and place cubes to form the figures that are indicated. For this reason, a Leap Motion device was used to recognize user gestures and translate them into actions in the virtual reality scene [10,12]. In this work, the design of the Yerkes' tests for a desktop application using Unity and Leap Motion for interaction is presented. Engine Unity is used to develop the virtual scene where the user interacts with the objects in order to perform the Yerkes' test. Finally, the gestures that have been selected for the actions and the tasks that the user can perform in the virtual Yerkes' tests are presented.

2   Yerkes' Test

The cube test belongs to the Beta-Army test battery designed by Robert Yerkes in the second decade of the 20th century. This test consists of showing the patient a three-dimensional figure made up of stacks of cubes, then the patient must build the figure by stacking cube by cube, taking into account the cubes that are hidden. The cube test allows an oculomotor evaluation and is related to spatial intelligence. The objective of this test is to evaluate a person's ability to identify the number of cubes in a three-dimensional image formed from these geometric objects. The cubes may be visible or partially hidden from the patient. Some examples of the exercises that must be solved with the Yerkes' test are shown in Fig. 1.

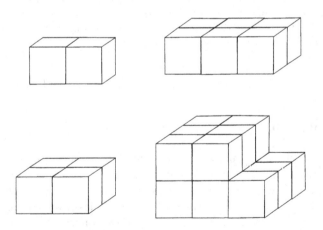

Fig. 1. Some examples for cube test

3   System Design

According to [9], Yerkes' test can be applied using a virtual reality application. Due to the oculomotor skills that the user must perform in the test, it is necessary to use a control to capture movement. As cube test focuses on the use of vision and hands, the Leap Motion device was used. This device allows capturing the movement of the hands and, with the help of the development framework, mapping this capture to a virtual reality environment.

Figure 2 shows the System Design for cubes' test. The user interaction with the application is based on user's event cycle. First, the user interact with the system using the Leap Motion device. Then the operating system send the event to the user application. With the device controller and Leap Motion framework the application recognizes the event and processes it. User events are interpreted into user gestures, which trigger tasks in the application. Depending on the tasks, some method of SDK Leap Motion is used or the application methods are used to move the cubes in the virtual environment through the Unity framework. The application's view object presents the result of the user event, which can be a change in the position of an object, or adding an object, to name a few. This is reflected in a change in the image of the virtual environment and is displayed in the application window for the user to obtain feedback from the system.

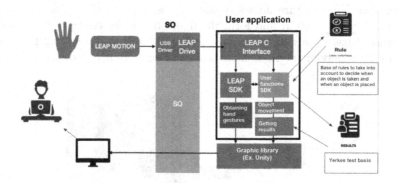

Fig. 2. System design

4   Leap Motion and Gestures Definition

Gestures definition is a key to get a useful user interaction. Fortunately, leap motion defines a set of basic hand gestures for interacting with 3D objects in the virtual environment, such as picking up or dropping an object. However, there are other gestures that are not related to tasks and that is where they should be added so that the interaction is adequate and the tasks of the application can be carried out.

The main tasks that you want to perform in the cube test are: Grab and drop cube, add new cube to scene, rotate view right, rotate view left, move plane up and down.

Grab and drop cube. This gesture is defined by the Leap Motion framework. And it is used naturally for the user. You just reach out to the 3D object you want and make a closing motion to grab onto the object. With the held object you can move it in the scene and with opening your hand you release it (Fig. 3).

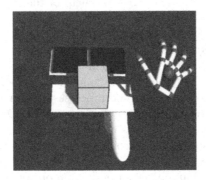

Fig. 3. Grab and drop gesture

Add cube. This gesture allows to add a new cube to the scene so that the user can manipulate it and form the figure of the Yerkes test that has been entrusted has been defined in this work and consists of bending the middle and ring fingers of the right hand while the rest are kept extended, Fig. 4.

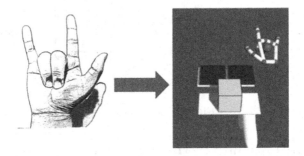

Fig. 4. Add cube gesture

Rotate view left and right. These gestures allow you to rotate the view of the scene. The gestures consist of raising the little finger of the left hand if a rotation to the left is wanted or raising the little finger of the right hand if a rotation to that side is wanted. These gestures are presented in Fig. 5.

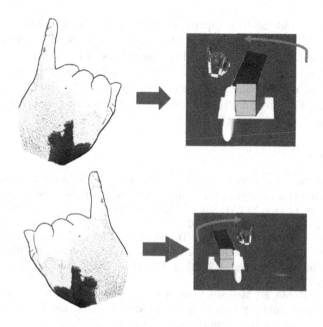

Fig. 5. Rotate left or right gestures

Plane up down. This gesture causes the plane to descend from its current position, or return to the original position. It was included so that the user can stack cubes that require greater height in a more comfortable way, Fig. 6.

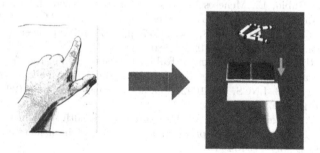

Fig. 6. Add cube gesture

For test application reasons, the delete cube gesture was omitted, although there is an undo function with the CTRL-Z key sequence.

5 Conclusions

Neuropsychological tests can be implemented in eHealth applications to help specialists so that more patients can perform them without the need for the doctor to be present. Motion capture devices, such as Leap Motion, allow some oculomotor test to be incorporated into eHeatlh applications. The frameworks included in the Leap Motion SDK allow these types of input devices to be easily incorporated into applications that use other development frameworks, such as Unity. Its possible to define new gestures or to use the ones that Leap Motion SDK includes. For the cube test it was necessary to add gestures to add cubes and manipulate the view of the scene.

References

1. Cruz Caballero, P., Meneses-Viveros, A., Hernández-Rubio, E., Zamora Arévalo, O.: Distributed user interfaces for Poppelreuters and Raven visual tests. In: Zhou, J., Salvendy, G. (eds.) ITAP 2017. LNCS, vol. 10298, pp. 325–338. Springer, Cham (2017). https://doi.org/10.1007/978-3-319-58536-9_26
2. De La Torre Díez, I., Alonso, S.G., Hamrioui, S., López-Coronado, M., Cruz, E.M.: Systematic review about QoS and QoE in telemedicine and eHealth services and applications. J. Med. Syst. **42**(10), 1–10 (2018). https://doi.org/10.1007/s10916-018-1040-4
3. Hernández-Rubio, E., Meneses-Viveros, A., Aguilar-Herrera, A.I., Zamora Arévalo, O., Hernández-Rubio, Y.L.: Cloud system for the management of neuropsychological test in Mexico. In: Stephanidis, C., Antona, M., Ntoa, S. (eds.) HCII 2021. CCIS, vol. 1421, pp. 323–327. Springer, Cham (2021). https://doi.org/10.1007/978-3-030-78645-8_40
4. Hernández-Rubio, E., Meneses-Viveros, A., Mancera-Serralde, E., Flores-Ortiz, J.: Combinations of modalities for the words learning memory test implemented on tablets for seniors. In: Zhou, J., Salvendy, G. (eds.) ITAP 2016. LNCS, vol. 9754, pp. 309–319. Springer, Cham (2016). https://doi.org/10.1007/978-3-319-39943-0_30
5. Hernández-Rubio, E., Meneses-Viveros, A., Muñoz Salazar, L.: User experience in older adults using tablets for neuropsicological tests in Mexico City. In: Rau, P.-L.P. (ed.) HCII 2019. LNCS, vol. 11577, pp. 135–149. Springer, Cham (2019). https://doi.org/10.1007/978-3-030-22580-3_11
6. Guerrero Huerta, A.G., Hernández Rubio, E., Meneses Viveros, A.: Augmented reality in tablets for the Yerkes test for older adults. In: Zhou, J., Salvendy, G. (eds.) ITAP 2018. LNCS, vol. 10927, pp. 36–48. Springer, Cham (2018). https://doi.org/10.1007/978-3-319-92037-5_4
7. Jimenez, P., Bregenzer, A., et al.: Integration of eHealth tools in the process of workplace health promotion: proposal for design and implementation. J. Med. Internet Res. **20**(2), e8769 (2018)
8. Kreps, G.L., Neuhauser, L.: New directions in eHealth communication: opportunities and challenges. Patient Educ. Couns. **78**(3), 329–336 (2010)
9. Miranda, J.A.H., Hernàndez Rubio, E., Meneses Viveros, A.: Analysis of Luria memory tests for development on mobile devices. In: Duffy, V.G. (ed.) DHM 2014. LNCS, vol. 8529, pp. 546–557. Springer, Cham (2014). https://doi.org/10.1007/978-3-319-07725-3_54
10. Leap Motion: Leap motion, San Francisco, CA, USA (2015)
11. Spring, J.H.: Psychologists and the war: the meaning of intelligence in the alpha and beta tests. Hist. Educ. Q. **12**(1), 3–15 (1972)
12. Weichert, F., Bachmann, D., Rudak, B., Fisseler, D.: Analysis of the accuracy and robustness of the leap motion controller. Sensors **13**(5), 6380–6393 (2013)

Athlete Data Logger: A Smartphone Application for the Management of Strength Training and Conditioning of Athletes

Masayoshi Kanoh[(⊠)], Kenta Kato, Yudai Nasu, Yoshikatsu Nakagawa, Yuki Nihei, Keisuke Miyake, and Yukio Oida

Chukyo University, Nagoya 466-8666, Japan
mkanoh@sist.chukyo-u.ac.jp

Abstract. Data on the strength training and conditioning of athletes have traditionally been recorded on paper. However, this method is inconvenient due to the cost of storage space, potential loss of record sheets, and difficulty in carrying them. To address this issue, we developed Athlete Data Logger, a smartphone application with two versions (one for coaches and one for athletes) that assists with managing the status of athletes' conditioning and strength training. We had two coaches and 62 athletes use the application for one week and then performed an evaluation based on the System Usability Scale (SUS). The results showed that the SUS score by the coaches was 88.8 points, and the training and conditioning functions of the application for athletes were rated 68.8 ± 13.2 and 79.8 ± 8.2, respectively. As the mean SUS score reported in other studies is 68.1, these results demonstrate that Athlete Data Logger has more usability than a typical application.

Keywords: Strength training · Conditioning · Smartphone application

1 Introduction

In order for athletes to reach peak condition on the day of a sports competition, daily management of their conditioning and strength training is important.

National initiatives in Japan such as the "Strategy for Sports Nation" formulated in 2010 have improved Japan's international competitiveness in sports, leading to the country winning a record number of medals at the Tokyo 2020 Olympic Games. To maintain a high level of competitiveness in the future, sports organizations and sports universities that train top athletes must manage and implement conditioning and training based on scientific evidence. In order to utilize the data obtained in the field to improve athletes' competitive performance, it is essential for athletes themselves to make accurate records and for coaches, trainers, and other staff to take appropriate actions on the basis of those records. However, evidence-based actions are not always provided at the scene of a sports

© The Author(s), under exclusive license to Springer Nature Switzerland AG 2022
C. Stephanidis et al. (Eds.): HCII 2022, CCIS 1581, pp. 287–293, 2022.
https://doi.org/10.1007/978-3-031-06388-6_38

practice, so the management of conditioning and training is often conducted on the basis of the subjective judgment of the athletes themselves. To address this issue, we developed a smartphone application called Athlete Data Logger (ADL) for managing and implementing conditioning and training to support athletes in improving their performance.

2   A Smartphone Application for Supporting Management

The Athlete Data Logger (ADL) application consists of two versions: one for athletes (described in Sect. 2.1) and one for coaches (described in Sect. 2.2).

2.1   ADL for Athletes

ADL for athletes implements functions for athletes to manage the status of their own strength training and conditioning.

Strength Training Management. This function has two sub-functions: (1) a function to automatically set the training load according to the user's muscle strength and the purpose of the training, and (2) a function to automatically set the appropriate rest time according to the purpose of the training. Function (1) eliminates the need for the user to manually adjust the load, thus enabling him or her to take on appropriate practice. Moreover, it reduces the amount of time the trainer needs to spend with the user, thus reducing the burden on the trainer. For this function, we implemented an automatic load adjustment algorithm based on the repetition maximum method [1], as shown in Fig. 1. We expect this algorithm to be helpful for eliciting a steady improvement in muscle strength. Function (2) is designed to give the muscles time to properly recover from fatigue, which enables the user to perform the next training set at full strength.

Conditioning Management. This function is for managing information on conditioning and injuries, including weight, body temperature, health status (headache, cough, runny nose, etc.), sleep status, appetite, bowel movements, and breakfast intake. In the injury management function, body parts are classified into 91 categories based on the IOC definition [2] and information on the injured part is recorded, including details, cause, level of pain, and recovery behavior.

Accessing Record Information. The recorded information can be accessed by three functions (shown in Fig. 2) as follows. The "daily conditioning list" view function (1) allows the user to check daily conditioning in a list format. The "injury pain locations" view function (2) provides a visualization of the day's injury status according to the positions of marks placed on a human-shaped diagram. Each mark is labeled with the pain level (1–6) at the site of injury, and

Automatic load adjustment algorithm
Input id: User ID
         Nt: Target total number of repetitions, which changes by the purpose of training
         Nf: Target number of repetitions in the first set of training
Output d_load: Amount of change of training load

```
1   if not have_injury(id):       # if the user does not have an injury
2       t = get_total_reps(id)     # get the total number of repetitions of training
3       if Nt ≤t:
4           d_load = 2.5           # plus 2.5 kilograms
5       else if Nt − 2 ≤ t and t≤ Nt − 1:
6           d_load = 0             # no change
7       else:                     # that is t ≤ Nt − 3
8           if have_fatigue(id):  # if the user has training fatigue
9               d_load = 0        # no change
10          else:                 # that is the user does not have fatigue
11              d_load = −2.5     # minus 2.5 kilograms
12  else:                         # if the user has an injury
13      d_load = 0                # no change
14  f = get_firstset_reps(id)     # get the number of repetitions in the first set of training
15  if f ≤ Nf:
16      d_load = −2.5             # minus 2.5 kilograms
17  else:
18      d_load = 0                # no change
19  return d_load
```

Fig. 1. Automatic load adjustment algorithm.

its shape indicates the changes of the injury pain level from the previous day. The "time-series graph" view function (3) allows users to examine changes in their training records and injury pain levels over time as line graphs.

2.2   ADL for Coaches

ADL for coaches has three functions: (1) an athlete registration authentication function that links a coach to athletes (Fig. 3(a)), (2) an athlete-data view function that allows the coach to check the information of each athlete (Fig. 3(b)), and (3) an injury information listing function that provides an overview of the injury status of all athletes (Fig. 3(c)). The athlete registration authentication function was designed to support a smooth linkage between coaches and athletes by means of a sports ID created by each coach. This function also adopts a login authentication using a Google account, thus providing high security and ease of login. The athlete-data view function displays a list of athletes, and tapping each athlete brings up a human-shaped diagram showing the pain level at each injury site, a list of conditioning over the past week, and training status over the past month. This function allows coaches to see the detailed status of individual athletes quickly. The injury information listing function displays a list of all athletes' human-shaped diagrams. This function allows coaches to compare the injury status of all athletes.

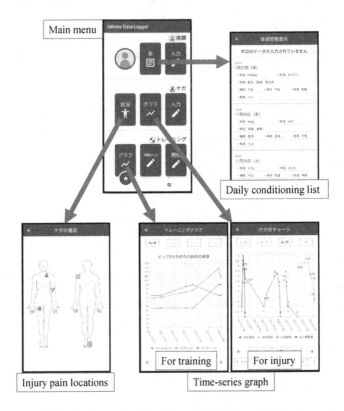

Fig. 2. Accessing functions of ADL for athletes.

3   Experiment

We had two coaches and 62 athletes use ADL for one week and then evaluated it based on the System Usability Scale (SUS) [3]. ADL for coaches was used by a judo coach and a softball coach. The strength training function of ADL for athletes was used by 40 judo athletes, and the conditioning function was used by 22 softball athletes. After using ADL for one week, the participants were asked to score the ten items in Table 1 with one of five responses that range from "strongly agree" to "strongly disagree." We then converted the original scores of 0–40 to SUS scores of 0–100. Figure 4 shows the results. The average SUS score by the coaches was 88.8 points, judo athletes rated the training function as 68.8 ± 13.2, and softball athletes rated the conditioning function as 79.8 ± 8.2. Note that 21 of the judo athletes could not use the training function, because All-Japan Collegiate Judo Weight Categorized Team Championships was held at next week of this experiment. Therefore, the results for the 19 who did use this function are also shown. The average score of the 19 judo athletes who used this function was 73.9 ± 13.0. A previous report has shown that the average score of SUS is 68.1 [4]. We performed a one-sample t-test to investigate whether the obtained

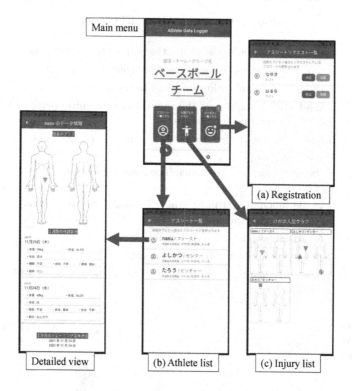

Fig. 3. Functions of ADL for coaches.

scores differed from the average and found a significant trend in judo athletes using the training function ($p = 0.068$) and a significant difference in the softball athletes (all of them are used the conditioning function) ($p = 0.000$). As for the coaches, we could not use a t-test because there were only two participants, so we referenced the work of Bangor et al. [5], who graded the SUS score from A to F, and found that the coaches' score is classified as grade B "Excellent," which indicates that the ADL for coaches is highly rated. The above results demonstrate that ADL has more usability than a typical application.

Table 1. Items of system usability scale.

1	I think that I would like to use this application frequently
2	I found the application unnecessarily complex
3	I thought the application was easy to use
4	I think that I would need the support of a technical person to be able to use this application
5	I found the various functions in this application were well integrated
6	I thought there was too much inconsistency in this application
7	I would imagine that most athletes would learn to use this application very quickly
8	I found the application very cumbersome to use
9	I felt very confident using the application
10	I needed to learn a lot of things before I could get going with this application

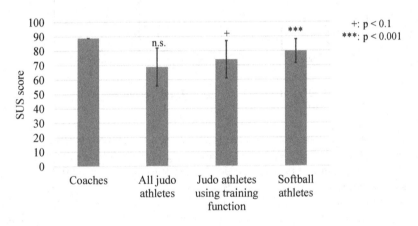

Fig. 4. Experimental results.

4   Conclusion

In this paper, we presented Athlete Data Logger, a smartphone application that allows coaches and athletes to manage the status of athletes' conditioning and strength training. There are two versions of the application, one for coaches and one for athletes. We had coaches and athletes at Chukyo University use the application for one week and then evaluated it based on the System Usability Scale. The results demonstrate that Athlete Data Logger has more usability than a typical application.

References

1. Haff, G.G., Triplett, N.T.: Essentials of Strength Training and Conditioning. Fourth Edition, Human Kinetics (2015)
2. Junge, A., et al.: Injury surveillance in multi-sport events: the international Olympic committee approach. Br. J. Sports Med. **42**(6), 413–421 (2008)
3. Brooke, J.: SUS - a quick and dirty usability scale. In: Jordan, P. W., Thomas, B., Weerdmeester, B.A., McClelland, A.L. (Eds.) Usability Evaluation in Industry. Taylor and Francis (1996)
4. Sauro, J.: A Practical Guide to the System Usability Scale. Measuring Usability LLC (2011)
5. Bangor, A., Kortum, P.T., Miller, J.T.: Determining what individual SUS scores mean: adding an adjective rating scale. J. Usabil. Stud. **4**(3), 114–123 (2009)

Research on Product Design of EMG Wearable Device Based on High-Density Electromyography

Jiayuan Lu and Xiangyu Liu[✉]

College of Communication and Art Design, University of Shanghai for Science and Technology,
Shanghai 200093, China
1820110219@st.usst.edu.cn, liuxiangyu@usst.edu.cn

Abstract. Core muscles play a fundamental role both in exercises and daily routines. Strong core muscles can enhance the Trunk stability and transition of strength. However, due to the weakness, most rookies can hardly feel the recruitment of core muscles and start compensating or using the wrong form. This may lead to cumulative fatigue in the short term and improper postures or spinal injuries in a long time. Thus, monitoring and protecting the unit for early core-muscle training is necessary. The study focuses on fitness rookies and designs an innovative waistband. High-density electromyography (HD-sEMG) can provide real-time monitoring of muscle conditions once it censors fatigue. The band will remind the user to take a break. And the shape memory polymer (SMP) can protect the waist and back from potential injury if necessary. With the continuous impact of the coronavirus, trainers spend more time at home and face the limitation of space and equipment. Nonetheless, isometric and simplified isotonic training will be enough for starters for core-muscle exercise. The study lists core-muscle strength exercises for athletes and core-muscle stability prescriptions for medical care, then reorganize them for rookies at home.

Keywords: High-density electromyography · Core muscle strength · Resistance exercise prescription · Wearable device · Human-computer interaction

1 Introduction

1.1 Research Background of Chinese Sports and Fitness

With the implementation of the national fitness strategy, the Chinese have achieved specific results in sports and health. By 2020, the sports area per capita has reached 2.2 square meters, the number of social sports instructors per 1,000 people has risen to more than 1.86, and the proportion of people who regularly participate has reached 37.2%. Increasing participation has also boosted the sports economy. From 2015 to 2019, the total scale of the national sports industry jumped from 1.71 trillion RMB to 2.95 trillion RMB, with an average annual growth rate of 14.6% [1]. The continuous global impact of the coronavirus has not taken away the passion for people to pursue health. According

© The Author(s), under exclusive license to Springer Nature Switzerland AG 2022
C. Stephanidis et al. (Eds.): HCII 2022, CCIS 1581, pp. 294–301, 2022.
https://doi.org/10.1007/978-3-031-06388-6_39

to the "2021 National Health Insights Report", 69% of respondents hope to pay more attention to the rationality of practice, and 66% expect to make changes in exercise frequency. However, only 33% and 32% of the respondents above made substantial changes [2].

Lack of Information about Body Condition and Resistance Training. Two factors may cause this. First, people do not acquire enough information from their bodies. Even though wearable monitoring devices like the apple watch have made a hit in wearable devices for years, the body information they provide can not fully reflect the body changes while working out, especially when taking resistance training. Muscle fatigue is so subjective that no one else can tell. Although the American College of Sport Science (ACSM) has made a prescription about resistance training and recommends the amount of time one should take based on different strengths [3], it can not monitor muscle fatigue and gives direct information.

Secondly, resistance training exercises that suit the public have not formed into a system yet. Take core-strength resistance training for an example. Core strength refers to the resistance ability of the muscles in the core area of the human body, which is an essential basis for people to engage both in a sports event and daily life [4]. One can achieve agility, balance, coordination, speed, explosiveness, and reflexes with a strong core muscle. Enhancing core strength can provide the human body with effective force recruitment, force transmission, and force control. The concept was originated from core stability, which can be traced back to the 1960s. Kibler first introduced it into competitive sports training in 2006 [5]. Core-strength helps force transmission in open-chain movements such as javelin throwing or basketball jump shot. However, core-strength training in competitive sports is mainly closed-chain exercises, which require multi-muscle and multi-joint participation. For rookies, starting a sophisticated training exercise like this at home or under-supervised can quickly increase the risk of fatigue injury in the short-term and improper postures or spinal injuries in the long term with their weak control of muscles.

Conclusion and Solution. To sum up, most people neither have little awareness of their body condition nor have no clue how to train correctly, especially the core muscles, and even if these problems had been solved, it is still hard to tell when to take a break, how long it should take, and when to start again.

The study focuses on core-strength resistance training for starters and designs a bright waist belt that offers muscle monitoring and protection. Using high-density electromyography (HD-sEMG), the microcosmic information such as motor unit action potential (MUAP) can be filtered from the macroscopical electromyography and infer the changes of the motor unit (MU) in the central nervous system (CNS). This can help make the response to the user even before fatigue occurs. Besides, the data collected during recruitment can also be transferred into repetition maximum (RM) to make a suitable training prescription. Using Shape memory polymer (SMP), the waist belt can offer extra support for the low back and waist if necessary without intervening in daily wearing.

1.2 Research Goal

Relying on HD-sEMG evidence-based research, the study has designed an intelligent wearable wristband that provides professional myoelectric monitoring, personalized training prescription, and extra supporting unit without disturbing daily wearing for users. The following steps will be conducted:

- Optimizing the layout under the premise of ensuring the accuracy of HD-sEMG through evidence-based research;
- Providing a basis for the subsequent design of fatigue-reminding mechanism by studying the process of muscle fatigue;
- Providing design reference and research basis for the next design through ergonomics, structure, and material.

2 Method

In the process of resistance training, the monitoring of training intensity has always been a need, especially for starters. At present, the evaluation of muscle fatigue in resistance training mainly relies on the experience of fitness trainers and the subjective feelings of fitness people themselves. Forming a habit requires frequent repetition; the more complex the pattern is, the higher the repetition frequency it takes. Muscle training required the user's continuous focus on the contraction of targeted muscle groups and body balance. As intensity increases, the muscle groups are prone to fatigue.

2.1 Technical Support: HD-SEMG

Like ECG and EEG, electromyographic (EMG) is a bioelectrical signal that generates muscle activity. The spatial and temporal superposition of motor unit action potentials (MUAP) is produced by numerous muscle fibers belonging to different motor units (see Fig. 1). A motor unit (MU) contains an α motor neuron in the spinal cord as the central nervous system and several muscle fibers under control. With external stimuli or central nervous system innervation, α motor neurons generate nerve impulses. At the same time, they reach muscle fibers, the final effector, along with each motor nerve fiber and develop motor unit action potentials (MUAP) [6–8].

Surface electromyographic signal (sEMG) is non-invasive to the subject's skin and corresponds to the targeted muscle. The high-density surface electromyogram (HD-sEMG), on the other hand, is derived from sEMG. It expands the number of channels sEMG has from only one to a two-dimensional densely arranged (3–6mm between each) channel array. More channels provide larger-capacity and higher-resolution spatiotemporal information, bringing a new perspective from microscopic muscle movement to the study.

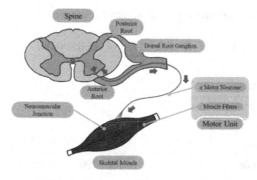

Fig. 1. Diagram of the motor unit.

Through the research of EMG, exercise intensity and specific action intents of people under non-injury conditions can be represented. The current research on EMG of muscle fatigue mainly focuses on the fatigue task induced by isometric contraction [9] and isotonic contraction [6]. Although muscle fatigue under dynamic tasks is more common in daily life, considering HD-sEMG requires large-scale electrodes fit on the skin, large trunk movements will lead the acquisition area shifted, which will affect the precision of the data. Thus, during the data collection, myoelectric changes of the abdominal muscles in the isometric contraction task will be considered.

2.2 Participants

Before the experiment, we have completed a tentative pre-acquisition investigation to ensure feasibility. Twelve subjects were invited, and information on each is shown (Table 1). None of them had congenital or acquired neuromuscular disease or spinal injury. All subjects had a complete acknowledgment of the details before the experiment, including:

- The overall process of the experimentation.
- The electromyography collection equipment and electrodes.
- Potential allergy risk of the paste used in the investigation.
- Short-term soreness and weakness of abdominal muscle after the experiment.

Table 1. Personal information of subjects participating in the experiment.

Subject	Gender	Age	Height (CM)	BMI
BHX	Male	22	175	22.7
CYF	Male	22	177	22.5
CSF	Male	22	175	22
DSD	Male	22	175	15.5
LXY	Male	32	175	22.9
LJY	Male	22	190	23.8
LWF	Male	22	177	22
TSK	Male	21	178	23.2
WY	Male	21	178	19.9
XZH	Male	22	168	20.3
YS	Male	22	175	15.5
ZRY	Male	21	177	20.1

Before the experiment, all the subjects were informed their private information would not be publicized, and they signed on the consents voluntarily.

2.3 Experiment

The experiment was carried out in an artificial lighting environment, and the room temperature was kept at 26 °C to 28 °C. During the experiment, subjects were required to perform a static crunch. As a typical isometric contraction task, it can easily stimulate the recruitment of abdominal muscles. The task required subjects to maintain at least 30 s or until exhaustion. From start to fatigue was recorded as one set, and each subject completed three sets in total. Each subject was allowed to have sufficient rest between the sequent set to avoid the effect of muscle fatigue (Fig. 2). After the preparation, subjects are ready to start (Fig. 3).

2.4 Results

We segmented the HD-sEMG signals using a 5 s window with a 3 s overlap. The initial window was seen as the pre-fatigue state, and the final window was the post-fatigue. The fast-ICA (independent component analysis) algorithm extracted the motor unit action potential (MUAP). We calculated the MUAP synchronization and found an increase in the Beta (15–30 Hz) band. The increased Beta synchronization will be the index of muscle fatigue to assist the product design.

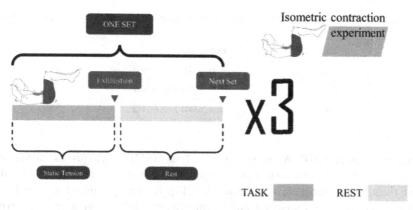

Fig. 2. Isometric contraction experiment process.

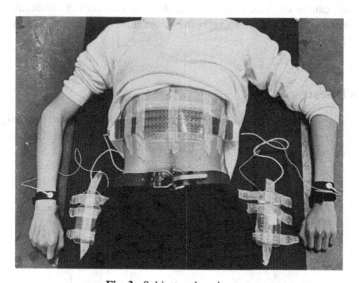

Fig. 3. Subject and equipment.

3   Product Design

3.1   Preliminary Preparation

Construction and Measurement of Waistband

The waistband comprises a breathable protection net, elastic belt, and reinforced belt. Tightening the belt to put external pressure on the muscles stimulates the muscles during exercise, accelerates the metabolism, and increases the intra-abdominal pressure to stabilize the core. The size, however, does not have a standard. Since the nation-wide body size measurement has not been taken since the 1980s, the study will base on the analysis of over 3,000 subjects over 50 measurement items taken out by Hu [10]. They found strong connections between body weight and chest width, waist width, and hipline (Table 2), which helps confirm the measurement of the final product.

Table 2. Linear Relationship between Measurement Items (MM) and Body Weight $W1$ (KG).

Items (MM)	Equation
Chest	$= 6,364W1 + 559.4$
Waist	$= 7.930W1 + 320.1$
Hips	$= 4.504W1 + 661.2$

Technical Support: SMP. A shape memory polymer (SMP) can adjust its state parameters (shape, position, strain, etc.) and return to the initial state after getting outside stimuli (heat, light, electricity, magnetism, etc.) [11]. Thermally-induced, light-induced, electro-induced, magnetic-induced, and Chemosensory SMP belong to the main types of SMP materials. Taking electro-induced SMP as an example, most are electrically insulating and cannot be driven by electrical devices. Embedding conductive fillers as a heating source to form a conductive network structure can make it easier to generate Joule heat [12].

3.2 Form Design

Based on core muscle area, support area, and restriction of movement, the design finally selects the coverage area as follows (Fig. 4), finalizes two projects of sketches and renders a model based on project A (Fig. 5).

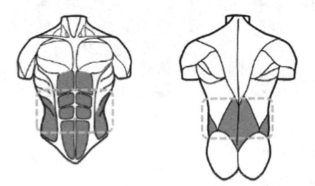

Fig. 4. Selected core-muscle area.

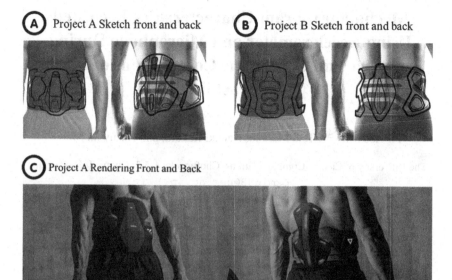

Ⓐ Project A Sketch front and back   **Ⓑ** Project B Sketch front and back

Ⓒ Project A Rendering Front and Back

Fig. 5. Sketches and renderings

Acknowledgment. This work is sponsored by the Shanghai Sailing Program (22YF1430800).

References

1. 14th Five-Year Plan for Sport. General Administration of Sport of China, China (2021)
2. Ding, X.: 2021 National Health Insights Report, China (2021)
3. Ratamess, N., Alvar, B., Evetoch, T., Housh, T., Kibler, W., Kraemer, W.J.: Progression models in resistance training for healthy adults. Med. Sci. Sports Exerc. **41**, 687–708 (2009)
4. Feng. J.J., Yuan. J.G.: Review of researches on core stability and core strength. J. Phys. Educ. **16**, 58–62 (2009)
5. Kibler, W., Press, J., Sciascia, A.: The role of core stability in athletic function. Sports Med. **36**, 189–198 (2006)
6. Liu, X.Y.: Study on the Adaption Design of Forearm Myoelectric Prosthesis. East China University of Science and Technology, China (2021)
7. Li, Q.L.: Study on sEMG Based Exoskeletal Robot for Upper Limbs Rehabilitation. Harbin Institute of Technology, China (2009)
8. Dong, H.Q.: Research on Upper Limb Pattern Recognition Technology Based on Surface Electromyography. Shanghai Normal University, China (2018)
9. Yang, H.M., Peng, Z., Sun, M.Y., Zhou, D.Q.: Study on Surface electromyographic characteristics of biceps brachii during static elbow flexion under fatigue. Contemp. Sports Technol. **11**, 33–37 (2021)
10. Hu, H.M., Chao, C.Z., Zhao, Z.Y., Zhang, X., Ran, L.H.: Correlation study on measurement of Chinese adults. Chin. J. Ergon. **8**, 49–53 (2014)
11. Li, M., Li. H.B.: Review of shape memory materials. Packag. J. **6**, 17–23 (2014)
12. Li, W.B., Wei, W.T., Li, J.R., Liu, J.H., Qian, K.: Research progress of shape memory polymer fibers and reinforced composites. Acta Materiae Compositae Sinica **39**, 77–96 (2022)

Mechanomyogram Characteristics Recorded Using Accelerometer and Microphone During Isometric and Concentric Contractions of Biceps Brachii

Pil Kee Min[✉], Tota Mizuno, Naoaki Itakura, and Kazuyuki Mito

The University of Electro-Communications, Chofugaoka 1-5-1, Chofu, Tokyo, Japan
pkmin88@uec.ac.jp

Abstract. The aim of our study was to find a suitable sensor for Mechanomyography (MMG) measurement during dynamic exercises. Ten healthy male volunteers participated in this study. The subjects performed isometric and concentric contractions of the right arm at elbow joint angles of 40° to 140°. The motion speeds for the concentric contraction was 10°/s and 20°/s. The motion speed for the isometric contraction was defined as 0°/s. The contraction forces were 20% and 40% of the maximum voluntary contraction (MVC) measured at the elbow joint angle of 90° during isometric contraction. MMG of biceps brachii muscle was recorded using two types of transducers: accelerometer and microphone. The two transducers were attached on the muscle belly using a double adhesive tape. The two MMG signals from the accelerometer (MMGacc) and microphone (MMGmic) were stored in a personal computer using an A/D converter with a 16-bit resolution; the sampling frequency was 1 kHz. The root mean square (RMS) and median frequency (MDF) were calculated using the signals recorded every 10° at elbow joint angles of 60° to 120°. Furthermore, the RMS value for each joint angle was normalized by the RMS at MVC (%RMS). The %RMS values of MMGacc and MMGmic increased as the increasing level of force, elbow angle, and motion speed increased. The MDF values of MMGmic increased with the increase in all factors; however, the MDF values of MMGacc increased only with the increase in motion speed. In a previous study, that is suggested that the accelerometer measured the mechanomyogram and the body movement. Results of the frequency analysis, indicate that the accelerometer was susceptible to disturbances, such as body movement; thus, microphone is considered more suitable for measuring the MMG.

Keywords: Microphone · Accelerometer

1 Introduction

Electromyography (EMG) and Mechanomyography (MMG) are objective, noninvasive methods for assessing muscle functions. During muscle exertion, electrical signals are sent from the brain to the muscle fibers, and electromyography is used to measure

C. Stephanidis et al. (Eds.): HCII 2022, CCIS 1581, pp. 302–307, 2022.
https://doi.org/10.1007/978-3-031-06388-6_40

these electrical signals using electrodes attached to the skin surface. In contrast, MMG measures the minute vibrations transduced to the skin surface using accelerometers and microphones during muscle exertion. MMG measures the vibration transducer signals of the micro-vibrations of the muscles during muscle contraction and the pressure waves (micro-vibrations) produced by the deformation of the diameter of the muscle fibers during muscle contraction [1]. The MMG plays an important role because it is located with the electromyogram, which reflects the mechanical activity of the muscles [2]. Accelerometers are used to measure mechanomyogram(MMG); however, they suscep-tible to motion artifacts due to vibration and movement [3]. It has been reported that microphones have less noise than acceleration sensors when used to evaluate muscle functions during static exercises [4]. However, in dynamic motion, which is more prone to motion, artifacts than static motion the effectiveness of microphones needs to be examined.

Therefore, the objectives of this study were to investigate the effectiveness of micro-phones and accelerometers in MMG measurements during dynamic exercise, compare the two types of sensors, and evaluate muscle functions.

2 Methods

This study employed ten men as subjects (average age was 23.5 ± 0.8). The subjects were given a full explanation of the experiment and consents were obtained from the participants.

A three-axis acceleration sensor (KXM52-1050) was installed behind the arm of each subject to measure the elbow joint angle. A wire was wound around the disk, and a weight was added to the end of the wire to give an appropriate load. An accelerometer (9G111BW, NEC-KOUEI, Japan) and a microphone (EM246, CO, Japan) were used in the tranducer. Table1 shows the characteristics of each sensor used in the experiment.

The muscle tested was the biceps brachii of the right arm, and the maximum voluntary contraction (MVC) was measured during isometric contraction at an elbow joint angle of $90°$. The highest value obtained was used as the MVC. The static exercise was repeated three times, in which the subjects exerted force for 5 s at $10°/s$ between $60°$ and $120°$ elbow joint angles. The load on the biceps brachii was set at 20% and 40% of the maximum exerted muscle strength. To compare with dynamic motion, the speed of the static motion was defined as $0°/s$. During the experiment, the subject was marked on the monitor to determine easily the elbow joint angle. In the dynamic exercise, the right arm of the subjects was subjected to three refractive movements between $40°$ and $140°$ elbow joint angle. The weight of the upper arm biceps was the same as that of the static exercise, that is, 20% and 40% of MVC, and the exercise speeds were$10°/s$ and $20°/s$. Similar to the static exercise, a monitor was installed to easily see the joint angle of the subject during the experiment.

The MMG of the upper right arm biceps was measured. The sampling frequency was 1 kHz, and each measured signal was stored in a computer using an A/D converter.

MMG (MMGacc) and MMGmic (MMGmic) using microphones employed a 2 Hz high-pass filter as a digital filter.

For statistical analysis, all values presented in the text and figures are means for all subjects. A repeated-measure analysis of variance (ANOVA), with muscle strength, exercise speed, and elbow joint angle as the independent factors was used to determine the Root Mean Square (RMS) and the Median Frequency (MDF) of two transducers (microphone and accelerometer).

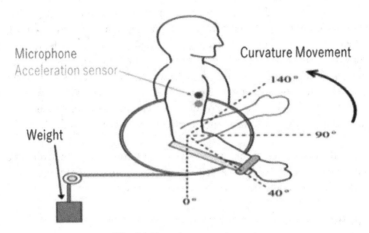

Fig. 1. Experiment equipment

Table 1. Transducer specification

Name	Model	Hz	Sensitivity	mm	g
Accelerometer	9G111BW	1–1.3 kHz	1.8 pc (m/s^2)	4 × 4 × 13	1.3
Microphone	EM246	05–11 kHz	−44 dB ± 4 dB at 0.5 Hz	Diamete: 6 Height: 2	0.2

3 Results

The RMS and MDF are shown in Figs. 2 and 3, respectively. The %RMS of MMGmic and MMGacc and MDF of MMGmic increased with increasing muscle strength, exercise speed, and elbow joint angle.

The result of the three way repeated-measure ANOVA of the %RMS of MMGmic indicate that all factors (muscle strength, contraction speed, and joint angle) had significant effects (F $(1,9)$ = 107.615, p < 0.001, F $(2,18)$ = 24.664, p < 0.05, F $(6,54)$ = 44.270, p < 0.001) and there were interactions between muscle strength and contraction speed and between muscle strength and elbow joint angle (F $(2,18)$ = 3.686, p < 0.05, F $(6,54)$ = 4.271, p < 0.05).

The results of the three-way repeated-measures ANOVA of the %RMS of MMGacc, indicate that the two factors muscle strength and contraction had significant effects (F$(1,9)$ = 117.141, p < 0.001, F$(2,18)$ = 8.601, p < 0.001) and there was interaction between muscle strength and contraction speed (F$(2,18)$ = 8.577, p < 0.05).

In MDFmic, muscle strength, contraction speed, and joint angle exhibited significant effects ($F(1,9) = 8.738$, $p < 0.05$, $F(2,18) = 17.419$, $p < 0.001$, $F(6,54) = 28.440$, $p < 0.001$), and there was interaction was found between contraction speed and elbow joint angle ($F(12,108) = 4.611$, $p < 0.001$).

In the MDFacc, there was a significant effect of contraction speed exhibited significant effect ($F(2,18) = 8.653$, $p < 0.001$).

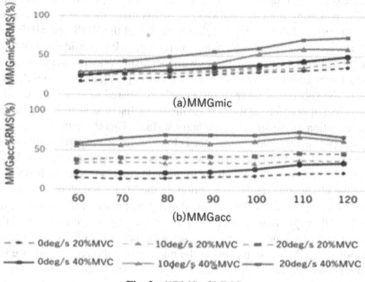

Fig. 2. %RMS of MMG.

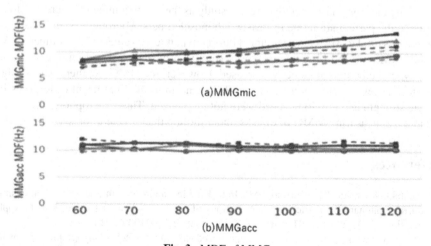

Fig. 3. MDF of MMG

4 Discussions

RMS and MDF of MMG generally increase with an increase in the muscle force exerted, which is attributed to the number of motor unit mobilization [5]. In this study, RMS increased with the increase in the exerted muscle force in MMG using accelerometers, and using the microphone, the RMS and MDF increased as the muscle force exerted increase. This could be due to the number of mobilized motor unit, which increased with the increase in the muscle force exerted. It has been reported that RMS and MDF increase with increasing velocity in MMG [6]. In this study, the RMS increased with the increasing velocity in MMG using accelerometers, and the RMS and MDF increased with the increasing velocity in MMG using microphones. It is considered that the participation rate of fast muscle fibers increases with increasing velocity. Because fast muscle fibers have a larger amplitude than slow muscle fibers [7, 8], and fast muscle fibers are distributed in the superficial layer of the muscle compared to slow muscle fibers, the attenuation effect of fast muscle fivers is smaller than that of slow muscle fibers considering the attenuation of the signal to the body surface. Therefore, the increase in RMS and MDF observed in this study as the speed cloud be due to the participation rate of the fast muscle fibers. It has been reported that RMS increases with increases in the number of motor unit mobilizations [9] and elbow joint angle [10]. In this study, RMS increased with increasing elbow joint angle. In addition, in the MMG, which reflects the number of mobilized motor units, the MMG obtained using the microphone showed an increase in RMS as the elbow joint angle increased. These findings suggest the possibility that the number of mobilized motor units increases with increasing elbow joint angle.

In addition, the MMG obtained using the microphone showed an increase in MDF. It has been reported that the electric velocity of muscle fibers increases with increasing elbow joint angle [10]. The increase in the electric velocity of muscle fibers suggests that the participation rate of fast-twitch muscle fibers increases with increasing elbow joint angle. The increase in MDF in the present study as the elbow joint angle increase cloud be due to the participation rate of fast-twitch muscle fibers. Microphones and acceleration sensors used to MMG measurement during dynamic movement were compared. As a result, RMSmic and MDFmic increased significantly as the exerted muscle strength, velocity, and elbow joint velocity increased. However, for MMGacc, there was no significant difference in arm joint speed in RMS, and in MDF, Significant differences in muscle strength and arm joint speed were not recognized. Thus, microphones are more suitable for measuring MMG of objects under motion than acceleration sensors.

References

1. Akataki, K., Mita, K., Watakabe, M., Itoh, K.: Mechanomyogram and force relationship during voluntary isometric ramp contractions of the biceps brachii muscle. Eur. J. Appl. Physiol. **84**(1), 19–25 (2001). https://doi.org/10.1007/s004210000321
2. Orizio, C.: Muscle sound: Bases for the introduction of a mechanomyographic signal in muscle studies. J. Crit. Rev. Biomed. Eng. **21**(3), 201–243 (1993)
3. Watakabe, M., Mita, K., Akataki, K., Itoh, Y.: Mechanical behavior of condenser microphone in mechanomyography. Med. Biol. Eng. Comput. **39**(2), 195–201 (2001). https://doi.org/10.1007/BF02344804

4. Mito, K., Misawa, H., Shirai, A., Mizuno, T., Itakura, N.: Comparison of frequency properties of mechanomyogram between accelerometer and microphone. In: Proceedings of 27th Congress of the International Society of Biomechanics, vol. 1148 (2019)

5. Maton, B., Petitjean, M., Cnockaert, J.C.: Phonomyogram and electromyogram relationships with isometric force reinvestigated in man. Eur. J. Appl. Physiol. **60**(3), 194–201 (1990). https://doi.org/10.1007/BF00839159

6. Coburn, J.W., et al.: Mechanomyographic and electromyographic responses to eccentric muscle contractions. Muscle Nerve Off. J. Am. Assoc. Electrodiagn. Med. **33**(5), 664–671 (2006). https://doi.org/10.1007/s004210050054

7. Marchetti, M., Felici, F., Bernardi, M., Minasi, P., Di Filippo, L.: Can evoked phonomyography be used to recognize fast and slow muscle in man. Int. J. Sports Med. **13**(1), 65–68 (1992)

8. Bichler, E.: Mechanomyograms recorded during evoked contractions of single motor units in the rat medial gastrocnemius muscle. Eur. J. Appl. Physiol. **83**(4), 310–319 (2000). https://doi.org/10.1007/s004210000261

9. Moritani, T., Muro, M.: Motor unit activity and surface electromyogram power spectrum during increasing force of contraction. Eur. J. Appl. Physiol. **56**(3), 260–265 (1987). https://doi.org/10.1007/BF00690890

10. Mito, K., Anzai, O., Kaneko, K., Sakamoto, K., Shimizu, Y.: Evaluation of muscular function by muscle fiber conduction velocity during static and dynamic contraction of biceps brachii muscle. J. Jpn. Soc. Welf. Eng. **9**, 40–46 (2007)

Analysis of Conducting Waves Using Multi-channel Surface Electromyogram Depends on Electrodes Supported Multiple Directions

Kohei Okura[✉], Yu Matsumoto, Kazuyuki Mito, Tota Mizuno, and Naoaki Itakura

The University of Electro-Communications, 1-5-1 Chofugaoka, Chofu, Tokyo, Japan
xzjb2957@gmail.com

Abstract. A surface electromyogram (EMG) is recorded based on the interference of the action potentials produced by certain motor units of a muscle. If the composition of the interference wave can be analyzed, the mechanisms of the muscle contraction can be elucidated in greater detail. Previously, we proposed a multi-channel method based on extraction of all of the conducting waves existing in a surface EMG, and examined the characteristics of each conducting wave. As a result, it became possible to consider the detailed mechanisms of muscle contraction. In the previous research, the triceps surae muscle was used as the test muscle using an arcuate electrode, and the obtained conducting wave can be extracted, but it is difficult to estimate the muscle fiber direction. To solve this problem, we proposed a new electrode. The feature of this is that four sterling silver wires with a diameter of 1 mm, a length of 10, 9, 8, 7, and 6 mm are arranged in multiple directions. In this study, the measurement was performed using the m-ch method and the proposed electrode, and the difference in the characteristics of the conducted wave obtained depending on the electrode width and direction was considered. In the experiment, the test muscles were the biceps brachii muscle and the triceps surae muscle, and a constant load was applied and maintained for 10 s to acquire myoelectric potential data. The experiment was performed in 3 patterns. As a results, it is possible to estimate the muscle fiber direction from the conducting waves obtained in each row for both the biceps brachii muscle and the triceps surae muscle. In the future, we will change the attachment position of the triceps surae muscle and examine the electrode shape, and this is a guideline to verify whether measurement is possible regardless of the test muscle.

Keywords: Surface electromyogram (EMG) · The interference wave · Multi-channel method

1 Introduction

The action potentials of the muscle fibers making up skeletal muscle are generated by chemical action at the neuromuscular junction; this action conducts along the muscle fibers from the neuromuscular junction to the tendons at both ends. The conduction

C. Stephanidis et al. (Eds.): HCII 2022, CCIS 1581, pp. 308–314, 2022.
https://doi.org/10.1007/978-3-031-06388-6_41

velocity of the action potentials is called the muscle fiber conduction velocity, and the conduction velocity is derived from the surface electromyogram (EMG) using, e.g., a cross-correlation method. The waveform obtained from the surface EMG is not the action potential in a single motor unit, but rather the interference potential in multiple motor units. Therefore, if we pay attention to the waveform shape as conducted over multiple channels, it is thought that a new index different from the conduction velocity can be derived.

In the previous research by Kosuga et al. [1], a multi-channel method (m-ch method) was investigated, aiming to quantitatively determine the conducted wave as obtained from the multi-channel surface EMG, its conditions, and a calculation method for the conduction velocity. According to this method, all conducting waves were extracted from the waveform of the surface EMG using array electrodes, and characteristics such as the conduction velocity, amplitude, and wavelength of each conducting wave were investigated. As a result, it became possible to consider the muscle contraction mechanisms in more detail.

In a previous study by Maeda et al. [2], we proposed a pair of ladder-shaped electrodes and an arc-shaped electrode for allowing gradual expansion, and conducted an experiment using the triceps surae muscle as the test muscle. From the experimental results, it was possible to extract the conducting wave; however, it remained difficult to estimate the muscle fiber direction of the pennate muscle.

To solve these problems, we propose the electrode shown in Fig. 1. The feature of this electrode is that four sterling silver wires (each with a diameter of 1 mm) and respective lengths of 10, 9, 8, 7, and 6 mm are prepared and arranged in multiple directions. In addition, a dual in-line package switch can be installed between the electrode and amplifier to turn it on (short circuit). As a result, it is possible to acquire myoelectric data by changing the electrode shape without re-pasting, and it is possible to acquire the same data multiple times, making it possible to provide redundancy.

The purpose of this study is to consider the differences in the characteristics of the conducting wave obtained depending on the electrode width and direction, based on measurements using the m-ch method and proposed electrode.

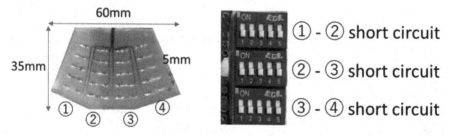

Fig. 1. Proposed electrode

2 Methods

2.1 Experimental Method

In Experiment 1, the subjects were 11 healthy adults, and the subject muscle was the biceps brachii muscle of the dominant arm (as determined according to the subject's self-report). The subject maintained the elbow joint angle at 90° in the sitting position, and the maximum exerted muscle strength (100% MVC) was measured. After that, the same posture was maintained for 10 s with a load of 20% MVC, and the surface myoelectric potential data were acquired.

In Experiment 2, the subjects were four healthy adults, and the test muscles were the lateral and medial heads of the gastrocnemius muscle of the triceps surae muscle of the dominant leg. The subject was allowed to maintain the heel in a standing position with the heel lifted from the floor for 10 s, and the surface myoelectric potential data was acquired. In consideration of the muscle fatigue between trials, sufficient breaks were provided. Multiple measurements were performed using the three patterns described in Table 1.

The sampling frequency in the experiment was 5 kHz. The amplifier settings were a High Cut of 1 kHz and Low Cut of 5 Hz, and the amplification factor was 80 dB. The data obtained from the experiment was subjected to an finite impulse response filter with a high cutoff frequency of 1 kHz, and the results were used for analysis.

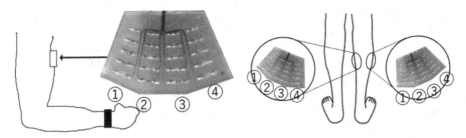

Fig. 2. Experimental system (left: Experiment 1, right: Experiment 2)

Table 1. Myoelectric potential data obtained in each column

Measurement channel [ch]	1–4	5–8	9–12	13–16
Fully open	①	②	③	④
Short circuit between ①–② and ③–④	①&②		③&④	
All short circuit	①&②&③&④			

2.2 Analysis Method

The m-ch method was used for the analysis. In the m-ch method, one of a pair of adjacent electrodes of the same shape is defined as a conduction source, and the other is defined as the conduction destination. The section where a zero crossing occurs twice from the source is extracted as one waveform. It is determined whether the signal has conducted over multiple channels, and then the conduction speed is calculated. When performing the conduction judgment, one waveform obtained from the conduction source is used as a conduction wave candidate. Then, the conduction wave candidate of the conduction destination existing 10 ms before and after the start point of the conduction wave candidate of the conduction source is extracted. To be able to calculate even when the waveforms have different wavelengths, the conduction wave candidates are resampled based on a sampling theorem, and the similarity ratio, amplitude ratio, and wavelength ratio are calculated.

When judging a conduction wave over multiple channels, thresholds are set for the similarity ratio, amplitude ratio, and wavelength ratio, based on the concept that if the waveform shapes between adjacent channels are similar, the action potential has conducted between the two channels. When the conduction wave candidate is equal to or larger than a threshold, it is determined as a conduction wave. The conduction speed is defined as the time difference Δt between channels, and the value is obtained by dividing the distance between channels (5 mm) by the Δt between channels. In addition, the conduction velocity variation coefficient (hereinafter referred to as CV) is used as a conduction determination condition to consider the velocity variable of the waveform for which the conduction is determined. In this study, the conduction judgment conditions were the similarity ratio, a wavelength ratio of 0.9 or more, an amplitude ratio of 0.7 or more, and a CV of 30% or less. Only conduction waves over three channels were extracted and used for analysis.

For the conducted wave(s) obtained using this analysis method, the relative frequency distribution of the amplitude and conduction velocity were compared for each electrode. The total number of conducted waves was set to 100%, and the amplitude and proportion of each conducted wave were calculated.

3   Result and Discussion

3.1   Relative Frequency Distribution and Number of Conducting Waves

Figure 3 shows the relative frequency distribution of subject B for the biceps brachii. From comparing Fig. 3(a) to (c), it can be seen that the more open the waves, the larger the number of conducted waves obtained. In addition, the extraction rate of the conducting wave with a conducting speed of 2.5 to 5.0 m/s increases as it is opened. In particular, there is a large difference between the number of conducted waves obtained when all short circuits are made and when there is no other short circuit. It is considered that this is because the muscle fibers related to the myoelectric potential obtained at each electrode differ greatly when the total short circuit occurs. In addition, the more the muscle fibers are opened, the lesser the difference; thus, it is considered that more detailed myoelectric potential data can be obtained.

Next, comparing Fig. 3(c) and (d), it can be seen that there is a large difference in the number of conducted waves. In addition, the relative frequency distribution is significantly different. It is considered that this is because the third row and fourth row are compared, and the third row is attached along the muscle fiber direction to a greater extent. As the numbers and characteristics of the obtained conducting waves differ depending on the direction, it is possible to estimate the muscle fiber direction.

Figure 4 shows the relative frequency distribution for subject B, with the medial gastrocnemius as the test muscle. Comparing Fig. 4(a) and (b), a large difference in the number of conducted waves is observed. In addition, the relative frequency distribution is significantly different. It is considered that this is because the third row and the fourth row are compared, and the third row is attached along the muscle fiber direction to a greater extent. As the number and characteristics of the obtained conducting waves differ depending on the direction, it is possible to estimate the muscle fiber direction, even in the triceps surae muscle.

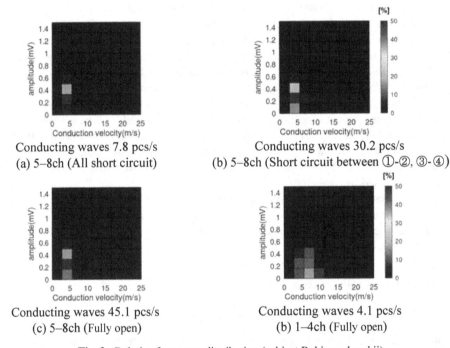

Conducting waves 7.8 pcs/s
(a) 5–8ch (All short circuit)

Conducting waves 30.2 pcs/s
(b) 5–8ch (Short circuit between ①-②, ③-④)

Conducting waves 45.1 pcs/s
(c) 5–8ch (Fully open)

Conducting waves 4.1 pcs/s
(b) 1–4ch (Fully open)

Fig. 3. Relative frequency distribution (subject B, biceps brachii)

3.2 Electromyogram (EMG) Data

Figure 5(a) and (b) show that the starting points of the conducted waves as conducted over three channels are almost the same, and that the myoelectric potential data before and after the starting points can be extracted.

In a "total short circuit," it is difficult to visually identify the waveform determined to be conducted from Fig. 5(a). From this result, it is considered that the phenomenon of a similar conduction waveform over multiple channels is not observed because the action potentials captured by each electrode are different.

In the "fully open" conditions, it can be confirmed that the conducted wave is crossed on 2–4ch. As the electrode was attached to the outside of the test muscle at this time, it

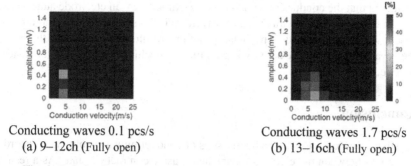

Conducting waves 0.1 pcs/s
(a) 9–12ch (Fully open)

Conducting waves 1.7 pcs/s
(b) 13–16ch (Fully open)

Fig. 4. Relative frequency distribution (Subject B, medial gastrocnemius head)

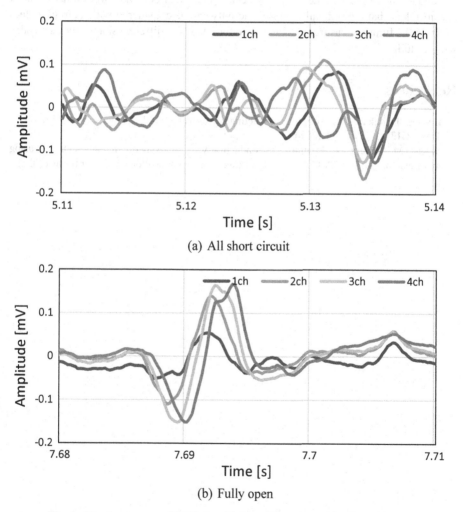

(a) All short circuit

(b) Fully open

Fig. 5. Electromyogram (EMG) data (Subject B, gastrocnemius lateral head)

is considered that the conducting wave could be extracted by an electrode attached near the center. It was also shown that the 1ch waveform is not smooth. This is thought to be because it was affixed near the end-plate. From this result, it is considered that a more detailed evaluation of muscle activity is possible by attaching electrodes to the inside of the muscle.

4   Conclusion

In this study, we examined the characteristics of conducting waves obtained according to differences between the electrode shape and muscle contraction state. As a result, it became clear that the extraction of the conducting waves was easy because the number of conducting waves obtained with the rectangular electrode was large. In addition, it became clear that more detailed muscle activity can be considered with a circular electrode. In the future, measurements will be continued, and different shapes for electrodes will be studied.

References

1. Kosuge, T., Itakura, N., Mito, K.: Conducting waves using multi-channel surface EMG. IEEJ Trans. **C134**(3), 390–397 (2014)
2. Maeda, M., Itakura, N., Mizuno, T.: Conduction wave analysis on arcuate electrodes using multi-channel surface EMG. University of Electro-Communications Bachelor thesis (2021)

Realtime Activity Recognition Using LSTM and Smartwatch Sensor Data

Sergio Staab[✉], Lukas Bröning[✉], Johannes Luderschmidt[✉],
and Ludger Martin[✉]

RheinMain University of Applied Sciences, 65195 Wiesbaden, Hesse, Germany
{Sergio.Staab,Lukas.Broening,Johannes.Luderschmidt,
Ludger.Martin}@hs-rm.de

Abstract. The aim of this work is to gain knowledge about finding, providing, and classifying interaction and health data during the course of disease of people suffering from dementia. In the following, we present a prototype that records interaction data of dementia patients using the smartwatch "Apple Watch Series 6" and that uses a recurrent neural network to provide information about the respective activity in real time. Based on three very similar activities, we systematically compare the prediction accuracy of different sensors in combination with a recurrent neural network.

Keywords: Human motion analysis · Health informatics · Recurrent neural network

1 Introduction

In this feasibility study, we present a system for live activity recognition in the context of people with dementia.

In cooperation with two care communities, fine-grained actions were identified that represent classic activities in the daily lives of people with dementia and whose documentation was previously carried out daily by care staff. These include activities such as cooking, reading, handicrafts, playing games, drinking, eating, going for walks, watching TV, painting, listening to music, and cleaning up.

We take the activities of writing, eating, and drinking and try to make statements about the current activity based on the movement data provided by the sensors of the Apple Watch 6 using a recurrent neural network with a memory called Long Short-Term Memory (LSTM).

Consultation with various care teams who work with dementia patients on a daily basis revealed that many patients wear smartwatches. Such clocks maintain low adjustment power for sensor positioning. The sensor technology used includes in particular accelerometers, position sensors, gyroscopes, and magnetometers.

In our paper, we present the application of our prototype in a test series with five subjects. In doing so, we demonstrate the accuracy of the memory-based classification network in interaction with the latest wearable sensor technology

© The Author(s), under exclusive license to Springer Nature Switzerland AG 2022
C. Stephanidis et al. (Eds.): HCII 2022, CCIS 1581, pp. 315–322, 2022.
https://doi.org/10.1007/978-3-031-06388-6_42

and discuss the future directions and possibilities in the wearable IoT field of dementia diagnostics.

This paper contributes:

- an approach to visually analyse sensor data to determine which sensor data are promising for the recognition of certain motion sequences
- a possibility for live recognition of similar movements of patients using smartwatches

After this introduction, Sect. 2 introduces related work in the field of health information technologies, human activity recognition and recurrent neural networks. Section 3 describes the project structure and elaborates on the aggregation of the sensor data as well as the machine learning tool. Section 4 shows the results of the tracking process and visualizes the different motion sequences based on the sensors. Section 5 summarizes the work.

2   Related Work

Health information technologies have been revolutionizing healthcare for years, according to Lau et al. [11]. In their work, they examine the current state of mobile devices and software related to health information. There are currently over 325,000 mobile applications available in app stores [18]. Identifying mental and physical disorders and supporting people with difficulties can significantly improve the health of users, according to Malu and Findlater [12]. Many of these applications rely on data collected by sensors on smartwatches, including heart rate monitor, GPS, accelerometer, and gyroscope. Various interaction techniques make smartwatches unique and ubiquitous as data tracking devices. The literature supports this statement in various works in recent years. Dong et al. [8] and Ramos-Garcia and Hoover [16] have measured eating cycles of users using smartphones. In their studies, they used accelerometer and gyroscope sensor data from the smartphones.

Xu et al. [21] classified hand and finger gestures as well as characters from smartwatch motion sensor data. Similarly, Riaz et al. [17] and Tautges et al. [19] attempted to reconstruct body motions using multiple wearable devices by comparing accelerometer data with data generated from motion capture.

Our work is most similar to the project by Serkan Balli et al. [7]. In their work, using accelerometer and gyroscope in a smartwatch, they extracted 14 features from the obtained sensor data, condensed them by a dimensionality reduction algorithm filter, and tested several methods (C4.5, SVM, random forest and kNN methods) for classifying human actions on five subjects to identify the following activities: brushing teeth, running, writing on paper, writing with a keyboard and vacuuming. The study demonstrates how well machine activity classifications can be realized using sensor technology from smartwatches. For example, writing using the kNN method was classified with a success rate of over 98%. Random forest and C4.5 methods classify running with 100% accuracy. Our project extends the applied motion sensors (accelerometer and gyroscope) to include the pedometer and heart rate sensors. We expect this to be an improvement beyond the state of the art.

Ashry et al. [6] developed a bidirectional long short-term memory (Bi-LSTM) that continuously detects human activity and incorporates future context unlike a standard LSTM. The model processes smartwatch sensor data that include triaxial accelerometer and gyroscope data as well as gravity and rotational displacement data at a sampling rate 50 Hz. The database was created by 25 volunteers performing ten daily activities. Finally, the online system developed by Ashry et al. allows real-time classification of the activities with an accuracy of 91%.

Mekruksavanich et al. [13] investigated activity recognition based on smartwatch sensor data. For this purpose, the authors used a hybrid LSTM that links a LSTM with a Convolutional Neural Network (CNN). For their data, the authors used the publicly available WISDM dataset. It includes triaxial accelerometer and gyroscope data recorded by 51 volunteers while performing 18 predefined activities at a sampling rate 20 Hz. Mekruksavanich et al. state that CNN-LSTM provide better activity recognition and outperform alternative models. In their study, the authors achieve an activity recognition accuracy of 96.2%.

In their study, Oluwalade et al. [14] also used the WISDM dataset and compared the performance of the deep learning models LSTM, Bi-LSTM, CNN-LSTM, and CNN. The classification of 15 activities succeeded with an accuracy of more than 91% for their best model. The best results were obtained with the smartwatch acceleration data and the CNN-LSTM as well as CNN.

This work demonstrates the potential of smartwatches in collaboration with recurrent neural networks in healthcare applications.

3 Project Structure

This paper presents a standalone, state-of-the-art watchOS application for the Apple Watch Series 6 that offers various functionalities. The application includes methods for retrieving motion and health data, a temporary backup to the smartwatch memory, methods for tagging data, and an interface for exchanging sensor data with a web server via WebSocket. In case of complications, the backup methods can initiate a resend of the sensor data generated in a session.

Figure 1 provides an overview of the work. Data generation, data handling, and data saving are part of the tracking, the visualization of the labeled data and the classification of the data.

In this work, the Apple Watch Series 6 is used, which is equipped with the latest sensor technology. The sensor technology in focus of this work consists of the accelerometer, gyroscope, magnetometer, position sensor, GPS sensor, and heart rate sensor.

3.1 Sensors

"Accelerometer": Accelerometers are electromechanical devices that detect accelerations due to physical effects and convert them into electrical signals

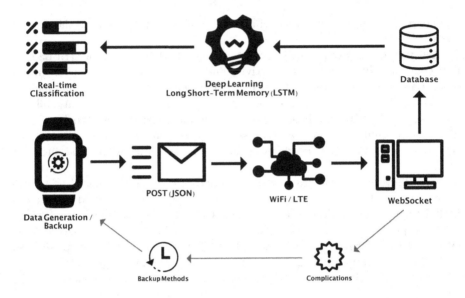

Fig. 1. Overview

for further processing, according to Hering and Schönfelder [9]. They are used to measure instantaneous acceleration in multidimensional space [1], which describes the rate of change of velocity over time [15].

"Gyroskope": According to Hering and Schönfelder, gyroscopes are rotation rate sensors that measure the rotational speed of a body. The rotational speed is measured as an angle in radians per second, rad/s, about a respective axis by the gyroscope, which measures the rotation values in three dimensions like the accelerometer of the Apple Watch [3].

"Attitude": In addition to accelerometer and gyroscope data, combined device orientation data, also called "attitude", is also provided by the processed data object, according to Apple Developer Documentation [5]. This is the combined values of Pitch, Roll and Yaw as specific attitude angles to describe the orientation of a device in three-dimensional space. Thus, the above three values reflect the position of a smartwatch in space relative to a defined reference frame. The rotation values are specified in Radiant rad and range from $-\pi$ to π around a specific axis.

"Magnetometer": A magnetometer is a measuring instrument for measuring magnetic flux density in T (Tesla) and is measured from 10^{-15} T to 10 [20]. In the Apple Watch, the magnetometer acts as a magnetic compass as well as for referencing the accelerometer and position sensor. The magnetometer, the accelerometer, and the gyroscope all contribute to the mathematical calculation of the device's position.

"Heart Rate Sensor": According to Apple Support [4], the heart rate sensor of the Apple Watch is used to record heart rate and thus in particular for health and activity monitoring. In addition to recording and analyzing heart rate, the generation of heart rate data also enables estimates of exercise intensity and calorie consumption, among other things. The optical heart rate sensor evaluates the heart rate in beats per minute (bpm).

The developed application is configurable and expandable, allowing further sensors and attributes to be integrated in the future if required.

Continuous polling of motion data is performed at a customizable time interval, the frequency. The maximum frequency 100 Hz (Hz) when using an Apple Watch Series 6 [2]. Thus, a maximum of 100 motion data objects can be generated per second.

3.2   Long Short-Term Memory

Long short-term memory (LSTM) originally dates back to the work of Hochreiter and Schmidhuber [10] and represents a special architecture of an artificial recurrent neural network (RNN). An LSTM is particularly suited to process sequential streams of sensor data due to a flexible gating mechanism, according to Ashry et al. [6]. In particular, according to the authors, the key advantage over comparable machine learning models is that an LSTM takes into account the temporal context of the sensor data. According to Oluwalade et al. [14], the neural network architecture is designed to learn time-related dependencies and remember significant sequences.

The data set for the present project was created by four users who each labeled the three activities of drinking, eating, and writing 20 times over a 10-second period. After pre-processing and an 80 to 20 train-test split of the data, the balanced dataset served as a generated time series with a step size of 120 as input to the LSTM. Architecturally, the input layer comprises 120 units accordingly, followed by a flatten layer, a dense layer with 64 units and another dense ouput layer with three units for the number of classes. The first dense layer includes the activation function Relu, the last one includes Softmax. In addition, the Adam optimizer was used during compilation. With all 12 features, the respective triaxial user acceleration, gravity, attitude, and gyroscope data, the trained model achieves an accuracy of more than 96% over 10 epochs.

4   Activity Recognition - Results

The protoype previously described was tested in a series of experiments; four subjects were included, each generating 20 label sequences, or eight labels. Figure 2 shows the three activities of writing, drinking, and eating.

The red arrows show the range of motion of the arm and wrist. It is particularly noticeable here that the movements of eating and drinking are almost identical. The arm moves in the direction of the face and only the position of the hand provides information about the respective activity. This is what makes the recognition of the respective activity rather complicated. In the following, different sensors with different classification algorithms are compared.

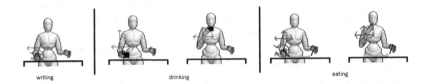

writing   drinking   eating

Fig. 2. Movement sequences - writing, drinking, eating (Color figure online)

The test series show how the best classification algorithms perform with different sensors (see Table 1). The different prediction performances are given as a percentage to the respective sensor.

Table 1. Comparison of different combinations of sensors and recurrent neural network with a memory called Long Short-Term Memory for classifying the activities writing, eating and drinking

Sensor combination	Prediction probability performance
Acceleration	58.85%
Attitude	64.97%
Gyro	98.18%
Gravity	89.88%
Acceleration, Attitude	94.65%
Acceleration, Gyro	98.18%
Acceleration, Gravity	88.60%
Attitude, Gyro	97.66%
Attitude, Gravity	86.92%
Gyro, Gravity	96.61%
Attitude, Gravity, Acceleration	94.19%
Attitude, Gyro, Acceleration	97.88%
Attitude, Gyro, Gravity	94.22%
Acceleration, Gyro, Gravity	95.76%
Acceleration, Attitude, Gyro, Gravity	96.35%

Based on the investigations presented here, the rotation speed of the hand measured by the gyroscope proves to be the best parameter for the classification of the three activities. It does not change if the speed of movement is included (acceleration, gyroscope).

5   Conclusion

In this work, we investigated the combination of state-of-the-art sensor technology and a recurrent neural network. We presented a prototype based on the Apple Watch 6 that communicates with a web server to classify live activities. Systematic comparisons of sensor technology were performed to see how well different combinations of sensors performed in detecting three very similar activities. Contrary to our expectations, activities can be detected with a probability of up to 98% based on hand movements and rotations only.

References

1. Apple Inc.: cMMotionManager: Apple developer documentation (2021). cMMotionManager. https://developer.apple.com/documentation/coremotion/cmmotionmanager
2. Apple Inc.: Getting processed device-motion data: Apple developer documentation (2021). https://developer.apple.com/documentation/coremotion/getting_processed_device-motion_data
3. Apple Inc.: Getting raw gyroscope events: Apple developer documentation (2021). Gyroscope. https://developer.apple.com/documentation/coremotion/getting_raw_gyroscope_events
4. Apple Inc.: Herzfrequenz mit der Apple watch überprüfen - Apple support (de) (2021). https://support.apple.com/de-de/HT204666
5. Apple Inc.: Understanding reference frames and device attitude: Apple developer documentation (2021). Attitude. https://developer.apple.com/documentation/coremotion/getting_processed_device-motion_data/understanding_reference_frames_and_device_attitude
6. Ashry, S., Ogawa, T., Gomaa, W.: CHARM-deep: continuous human activity recognition model based on deep neural network using IMU sensors of smartwatch. IEEE Sens. J. **20**(15), 8757–8770 (2020). https://doi.org/10.1109/jsen.2020.2985374
7. Balli, S., Sağbaş, E.A., Peker, M.: Human activity recognition from smart watch sensor data using a hybrid of principal component analysis and random forest algorithm. Measur. Control **52**(1–2), 37–45 (2018). https://doi.org/10.1177/0020294018813692
8. Dong, Y., Scisco, J., Wilson, M., Muth, E., Hoover, A.: Detecting periods of eating during free-living by tracking wrist motion. IEEE J. Biomed. Health Inform. **18**(4), 1253–1260 (2014). https://doi.org/10.1109/jbhi.2013.2282471
9. Hering, E., Schönfelder, G. (eds.): Sensoren in Wissenschaft und Technik: Funktionsweise und Einsatzgebiete, IArC Monographs on the Evaluation of Carcinogenic Risks to Humans, 1st edn, vol. 102. Vieweg+Teubner Verlag, Wiesbaden (2012). https://doi.org/10.1007/978-3-8348-8635-4. https://monographs.iarc.fr/wp-content/uploads/2018/06/mono102.pdf
10. Hochreiter, S., Schmidhuber, J.: Long short-term memory. Neural Comput. **9**(8), 1735–1780 (1997). https://doi.org/10.1162/neco.1997.9.8.1735
11. Lau, F.: Improving Usability, Safety and Patient Outcomes with Health Information Technology: From Research to Practice. IOS Press, Amsterdam (2019)
12. Malu, M., Findlater, L.: Toward accessible health and fitness tracking for people with mobility impairments. In: Toward Accessible Health and Fitness Tracking for People with Mobility Impairments, p. 8. ACM, New York, June 2016. https://doi.org/10.4108/eai.16-5-2016.2263329

13. Mekruksavanich, S., Jitpattanakul, A., Youplao, P., Yupapin, P.: Enhanced hand-oriented activity recognition based on smartwatch sensor data using LSTMs. Symmetry **12**(9), 1570 (2020). https://doi.org/10.3390/sym12091570

14. Oluwalade, B., Neela, S., Wawira, J., Adejumo, T., Purkayastha, S.: Human activity recognition using deep learning models on smartphones and smartwatches sensor data. In: Proceedings of the 14th International Joint Conference on Biomedical Engineering Systems and Technologies - HEALTHINF, Vienna, Austria. arXiv (2021). https://doi.org/10.48550/ARXIV.2103.03836. https://arxiv.org/abs/2103.03836

15. Prechtl, A.: Zeit. raum. bewegung. In: Prechtl, A. (ed.) Vorlesungen über die Grundlagen der Elektrotechnik, pp. 1–14. Springer, Vienna (1994). https://doi.org/10.1007/978-3-7091-3833-5_1

16. Ramos-Garcia, R.I., Hoover, A.W.: A study of temporal action sequencing during consumption of a meal. In: Proceedings of the International Conference on Bioinformatics, Computational Biology and Biomedical Informatics, vol. 13, pp. 68–75. ACM, New York, September 2013. https://doi.org/10.1145/2506583.2506596

17. Riaz, Q., Tao, G., Krüger, B., Weber, A.: Motion reconstruction using very few accelerometers and ground contacts. Graph. Models **79**, 23–38 (2015). https://doi.org/10.1016/j.gmod.2015.04.001

18. Roche, D.: mHealth app economics current status and future trends in mobile health. Technical report 1, The Digital Health Strategy Company (2017)

19. Tautges, J., et al.: Motion reconstruction using sparse accelerometer data. ACM Trans. Graph. **30**(3), 1–12 (2011). https://doi.org/10.1145/1966394.1966397

20. Loreit, U., Dettmann, F., Andrä, W.: Der elektronische kompaß. In: Design & Elektronik Sensortechnik, pp. 28–30 (1995)

21. Xu, C., Pathak, P., Mohapatra, P.: Finger-writing with Smartwatch. In: HotMobile 2015: Proceedings of the 16th International Workshop on Mobile Computing Systems and Applications, pp. 9–14. no. 6 in 1. ACM, New York, February 2015. https://doi.org/10.1145/2699343.2699350

IoT and Intelligent Living Environments

Smart Armband for Tracking Children Using a Mobile Application

Franklin Castillo[1], Lisseth Guangasi[1], Guillermo Palacios-Navarro[2],
and José Varela-Aldás[1,2(✉)] ⓘ

[1] SISAu Research Group, Facultad de Tecnologías de la Información y la Comunicación,
Universidad Tecnológica Indoamérica, Ambato, Ecuador
{franklincastillo,josevarela}@uti.edu.ec,
lguangasi2@indoamerica.edu.ec
[2] Department of Electronic Engineering and Communications, University of Zaragoza,
Zaragoza, Spain
guillermo.palacios@unizar.es

Abstract. Today, children are exposed to many dangers, so it is necessary to know their current location continuously. New technology allows connection to the internet almost anywhere, this can be used to track people through a remote device. Mobile apps have become popular with the help of ever-cheaper smartphones. This work develops a wearable device in the form of a smart armband for user tracking from a mobile location. The system is designed for use by children ages 5–12 in large areas with Internet coverage. Both stations are linked to a cloud database created in Firebase, this allows the exchange of information through the internet. In addition, the system allows the sending of audio notifications from the mobile application to notify the user at the remote site. Notifications are pre-stored on the electronic board for remote playback without overloading the network. In the testing stage, the children are monitored within a controlled area by tracking location and sending audio messages. The results show the functioning of the system, and the acceptance test applied is favorable for the characteristics of this proposal, although the audio notifications have the worst acceptance.

Keywords: Smart armband · ESP32 board · GPS · Mobile application

1 Introduction

The so-called smart cities have the objective of controlling the greatest number of elements within their environment, including tracking people remotely [1]. For this purpose, wearables are developed that allow the acquisition of data in real-time the different states of the user [2–4]. Smart armbands are used to monitor the quality of life of people, as well as remote control through a user interface [5].

Child health is one of the sectors benefited by these proposals, through a monitoring system for chronic childhood diseases [6]. On the other hand, child safety has also benefited from these new technologies. Developing location systems for child tracking

C. Stephanidis et al. (Eds.): HCII 2022, CCIS 1581, pp. 325–331, 2022.
https://doi.org/10.1007/978-3-031-06388-6_43

using different technologies [7]. The main technologies that have driven these proposals are the Internet of Things (IoT) and mobile applications [1, 8–10], and even more so with the cost reduction of these technologies.

This work develops a smart armband based on a System on Chip (SoC) that allows the location of the user to be tracked and communicate remotely through audio messages. The system is managed through a mobile application and is evaluated in children from 5 to 12 years old through an acceptance test.

2 Methods and Materials

The materials used in this project are presented in the scheme of Fig. 1. The local system is based on an electronic SoC board, an independent power source, a global positioning sensor, and an audio output. The electronic board communicates with a Wi-Fi network for connection to the cloud database. On the other side is the mobile application that also connects to the cloud to obtain the user's position and send remote commands to the smart armband.

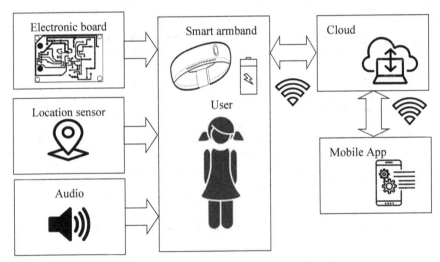

Fig. 1. General scheme of the proposal for tracking children using a mobile application.

2.1 Electronic Design

The electronic design is presented in the circuit of Fig. 2. The ESP32 board is the main element of the circuit and is responsible for reading and controlling the information. The global positioning sensor used is the GPS NEO 7M which requires serial communication via 2 digital pins. For the audio output, a speaker connected to the LM386 audio amplifier is used, which receives the analog data to reproduce audio. The main board and the audio amplifier are powered by a 9 V DC battery.

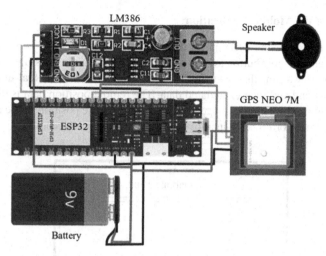

Fig. 2. Electronic circuit

2.2 Program Design

The main program of the ESP32 board consists of sending the position of the armband and receiving the audio playback order. Figure 3 presents the flow diagram of the program, once the necessary libraries, objects, and variables have been initialized, the main repetitive loop is carried out. The latitude and longitude of the GPS are obtained to send this information to Firebase. Then data is received from the cloud to play the audio if required or restart the main program.

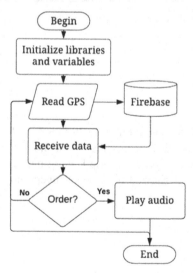

Fig. 3. Program flowchart for ESP32

2.3 Design of the Mobile Application

In Fig. 4 the design of the user interface for the mobile application is presented. The interface contains a single button to send an order to play the audio message, the message has the purpose of warning the user to return. The app is connected to a Real-time database on Firebase to send and receive updated data. The remote position data is displayed in 2 labels, latitude and longitude, respectively. In addition, the position of the armband is marked on the map for tracking its movements through the data received.

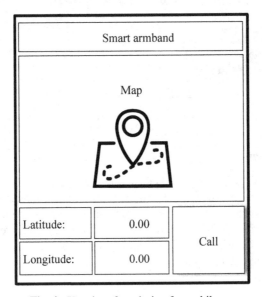

Fig. 4. User interface design for mobile app.

3 Results

3.1 Operation Tests

Figure 5 shows images of the operation of the proposal, including photos of the smart armband and the mobile application installed on a Smartphone. The components of the armband were mounted in a leather case leaving out the speaker for better audio output. The tests carried out showed the correct functioning of all the implemented characteristics.

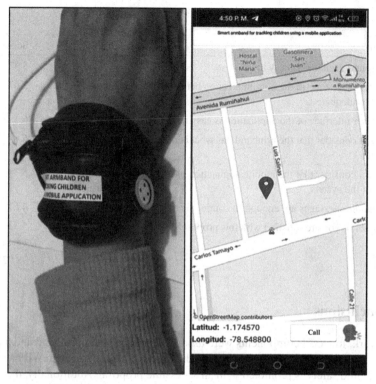

Fig. 5. Images of the armband and the mobile application

3.2 Acceptance Evaluation

The acceptance tests were carried out with 3 children from 5 to 12 years of age using a long-range WiFi network within a controlled area, after using the system a survey was applied to the children's parents. The questionnaire is made up of 7 questions related to the characteristics of the system, including the armband and the mobile application. The questions were rated at 7 levels on a Likert scale, where 7 means totally agree and 1 means totally disagree. The results indicate a rating of 78.22% acceptance (see Table 1), a favorable value for the proposal. Although it is evident that the audio message is not the best form of communication.

Table 1. Acceptance test results

Question	Score
1. - The smart armband is easy to use	5.33
2. - The response time in the communication between the application and the armband is adequate	5.67
3. - The user interface of the application is easy to use	6
4. - Do you consider that the armband has what is necessary for the purpose of the system	6
5. - Do you consider that the mobile application has what is necessary for the purpose of the system	5.33
6. - The audio messages are enough to communicate with the armband	4.67
7. - In general, you are satisfied with this proposal	5.33
Total	38.33/49 78.22%

4 Conclusions

In this work, low-cost components were used to develop a smart armband and a mobile application. For tracking the position of children in a controlled area with WiFi access. In this way, child safety is promoted with an accessible proposal. Additionally, the parents sent audio messages through an option in the user interface, telling the child that they should return. In the application of the acceptance test, a score of 78.22% was obtained, although it is a favorable score, there are certain discontents, especially in the form of communication. In the future, it is intended to incorporate the fluid voice communication in both directions.

References

1. Alam, T., Hadi, A.A., Najam, R.Q.S.: Designing and implementing the people tracking system in the crowded environment using mobile application for smart cities. Int. J. Syst. Assur. Eng. Manage. **13**, 1–33 (2021). https://doi.org/10.1007/s13198-021-01277-7
2. Peraković, D., et al.: Smart wristband system for improving quality of life for users in traffic environment. In: Cagáňová, D., Balog, M., Knapčíková, L., Soviar, J., Mezarcıöz, S. (eds.) Smart Technology Trends in Industrial and Business Management. EAI/Springer Innovations in Communication and Computing, pp. 429–450. Springer, Cham (2019). https://doi.org/10.1007/978-3-319-76998-1_32
3. Duncker, D., et al.: Smart wearables for cardiac monitoring—real-world use beyond atrial fibrillation. Sensors **21**, 2539 (2021). https://doi.org/10.3390/s21072539
4. Varela-Aldás, J., Guamán, J., Paredes, B., Chicaiza, F.A.: Robotic cane for the visually impaired. In: Antona, M., Stephanidis, C. (eds.) HCII 2020. LNCS, vol. 12188, pp. 506–517. Springer, Cham (2020). https://doi.org/10.1007/978-3-030-49282-3_36

5. Kim, H., Park, S., Na, N., Kim, J., Moon, Y., Kim, J.: The smart armband: expanding wearable interface area and suggesting interaction scenarios. In: Kim, K., Joukov, N. (eds.) Information Science and Applications (ICISA) 2016. LNEE, vol. 376, pp. 1361–1365 (2016). Springer, Singapore (2016). https://doi.org/10.1007/978-981-10-0557-2_128
6. Sendra, S., Parra, L., Lloret, J., Tomás, J.: Smart system for children's chronic illness monitoring. Inf. Fusion. **40**, 76–86 (2018). https://doi.org/10.1016/j.inffus.2017.06.002
7. Sakphrom, S., Suwannarat, K., Haiges, R., Funsian, K.: A simplified and high accuracy algorithm of RSSI-based localization zoning for children tracking in-out the school buses using bluetooth low energy beacon. Informatics. **8**, 65 (2021). https://doi.org/10.3390/inform atics8040065
8. Memon, I., Fazal, H., Shaikh, R.A., Mallah, G.A., Arain, R.H., Muhammad, G.: Smart intelligent system for mobile travelers based on fuzzy logic in IoT communication technology. In: Bajwa, I.S., Sibalija, T., Jawawi, D.N.A. (eds.) INTAP 2019. CCIS, vol. 1198, pp. 22–31. Springer, Singapore (2020). https://doi.org/10.1007/978-981-15-5232-8_3
9. Varela-Aldás, J., Pilla, J., Andaluz, V.H., Palacios-Navarro, G.: Commercial entry control using robotic mechanism and mobile application for COVID-19 pandemic. In: Gervasi, O., et al. (eds.) ICCSA 2021. LNCS, vol. 12957, pp. 3–14. Springer, Cham (2021). https://doi.org/10.1007/978-3-030-87013-3_1
10. Varela-Aldás, J., Buele, J., Cumbajin, M.: Smart home control system using echo dot. In: Rocha, Á., Ferrás, C., López-López, P.C., Guarda, T. (eds.) ICITS 2021. AISC, vol. 1330, pp. 303–312. Springer, Cham (2021). https://doi.org/10.1007/978-3-030-68285-9_29

Pet Access Control System Using a Mobile Application

Carlos Cuzme[1], Mario Miranda[1], Víctor H. Andaluz[1,2], Guillermo Palacios-Navarro[3],
and José Varela-Aldás[1,3(⊠)] (iD)

[1] SISAu Research Group, Facultad de Tecnologías de la Información y la Comunicación,
Universidad Tecnológica Indoamérica, Ambato, Ecuador
ccuzme@indoamerica.edu.ec, {mariomiranda,josevarela}@uti.edu.ec
[2] Universidad de las Fuerzas Armadas ESPE, Sangolquí, Ecuador
vhandaluz1@espe.edu.ec
[3] Department of Electronic Engineering and Communications, University of Zaragoza,
Zaragoza, Spain
guillermo.palacios@unizar.es

Abstract. This work develops a system consisting of a mobile application and an automatic gate implemented with low-cost technology. The devices are linked to a cloud server through the internet. The design of the system consists of a gate that incorporates a motion sensor to detect the pet, for this a passive infrared sensor is used. The electronic circuit of the gate is based on the ESP32 board. This device sends notifications to monitor when the pet approaches this area. The system consists of two modes, manual and automatic. In manual mode, the user decides to open the gate or not, while in automatic mode the gate opens whenever it detects the pet. On the other hand, the mobile application has been designed to control the operating mode. The application's user interface presents a warning when the presence of the pet is detected and allows the gate to be activated remotely only when it is in manual mode. The cloud platform used is Firebase, this remote database records the latest states of the fields shared by both devices. 3 pets were tested for 1 week to ensure continued system performance. As a result, adequate communication was obtained between the elements installed in the gate and the mobile application.

Keywords: Pet access control · ESP32 board · Firebase · Mobile application

1 Introducción

Today everyone is facing a new era of computerized communication in a globalized environment due to the Internet. Because of this, it has become essential to use access control systems in both conventional and corporate environments [1]. Access control systems are electronic systems based on identification to restrict entry to specific sites or access to resources using different types of reading [2]. The identification can be done through keypads, biometric signals, simultaneously controlling an actuator such as a motor or lock, these electronic devices can be connected to the internet of things (IoT) [3, 4].

Currently, several autonomous mechanisms allow the control of several devices without the need to be interconnected through a local network or computer. A cloud platform is one of these, allowing the management of system resources from remote connections with high response speeds [5]. On the other hand, the use of electronic devices has drastically changed human life to such an extent that it has become essential [6, 7]. As in the case of smartphones, these have functions that facilitate daily life, some of which are essential for communication between people as well as for optimizing basic activities through mobile applications [8]. As a result, applications have evolved to the point of offering total information management, including remote control of home devices [9].

This paper develops an access control system for pets through a mobile application based on IoT and using low-cost technology. The proposal allows to control a gate remotely and to know if there is a pet trying to use this output. Although commercially there are several options, this work offers a low cost and easily replicable option. Section 2 presents the materials and methods used, Sect. 3 presents the results, and Sect. 4 presents the conclusions.

2 Methods and Materials

This proposal uses a system on chip to manage the different modules of the system, this is an electronic card with WiFi connectivity features. Figure 1 shows the elements of the proposal. The additional devices are a passive infrared (PIR) sensor and a servo motor. The PIR detects the presence of the pet to trigger different actions. The servo motor allows the control of the gate so that the pet can get out or stay inside. The system is controlled remotely from anywhere with the internet through a mobile application, the screen notifies the presence of a pet, and the user can open or close the gate as required.

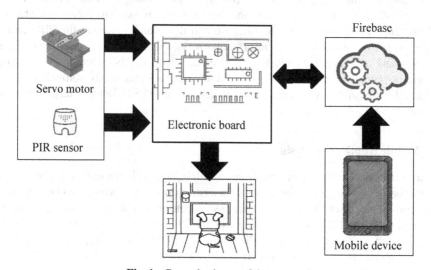

Fig. 1. General scheme of the proposal

2.1 Electronic Design

The electronic design is developed in the Fritzing application, the circuit in Fig. 2 shows the connection of the devices to the main microcontroller (ESP32). The ESP32 board integrates a WiFi communication module. The PIR sensor (HC-SR501) uses a digital input for motion detection and the servo motor (MG996R) a digital output to generate the modulated control pulses.

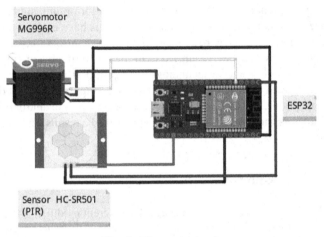

Fig. 2. Electronic circuit

2.2 Program Design

The coding is done using the Arduino IDE application using the flowchart in Fig. 3. In the initialization, the connection to the WiFi network is made to access the internet and exchange information with the Firebase real-time database. First, the PIR sensor reading is performed to send this information to Firebase. Then the order is received from Firebase to control the gate, depending on the mode and the order the servo motor changes position to open or close the gate. In manual mode, the servo motor changes its position directly, and in automatic mode, the gate opens when it detects the presence of the pet.

2.3 Mobile Application Design

The user interface for the mobile application is designed as shown in Fig. 4. The design consists of the labels and buttons required for system operation. Two buttons are required for operation mode selection and two buttons for gate control in manual mode. In addition, a label is used to display the states of the PIR sensor, this warning is complemented by an audible alert. This application is developed using App inventor, adding the experimental functions for connection with Firebase.

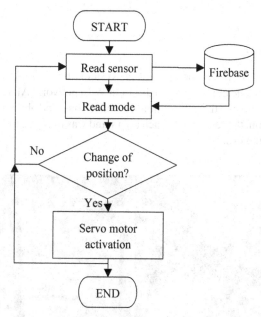

Fig. 3. Program flowchart in ESP32

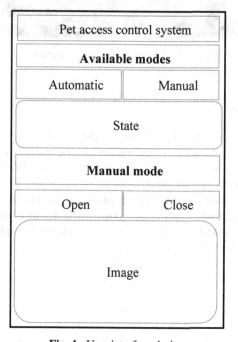

Fig. 4. User interface design

3 Results

3.1 Operation Tests

The images in Fig. 5 show the operation of the system, the Smartphone is in a different location than the gate and connected to a different WiFi network. All tests had successful results, opening and closing the gate without complications, and obtaining the real state of the sensor. In addition, the response to each command was immediate, with no noticeable delay in executing the orders.

Fig. 5. Images of the system in operation

3.2 Acceptance Tests

To analyze the acceptance of the proposal, a questionnaire consisting of six questions designed to evaluate the characteristics of the system was used. To carry out this process, the questionnaire was randomly applied to five pet owners interested in the subject. The selection answers are established on an ascending scale, where 1 means strongly disagree and 7 means strongly agree. This method was used to facilitate data collection and to obtain a final indicator to define acceptance. The results of the acceptance test are presented in Table 1, obtaining a score of 98.57%, which is favorable for this proposal.

Table 1. Acceptance questionnaire

Question	Score
1. - You believe that this system is useful for your pet	6.6
2. - It was easy to use the mobile application	7
3. - The functions of the mobile application are sufficient for the intended purpose	7
4. - Communication between the devices responds efficiently	7
5. - The system is useful for everyday life	7
6. - In general, I am satisfied with the system	6.8
Total	41.6/42 98.57%

4 Conclusions

The proposal presented in this article is of public interest, with direct application in the daily life of pet lovers. This work develops an access control system for pets, allowing the pet owner to control a gate with access to another part of the house, such as a yard. Analyzing the results of the acceptance test, it is determined that the system meets the requirements, is simple to use and benefits the pets. This proposal can be complemented by adding more sensors to confirm that the pet is using the access, as well as the detection in the opposite direction for the return of the pet. In addition, there is no difference between the pet and a person. These issues can be added in future work.

References

1. Kang, W.M., Moon, S.Y., Park, J.H.: An enhanced security framework for home appliances in smart home. HCIS **7**(1), 1–12 (2017). https://doi.org/10.1186/s13673-017-0087-4
2. Aluvalu, R., Uma Maheswari, V., Chennam, K.K., Shitharth, S.: Data security in cloud computing using ABE-based access control. In: Das, S.K., Samanta, S., Dey, N., Patel, B.S., Hassanien, A.E. (eds.) Architectural Wireless Networks Solutions and Security Issues. LNNS, vol. 196, pp. 47–61. Springer, Singapore (2021). https://doi.org/10.1007/978-981-16-0386-0_4
3. Sanjay, B.S., Kaushik, N., Srinivasan, V., Prabhakar, S., Jayavel, K.: Design and implementation of smart garage- an IoT perspective. In: 2017 International Conference on Energy, Communication, Data Analytics and Soft Computing (ICECDS), pp. 2712–2716. IEEE (2017). https://doi.org/10.1109/ICECDS.2017.8389947
4. Varela-Aldás, J., Pilla, J., Andaluz, V.H., Palacios-Navarro, G.: Commercial entry control using robotic mechanism and mobile application for COVID-19 pandemic. In: Gervasi, O., et al. (eds.) ICCSA 2021. LNCS, vol. 12957, pp. 3–14. Springer, Cham (2021). https://doi.org/10.1007/978-3-030-87013-3_1
5. Koyasako, Y., Suzuki, T., Yamada, T., Shimada, T., Yoshida, T.: Demonstration of real-time motion control method for access edge computing in PONs. IEEE Access. **10**, 168–175 (2022). https://doi.org/10.1109/ACCESS.2021.3136876
6. Varela-Aldás, J., Guamán, J., Paredes, B., Chicaiza, F.A.: Robotic cane for the visually impaired. In: Antona, M., Stephanidis, C. (eds.) HCII 2020. LNCS, vol. 12188, pp. 506–517. Springer, Cham (2020). https://doi.org/10.1007/978-3-030-49282-3_36

7. Gluhak, A., Krco, S., Nati, M., Pfisterer, D., Mitton, N., Razafindralambo, T.: A survey on facilities for experimental internet of things research. IEEE Commun. Mag. **49**, 58–67 (2011). https://doi.org/10.1109/MCOM.2011.6069710

8. Varela-Aldás, J., Moreira, A., Criollo, P., Ruales, B.: Body temperature control using a robotic arm. In: Botto Tobar, M., Cruz, H., Díaz Cadena, A. (eds.) CIT 2020. LNEE, vol. 762, pp. 280–293. Springer, Cham (2021). https://doi.org/10.1007/978-3-030-72208-1_21

9. Varela-Aldás, J., Buele, J., Cumbajin, M.: Smart home control system using echo dot. In: Rocha, Á., Ferrás, C., López-López, P.C., Guarda, T. (eds.) ICITS 2021. AISC, vol. 1330, pp. 303–312. Springer, Cham (2021). https://doi.org/10.1007/978-3-030-68285-9_29

Localizing Climate-Smart Applications Through Participatory Design: A Case Study of the Beekeeper's Companion

Sarah-Beth Hopton[1](✉), Max Rünzel[2], and Laura Becker[3]

[1] Appalachian State University, Boone, NC 28607, USA
hoptonsb@appstate.edu
[2] Hive Tracks, Boone, NC 28607, USA
max@hivetracks.com
[3] ICARDA, Beirut, Lebanon
l.becker@cgiar.org

Abstract. This paper details the need for more localization and customization of climate-smart applications in development contexts and demonstrates how practitioners' commitment to participatory design methods can improve uptake and use of technological interventions that support environmental justice and indigenous knowledge.

Keywords: Participatory design · Localization · Application development · Climate-smart technology · Environmental justice · Technical communication

1 Introduction

1.1 Climate Change and the Need for Climate-Smart Application Development

Humanity depends on services that nature provides. We are especially dependent on pollination services, through which human food systems either flourish or fail. As global warming and anthropogenic climate change threatens, disrupts or devastates natural ecosystems, human rights to clean food and water, economic stability, and personal health and safety are also in jeopardy.

While many climate-mitigation and adaptation policies and technologies treat biodiversity loss, global warming, and human rights as independent of each other, they are not. Disruption in one system disrupts the other systems to which they are connected. For example, the overapplication of agricultural chemicals that support a monocrop system of food production needed to feed seven billion people, results in habitat loss for pollinators. Habitat loss is a key contributor to recent declines in honeybee populations, which impacts the human right to health and food [1].

Thus, any mitigating technical solutions, policy changes, or practices should be designed holistically, with consideration given to global warming, biodiversity loss, and human rights impacts collectively [2] and those solutions should be co-designed with the

C. Stephanidis et al. (Eds.): HCII 2022, CCIS 1581, pp. 339–346, 2022.
https://doi.org/10.1007/978-3-031-06388-6_45

very people who are disproportionately affected by climate change: women, children, and Black, Indigenous people of color [3].

Worldwide, women have proven that they are not only key contributors to agricultural labor, making up 50% of the workforce, but that they can drive innovative technical solutions that positively affect their communities and climate [4]. The *AI-Driven Climate-Smart Beekeeping (AID-CSB) for Women* project worked with beekeepers in Ethiopia and Uzbekistan to co-design and localize the "Beekeeper's Companion", a climate-smart information communication technology for development (ICT4D) application designed to support beekeepers' hive management practices and improve honey production. With the goal of applying advanced machine learning models on standardized biodiversity data to mitigate bias and maintain spatial and temporal accuracy, the project leveraged the participation and local knowledge of women beekeepers and national experts, incorporating their traditional and local knowledge into the algorithms that then push information to the beekeepers. Recognizing the need for an agricultural solution that does not require more time from women, the app was designed so that uploading data points required a minimal time investment.

One of the project's many goals included narrowing the gender digital divide by increasing women's digital literacy while giving users valuable information they could use to manage and grow their operations. Notably, many global digital projects fail because development firms too frequently design *at* users not *for* them. The participatory design method used in this project reversed this process and involved stakeholders, designers, researchers, and end users in the design process, ensuring the final product met the needs of its audience, not the will of the developer [5–9].

Gender-responsive tech-enabled beekeeping can unlock a low-barrier economic activity that also improves local biodiversity, crop yields, and the health of bee populations. By supporting healthy hive management practices in small-scale operations, the application also supports resiliency in the face of the COVID-19 pandemic, as beekeepers can access resources and knowledge wherever they are, even when in-person extension services are not possible. Access to such information can help women and their communities become climate-resilient by offering ways to adapt practices to new climatic realities.

Close to half the world remains offline and the majority of those without access to internet connection in developing countries are women [10] but lack of accessibility only explains part of the digital gender divide. For the past 30 years, experts working at the intersections of gender and ICT4D theorized that digital literacy and skills, cost, and availability of delivery mechanisms (like cell phones) were the principal reasons for the gender digital divide [11]. New research however, suggests that norms have an equal and sometimes greater impact on women's access to and use of technology [12, 13]. Many women in low-income countries have cell phones or access to communication technology because they are *allowed* to. However, millions of women do not have access to tech because of family, community, legal [14] or religious regulations [15, 16] that order women to protect themselves or preserve their dignity by abstaining from use. Even in more relaxed cultural settings, technology is often considered a tool specific to and appropriate for men and community members sometimes regard women who use technology with suspicion or scorn [17]. Furthermore, the COVID-19 pandemic exacerbates challenges of affordability, accessibility, and technology use and has been particularly difficult to manage for women in rural communities already living at the economic margins. Degendering the digital divide and technology solutions requires development partners to improve digital literacy, skills, decrease cost of access, customize delivery mechanisms, consider and–where possible–incorporate or disrupt the normative values and attitudes associated with gender and technology [18–20].

While technology is not a panacea, ICT4D solutions can catalyze and empower women and BIPOC communities, especially in agriculture. Coupling women's existing knowledge about agri- and apiculture with responsively-designed technology could result in a force-multiplier effect in mitigating and adapting to climate-related problems like pollinator decline. Technology acts as a gateway for women to access information that can radically improve their livelihoods and those of their family and community. By some estimates, doubling the number of women online in developing countries has the potential to increase global gross domestic product (GDP) by an estimated U.S. $13–18 billion [21].

2 Methodology

2.1 Participatory Design and the Development Cycle

To participate in narrowing the gender digital divide, improve women's livelihoods, and reverse pollinator declines, ICARDA's MEL team, HiveTracks and *icipe*, partnered to make available and localize a beekeeping application for beekeepers in Uzbekistan and Ethiopia called The Beekeeper's Companion, which helps beekeepers more effectively manage their hives and collects data important to scientific research on pollinator populations.

Launched in 2010, the first HiveTracks' app was designed to help beekeepers manage hive data that had traditionally been recorded by hand and was often difficult to assess longitudinally and therefore of limited value both to the beekeeper or the scientific community. Through the AID-CSB project, the new 2.0 version of the app—The Beekeeper's Companion—underwent iteration to localize the app for use in Uzbekistan and Ethiopia. This process required extensive desk and user research to understand and later customize the user interface and application functions across three different languages (Uzbek, Russian, and Amharic), two different climates, for vastly different user profiles and to accommodate different indigenous beekeeping practices.

The app is mobile only, offline capable, and creates a true digital companion for beekeepers, generating season and location-based information, reminders, and decision-making aids that beekeepers need to protect hives from weather and climate risks, pests, disease, and nutritional deficiencies and malpractices. Though the beekeepers own their data and that data is protected—thus protecting privacy of women users—in the future, scientists and researchers will be able to access non-identifiable aggregated data hosted on the HiveTracks server, to understand the variables associated with honeybee health and the local conditions exacerbating pollinator declines, while giving voice to women whose voices in agricultural policy and technological production have been historically silenced.

The AID-CSB project leveraged a 3-step process to localize The Beekeeper's Companion App that independently supported the mitigation of bias and protection of user privacy:

Desk research was conducted to gather both a general understanding of the honey sector and beekeeping practices, as well as collect specific data points to be used later on in the app development, such as flowering calendars.
Preliminary user interviews were conducted to understand the day-to-day beekeeping experience, practices, and challenges of project beekeepers in order to design the app prototype.
Prototype testing enabled women beekeepers to interact directly with the app prototype to identify problems and areas of improvement early, so designers could make the necessary changes prior to development and build products that meet user needs and expectations.

The AID-CSB project participants included 24 beekeepers in Uzbekistan (20 women and four men) across two regions: Tashkent (agricultural/rural) and Bukhara (desert). In Ethiopia, 15 beekeepers (12 women and three men) were selected from *icipe's* More Young Entrepreneurs in Silk and Honey (MOYESH) project across three sites in the Amhara region. After communicating the purpose of the interview/prototype testing and receiving beekeeper consent, meetings were conducted and recorded over Zoom with the HiveTracks UX/UI designer and a local translator, and later transcribed. Additionally, information was recorded via physical notetaking, which was then recorded in electronic documents for reference and qualitative analysis by HiveTracks and ICARDA.

3 Results

3.1 Customization and Localization of Climate-Smart Applications

When asked about challenges specific to women beekeepers, interviewees remarked that beekeeping is physically demanding. Further, the responsibility of raising a family makes it difficult for beekeepers to balance caring for their bees with caring for their families, as it is viewed as culturally unacceptable for women to stay at apiaries past dark in traditional households; thus, there is particular importance on the flexibility needed for improved timing of beekeeping practices.

Additionally, the importance of the one-on-one user interview approach was validated during mixed-gender beekeeper discussion groups at the final workshops in Uzbekistan, where men dominated the conversation and women felt less comfortable speaking up. Other important findings included differences in language and terminology. For example, the U.S. version of the app refers to pests and diseases as "stressors"; however, in Uzbek culture "stress" only makes sense in context to human beings. While such linguistic nuance may seem minor, these differences can frustrate understanding of the app, which can affect the uptake and use of it. Consistency of language and iconography was another important feedback point that will affect future iterations of the user interface.

The AID-CSB project illuminates the importance of understanding how information travels within beekeeping communities and the ways that communicative culture impacts the flow of information. In Uzbekistan, the most common communication between bee-keepers occurs in a large Telegram group to exchange information on markets, share beekeeping photos, ask questions, and sell honey and byproducts. Beekeepers also com-municate and access information through membership in beekeeping organizations and knowledgeable family members and mentors. Despite the grassroots-level organization of the Telegram group, several types of information (such as pesticide use) and key deci-sions (such as honey pricing) flow top-down. Details like this are important in order to maximize networks of people effectively, and they could also have significant impacts on adoption and use of the application.

Unlike Uzbek beekeepers, Ethiopian beekeepers do not keep written records of hive inspections or plan out beekeeping tasks in advance. Hives may be identified by a number, their hive type, a certain color, their position in the apiary, or nothing at all. Building these habits will be critical to the successful adoption of the Beekeeper's Companion app.

In Ethiopia, one of the main challenges to overcome is the gender digital divide, in which rural, low-income women are less likely to be able to access and use digital technologies. To better understand the baseline level of beekeepers' digital knowledge and plan project activities accordingly, a survey was conducted with the 15 beekeepers on their use and comfort using technology. Four women had never used a smartphone, and only two women felt 100% confident using a smartphone. However, all but two beekeepers actively used social media, which requires many of the same digital skills as the Beekeeper's Companion app.

Considering these findings, an ICARDA intern developed and implemented smart-phone training to build off beekeepers' existing knowledge and familiarity with similar concepts (e.g. social media and basic mobile phone functions such as sending a text mes-sage and making a call). To build a comfortable learning environment, beekeepers were encouraged to bring a tech-savvy family member who could help provide extra support during the training, which included many peer-to-peer exercises. Today, the beekeepers exchange beekeeping photos in a Telegram group, practicing their new skills and sharing information and experiences.

As with Uzbekistan, traditional gender roles do not encourage women to express their opinions or speak up. Similar to observations in Uzbekistan mixed-gender workshops, during the smartphone training (mixed-gender small groups of five to nine beekeepers with family members and two field assistants), it was evident that some women beekeep-ers were not comfortable actively participating in group discussion. This challenge was anticipated and mitigated by including many peer-to-peer smartphone exercises in which women could practice directly with one another or family members, thus increasing their agency but also normalizing their use of technology. Nonetheless, this experience underscores the importance of one-on-one prototype testing sessions and highlights the broader barriers to inclusive and participatory design.

It became clear early in the UX design process that changes needed to be made in the app's design for it to truly be localized. Most notably, the Beekeeper's Companion app was originally designed for hobbyist beekeepers. Project beekeepers often managed 20 to 100+ hives. An inspection process at the individual hive-level did not meet user needs for the Ethiopian (as well as Uzbek) beekeepers who managed large apiaries and it became clear that an additional inspection process at the apiary-level will be a necessary addition to the application if it is to be beneficial to larger or commercial users.

Not having direct access to communication with beekeepers or fully understanding their operations and challenges makes it difficult for beekeepers to access the right information at the right time. The co-designed Beekeeper's Companion app unlocks the opportunity for local extension services, researchers, and project management to monitor and assess the data entered by beekeepers in an anonymized manner, if given consent.

4 Discussion

4.1 Recommendations for Practitioners from Lessons Learned

Practitioners and researchers wishing to conduct similar transnational usability projects will benefit from AID-CSB's lessons learned on what worked and what still needs work:

- **Get to know project participants** through preliminary interviews; this not only provides critical baseline information for technology development, but also builds relationships and trust;
- **Test your technology with the users** through prototype testing by an experienced UX/UI designer to ensure the technology suits them and is adapted to local contexts and practices accordingly;
- **Leverage 1:1 interviews to hear all voices**; this technique is particularly helpful when collecting information from different genders and socioeconomic classes, as women and disadvantaged groups may be uncomfortable sharing opinions in large group discussions;
- **Involve family members for digital literacy training**, as trainees in certain cultural contexts will be more comfortable asking family members questions, and they can provide continued training and support at home;
- **Manage expectations and clearly communicate**; because participants are co-designing the technology, they will experience many bugs and see imperfect versions of the technology;
- **Implement a multi-step translation process** with both a professional translator and local subject matters experts to ensure that text is not only translated, but fits local terminologies and expressions, is gender-inclusive, and visually corresponds to the desired user action in the app design;
- **Avoid designing technology to Western norms** by continuously iterating and clarifying that the technology is being made to suit participants' best subject matter practices. For example, in the first round of desk research all Ethiopian flowering data was provided in the Gregorian calendar, as this is the international standard. However, beekeepers use the Ethiopian calendar, and therefore the app needed to be designed as such;
- **Reduce bias in technology design** by (1) identifying and acknowledging pre-existing societal biases within marginalized groups; (2) using real data when possible to avoid measurement bias, but when necessary, carefully leveraging proxy data; (3) ensure appropriate aggregation and evaluation measures within the technology; (4) ensure a focused scope (that the app is used for the intended purpose).

If smallholder farmers and beekeepers are expected to adopt climate-smart technology practices, they should be the first experts consulted in the design of such technology. Data collection methods must respect the user's wide diversity of knowledge and specific challenges based on location, language, climate, gender, and digital skills. This is particularly true when carrying out a gender-responsive participatory development process. Encouraged through one-on-one dialogue, women's input was at the center of this project, informing how the app interface, features, and gender-sensitive translations should be designed to best support their livelihoods as beekeepers and respect their indigenous knowledge practices. In addition to the direct support to beekeepers, the hive management practices facilitated through the application customization promotes pollination services to support healthy, biodiverse ecosystems critical to managing and mitigating climate change and protecting global human rights to food.

References

1. Willige, A.: 75% of Crops Depend on Pollinators: they must be protected. https://www.weforum.org/agenda/2019/12/protect-pollinators-food-security-biodiversity-agriculture/. Accessed 21 Dec 2022
2. Pörtner, H.O., et al.: IPBES-IPCC co-sponsored workshop report on biodiversity and climate change. IPBES and IPCC, pp. 1–28 (2021)
3. Boyd, D.R.: Report of the special rapporteur on the issue of human rights obligations relating to the enjoyment of a safe, clean, healthy and sustainable environment. United Nations General Assembly, A/76/150, pp. 1–26 (2021)
4. Women as Agents of Change. United Nations Climate Action. https://www.un.org/en/climatechange/climate-solutions/womens-agents-change
5. Steinke, J., Ortiz-Crespo, B., Etten, J., Müller, A.: Participatory Design of Digital innovation in Agricultural Research-for-Development: Insights from Practice. Alliance of Biodiversity International and CIAT, Digital Inclusion, Montpellier, France (2022)
6. Acharya, K.R.: Usability for social justice: exploring the implementation of localization usability in Global North technology in the context of a Global South's country. J. Tech. Writing Commun. 49(1), 6–32 (2017)
7. Bannon, L.J., Ehn, P.: Design matters in participatory design. In: Simonsen, J., Robertson, T. (eds.) Routledge Handbook of Participatory Design, pp. 37–63. Routledge, New York, NY (2013)
8. Spinuzzi, C.: The methodology of participatory design. Tech. Commun. 52(2), 163–174 (2005)
9. Zachry, M., Spyridakis, J.H.: Human-centered design and the field of technical communication. J. Tech. Writing Commun. 46(4), 392–401 (2016)
10. Iglesias, C.: The Gender Gap in Internet Access: using a women-centered method. Web Foundation (2020)
11. Steele, C.: What is the Gender Divide? Digital Divide Council (2019). http://www.digitaldividecouncil.com/what-is-the-digital-divide/.
12. Revi, S., Grubbs, L., Koutsky, T.: Breaking through the gender digital divide: technology, social norms, and the WomenConnect challenge. ERN: Information Asymmetry Models (Topic) (2020)
13. Joiner, R., Stewart, C., Beaney, C.: The Wiley handbook of psychology, technology, and society. In: Rosen, L.D., Cheever, N., Carrier, L.M. (eds.) Gender Digital Divide: Does it Exist and What are the Explanations? pp. 74–89. Wiley, Hoboken, NJ (2015)

14. Chandran, R.: Indian Villages Ban Single Women from Owning 'Distracting' Mobile Phones, Reuters (2016). https://www.reuters.com/article/us-india-women-phone/indian-villages-ban-single-women-from-owning-distracting-%20mobile-phones-idUSKCN0VZ1AA

15. Grant, M.: Egyptian Islamic Authority Issues Fatwas Against Selfies and Chatting Online, Newsweek (2014). https://www.newsweek.com/egyptian-islamic-authority-issues-fatwas-against-selfies-and-chatting-online-%20267832

16. Dodson, L.L., Sterling, L.R., Bennett, J.K.: Minding the Gaps: Cultural, technical and gender-based barriers to mobile use in oral-language Berber communities in Morocco. In: Proceedings of the Sixth International Conference on Information and Communication Technologies and Development, vol. 1, pp. 79–88 (2013)

17. Bellman, E., Malhotra, A.: Why the vast majority of women in india will never own a smartphone. Wall Street J. (2016). https://www.wsj.com/articles/why-the-vast-majority-of-women-in-india-will-never-own-a-%20smartphone-1476351001

18. Feeney, M., Fusi, F.: A critical analysis of the study of gender and technology in government. Inf. Polity **26**(2), 115–129 (2021)

19. Sun, H.: Exploring cultural usability. In: Proceedings of IEEE International Professional Communication Conference, pp. 319–330 (2002)

20. Weber, J., Bath, C.: Social' Robots and 'Emotional' software agents: gendering processes and de-gendering strategies for 'technologies in the making. In: Zorn, I., Maass, S., Rommes, E., Schirmer, C., Schelhowe, H. (eds.) Gender Designs IT, pp. 53–63 (2007)

21. Globescan, D.: Women and the Web: bridging the internet gap and creating new global opportunities in low and middle-income countries. Intel, pp. 1–104 (2012). https://www.intel.la/content/dam/www/public/us/en/documents/pdf/women-and-the-web.pdf.

Building Connected Home Scenarios (IoT) Using Computers

Mary Luz Mouronte-López[1]([⊠]) [iD], Ángel Lambertt Lobaina[2],
Elizabeth Guevara Martínez[2] [iD], and Jorge Alberto Rodríguez Rubio[3]

[1] Higher Polytechnic School, Universidad Francisco de Vitoria, Madrid, Spain
maryluz.mouronte@ufv.es
[2] Faculty of Engineering, Universidad Anáhuac México, Huixquilucan, Estado de México, Mexico
[3] Cisco Academy – Investigaciones y Estudios Superiores S.C., Huixquilucan, Estado de México, Mexico

Abstract. The construction of scenarios showing the operation of real communication networks is useful not only for industry but also for academia. The fast development of the Internet of Things (IoT) and its use in the most diverse human – computer interaction activities have motivated universities all over the world to organize courses in order to train and make students familiar with the use of this technology. The use of tools that simulate IoT networks functioning is crucial to facilitate the teaching and training of future engineers in this area.

This contribution shows two scenarios which have been used in a seminar of IoT for undergraduate students of Computer Engineering at the Universidad Francisco de Vitoria in Madrid and Computer Engineering and Telecommunications at the Universidad Anáhuac México Norte in Mexico, both related to the application of IoT to create smart building. One scenario is the design and simulation of the networks of a smart building; the second one is the use of an Arduino board to create a small and simple IoT system connected to the cloud.

The software used in the simulation was Cisco Packet Tracer, a multiplatform tool from Cisco System Inc. that allows the "construction" of networks without using hardware and/or physical network. The board used to develop a real IoT system was the Arduino Nano 33 IoT connected by Internet to Arduino IoT Cloud via wireless network.

The scenarios presented were successfully used with undergraduate students in both universities.

Keywords: Internet of Things · CISCO Packet Tracer · Network simulation · Smart buildings · Arduino boards · Cloud · Educational tools

1 Introduction

The term Internet of Things (IoT) first coined by Kevin Ashton in 1999 [1] is consequence of Internet evolution. The IoT refers to the use of intelligently connected devices and systems of heterogenic technologies to leverage data gathered by embedded sensors

C. Stephanidis et al. (Eds.): HCII 2022, CCIS 1581, pp. 347–354, 2022.
https://doi.org/10.1007/978-3-031-06388-6_46

and actuators in machines and other physical objects. It makes the objects themselves identifiable, intelligent, convey information about them and can access information gathered by other things. IoT lets us connect with people and things anytime and anywhere [2].

The use of IoT offers many advantages by enabling the deployment of new services by creating smart cities, buildings, and factories among many other applications [3]. The use of data obtained through IoT devices would generate significant revenues. The 2021 Gartner Report [4] predicted that wireless communications will be of key importance for Industry 4.0 and smart factories. Some analyses refer to the integration of 5G technology with IoT applications, and address aspects related to improving some communications functions [5, 6]. Other investigations refer to security issues, suggesting solutions helping to preserve privacy in IoT environments [7, 8]. They also refer to the application of IoT in buildings in order to save energy and increase the comfort of residents [9].

This paper describes the development of two scenarios: an IoT network simulation and a simple real IoT system connected to the cloud. Their purpose was to employ them as educational tools helping students of our universities to learn and understand the benefices of IoT. Both scenarios are intentionally very simple because during the seminars they would be modified by the students themselves, creating more complex networks which will meet the requirements of more realistic environments. During seminars students acquired deeper knowledge about IoT meanwhile developing skills using simulation and developing tools.

2   Tool

2.1   Simulation

The tool selected for network simulation was Cisco Packet Tracer, a Cisco System Inc. proprietary multi-platform tool that enables students to create networking and IoT simulations without need of hardware and/or existing network. The tool can be downloaded freely by students and runs on the principal operating systems.

Cisco Packet Tracer offers a wide variety of standard network components that can be connected and configured to simulate real networks (see Fig. 1). The release of the version 7.0 of the tool [10] introduced IoT network simulation capabilities.

Working with Cisco Packet Tracer is highly intuitive. Components used to build networks are selected among sets of different kind of components which are then placed in the working area of the main window. IoT components include smart devices (those that can connect directly to network's servers or gateways through their own network interfaces), non-intelligent components (some sensors and actuators) and processing boards named MCU (microcontroller unit) and SBC (single board computer) which simulate the popular and well known Arduino and Raspberry Pi boards. Once the devices are selected, they are connected and configured.

In addition to the logical simulation, Cisco Packet Tracer allows the simulation of networks at physical level creating different environments: cities, buildings, physical containers and wired cabins. It is possible to setup the values of environmental variables at different times of the day to simulate the behavior of many IoT devices.

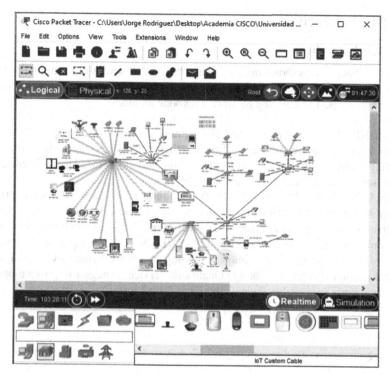

Fig. 1. Building network

2.2 Arduino Development Platforms

Arduino Nano 33 IoT board was selected because it is a cheap but very powerful board specially designed to be used in IoT applications. It has a powerful ARM processor, a BLE-WiFi module and an inertial unit which, working together the traditional I/O lines and communication ports of Arduino boards, make this board an excellent choice to be used in academic environments.

Arduino IDE, the open source develop environment was used to develop the software running on the Arduino Nano 33 IoT board [11]. It makes it easy to write code and upload it to Arduino compatible boards.

Arduino IoT Cloud [12] is an open-source platform based on easy-to-use hardware and software. It can be used for free with low cost Arduino compatible boards. Its friendly interface facilitates students to learn and train the development of IoT applications on the cloud. Arduino IoT Cloud facilitates students to get familiar with developments of IoT projects on the cloud.

3 Network Structure

3.1 Network Backbone

The network backbone is shown in Fig. 2. It is composed by several conventional network devices which connect the Internet Service Provider (ISP) with subnets of apartments and common areas. The building network backbone includes:

- Router INPUT: which connects the building network to the ISP;
- ASA (Adaptive Secure Appliance) firewall: that enables a secure connection of the building network with the ISP, protecting it from access by intruders and penetration of viruses and malware that may affect its operation;
- Router COMMON: which permits: (1) IP telephony devices configuration to provide telephony services, including the creation of Virtual Local Area Networks (VLANs) to separate data and voice traffics; (2) isolation of data traffic between apartments and common areas networks by creating four VLANs; (3) developing a dynamic and static routes to communicate subnets, including an extended Access Control Lists to control traffic between subnets; (4) Quality of Service strategies to provide optimal use of network: bandwidth, latency, jitter and packet loss.
- Switch COMMON: that separates apartments and common areas subnets.

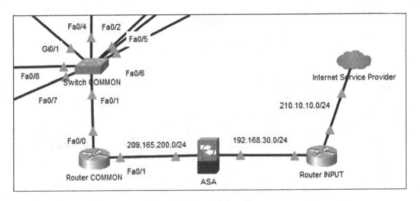

Fig. 2. Network backbone

3.2 Common Areas Network

Include standard network devices (PC COMMON, IP phone, COMMON IoT Server and COMMON Access Point) and some IoT devices (Garage Door, CO sensor, Main door, RFID COMMON reader, RFID COMMON card, Movement sensor, Outdoor sprinkler, SBC0, Movement lamp and Street lamp) as shown in Fig. 3. All devices used in the common areas network are connected to the VLAN20.

The IoT devices connected to the common areas permit to create several systems to automate areas like garage access, illumination, garden irrigation and building access. SBC0 running a simple java program is used to illustrate how connect a low-cost actuator (outdoor sprinkle) which doesn't have a network interface.

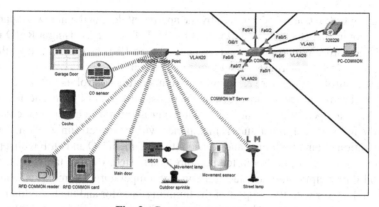

Fig. 3. Common areas network

3.3 Apartment Networks

All apartment networks are connected to different VLANs but have very similar configurations. They have several standard network devices and IoT devices connected to the IoT Server which permits to create the control algorithm of the different systems.

Apartment Network Standard Devices. Standard network devices include the apartment switch which connects standard devices like IP phones, smartphones, PC, laptops, server and access point (see Fig. 4). Eventually the apartment switch could connect some IoT wired devices (for example the air conditioner device in our simulation).

The apartment access point is used to provide communication to the IoT devices and also to the wireless standard devices used by residents like smartphones, laptops, notebook, etc.

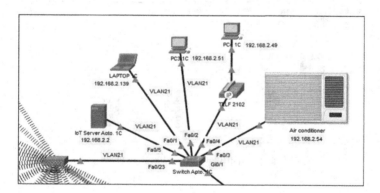

Fig. 4. Apartment network standard devices

Apartment Network IoT Devices. IoT network devices include a wide variety of devices which permit the functioning of several systems: climate, access, fire-protection, illumination and stand-alone electro domestic and recreational devices as shown in Fig. 5.

- Access control: It controls the access by the apartment door and windows. Apartment door is controlled (locked and unlocked) by the IoT server by using a RFID reader and RFID cards. Windows access is detected by an IR sensor access; thus the IoT server turns ON the alarm siren and sends an alarm message.
- Climate control (temperature & humidity): Temperature control includes the air conditioner, the furnace and a thermostat. Thermostat read and inform the IoT server about local temperature and then air conditioner and furnace are remote controlled from the IoT server. Temperature is maintained within comfort limits. By alternating the operation of air conditioner and furnace (turning them NO and OFF with a proper hysteresis algorithm), the room temperature is adjusted. Ceiling fan will be turned ON and OFF helping to reach faster a comfort temperature. Humidity is controlled by the IoT server with the support of the humidity monitor and the humidifier.
- Fire control: includes fire and smoke detectors, CO_2 sensor, ceiling fan, fire sprinkler and an alarm siren controlled by the IoT server. If a fire is detected, the water sprinkles located on the ceiling are put into operation, the door and windows are opened, the fan is turned on and the alarm siren sounds.
- Household and recreational devices (smart TV, watching machines, refrigerators and many others) could be included on the systems or remotely controlled to increase the comfort of the residents.

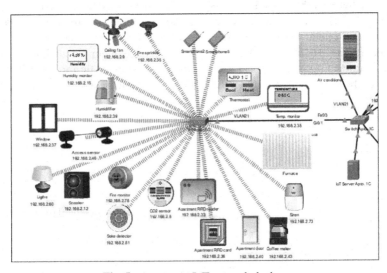

Fig. 5. Apartment IoT network devices

4   Example of a Real IoT System

To complement the scenarios created for teaching purposes, a real IoT system was developed based on the Arduino Nano 33 IoT board that collects data from temperature and acceleration sensors and sends them to a dashboard created in the cloud.

The dashboard allows the exchange of information between the system and an external user by internet connection on any place outside the system under control. Figure 6 shows the breadboard with the components used to develop the real IoT system.

Fig. 6. IoT systems developed with Nano 33 IoT

Figure 7 shows the dashboard SENSORS created in the cloud. This includes some analog data (ROOM TEMPERATURE and X, Y, Z ACCELERATION) obtained from the environment and a Boolean output used to activate a fan motors.

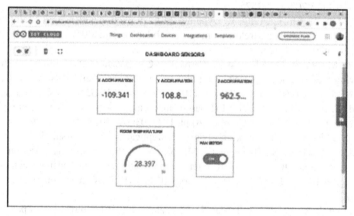

Fig. 7. Dashboard of the IoT systems developed with Nano 33 IoT

The use of the real IoT system developed as an example that can be extrapolated not only to a smart building, but to any other IoT application.

5   Conclusions

The simulation described in this paper allowed undergraduate students of Computer Engineering at Universidad Francisco de Vitoria in Madrid and Information Technology and Telecommunications Engineering at Universidad Anáhuac México Norte in Mexico, to reinforce the knowledge and skills acquired during the IoT seminars.

During the seminars students created, designed and simulated IoT more complex networks letting them to work in scenarios with new requirements closer to real requirements of apartment buildings.

The experience gained will allow professors to improve the educational tools developed to be used in other future IoT courses or seminars.

References

1. Gabbai, A.: Kevin Ashton describes the Internet of Things. Interview. Smithsonian Magazine (2015). https://www.smithsonianmag.com/innovation/kevin-ashton-describes-the-internet-of-things-180953749/
2. GSM Association: Understanding the Internet of the Things (IoT). GSMA Connected Living (2014). https://www.gsma.com/iot/wp-content/uploads/2014/08/cl_iot_wp_07_14.pdf
3. Panetta, K.: Gartner top 10 strategic technology trends 2020 (2019). https://www.gartner.com/smarterwithgartner/gartner-top-10-strategic-technology-trends-for-2020/
4. Panetta, K.: Gartner top 10 strategic technology trends 2021 (2020). https://www.gartner.com/smarterwithgartner/gartner-top-strategic-technology-trends-for-2021/
5. Rong, B., Han, S., Kadoch, M., Chen, X., Jara, A.: Integration of 5G networks and internet of things for future smart city. Wireless Commun. Mobile Comput. **2020**, 1–2 (2020). https://doi.org/10.1155/2020/2903525
6. Wu, S., Mao, W., Liu, C., Tang, T.: Dynamic traffic prediction with adaptive sampling for 5G HetNet IoT applications. Wireless Commun. Mobile Comput. **2019**, 1–11 (2019). https://doi.org/10.1155/2019/4687272
7. Gheisari, M., Wang, G., Khan, W.Z., Fernández-Campusano, C.: A context-aware privacy-preserving method for IoT-based smart city using Software Defined Networking. Comput. Secur. **87**, 101470 (2019). https://doi.org/10.1016/j.cose.2019.02.006. Accessed 18 Feb 2022
8. Majeed, U., et al.: Blockchain for IoT-based smart cities: recent advances, requirements, and future challenges. J. Network Comput. Appl. **181**, 103007 (2021). https://www.sciencedirect.com/journal/journal-of-network-and-computer-applications/vol/181/suppl/C
9. Havard, N., McGrath, S., Flanagan, C., MacNamee, C.: Smart building based on Internet of Things technology (ICST). In: 12th International Conference on Sensing Technology, 4–6 December 2018, pp. 278–281. https://doi.org/10.1109/ICSensT2018.8603575. Accessed 18 Feb 2022
10. What's new in Cisco Packet Tracer 7.0. Update 18/06/2017. https://www.packettracernetwork.com/features/packettracer-7-newfeatures.html
11. Arduino. Arduino IDE 1.8.19. https://www.arduino.cc/en/software. Accessed 18 Feb 2022
12. Söderby, K.: Getting Started With the Arduino IoT Cloud. LAST REVISION: 10/03/2022. https://docs.arduino.cc/cloud/iot-cloud/tutorials/iot-cloud-getting-started

Monitoring System for Plants Based on a Smart Plant Pot

Marco Salazar[1], Franklin Castillo[1], Víctor H. Andaluz[1,2],
Guillermo Palacios-Navarro[3], and José Varela-Aldás[1,3]($\boxtimes$) (iD)

[1] SISAu Research Group, Facultad de Tecnologías de la Información y la Comunicación,
Universidad Tecnológica Indoamérica, Ambato, Ecuador
`msalazar26@indoamerica.edu.ec`, `{franklincastillo,`
`josevarela}@uti.edu.ec`
[2] Universidad de las Fuerzas Armadas ESPE, Sangolquí, Ecuador
`vhandaluz1@espe.edu.ec`
[3] Department of Electronic Engineering and Communications, University of Zaragoza,
Zaragoza, Spain
`guillermo.palacios@unizar.es`

Abstract. The occupations of the modern world neglect important things like the environment and sustainable development. This work develops a monitoring system for plants, based on a smart plant pot that can be supervised and configured through a mobile application. The electronic design consists of the use of two sensors that constantly send the temperature and humidity of the plant to the mobile application. In addition, a submersible pump provides water to the interior of the plant pot to monitor the condition of the plant. The optimal temperature and humidity settings will depend on the type of plant; these options can be configured remotely. Alerts are sent in the form of notifications or appear on the display of the plant pot when a different status than recommended is detected. Information is reflected locally on the plant pot display as facial expressions. The local operating code is designed so that the facial expression displayed on the screen changes automatically based on the conditions presented on the plant pot. As a result, adequate communication was obtained between the mobile application and all the devices installed in the smart plant pot. Finally, an acceptance test is applied that qualifies this proposal as suitable for domestic use.

Keywords: Smart plant pot · Mobile application · Monitoring system · Firebase

1 Introduction

Plants play a very important role in maintaining the ecological cycle and form the base of the food chain pyramid. Therefore, plants require adequate monitoring and control, based on an integrated and multidisciplinary design approach [1, 2]. The integration of a system for plant monitoring facilitates agriculture and makes use of the concept of ambient intelligence. In addition, the increasing adoption of the Internet of Things

© The Author(s), under exclusive license to Springer Nature Switzerland AG 2022
C. Stephanidis et al. (Eds.): HCII 2022, CCIS 1581, pp. 355–361, 2022.
https://doi.org/10.1007/978-3-031-06388-6_47

(IoT) in consumer, commercial, industrial and service applications allows their use in disciplines other than agriculture [3–5].

There are works on the design and development of monitoring systems capable of reporting several metrics of a common indoor plant, these metrics include temperature and soil moisture [2, 6]. In addition, sensors are used in smart plants that communicate and activate electronic devices to monitor and optimize individual plant productivity and resource use [7, 8].

This paper develops a smart plant pot with a display to show emotions according to plant status using low-cost technology. Sensors are installed inside the pot to provide information to be presented in a mobile application. The system is implemented with an internet of things card, and all the developed features are managed using the mobile application. For this purpose, the paper has been organized into 4 sections; starting with the current section containing a brief introduction to the topic; Sect. 2 describes the methodology to be used; Sect. 3 presents the results obtained, and Sect. 4 contains the main conclusions.

2   Methods and Materials

For the development of this work, an electronic board with wireless communication (WiFi) is used to control the different components, Fig. 1 shows the proposed scheme. This electronic card stores the necessary programming for the management of the intelligent plant. The installed modules are a temperature sensor and an analog hygrometer included inside the pot to obtain all the data coming from the temperature and humidity of the soil, respectively. There is also a submersible pump and an electrical relay to supply water to the plant. All data is sent to a mobile application through the cloud using the internet.

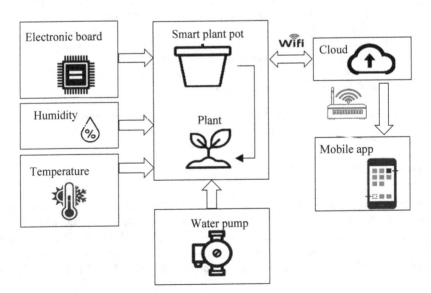

Fig. 1. General scheme of the smart plant pot

2.1 Electronic Design

The electronic design includes the connection of the sensors, such as the DHT-22, which is the temperature sensor connected to one digital pin of the ESP32 board. Similarly, the FC-28 hygrometer is connected to a port configured as an analog input. The display used is an I2C OLED of 128×64 pixels, this device is connected to the SDA and SCL ports of the I2C communication of the ESP32. For the submersible pump, a 12 V DC supply is used and a relay connected to a digital output for power control (Fig. 2).

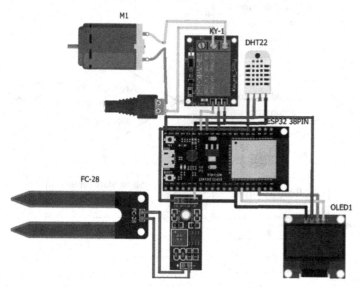

Fig. 2. Electronic circuit

2.2 Program Design

The actions of the program implemented in the ESP32 are shown in the flowchart in Fig. 3. Once the program is started, the temperature and humidity sensor data are read, this information is sent to the Firebase database. Then the operating mode up-date is received, this data allows to define the actions of the manual or automatic mode. In manual mode, the user directly controls the pump operation. In automatic mode, the pump is activated only with values outside the moderate range for temperature and humidity. In either case, the pump activation is by time short (2 s) and not permanent. In addition, the status of the plant is shown on the OLED display in the form of a sad or happy face.

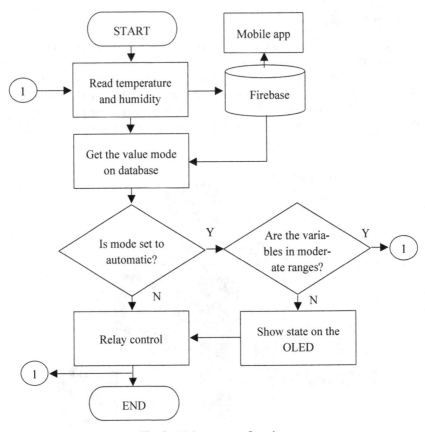

Fig. 3. Main program flowchart

2.3 Mobile Application Design

The user interface of the mobile application consists of the basic operating elements. Two labels display the temperature and soil moisture data, respectively. Two buttons allow to control the operating mode, in the manual mode the activation direct order for the pump is sent. Figure 4 shows the arrangement of the elements for the user interface.

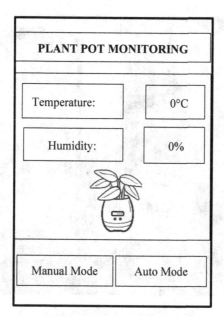

Fig. 4. User interface design

3 Results

3.1 Functional Tests

Figure 5 shows images of the operation of the smart plant pot, highlighting elements such as the display and the submersible pump. On the other hand, the mobile application located in a remote location shows the temperature and humidity values. The different tests were carried out successfully, constantly acting on the values acquired by the sensors and with an immediate response when the control buttons were pressed.

3.2 Acceptance Evaluation

To evaluate the characteristics of this proposal, an acceptance questionnaire was applied. The questionnaire consists of 7 questions to evaluate different components of the proposal. The questions are answered using a 7-level Likert scale, where 7 indicates strongly agree and 1 indicates strongly disagree. The results of the acceptance test are presented in Table 1, with a final rating of 85.71% acceptance, considered a favorable value for this proposal. The evaluation shows favorable reactions to the smart plant pot prototype, although it can be improved with its physical components and graphic interface.

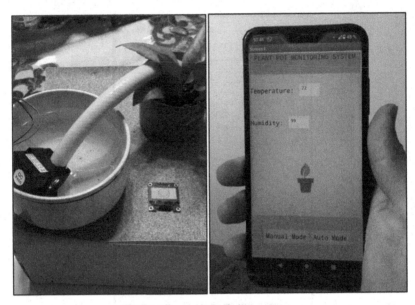

Fig. 5. Images of the functional tests.

Table 1. Acceptance test

Question	Score
1. You might use the smart plant pot properly	7
2. You are satisfied with the response time in the co-communication between the application and the device	6
3. It was easy to use the interface options in the application	7
4. It was easy to learn how to use the smart plant pot	7
5. It was not physically difficult to locate the smart plant pot	5
6. The indicators were efficient when using the system	5
7. Overall, I am satisfied with the system	5
Total	43/49 85.71%

4 Conclusions

This work presents a smart plant pot managed through a mobile application. This proposal is important in everyday life because the occupations of the modern world make people neglect the environment. Based on the acceptance test with a score of 85.71%, it is determined that the system meets the expectations raised, mainly because it is easy to use. The proposal has some limitations, the size of the plant pot is large, and the location of the devices is dispersed; in the future, the design can be simplified with a compact model that optimizes the space in the elements.

References

1. Giraldo, J.P., Wu, H., Newkirk, G.M., Kruss, S.: Nanobiotechnology approaches for engineering smart plant sensors. Nat. Nanotechnol. **14**, 541–553 (2019). https://doi.org/10.1038/s41565-019-0470-6
2. Maxey-Vesperman, J., Goldasich, Z., Tewolde, G.: Smart plant life monitoring system. In: 2019 IEEE 16th International Conference on Smart Cities: Improving Quality of Life Using ICT & IoT and AI (HONET-ICT), pp. 238–240. IEEE (2019). https://doi.org/10.1109/HONET.2019.8907989
3. Kohli, A., Kohli, R., Singh, B., Singh, J.: Smart plant monitoring system using IoT technology. In: Handbook of Research on the Internet of Things Applications in Robotics and Automation, pp. 318–366 (2020). https://doi.org/10.4018/978-1-5225-9574-8.ch016
4. Varela Aldás, J., Pilla, J., Andaluz, V.H., Palacios-Navarro, G.: Commercial entry control using robotic mechanism and mobile application for COVID-19 pandemic. In: Gervasi, O., et al. (eds.) ICCSA 2021. LNCS, vol. 12957, pp. 3–14. Springer, Cham (2021). https://doi.org/10.1007/978-3-030-87013-3_1
5. VarelaAldás, J., Buele, J., Cumbajin, M.: Smart home control system using echo dot. In: Rocha, Á., Ferrás, C., López-López, P.C., Guarda, T. (eds.) ICITS 2021. AISC, vol. 1330, pp. 303–312. Springer, Cham (2021). https://doi.org/10.1007/978-3-030-68285-9_29
6. Ariyaratne, U.H.D.T.N., Vitharana, V.D.Y., Deelaka, L.H.D.R., Herath, H.M.S.M.: IoT Smart Plant Monitoring, Watering and Security System (2022)
7. Al-Mayahi, A., et al.: A smart capillary barrier-wick irrigation system for home gardens in arid zones. Irrig. Sci. **38**(3), 235–250 (2020). https://doi.org/10.1007/s00271-020-00666-3
8. Fan, S., Wang, T., Wang, B., Zhang, Y., Cai, Y., Liu, B.: Flower "Dock"-smart flowerpot based on microcontroller. In: Jansen, B.J., Liang, H., Ye, J. (eds.) International Conference on Cognitive based Information Processing and Applications (CIPA 2021). LNDECT, vol. 85, pp. 826–830. Springer, Singapore (2022). https://doi.org/10.1007/978-981-16-5854-9_108

Incorporating the Public Perspective into the Future Design of Smart Home Living'

Valentine Seymour[1]([⊠]), Maria Xenitidou[2], Lada Timotijevic[1], Charo Hodgkins[1], Eleanor Ratcliffe[1], Birgitta Gatersleben[1], Nigel Gilbert[2], and Chris R. Jones[1]

[1] School of Psychology, University of Surrey, Guildford GU2 7XH, UK
`v.i.seymour@surrey.ac.uk`
[2] Department of Sociology, University of Surrey, Guildford GU2 7XH, UK

Abstract. User-Centred Design (UCD) researchers have been investigating smart homes for 20 years and have highlighted the approaches' effectiveness in identifying the requirements of users. Despite the growing interest in smart homes, research has shown that its adoption remains low. This owes to the tendency for research to often use a technological-centred approach to improve a pre-existing product or tailor it to target users. Visions of smart homes may therefore not have been fully based on a clear understanding of users' needs and sociotechnical issues of concern.

Enabling the public to have a role in shaping the future of smart home technologies and related sociotechnical issues of concern in the early stages of the UCD process have been widely recommended. Specifically, there have been calls to engage the public in sharing responsibility for developing data privacy agreements, data governance frameworks, and effectively domesticating technologies into life and 'home' systems.

This paper introduces the citizens' jury method to enable the public to have a role in shaping the future of smart homes and related sociotechnical issues. This is an understudied area of research that would be considerably valuable for practitioners in the usability and smart technology sectors. Findings from this paper are based on a cross-section of UK citizens', exploring their opinions on sociotechnical issues of data security, accessibility to and control over use of devices and technological appliances associated with smart homes. A set of recommendation are developed to provide guidance and suggested actions on approaching these issues in the future.

Keywords: Smart homes · Citizens jury method · Data security · data governance · Public involvement

1 Introduction

'Smart homes' is a widely used concept. It is, however, beyond the scope of this article to review the many ways this concept has been previously explored [1]. Instead, we adopt the view that a 'smart home' is one that is equipped with a layering together of different technological features aimed at providing tailored services for the people using them.

C. Stephanidis et al. (Eds.): HCII 2022, CCIS 1581, pp. 362–367, 2022.
https://doi.org/10.1007/978-3-031-06388-6_48

This makes it possible to monitor, control and support people using smart technologies, thus enhancing the quality of life and promoting independent living [1].

Economic forecasts suggest that the ownership of smart home devices will climb to an estimated 25.4 million UK users by 2026 [2]. This drive towards smart home technologies is partially motivated by the underlying purpose "to improve people's living experience" [3: 463]. Despite this, some research has shown that agreeing to live in smart homes remains low [4].

The barriers to opting for smart homes have been linked to various sociotechnical issues of concern to users. Others also highlight the need for a clearer understanding about the relationship between users' perceived risks associated with data sharing and trust towards the smart home industry [4]. Instead, research to date has tended to focus on technological features of smart homes [3]. It is easy therefore to see how visions of smart homes and their technological features may not have been fully based on a clear understanding of users' needs and sociotechnical issues of concern. As such there have been calls for more research activity to address these concerns [4].

Understanding both the benefits and challenges of smart homes is critically important given that their overall success hinges on their adoption [5]. The inclusion of public interventions in future research, such as those involving a deliberative decision-making process, have been widely recommended [6]. The citizens' jury is one such method that has not yet been applied to enable the public to have a role in shaping the future ethical issues and governance practices in data-driven smart environments [7].

The contribution of this article is that it applies a citizens' jury method to create a set of recommendations that can be used to provide guidance and suggested actions on approaching these ethical and governance issues associated with smart home living in the future. Specifically, the study aims to:

- explore the UK public's opinions on data security and governance issues associated with smart homes using a deliberative decision-making method (i.e., the citizens' jury method); and,
- create a set of recommendations to provide future guidance on data security and governance issues associated with smart homes.

2   Method

2.1 Participants

20 members of public volunteered to participate in this study. Participants were organized into four groups, controlling for age (e.g., younger, and older adults) as well as their orientations to smart technologies (e.g., techno-sceptic).

2.2 Expert Witnesses

4 expert witnesses were chosen to provide relevant information about socio-technical issues associated with smart homes. Witnesses were identified through author's existing contacts and cross-referencing methods from publicly accessible online sources.

2.3 Citizens' Jury Design

A two-day online citizens' jury was held in June 2021 and consisted of two 2-h sessions held each day (n = ten hours). Participants were provided with pseudonyms to protect their identities and an audio recorder was used to record the sessions [8].

Two witness talks occurred at the start of each day. On the first day, participants listened to witnesses 1 and 2 on issues of sense of control, accessibility of smart homes and the 'meanings of home' associated with smart home living. On the second day, jury participants listened to expert witnesses 3 and 4 on issues of data sharing, data management and ethical issues associated with smart home living.

Following this, small group discussions were used immediately after the witness talks. Participants were encouraged to deliberate, listen, and respond to the thoughts expressed by other participants in response to the issues presented in each of the with talks.

At the commencement of each day, participants were presented with three statements put to the jurors for deliberation were as follows:

Overarching statement: "Smart homes will are rapidly changing the way we live at home and what we mean by home".

Sub-statement 1: "Smart homes could monitor your lifestyle and living environment and identify areas for improvement. We should be willing to cede control to our home to make more decisions about how we should live our lives".

Sub-statement 2: "Smart living will require data-sharing. The benefits of living in smart homes outweigh the risks of data-sharing".

The design of these statements and small group discussions was informed by a literature review exploration. Participants were asked to individually vote either "yes" or "no" based on whether they 'agreed' or 'disagreed' with these two statements, discussing reasons for their vote afterwards. After the voting sessions, participants developed recommendations relevant to data security and governance issues discussed within their small groups.

2.4 Data Analysis

Citizens' jury discussions were transcribed and analyzed using thematic methods as outlined by Braun and Clark [9], identifying key themes that evidently emerged relevant to the study's aim.

3 Results

Participant's grouped aggregated voting responses to the two statements are shown in Table 1. Overall, most participants disagreed with the two statements. These voting outcomes reflect underlying discussions points, opinions, arguments, and issues raised during the citizens' jury.

Participants acknowledged various public benefits, associated with data sharing in smart environments, both individual and on society. These include providing assistive living, improvements in technology performances, and healthcare support to ensure vulnerable people (e.g., elderly and those with disabilities) remain autonomous, independent, safe, and well at home.

Table 1. Participant responses to the statements they were asked to vote on.

Statements	Participant responses			
	Group 1	Group 2	Group 3	Group 4
Overall statement: "Smart homes are rapidly changing the way we live at home and what we mean by home"	Majority agreed [4 = Yes, 1 = No]	Majority disagreed [4 = No, 1 = Yes]	Majority disagreed [2 = Yes, 3 = No]	Majority disagreed [4 = No, 1 = Yes]
Sub-statement 1: "Smart homes could monitor your lifestyle and living environment and identify areas for improvement. We should be willing to cede control to our home to make more decisions about how we should live our lives"	All disagreed [0 = Yes, 5 = No]	Majority disagreed [1 = Yes, 4 = No]	All No [0 = Yes, 5 = No]	All No [0 = Yes, 5 = No]
Sub-statement 2: "Smart living will require data-sharing. The benefits of living in smart homes outweigh the risks of data-sharing"	All No [0 = Yes, 5 = No]	Majority Yes, [4 = Yes, 1 = No]	All No [0 = Yes, 5 = No]	Majority no [1 = Yes, 4 = No]

Participants also expressed concerns over existing ethical procedures and data governance practices in data-driven smart environments, highlighting challenges associated with data protection responsibilities, accessibility of existing information about data sharing, consent management tools, and the appropriateness of data shared.

Generational and technological orientational differences were also identified and mattered when weighing up the risks and benefits of living in smart homes. The majority felt the risks of data sharing outweighed the benefits; this view was not shared by younger techno-enthusiasts who instead expressed their acceptance of intrusive data sharing as an inevitable part of our lives.

Discussions revealed a relationship between participants' sense of trust towards actors in the smart technology industry and participants willingness to share data. Most participants owed their distrust on a lack of transparent and inaccessible communications presented to users by industry developers for user guidance, clarity of 'data ownership', and consent management purposes.

At the end of the 2-day citizen jury, participants created a list of 'data privacy and governance' recommendations for future data-driven smart environments based on group discussions (Table 2).

Table 2. Participant recommendations.

Recommendations
1. Improve the transparency and accessibility of information on issues around data sharing, privacy, and security to ensure smart users are better informed to make decisions
2. Develop a representative and independent governing body that regulates and oversees decisions on future smart home technology use
3. Improve and regularly seek consent management practices from 'all' smart users (e.g., multiple users and capacities) to use their data
4. Provide assurances that any data sharing will be done responsibly and appropriate to fulfil the purpose for which it is used as well as user needs
5. Create further opportunities for the inclusion of smart users in data governance framework and decision making
6. More research is needed to address future issues on data sharing, privacy, governance, and security

4   Conclusion

Understanding the relationship between smart users' perceived risks and distrust towards the smart home industry is of central importance when planning an effective ethical and data governance practices response for future data-driven smart environments.

The research also revealed various public benefits associated with data sharing in smart environments, both individual and on society, such as assistive living and healthcare support. We also found that there were diverging views associated with smart technology adoption, with further research needed to address privacy concerns and other ethical issues which remain the main obstacles to smart technology adoption (e.g., accessible communications, responsible data sharing, consent management, and clarity over data ownership).

Our research highlighted the potential for using the citizens; jury method as a novel contribution, to explore public opinions on data security and governance issues. This approach also allowed the public to have a role in shaping the future of smart homes. However, it is important to note that due to the COVID-19, the citizens jury was held using an online video conferencing approach. Further research is therefore needed to explore these methodological implications on citizens jury discussions.

References

1. Sovacool, B.K., Turnheim, B., Hook, A., Brock, A., Martiskainen, M.: Dispossessed by decarbonisation: Reducing vulnerability, injustice, and inequality in the lived experience of low-carbon pathways. World Dev. **137**, 105116 (2021)

2. Koolen, C.: Transparency and Consent in Data-Driven Smart Environments. Intersentia, Antwerpen, Cambridge (2020)
3. Wilson, C., Hargreaves, T., Hauxwell-Baldwin, R.: Smart homes and their users: a systematic analysis and key challenges. Pers. Ubiquit. Comput. **19**(2), 463–476 (2015)
4. De Ruyck, O., Conradie, P., De Marez, L., Saldien, J.: User needs in smart homes: changing needs according to life cycles and the impact on designing smart home solutions. In: Lamas, D., Loizides, F., Nacke, L., Petrie, H., Winckler, M., Zaphiris, P. (eds.) INTERACT 2019. LNCS, vol. 11747, pp. 536–551. Springer, Cham (2019). https://doi.org/10.1007/978-3-030-29384-0_33
5. Martins, F., Almeida, M.F., Calili, R., Oliveira, A.: Design thinking applied to smart home projects: a user-centric and sustainable perspective. Sustainability **12**, 10031 (2020)
6. Ghaffarianhoseini, A., et al.: Intelligent or smart cities and buildings: a critical exposition and a way forward. Intell. Build. Int. **10**(2), 122–129 (2018)
7. Devaney, L., Torney, D., Brereton, P., Coleman, M.: Ireland's citizens' assembly on climate change: lessons for deliberative public engagement and communication. Environ. Commun. **14**(2), 141–146 (2020)
8. Patton, M.Q.: Qualitative Research and Evaluation Methods, 3rd edn. Sage Publishers, London (2002)
9. Braun, V., Clark, V.: Using thematic analysis in psychology. Qual. Res. Psychol. **3**(2), 77–101 (2006)

Development of a Scale Prototype of Smart Bed Controlled Using a Mobile Application

Juan Carlos Soberon[1], Gissela Gamboa[1], Franklin Castillo[1],
Guillermo Palacios-Navarro[2], and José Varela-Aldás[1,2(✉)] ⓘ

[1] SISAu Research Group, Facultad de Tecnologías de la Información y la Comunicación,
Universidad Tecnológica Indoamérica, Ambato, Ecuador
{jsoberon,ggamboa3c}@indoamerica.edu.ec, {franklincastillo,
josevarela}@uti.edu.ec
[2] Department of Electronic Engineering and Communications, University of Zaragoza,
Zaragoza, Spain
guillermo.palacios@unizar.es

Abstract. The need for a technological system for health care for sick people is evident. This work develops a scale prototype of a smart bed controlled through a mobile application. The electronic design consists of two servomotors that act to position the bed; these actions can be activated through the mobile application. At the same time, the patient can be monitored by a camera and an infrared thermometer that sends the data to the application through the Internet. The local operating code is designed so that the position of the bed changes automatically according to a preset sequence. The electronic system is based on the ESP32 board; this chip integrates WiFi communication that allows the connection of the bed with the cloud-based in Firebase. Temperature tests were carried out with the help of people to ensure that the data taken was correct. In addition, bed positions and reception of camera images were tested on a mannequin. As a result, adequate communication was obtained between the mobile application and all the devices installed in the smart bed. Finally, an acceptance test is applied that validates this proposal with a good score.

Keywords: Smart bed · Mobile application · Firebase · ESP32Cam

1 Introduction

Smart beds are integrated solutions for patient care, support and monitoring [1], based on an integrated, multidisciplinary design approach [2]. Research in this field is critical in the context of global aging and is driven by increased opportunities for accessibility solutions that are seamlessly integrated into the healthcare system [3–5], have a unique opportunity to enable more efficient efforts for caregivers and more responsive environments for patients [6].

Reviewing related works, continuous monitoring of vital signs using multiple radars has been realized; the radar is designed to be installed in hospital beds [7]. Another work

© The Author(s), under exclusive license to Springer Nature Switzerland AG 2022
C. Stephanidis et al. (Eds.): HCII 2022, CCIS 1581, pp. 368–374, 2022.
https://doi.org/10.1007/978-3-031-06388-6_49

builds an infrared thermometer with an electronic chip that can measure temperature accurately [8]. In addition, sensors are used to measure the patient's weight and use a user interface to analyze the pressure variation of the patient when changing positions in the bed [9]. In general, different applications have been developed with information and communication low-cost technologies that have changed people's lives and that use some combined tools [10, 11].

This paper develops a scaled prototype of a smart bed controlled through a mobile application using low-cost technology. For this it was implemented the system with an internet of things board, all the developed features are managed remotely. The paper has been organized into 4 sections; starting with the current section containing a brief introduction to the subject; Sect. 2 describes the methodology to be used, detailing the elements involved, Sect. 3 presents the results obtained, and Sect. 4 contains the main conclusions.

2   Methods and Materials

For the development of this proposal, an electronic board is used to control the different modules of the prototype to scale, Fig. 1 presents the scheme of the proposal. In this electronic board, the necessary programming for the operation of the prototype is installed, a camera that captures the patient from a suitable distance is included, the temperature is also monitored with an infrared thermometer next to the bed, and finally there are two servomotors to perform the necessary movements of the bed. All data is sent via the internet to a mobile application using a cloud-based database.

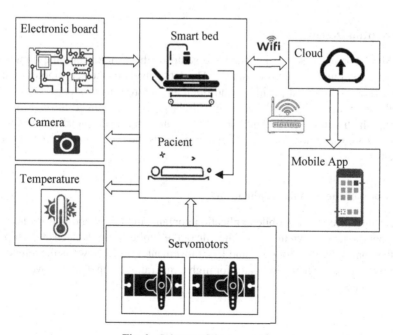

Fig. 1. Scheme of the proposal.

2.1 Electronic Design

This circuit is developed with a 5 V DC supply that provides the power for the two servo motors, the ESP32CAM, a temperature sensor, and the other ESP32, as shown in Fig. 2. All components are connected to the esp32 board, one servo motor to pin 4 and the other is connected to pin 14, the temperature sensor is connected to the SCL and SDA pins. Finally, the camera works with its chip integrated into the ESP32Cam.

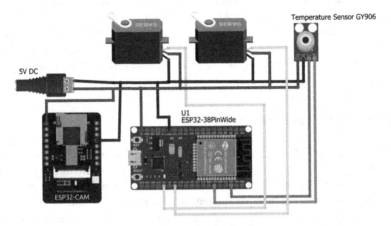

Fig. 2. Electronic circuit

2.2 Program Design

The ESP32 board is used to program the setup of the components, the temperature sensor, the servomotors and the camera. The movements of the servomotors are also encoded through different positions and the temperature sensor is read. On the other hand, the communication to the Internet (Firebase) is programmed through the WiFi network, which allows sending data, receiving commands and uploading images from the ESP32cam for remote viewing. Figure 3 presents the programmed functions using a flowchart.

2.3 Design of the Mobile Application

The user interface of the mobile application contains the labels and buttons necessary for its operation, as shown in Fig. 4. The title of the application is located at the top, then it has the control buttons for head and foot movement. Further down is the temperature label next to the emergency indicator for high temperatures. Finally, we have the image box for the camera.

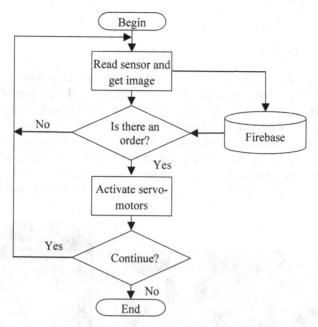

Fig. 3. Flow diagram of programmed actions

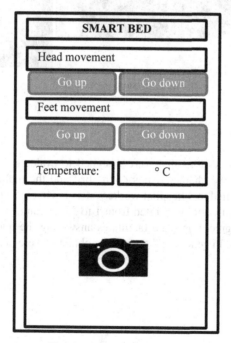

Fig. 4. User interface design

3 Results

3.1 Operation Tests

Figure 5 shows the prototype of the smart bed with its mobile application, in the tests carried out to check its operation. The bed and the phone used were located in different places with different WiFi networks. First, it was ensured that both devices are connected to the internet, then it is chosen which movement you want the bed to perform, both for the head and the feet, in the tests a dummy was placed. The temperature reading was also checked using a commercial thermometer, and finally, the quality of the images obtained by the camera was observed when movement was applied to the dummy. All the tests were successful and the communication between both places was fast.

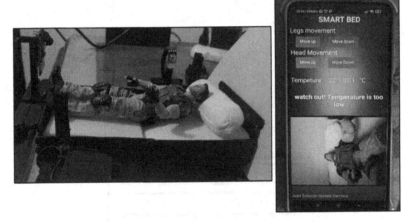

Fig. 5. System in operation

3.2 Acceptance Test

Table 1 shows the 7 questions that were designed to evaluate the acceptance of the proposal, considering the characteristics of the bed and the mobile application. This questionnaire was applied to 4 hospital workers after having used the scaled prototype. The answers to each question were rated from 1 to 7, 1 meaning strongly disagree and 7 meaning strongly agree, this scale facilitates answering the questions and for later averaging the answers. In general, all the ratings obtained were high, none below 6.

Table 1. Acceptance test

Question	Score
1. The system can be properly used to control the bed	6.75
2. Are you satisfied with the response time in the communication between the application and the bed?	7
3. It was easy to use the interface options in the mobile application	6.75
4. It was easy to control the postures of the bed	6.75
5. It was not physically difficult to use the bed	7
6. The camera has good image resolution	6.75
7. In general, I am satisfied with the system	6.75
Total	47.75/49 97.44%

4 Conclusions

The scale smart bed prototype presented in this document has several functions that allow monitoring of patients in need of special care, the camera allows to observe the patient in real-time and react to a sign of seriousness. In a complementary way, the patient's temperature is acquired, obtaining more information to make decisions regarding health care. In addition, the remote bed posture control allows the height of the head and feet to be adjusted, providing a means of action for better patient recovery and comfort.

Finally, the score obtained in the acceptance test is favorable for the proposal with a score of 97.44%. Although there is a limitation, this is not a real prototype but a scale model, so in future works, the proposal can be implemented in real size to analyze its characteristics.

References

1. Ghersi, I., Mariño, M., Miralles, M.T.: Smart medical beds in patient-care environments of the twenty-first century: a state-of-art survey. BMC Med. Inform. Decis. Mak. **18**, 63 (2018). https://doi.org/10.1186/s12911-018-0643-5
2. Davoodnia, V., Slinowsky, M., Etemad, A.: Deep multitask learning for pervasive BMI estimation and identity recognition in smart beds. J. Ambient. Intell. Humaniz. Comput. (2020). https://doi.org/10.1007/s12652-020-02210-9
3. García-Peñalvo, F.J., Conde, M.Á., Matellán-Olivera, V.: Mobile apps for older users – the development of a mobile apps repository for older people. In: Zaphiris, P., Ioannou, A. (eds.) LCT 2014. LNCS, vol. 8524, pp. 117–126. Springer, Cham (2014). https://doi.org/10.1007/978-3-319-07485-6_12
4. Varela-Aldás, J., Moreira, A., Criollo, P., Ruales, B.: Body temperature control using a robotic arm. In: Botto Tobar, M., Cruz, H., Díaz Cadena, A. (eds.) CIT 2020. LNEE, vol. 762, pp. 280–293. Springer, Cham (2021). https://doi.org/10.1007/978-3-030-72208-1_21
5. Varela-Aldás, J., Guamán, J., Paredes, B., Chicaiza, F.A.: Robotic cane for the visually impaired. In: Antona, M., Stephanidis, C. (eds.) HCII 2020. LNCS, vol. 12188, pp. 506–517. Springer, Cham (2020). https://doi.org/10.1007/978-3-030-49282-3_36

6. Restrepo, M., Huffenberger, A.M., Hanson, C.W., Draugelis, M., Laudanski, K.: Remote monitoring of critically-ill post-surgical patients: lessons from a biosensor implementation trial. Healthcare **9**, 343 (2021). https://doi.org/10.3390/healthcare9030343

7. Schellenberger, S., Shi, K., Michler, F., Lurz, F., Weigel, R., Koelpin, A.: Continuous in-bed monitoring of vital signs using a multi radar setup for freely moving patients. Sensors **20**, 5827 (2020). https://doi.org/10.3390/s20205827

8. Piccinini, F., Martinelli, G., Carbonaro, A.: Reliability of body temperature measurements obtained with contactless infrared point thermometers commonly used during the COVID-19 pandemic. Sensors **21**, 3794 (2021). https://doi.org/10.3390/s21113794

9. Seon, M., Lee, Y., Moon, C.: Medical robotic bed to prevent pressure sores. Appl. Sci. **11**, 8459 (2021). https://doi.org/10.3390/app11188459

10. Goh, N.W.-J., et al.: Design and development of a low cost, non-contact infrared thermometer with range compensation. Sensors **21**, 3817 (2021). https://doi.org/10.3390/s21113817

11. Varela-Aldás, J., Fuentes, E.M., Ruales, B., Ichina, C.: Construction of a WBGT index meter using low cost devices. In: Rocha, Á., Ferrás, C., Montenegro Marin, C.E., Medina García, V.H. (eds.) ICITS 2020. AISC, vol. 1137, pp. 459–468. Springer, Cham (2020). https://doi.org/10.1007/978-3-030-40690-5_45

The Typology of Plant-Computer Interaction Under the Sustainability Dialogue - Take Plant-Smart Furniture as an Example

Hang Su[1] and Yuan Liu[2(✉)]

[1] Central Saint Martins, London, UK
[2] Beijing Institute of Fashion Technology, Beijing 100029, China
yuan.liu@polimi.it

Abstract. The research aims to explore the role of plants in today's society and the added values and sustainable potentials through interaction with machines under the concept of DFS (design for sustainability). The major research methods include a literature review and case study, as an output, we both classify the typologies of plant-computer interaction under the sustainability dialogue, along with the project-based discussion of interactive furniture, implementing to explain the sustainable role of plants in new directions for future lifestyles.

The research is not only a response to the trend of biology-human-science integration but also an exploration of the harmonious symbiosis of humans and other forms of life under the framework of HCI and DFS. A typological is useful to provide guidance and reference for the study of the symbiotic relationship between plants, machines, and people under a sustainable context.

Keywords: Plant-computer interaction · Sustainability · Symbiotic design

1 Introduction

With the development of AI and electronic techniques, scenarios of HCI, represented by smart homes, have extensively integrated and improved people's quality of life. The relentlessly built environment brought by industrialization has led us to value our relationships with nature. "Multispecies ethnography (Kirksey and Helmreich 2010) has led to a reflection on the complicated relationships and interdependence between humans and other species. This gave rise to Animal-Computer Interaction (ACI), which is thought to enrich the HCI framework in terms of methodological and theoretical aspects and interface solutions (Mancini 2013). ACI claims to re-think non-human species as "users," which enables us to understand better and build symbiotic relations with other species for creating sustainable societies. However, although many recent advances in plant science argue the senses and ways of plants showing "intelligence" when dealing with problems (Mancuso and Viola 2015), we still found there is a clear gap in the discussion of plants compared to animals, while researching non-human species interacting with machines.

As an irreplaceable part of nature, plants are used as renewable sources from nutrition to cultural symbols to create value for humans with the help of artificial tools. However, as

C. Stephanidis et al. (Eds.): HCII 2022, CCIS 1581, pp. 375–382, 2022.
https://doi.org/10.1007/978-3-031-06388-6_50

people transform nature, the space that coexists with plants is constantly being invaded. Michael Marder (2013) described our relative neglect of plants as they are considered "the margin of the margin." Plants are also defined as the secondary role in the modern domestic hierarchy, where humans and animals (pets) are the primary roles. Because of their immobility and weak interaction with humans, they have been treated as "barely alive objects" in the context of human-animal interaction.

Out of environmental awareness, people's desire for a return to nature has never been stronger, and the search for sustainable interaction with the environment and socio-ethics has started to grow. Plants are increasingly being presented in various artificial environments. Their interactions with people no longer remain the simple nutritional demands of agrarian civilization but more broadly extended to health, emotional, and environmental interactions. The importance of research into plant-computer interactions is highlighted. Some interactive designs under the ACI and HCI framework have been discussed as the hybrid of integrating plants and machines. For instance, Aspling (2016) classified the plant-computer interaction based on the functions of plant intervention in computer systems, including plants as input/output devices, nurturing systems, etc. However, this does not provide an intuitive picture of the role in which the interaction can bring value to people and its potential impacts on sustainability.

This paper, therefore, seeks to ask about the role of plants in today's society and the potential values through interaction with machines under the concept of DFS (design for sustainability). We identify case studies to analyze the types and methods of plant-computer interaction, to discuss the added value and potentials for sustainability and new directions for future lifestyles.

2 Sustainability Factors in Plant-Computer Interaction

We refer to the commonly accepted definition of three dimensions of sustainability following the framework of DFS: economy, environment, and socio-ethics, which are derived from the SDGs (sustainable development goals) set out by the United Nations (2015). We then combine them with discussing individual needs in the hierarchical theory of needs (Maslow 1943) to summarize standard sustainability-based factors for evaluating each type of plant-computer interaction.

This study assesses the potential added value and significance of plant-computer interaction, mainly in environmental and socio-ethically sustainability. Environmental sustainability factors mainly include health values at the individual level and ecological values. Socio-ethical sustainability factors are more complex, mainly in terms of promoting individual emotional/empathic values by plants and the means of interspecies equality, inclusiveness, and symbiosis at the social level.

The above factors were used as criteria to analyze and classify the selected cases, resulting in four main types: sustainable sensory extension, environmentally-based sustainable internal circulation systems, empathetic interaction based on emotional values, and systematical-mutualistic symbiosis. Additionally, as plant-computer interaction is not currently considered as an independent discipline with a detailed methodology, Clara Mancini's (2013) suggestion and argument for distinguishing between animal technology and technology informed by animal-computer interaction are well referenced. Therefore, the plant-computer interaction mentioned in this paper is defined as the systematic application of design principles that place the plant at the center of an iterative development process as a legitimate user and design contributor.

3 Typology of Plant-Computer Interaction

3.1 Case Selection and Analysis Methods

We selected 24 plant-computer interaction cases that range from academic research, speculative or conceptual design practices, to commercial projects. We define the contribution of this typological analysis as a practical and thought-provoking typological reference for explorations in the near future.

Using the sustainability value factors summarized above as the leading evaluation indicators, we classify these plant-computer interaction cases into typology under the sustainability dialogue. We refer to Aspling (2016) for a classification of plant functions in computer systems. Specifically, the core criteria for the classification are based on whether and in what designed roles the interaction strategy can achieve different levels of sustainability or in what way it contributes (Table 1).

Table 1. Types of plant-computer interaction and the related case studies.

Types of plant-computer interaction	Project list	Link(s)
Sustainable sensory extension	Argus	https://www.media.mit.edu/projects/argus-sensors-inside-plants/overview/
	Botanicalls	https://www.botanicalls.com/
	Botanicus Interacticus	https://www.youtube.com/watch?v=EcRSKElucjk
	Elowan	https://www.media.mit.edu/projects/elowan-a-plant-robot-hybrid/overview/
	ListenTree	https://listentree.media.mit.edu/
	Other Intelligences	http://www.mariacastellanos.net/?/=/seccion/projects/entrada/other_intelligences
	project Florence	https://www.microsoft.com/artist-in-residence/collaborations/project-florence.html
	Pleased	https://pleased-fp7.eu/
Environmental-based sustainable endocyclic systems	Aria Hybrid Air Purifier	https://www.mateko.pl/aria-by-mateko/?lang=en
	Air O	https://www.gizmodo.cz/?tag=sheng-wen-wang
	Hortum machina B	http://www.interactivearchitecture.org/lab-projects/reearth
	OLUS	https://louieduncan.co.uk/olus-clean-air-zero-waste
	Plantas Nómadas	http://www.plantasnomadas.com/
	Pleura Pod	http://www.beomki.com/pleura-pod
Emotional-based empathetic interactor	BioCaller	https://ciid.dk/education/portfolio/idp20/courses/connected-objects-tui/projects/biopermit/
	EmotioPot	https://www.hackster.io/abid_hossain/emopot-a-plant-pot-that-can-show-a-plant-s-emotions-254ea4
	Plantio	https://dl.acm.org/doi/10.1145/1255047.1255075
	PotPet	http://sappari.org/pdf/potpet_tei2011.pdf
	MyGreenPet	https://www.youtube.com/watch?v=9HTxxT4ds64
	The Plants Sense	http://www.mariacastellanos.net/?/=/seccion/projects/entrada/plants_sense_eng
Systematic-mutualistic symbiosis	Urban Algae Canopy	https://www.ecologicstudio.com/projects/expo-milano-2015-urban-algae-folly
	Vertical Forest	https://www.stefanoboeriarchitetti.net/en/project/vertical-forest/
	Kinetic Green Canvas	http://greenstudios.net/smart-hydroponic-skin/art-innovation

3.2 Four Types of Plant-Computer Interaction

Environmental-Based Sustainable Endocyclic Systems

The emphasis in environmental-based sustainable endocyclic systems is on developing certain independence (or autonomy) of plants with the assistance of machines, which contributes to the improvement or enhancement of the human living environment or ecology. It is usually in the form of functional products or hybrids that play a sustainable value as environmental improvers within a limited range. The classification includes two strategies.

The first strategy focuses on enhancing or accelerating the positive environmental/health effects in the plant's biological properties through electronic devices. OLUS is an air filter that is claimed to be totally biodegradable. Since its material is derived from corn, it solves the pollution problem of the purifier itself on top of using the biological filtration of plants with dried moss. Similar examples are Air O and Aria Hybrid Air Purifier, which is also an air purifier based on plant roots' purifying and filtering capacities. Pleura Pod is another typical representative but more complex and efficient. It explores a wall cavity component containing cavities filled with algae that take advantage of the algae's ability to convert carbon dioxide into oxygen, which can be stacked to form an artificial lung wall that purifies the air and oxygenates the surrounding environment through automatic electronic control.

Another strategy translates the effectiveness of the plant's biological properties on the environment. In Plantas Nómadas, a hybrid symbiotic species with the symbiosis of micro-organisms and resident rooted plants and a photovoltaic fuel cell and robotic systems are presented. When the plants and "bacteria" need sustenance, the self-reliant robotic hybrid automatically moves towards the polluted river and "drinks" water from it. Then, the water is broken down by colonies of native bacteria in the fuel cell. This process improves the quality of the water and provides energy for the plant species that generate electricity through metabolism.

Meanwhile, the plants thrive and release oxygen into the atmosphere. Hortum Machina B is a kinetic urban cyber-gardener that senses its surroundings. It consists of a giant spherical exoskeleton with flora and electronics in the middle. The plants sense the environmental conditions around them. They can drive the hybrid autonomously to move to different city places to bring greenery and clear air. The exploration of this type of plant-computer interaction demonstrates its sustainable potential for ecological cycles and environmental purification.

Sustainable Sensory Extension

The type of Sustainable Sensory Extension introduces the value that plants can provide to humans as a usable, sustainable, and renewable natural sensor with the assistance of machines and the use of plant biology as an interactive resource to serve as a human interface to "natural" information. To some extent, exploring this type of plant-computer interaction will hopefully enrich the way humans sense nature.

For example, Argus, designed by Harpreet Sareen, is able to instantly detect irregularities in water quality of surrounding water sources with DNA nano-sensors inside a living plant, such as the levels of heavy metal and other toxic chemicals. It illustrates plants' ability in helping us learn more about our environment. Similarly, the Pleased project uses plants (roots) as biosensors to detect chemicals in the ground. Botanicus Interacticus transforms any plant into a touch-sensitive control device. The plant acts as a circuit that supports different kinds of touch gestures. Although the initial motivation for the project might be experiential, entertainment, and aesthetic uses, it objectively acts as a communication medium to promote people's engagement with nature. Besides, projects such as Project Florence, ListenTree, Other Intelligences, and Botanicalls aim to enable people to "communicate" or "talk" directly with plants through computer systems.

Empathetic Interactor Based on Emotional Values
This category of interaction emphasizes concepts that allow a strong emotional empathy with people or with the artificial environment, usually in the form of anthropomorphic designs or solutions. Combining the above emotional values with ethical sustainability, this strategy achieves sustainability by establishing a win-win emotion-based human-plant relationship through a positive emotional connection, where people will care more for the plants after gaining emotional satisfaction. This appears to positively impact enhancing inter-species communication and sustainable symbiosis.

BioCaller, for example, creates a family member relationship in the form of a plant interacting tactilely with a human through a wearable device worn around the neck. Likewise, Plantio and The Plants Sense aim to create a sense of empathy and intimacy between humans and plants and define the plant as a 'communication partner.'

Building on this, some explorations tend to help people obtain more positive emotional rewards through more hedonic interactive feedback. PotPet implements this strategy by enhancing the capacity for self-movement of plants. For instance, the plant-machine circles around its owner when it needs watering and spins happily when receiving the water. MyGreenPet, Plant-Smart Furniture, and EmotioPot have adopted a similar strategy. These strategies of allowing plant hybrids to mimic animals (pets) to achieve sustainable symbiosis are even more compelling after the benefits of keeping pets for human well-being have been proven (Friedmann 2013).

Systematic-Mutualistic Symbiosis
Systematic-Mutualistic Symbiosis is defined as an interaction strategy that achieves integrated ecological, economic, and ethical sustainability values by creating a systemic symbiosis of plants, artificial systems, and people. It takes the form of relatively large and integrated interactions, primarily realized in architecture.

Vertical Forest is a type of urban high-rise that allows for the symbiosis of people and other species. They integrate plants with the design of the buildings, providing an amount of vegetation equivalent to 30,000 square meters of woodland and undergrowth, concentrated on 3,000 square meters of urban surface. From the perspective of people living in it, the plant façade acts as a giant green filter that absorbs fine particles caused by urban traffic, absorbs carbon dioxide to produce oxygen, reduces indoor heat, and avoids noise pollution. From a natural point of view, it helps to improve the quality of air and water throughout the city and nurtures the habitat of many animal species, contributing to the spread and development of the city's ecological diversity. Another representative example is the Urban Algae Canopy, which takes advantage of the biological properties of an algae plant - Spirulina, which is technically integrated into the glass surface of the building's roof and skin, grows to enhance the shade of the glass surface and can be harvested periodically for consumption. It creates a sustainable and mutually beneficial symbiosis that co-evolves with the environment. In the same way, Kinetic Green Canvas is a systematic solution that electronically controls a number of plant blocks to change the pattern of a building surface wall.

4   The Project: Plant-Smart Furniture

4.1   Project Description

We specifically study empathetic interactors based on emotional values, since it has a relatively stronger potential to promote sustainability. A design project called Plant-Smart Furniture was implemented to visualize the value of the emotional expression of plants and the empathic role of plant-computer interaction in future sustainable living.

The project presents a collection of interactive furniture controlled by the "intelligence" of plants, including a "Bamboo palm chair," a "Vine coat stand," and a "Moss robot vacuum." By adopting computer technology, it empowers plants the right to survival and secures the rights of choice making and emotional expression under the interactive form of plants-computer symbiosis driving machines (Fig. 1).

Fig. 1. The scenarios of interaction and symbiotic exploration (*Plant-smart furniture*)

The collection includes a chair in symbiosis with a plant called bamboo palm. Different responses to the environment (water, temperature, and sunlight) are detected to reflect their health and emotions in real-time with the help of sensors. When the plants are dissatisfied with the environment, they resort to "violent means" to protest by crazily rotating the seat plate. The same situation happens in another piece of furniture – a coat stand controlled by ivy. By capturing and analyzing the PH value of the roots of ivy, eight branches on the stand can inflate and deflate depending on the state of the plant.

The third one is a moss-controlled robot vacuum. It can freely move around the house according to the moss' preferences for humidity temperature, and air quality, and at the same time clean and purify difficult-to-clean corners.

4.2 Reflections on Plant-Computer Interaction and Symbiotic for Sustainability

As an experimental innovation, this project offers a new way of thinking for DFS theory from the perspective of emotionally based symbiotic relationships between humans and nature. People need to flourish together with nature, and symbiosis becomes a key entry point for sustainable deployment and a promising trend towards sustainable lifestyles in the future.

According to Kobayashi (2015), satisfying people's spiritual and psychological needs for an intimate relationship with nature is critical for achieving quality and sustainable coexistence. Through an emotional anthropomorphic strategy, the project enables plant-machine interaction to stimulate the desire for human interaction with nature. In addition to the emotional benefits, the practical functions of these products, such as cleaning the floor and purifying the air in the house, all demonstrate a sustainable living style in which people and plants are equal and mutually beneficial.

Giving plants the ability of emotional expression and survival initiative is inspired by Michael Pollan's (2001) perspective on plants' survival needs. It changes the way they interact and symbiosis with people. Consequently, the role of plants in the domestic environment is able to transition from a secondary to a primary role by actively partici-pating in people's life scenarios. As Clara Mancini explained (2013), "This could help us reassess what sustainability is about and reconsider our place within a shared, fragile ecosystem." It also paves the way to discussion on how non-human species present a promising sustainable lifestyle of living with nature in the future.

5   Conclusion

This research is not only a response to the trend of biology-human-science integration but also an exploration of the harmonious symbiosis of humans and other forms of life under the framework of HCI and DFS. This study demonstrates the potential added values that the combination of plants and machines can bring to human life and the new possibilities in sustainability. A typological is helpful to provide guidance and reference for the study of the symbiotic relationship between plants, machines, and people under a sustainable context. From McGrath's (2009) perspective, this helps to inspire design practitioners to experiment with new, non-human-centric interfaces and thus advance the development of interaction design.

At last, we use a project to demonstrate the idea that emotional interactions help to reinforce sustainable values. According to Maslow's hierarchy of needs, we argue that spiritual and emotional needs will be the focus of people in a modern society where material life is relatively abundant. Therefore, this type of plant-computer interaction will have potential by fostering interspecies relationships. Although the project does not offer a perfect solution, digital technology development may support better solutions for sustainable symbiosis both emotionally and commercially, which, the author believes, will be achieved in the family settings of the future.

References

Danielle, D., Jacques, B., Tim, D.F.: The role of plants in bioretention systems; does the science underpin current guidance? Ecol. Eng. **120**, 532–545 (2018)

David, H., John, K., Amy, H., Jodi, F., Peng-Hui, W.: Infotropism: living and robotic plants as interactive displays. In: DIS 2004, pp. 215–221 (2004)

David, S.R., Fraser, B., Thomas, I.: The wonder of design with-in nature: towards an ecotechnic future. In: 10th European Academy of Design Conference - Crafting the Future (2013)

Veselova, E., Gaziulusoy, A.İ.: Implications of the bioinclusive ethic on collaborative and participatory design. TRACK 6. Co-Designing with Nature Towards Resilience and Diversity. THEME: Ethical Resilience, pp. 1571–1586 (2019)

Fredrik, A., Jinyi, W., Oskar, J.: Plant-computer interaction, beauty and dissemination. In: The Third International Conference on Animal-Computer Interaction (2016)

Harpreet, S., Pattie, M.: Cyborg botany: exploring in-planta cybernetic systems for interaction. In: CHI 2019 (2019)

Hwang, S., Lee, K.M., Yeo, W.: My green pet: a plant-based interactive plant for children. In: Proceedings of IDC 2010 (2010)

Kirksey, S.E., Helmreich, S.: The emergence of multispecies ethnography. Cult. Anthropol. **25**(4), 545–576 (2010)

Kuribayashi, S., Sakamoto, Y., Morihara, M., Tanaka, H.: Plantio: an interactive pot augmenting plant's expressions. In: Proceedings of ACE 2007. ACM (2007)

Mancuso, S., Viola, A.: Brilliant Green: The Surprising History and Science of PlantIntelligence. Island Press (2015)

McGrath, R.E.: Species-appropriate computer mediated interaction. In: Proceedings of CHI 2009, pp. 2529–2534. ACM Press (2009)

Mancini, C.: Animal-computer interaction (ACI) changing perspective on HCI, participation and sustainability. In: CHI 2013 Extended Abstracts on Human Factors in Computing Systems, pp. 2227–2236 (2013)

Marder, M.: Plant Thinking – A Philosophy of Vegetal Life. Columbia University Press, New York (2013)

Maslow, A.H.: A theory of human motivation. Psychol. Rev. **50**(4), 370 (1943)

Park, S., Oh, S., Hahn, M.: Emotio-pot: the interaction design of an affective flowerpot. In:Proceedings of ACE 2008. ACM (2008)

Pollan, M.: The Botany of Desire: A Plant's-Eye View of the World. Random House (2001)

Thompson, R., Prasad Mukhopadhyay, T.: Aesthetics of biocybernetic designs: a systems approach to biorobots and its implications for the environment. In Leonardo **47**(4) (2014)

UN General Assembly: Transforming our world: the 2030 Agenda for Sustainable Development, 21 October 2015, A/RES/70/1 (2015). https://www.refworld.org/docid/57b6e3e44.html

Investigating Aquatic Ecosystems with Computer Vision, Machine Learning and the Internet of Things

Tristan Y. H. Tay[1], Terence L. Y. Teo[1], and Kenneth Y. T. Lim[2]([⊠]) [iD]

[1] Singapore, Singapore
[2] National Institute of Education, 1 Nanyang Walk, Singapore 637616, Singapore
kenneth.lim@nie.edu.sg

Abstract. This paper describes an independent research project undertaken by a pair of high school students in Singapore under the mentorship of a Research Scientist at the National Institute of Education. The importance of Artificial Intelligence (AI) and Machine Learning (ML) continues to increase every day in our constantly advancing society. This investigative study aims to uncover the practicality of both AI and ML by utilizing it in a real world context, more specifically, to monitor aquatic behaviour. The aim of this investigation focuses on how ML can be used alongside appropriate hardware to effectively monitor the behaviour of aquatic organisms in response to changes in environmental factors. This paper describes the design, construction, testing and design decisions behind the development of a module which allows us to use ML in tandem with IoT sensors to fulfill the above aim. This investigation ultimately concludes that we were able to successfully conceptualize and create two designs and accompanying prototypes where their strengths lie in the presence of an ecosystem in which sensor data measured can be easily compared to the number of fishes detected by our object detection model to draw relationships between aquatic behaviour and different environmental factors. However it is limited due to the main hindrance of the prototypes' incapability of maintaining clear visibility of fish in murky waters with high turbidity.

Keywords: Machine Learning · Arduino · Raspberry Pi

1 Introduction

Machine Learning (ML) and Artificial Intelligence (AI) has increasingly found itself in the centre focus of the commercial and academic world, mainly because of the excitement and endless possibilities it brings for the world. When deliberating over what situation we should contextualize our usage of ML in, we stumbled upon a phenomenon at the Serangoon Gardens Secondary School pond. There, we noticed something curious: All the fishes were congregated together in one area of the pond and not at the other opposite end of the pond. We realised that periodically the fish would travel together between the two ends of the pond, and we wondered what factors were responsible for this phenomenon.

As such, this situation presented an opportunity for us to seize, in which we could utilize machine learning, accompanied with Internet of Things (IoT) sensors, to study aquatic behaviour in a localized environment, i.e. what are the microenvironmental factors which affect the behaviour of the fish in the pond.

Through this, we can contextualize our investigation in the field of marine biology, drawing relationships between abiotic factors, attained from sensors which monitor different environmental factors, and biotic behaviour, monitored using ML and its object recognition capabilities.

1.1 Objectives

In undertaking this study, we will be exploring how AI, or more specific to this application, ML, can be utilized and integrated with other data sensors to monitor aquatic biological behaviours, primarily, the behaviour of carp and other common fish used in Singapore school ponds. In doing so, we arrive at our main objectives for this investigation.

- designing an all-encompassing sensor module which comprises of image capturing and environmental monitoring capabilities, of which data recorded can be automatically uploaded onto the internet for analysis;
- training a object detection ML model so that the process of monitoring fish populations at opposite ends of the school pond can be automated by feeding the trained model with images captured by the sensor modules placed in the school pond; and
- utilize the sensor modules and trained ML model obtained from completing the two prior objectives in a real world application, placing them in the school pond to gain data on the microenvironmental factors as well as the respective fish populations at each end of the pond. Then, utilizing the data to draw relationships between the different microenvironmental factors and fish behaviour to arrive at conclusions as to how fish behaviour is affected by the present microenvironmental factors in the pond.

This paper will thus be organized accordingly, beginning with the literature which inspired us and directed us through this investigation, followed by the attempts at achieving the objectives listed above, with the main focus revolving around the hardware and software aspects of the prototypes we developed, in which we will be combining our methodology and results and discussion sections. We will then conclude with the general limitations with our investigation, as well as what our findings suggest for future research and prototyping.

2 Literature Review

2.1 Necessity of Investigation

Upon further research on the applicability of this investigation in real world contexts, it became apparent, from the Living Report 2020 by World Wildlife Fund (WWF), that the need to monitor aquatic behaviour in response to changing environmental factors is a must in the face of growing climate change and habitat destruction brought about by human activities, such as overfishing and coastal developments. Such human activities have led to the worsening of several environmental factors, such as the pH level, temperature and oxygen concentration of aquatic habitats, affecting the aquatic life which resides within them [1]. Hence this investigation is important and highly applicable in today's reality.

2.2 Application of Machine Learning

There have been existing studies which have already inculcated the usage of Artificial intelligence into aquatic biology monitoring systems. Salman *et al.* utilizes Gaussian Mixture Modelling (GMM), to model the background in a live video feed to detect objects such as fish which are not part of the background, optical flow, which detects movement in the video feed, and Region-based Convolutional Neural Network (R-CNN), which detects and proposes several regions where the object might be and limits object recognition to those areas for detection, with images from the Fish4Knowledge database for their usage in live fish sampling for estimation of fish populations [2]. Lu *et al.* on the other hand used transfer learning, utilizing pre-trained deep Convolutional Neural Network (CNN) models to train their own CNN model for fish species detection to detect different species of fish that have been caught to prevent overfishing [3].

However, an inherent flaw with the systems above is that despite them all having the ability to capture data (videos, pictures), the only data these systems are capable of collecting are pictures and videos. For commercial or recreational purposes, videos and pictures may be sufficient. But for research purposes, a lot more data is needed. In the context of biological or aquatic research, sensors like dissolved oxygen sensors, turbidity sensors, pH sensors, temperature sensors etc. are needed to understand and explain the biological behaviours of aquatic organisms in response to their surroundings.

Therefore, given the task, we would imagine an ideal version of a system, based on the above literature review, which would be: building a system that builds upon the above research and projects. Our system, which would be capable of remaining underwater for a sustained period of time (at least a week) autonomously, would include: a camera, multiple sensors that will work underwater which are relevant to aquatic research and the deployment of ML to help sift through all the data captured through the camera to aid identification of aquatic life.

From Fishcam [4] and Pipecam [5], we realised that a cylindrical pipe structure is commonly utilized for underwater monitoring of aquatic organisms and that Raspberry Pi is widely used in such underwater systems. Hence, we will be adapting both into our modules that we will be using for data collection.

2.3 Ideal Aquatic Environment

From literature review, we determined that the microenvironmental factors that make up good water quality for fish to reside in are >4 mg/m^3 of dissolved oxygen, pH level of around 7.5–8.5 as the average blood pH of fish is around 7.4, a turbidity value of 30 NTU (Nephelometric Turbidity Unit), and an optimum temperature which is dependent on the species of fish in question [6]. We realised that most of the fish in the school pond were koi fish, a subspecies of the common carp, hence the ideal temperature range would be around 20–25 °C [7].

These values will be kept in mind during our investigation, being useful in verifying the conclusions drawn from the obtained data, and should be considered if readers were to carry out similar investigations on carps as well.

3 Prototypes

3.1 Hardware

First Prototype. We set out to create a pipe that is assembled from simple and cheap materials, as inspired by FishCam and PipeCam. For our module, we determined that we want to include a pH meter, dissolved oxygen sensor, temperature sensor, turbidity sensor. The dissolved oxygen sensor has to be calibrated for it to provide accurate readings. We have considered that should the sensor not be calibrated, the values obtained from the sensor would still be usable in our present context because we are merely comparing between dissolved oxygen readings. Their discrepancy from the actual value would be constant. However, to a researcher, accurate dissolved oxygen readings are critical. To calibrate the sensor, we needed Sodium Hydroxide (NaOH) solution. The manufacturer of the dissolved oxygen sensor is DFRobot, and it is specified that 0.5 Molar (M) of NaOH solution is required for proper calibration. The sensors would be connected to an Arduino board. The Arduino would be connected to a Raspberry Pi board, which controls the frequency of sensor readings being taken and images captured by the camera. The external shell of the module - which houses all the sensors and electronics - is a simple PVC pipe brought from a hardware store. To modify the pipe to fit our purpose, that is to allow the sensor to extend outside the PVC, we cut circular holes into the PVC pipe. In our attempt to make use, as much as possible, of equipment we have, we improvised and used a soldering tool to melt through the plastic and make holes in the PVC pipe. Following which, we fit the sensors and cameras into the pipe. For the camera we used a dome (improvised from Daiso's transparent christmas ball) to fit the camera within, allowing the camera to be adjusted in all x, y and z axis without the pipe itself needing to be tilted. The result was an integrated module which combines a multitude of sensors, cameras and internal computers. The pipe was sealed physically with duct tape and silicone sealant. We approached a Vocational Institute for help to professionalise the pipe construction. A rubber gasket was added, along with other waterproofing improvements. However, water could still enter the pipe after a period of time, rendering it incapable for long-term data collection. Although this pipe idea was, as one might say, a failure, we think that on the contrary, it is useful conceptually. This is because this present iteration is highly practical for research purposes as it is an integrated module for sensors and imaging capabilities. Should there be many data collection points, logistically it would be an issue for researchers. With a singular module that is capable of utilizing IoT, data collection can be done quicker and with greater frequency because data is uploaded to the cloud and transfer of equipment from one location to another is also efficient and easy. Hence, we believe that our hardware design works conceptually, the only problem is the lack of professional tools, knowledge, materials and machinery.

Second Prototype. We were advised that, given our present situation, namely a lack of professional knowledge of waterproofing and the lack of equipment, an option would be to purchase IP68 boxes to house our components. This thought did occur to us at the very beginning, however we avoided it for our priority was to build an integrated module where all components fit into one common shell.

For the second prototype, we bought an IP68 waterproof box with a transparent cover, as well as a splash-proof box.

The choice of camera was also deliberated upon. We had two options: (1) Raspberry Pi Camera V2.1 is the standard camera that is typically used for Raspberry Pi units. This camera is equipped with the Sony IMX219 8-megapixel sensor, or (2) Raspberry Pi Infrared Camera Module is equipped with the 5-megapixel OV5647 sensor. This camera is unique as it emits infrared light, allowing it to capture images even in the dark.

We observed that the infrared camera had a wider field of view and could capture more in the picture it takes. We hence chose the infrared camera over the standard camera. However, the infrared light reflects off the transparent panel, resulting in glare in the picture. To resolve this problem, we unscrewed and removed the infrared lamps from the camera module itself. But, without the infrared light, the camera performs poorly in low light, thus needing a lot of light even in reasonably lit conditions.

After deciding on the most appropriate camera which should be utilized for our investigation, we faced another issue where we needed to ensure that the IP68 box which houses the camera module is able to sink to the bottom of the waterbody in which we are taking pictures of fish. It is here where buoyancy comes into play, given the equation from Archimedes Principle:

$$F_B = V \rho g$$

where F_B represents buoyancy force, V the volume of liquid displaced by the object, ρ represents the density of the liquid, and g represents gravitational field strength. In order for the IP68 box to sink, its weight has to be greater than the buoyancy force, such that there is a net downwards force. Hence we get the following:

$$mg > V \rho g$$
$$m > V \rho$$

where m represents the mass of the object, which in this case is the IP68 box. Given that the volume of the IP68 box is around 0.00181 m^3 and the density of water is approximately 1000 kgm^{-3}, the minimum mass needed for the IP68 box to sink would be 1.81 kg. Hence we bought a weight which has a mass nearest to this value, which was 2.5 kg, which we used to enable the IP68 box to sink.

Another problem we faced was imaging in harsh conditions. From our experience, murky water is an especially huge issue for the camera because the camera simply is not capable of capturing anything more than approximately 1 m from it. Because our intention is to apply ML to recognise fishes, the images must be reasonably clear to at least distinguish vague lines of the fishes' silhouettes and outlines. To further investigate how water murkiness affects the image quality, we put our cameras to test in three locations, namely the pond in Serangoon Gardens Secondary, the Institute of Technical

Education's (ITE) ecogarden pond - before and after pond cleaning, and an aquarium we set up at home just for this present testing purpose.

The pond in Serangoon Gardens secondary was extremely murky, with no fishes visible at all. The pond in ITE, prior to cleaning, was considerably murky but faint shapes of the fishes can be identified. After cleaning, more fish were visible. The home aquarium was the clearest, mostly because we can control the murkiness by replacing the water in the tank.

Thus for the investigation, the home aquarium served as the best-case scenario in which the water is not murky, and the pond at ITE was seen as a more realistic application of our prototype, where the water was murky but fish was still visible. The usage of the three different locations, in a sense, served as a litmus test for the effectiveness of our prototype, from which we realised that the largest limitation of our investigation would be that it is not applicable in water bodies that are too murky.

3.2 Software

Given the success of our more orthodox approach to this investigation, splitting the camera and sensors into two separate modules, we were able to obtain underwater pictures of fish for the training of our object detection model. Using about 200 pictures each, annotated with LabelImg, we trained two models, one to detect fish in the ITE pond, and the other to detect fish in the home aquarium. Training the models took about four hours each, but object detection itself was much faster, giving us images with drawn bounding boxes and labels around the fish in both locations (see Figs. 1 and 2 as examples).

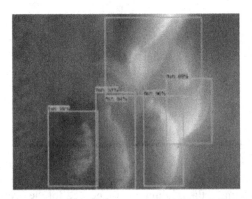

Fig. 1. Results with bounding boxes and labels for ITE pond

The bounding boxes also come with accompanying labels with the percentage match stated as well. The object detection model can be easily configured to only draw out bounding boxes for matches that are only above a fixed percentage match. For our investigation, and in the above images, we restricted the model to only draw bounding boxes for matches above a 20% match. We also scripted the object detection model to output the number of objects detected in each image in an Excel spreadsheet so that easy

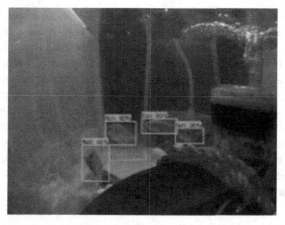

Fig. 2. Results with bounding boxes and labels for home aquarium

comparisons, graphs and conclusions can be drawn from the fish population detected and the sensor readings.

We utilised the xlsxwriter python package to output the probability and number of fishes onto an excel file. Below is the function which draws the images and outputs the accompanying data into an excel sheet.

4 Concluding Remarks

In conclusion, with respect to the three objectives mentioned at the beginning of this paper, we were successful in achieving two out of the three intended objectives for this investigation, namely designing an all-encompassing sensor module as well as training an object detection ML model to work in tandem with our sensor module. In the process, we were able to conceptualize two designs for the hardware, one being the cylindrical all-in-one pipe which would be successful given proper professional equipment and techniques for waterproofing, and the other being the two boxes one ecosystem model which relies more heavily on IoT for data from both environmental sensors and camera to be synced, taken simultaneously and uploaded onto the internet for analysis.

The remaining objective – applying the hardware and software developed from the preceding two objectives respectively into a real world application – could not be achieved due to the visibility of the water in the school pond. This problem arose from the murkiness of the water and the lack of professional equipment for enhanced visibility in such turbid environments. However, even with this setback, our investigation through the physical creation and testing of our conceptualized models still functions as a proof of concept, where both our hardware and software are able to function successfully together to allow for more fruitful investigations and research work in monitoring aquatic behaviour in response to environmental change.

The findings from our investigation also pose several future implications. Although the usage of AI and ML are achieving greater and greater prevalence in society, many still view its usage as complicated and too expensive, not to mention inculcating its usage in tandem with other supporting pieces of hardware to achieve a specific goal such as monitoring aquatic behaviour. Our investigation seeks to go against this perception, to show that creating hardware and utilizing AI alongside it can be as simple and affordable as creating a Do It Yourself (DIY) model with a PVC Pipe, or using an IP68 box and a socket box. The authorial team began this investigation without knowledge on AI and ML. But through guidance and independent learning, as well as a little of a maker spirit, we were able to accomplish the aforementioned objectives. However, with all projects comes its limitations, and some questions still have to be explored to affirm the validity of our achievements, and extend its usage beyond the localized context of school ponds and aquariums. How can the existing designs for monitoring aquatic behaviour be improved to allow for clearer imaging in turbid environments? How can such modules be utilized in response to the aforementioned issue of growing climate change?

References

1. Almond, R.E.A., Grooten, M., Petersen, T. (eds.): Living Planet Report 2020 – Bending the Curve of Biodiversity Loss. World Wildlife Fund, Gland (2020)
2. Salman, A., et al.: Automatic fish detection in underwater videos by a deep neural network-based hybrid motion learning system. ICES J. Mar. Sci. **77**, 1295–1307 (2019)
3. Lu, Y.-C., Tung, C., Kuo, Y.-F.: Identifying the species of harvested tuna and billfish using deep convolutional neural networks. ICES J. Mar. Sci. **77**, 1318–1329 (2019)
4. Mouy, X., et al.: FishCam: a low-cost open source autonomous camera for aquatic research. HardwareX **8**, e00110 (2020). https://doi.org/10.1016/j.ohx.2020.e00110
5. Fourie, F., Thomson, D.: PipeCam: low-cost autonomous underwater camera. Hackaday.io. Accessed 9 Sept 2021
6. Monitoring pond water quality to improve production. Thefishsite.com. Accessed 12 Jan 2022
7. FAO: natural food and feeding habits. Fao.org. Accessed 12 Jan 2022

Control of a Security Door Through the Internet of Things

Jonathan Toapanta[1], Mario Miranda[1], Víctor H. Andaluz[1,2],
Guillermo Palacios-Navarro[3], and José Varela-Aldás[1,3(✉)] (iD)

[1] SISAu Research Group, Facultad de Tecnologías de la Información y la Comunicación,
Universidad Tecnológica Indoamérica, Ambato, Ecuador
jtoapanta16@indoamerica.edu.ec, {mariomiranda,
josevarela}@uti.edu.ec
[2] Universidad de las Fuerzas Armadas ESPE, Sangolquí, Ecuador
vhandaluz1@espe.edu.ec
[3] Department of Electronic Engineering and Communications, University of Zaragoza,
Zaragoza, Spain
guillermo.palacios@unizar.es

Abstract. Home security has increased in recent years with the help of technology. Even more, the appearance of the internet of things (IoT) allows it to control and monitor devices from anywhere in the world. This work develops a proposal that alerts the user about the status of a door through a mobile application using low-cost devices. For the electronic design, a magnetic contact sensor has been used that detects if the door is open. An electric lock is also used to control the door with the mobile application from anywhere in the user. The electronic system is based on an ESP32 board that has WiFi communication, this board sends the door status data to the mobile application. The electric lock can be activated in three ways: manually from the door, automatically according to a programmed routine, and remotely using the mobile app. The platform used for the IoT is Firebase, which allows the exchange of information between the local site and the remote site. The tests carried out around the prototype have responded correctly, the installed sensor continuously reports on the status of the door, and the control is executed according to the orders sent through the cloud. In addition, an acceptance test is used that guarantees the correct operation of the proposal.

Keywords: ESP32 board · IoT · Firebase · Mobile application · Security door

1 Introduction

Home security is an important issue for people, everyone requires a protected space because most family members work and study, away from home. For this reason, security systems must be taken seriously, analyzing the possible problems [1]. The smart home appeared for controlling and monitoring the home, providing greater peace of mind through monitoring and staying connected anytime, anywhere [2].

© The Author(s), under exclusive license to Springer Nature Switzerland AG 2022
C. Stephanidis et al. (Eds.): HCII 2022, CCIS 1581, pp. 391–397, 2022.
https://doi.org/10.1007/978-3-031-06388-6_52

In recent years there is a trend to use the technology of the internet of things (IoT) to communicate smartphones to a conventional device such as an electric lock, this allows a door to be opened or closed remotely through authentication [3–5]. This is one of many services in the knowledge-based information society. In addition, there is a growth in convergent services that use two or more components for the same purpose.

The IoT requires that all objects provide information, in this way the states are updated in the cloud to make decisions automatically or by the user [6]. Some components of this technology are interactive services, user identification, wired and wireless sensors, carrier networks, advanced communication protocols, and distributed intelligence in different objects, all are common features today [7]. Currently, providing homes with a security system has become an important topic of analysis, in which the latest technologies are applied [8]. Of these technologies, the cloud platform is an important component to monitor and control home devices remotely [9].

This work develops a proposal that allows reading and controlling the status of a door through a mobile application using low-cost devices based on IoT. This document contains 4 sections, including the introduction. Section 2 presents the methods and materials, Sect. 3 shows the results and Sect. 4 presents the conclusions.

2 Methods and Materials

The materials used in this project are presented in the scheme of Fig. 1. The system consists of a magnetic contact sensor, an electric lock and a processor board for door control. The electronic board has WiFi communication for connection to a remote database. This database is installed on a cloud platform that is accessed from both ends. The other end is made up of the mobile application, from this position the door is controlled and monitored remotely.

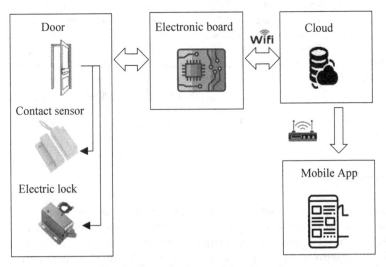

Fig. 1. General scheme of the proposal.

2.1 Electronic Design

The electronic circuit is designed as shown in Fig. 2. The ESP32 board is the central component of the circuit because it includes a WiFi communication module, and is responsible for data acquisition, control and processing. The magnetic contact sensor is connected to a digital port as input. The electric lock uses a relay to control the power supply at 12 V DC. The relay is controlled using a digital pin configured as an output.

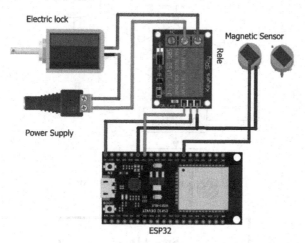

Fig. 2. Electronic circuit

2.2 Program Design

The main program designed for this project is presented in the flowchart of Fig. 3. The ESP32 board reads the sensor status to determine if the door is open or closed, and sends this information to the database in Cloud. The ESP32 also receives the information from the database and processes the received order, this order activates the electric lock if required, and thus opens the door. The remote database is updated with new data from both ends, in this case, the ESP32 updates the gate status. This read and control cycle is constantly repeated within the infinite loop function.

2.3 Design of the Mobile Application

Figure 4 shows the user interface design for the mobile application. The interface contains 3 buttons, an open button, a close button and a button to exit the application. The app connects to Firebase which is where the remote database is hosted. Through the open and close buttons, it sends the control orders for the door. In addition, it receives data from the magnetic contact sensor to display a message when the status of the door changes, whether it is manually or electronically operated.

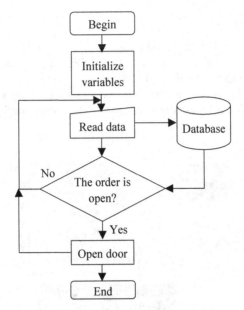

Fig. 3. Program flow chart for ESP32

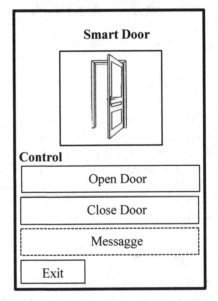

Fig. 4. User interface of the mobile application.

3 Results

3.1 Function Tests

In Fig. 5 it can see images of how the proposal works, both the elements of the door located in a house, and the mobile application located in a remote place. The tests carried out were carried out successfully, constantly updating the status of the door and activating the electric lock without problems.

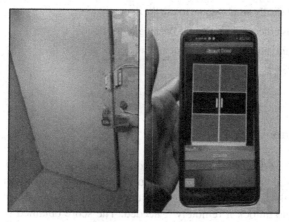

Fig. 5. Functionality test images.

3.2 Acceptance Evaluation

To evaluate the characteristics of this proposal, an acceptance questionnaire was applied to the 4 members of the house. The questionnaire is made up of 7 questions to evaluate different components of the proposal. The questions are answered using a 7-level Likert scale, where 7 strongly agree and 1 strongly disagrees. The results of the acceptance test are presented in Table 1, with a final evaluation of 78.06% acceptance, a favorable value for this proposal. Although this evaluation shows some dissatisfaction with the physical use of the door, this component can be improved with a local interface for door control.

Table 1. Acceptance test.

Question	Score
1. - The system can be used appropriately to control the door	5.75
2. - Are you satisfied with the response time in the communication between the application and the door	5.00
3. - It was easy to use the interface options in the app	5.50
4. - It was easy to learn how to use the system	5.75
5. - It was not physically cumbersome to use the door	4.50
6. - The alarm was efficient notifying the opening of the door	5.50
7. - In general, I am satisfied with the system	6.25
Total	38.25/49 78.06%

4 Conclusions

The use of low-cost devices to implement projects based on IoT is very common today. This has facilitated the increase in home security, allowing the development of reduced systems such as the one presented in this document. This way homeowners can monitor the front door and unlock it remotely if needed. The score obtained in the acceptance test indicates acceptable characteristics for users (78.06%) but leaves a point to improve with the difficult local use of the door. In future works, it is intended to automate an entire house by managing the different devices from the same mobile application.

References

1. Hariprakash, R., Ramu, G.V., Rajakumari, T., Ananthi, S., Padmanabhan, K.: Some problems & methods for remotely controllable automatic home security systems. In: 2008 Third International Conference on Systems and Networks Communications, pp. 400–403. IEEE (2008). https://doi.org/10.1109/ICSNC.2008.41
2. Varela-Aldás, J., Buele, J., Cumbajin, M.: Smart home control system using echo dot. In: Rocha, Á., Ferrás, C., López-López, P.C., Guarda, T. (eds.) ICITS 2021. AISC, vol. 1330, pp. 303–312. Springer, Cham (2021). https://doi.org/10.1007/978-3-030-68285-9_29
3. Jeong, J.-I.: A study on the IoT based smart door lock system. In: Kim, K.J., Joukov, N. (eds.) Information Science and Applications (ICISA) 2016, pp. 1307–1318. Springer, Singapore (2016). https://doi.org/10.1007/978-981-10-0557-2_123
4. Chávez-Chica, E., Buele, J., Salazar, F.W., Varela-Aldás, J.: Prototype system for control the ScorBot ER-4U robotic arm using free tools. In: Zallio, M., Raymundo Ibañez, C., Hernandez, J.H. (eds.) AHFE 2021. LNNS, vol. 268, pp. 158–165. Springer, Cham (2021). https://doi.org/10.1007/978-3-030-79997-7_20
5. Varela-Aldás, J., Guamán, J., Paredes, B., Chicaiza, F.A.: Robotic cane for the visually impaired. In: Antona, M., Stephanidis, C. (eds.) HCII 2020. LNCS, vol. 12188, pp. 506–517. Springer, Cham (2020). https://doi.org/10.1007/978-3-030-49282-3_36

6. Atzori, L., Iera, A., Morabito, G.: The Internet of Things: a survey. Comput. Netw. **54**, 2787–2805 (2010). https://doi.org/10.1016/j.comnet.2010.05.010
7. Hussein, N.A., Al Mansoori, I.: Smart door system for home security using Raspberry pi3. In: 2017 International Conference on Computer and Applications (ICCA), pp. 395–399. IEEE (2017). https://doi.org/10.1109/COMAPP.2017.8079785
8. Chitnis, S., Deshpande, N., Shaligram, A.: An investigative study for smart home security: issues, challenges and countermeasures. Wirel. Sens. Netw. **08**, 61–68 (2016). https://doi.org/10.4236/wsn.2016.84006
9. Jose, A.C., Malekian, R.: Smart home automation security: a literature review. Smart Comput. Rev. (2015). https://doi.org/10.6029/smartcr.2015.04.004

Correction to: Whole-Body Interaction and Representative Applications in Virtual Reality

Xiaolong Lou, Xinyi Li, Yuhaozhe Zheng, and Yan Shi

Correction to:
Chapter "Whole-Body Interaction and Representative Applications in Virtual Reality" in: C. Stephanidis et al. (Eds.): *HCI International 2022 Posters*, CCIS 1581, https://doi.org/10.1007/978-3-031-06388-6_7

In the originally published version of chapter 7 an incorrect grant number was erroneously used in the acknowledgements section. The grant number has been corrected.

The updated original version of this chapter can be found at
https://doi.org/10.1007/978-3-031-06388-6_7

Author Index

Printed in the United States
by Baker & Taylor Publisher Services